D0561743

Seraph of the End
—VAMPIRE REIGN—

13

STORY BY **Takaya Kagami**
ART BY **Yamato Yamamoto**
STORYBOARDS BY **Daisuke Furuya**

CHARACTERS

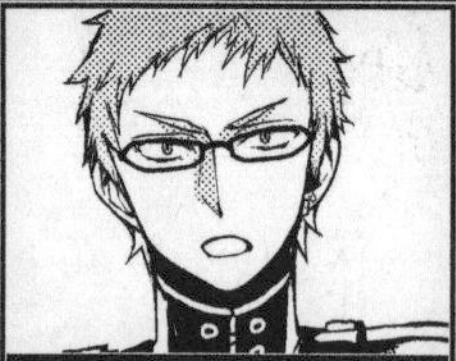

SHIHO KIMIZUKI

Yuichiro's friend. Smart but abrasive. His Cursed Gear is Kiseki-o, twin blades.

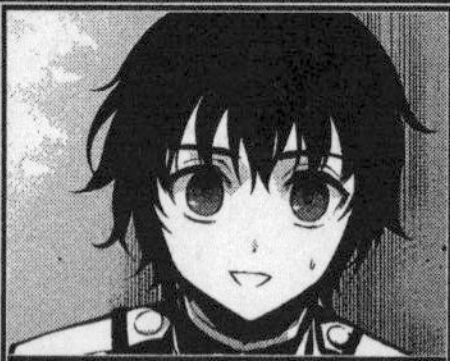

YOICHI SAOTOME

Yuichiro's friend. His sister was killed by a vampire. His Cursed Gear is Gekkouin, a bow.

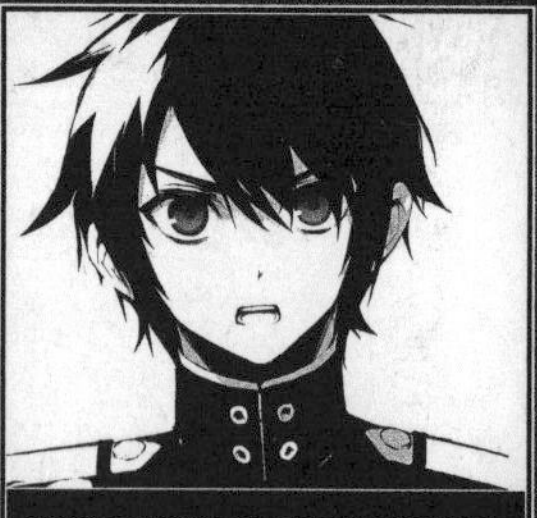

YUICHIRO HYAKUYA

A boy who escaped from the vampire capital, he has both great kindness and a great desire for revenge. Lone wolf. His Cursed Gear is Asuramaru, a katana.

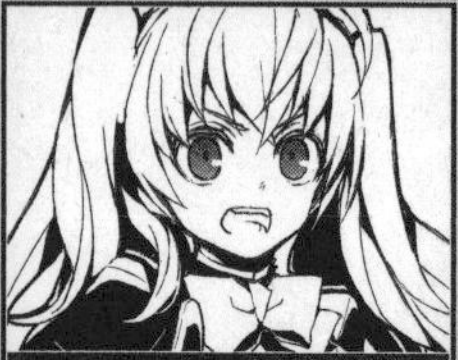

MITSUBA SANGU

An elite soldier who has been part of the Moon Demon Company since age 13. Bossy. Her Cursed Gear is Tenjiryu, a giant axe.

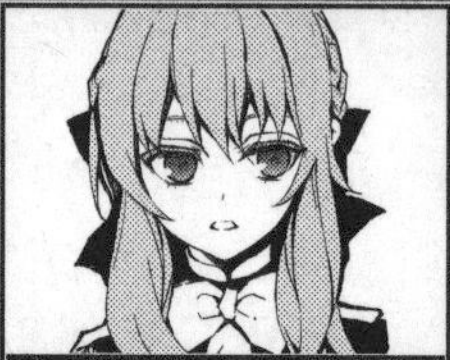

SHINOA HIRAGI

Guren's subordinate and Yuichiro's surveillance officer. Member of the illustrious Hiragi family. Her Cursed Gear is Shikama Doji, a scythe.

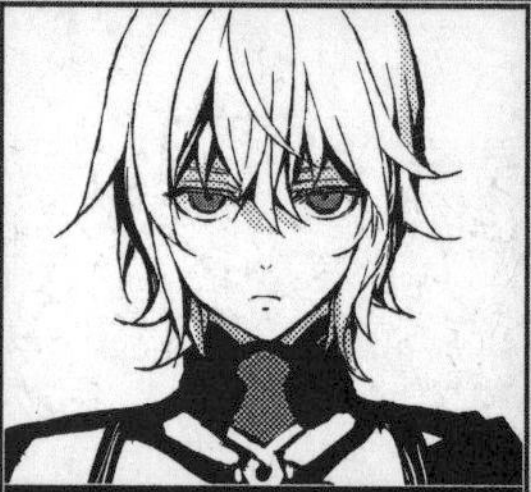

MIKAELA HYAKUYA

Yuichiro's best friend. He was supposedly killed but has come back to life as a vampire. Currently working with Shinoa Squad.

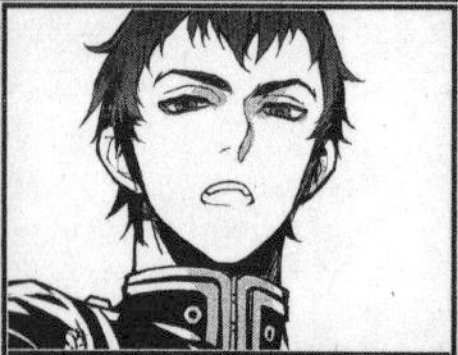

KURETO HIRAGI

A Lieutenant General in the Demon Army. Heir apparent to the Hiragi family, he is cold, cruel and ruthless.

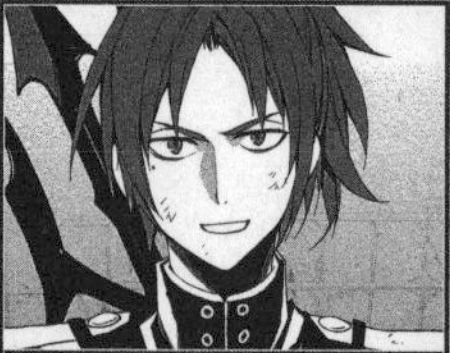

MAKOTO NARUMI

Former leader of Narumi Squad. After his entire squad died during the battle of Nagoya, he deserted the Demon Army with Shinoa Squad.

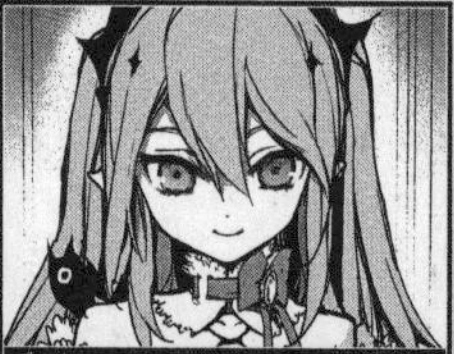

KRUL TEPES

Queen of the Vampires and a Third Progenitor. Currently held captive by Ferid.

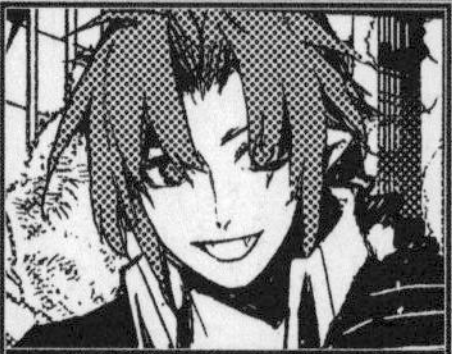

CROWLEY EUSFORD

A Thirteenth Progenitor vampire. Part of Ferid's faction.

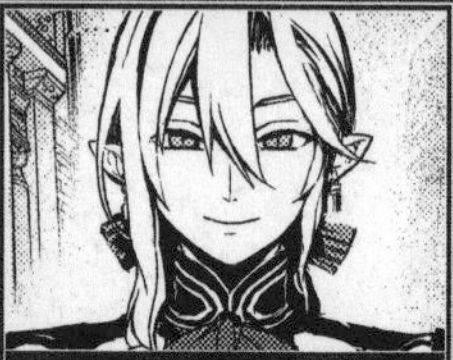

FERID BATHORY

A Seventh Progenitor vampire, he killed Mikaela.

SHIGURE YUKIMI

A 2nd Lieutenant and Guren's subordinate along with Sayuri. Very calm and collected.

SAYURI HANAYORI

A 2nd Lieutenant and Guren's subordinate. She's devoted to Guren.

GUREN ICHINOSE

Lieutenant Colonel of the Moon Demon Company, a Vampire Extermination Unit. He recruited Yuichiro into the Japanese Imperial Demon Army. He's been acting strange ever since the battle in Nagoya... His Cursed Gear is Mahiru-no-yo, a katana.

SHINYA HIRAGI

A Major General and an adopted member of the Hiragi Family. He was Mahiru Hiragi's fiancé.

NORITO GOSHI

A Colonel and a member of the Goshi family. He has been friends with Guren since high school.

MITO JUJO

A Colonel and a member of the Jujo family. She has been friends with Guren since high school.

STORY

A mysterious virus decimates the human population, and vampires claim dominion over the world. Yuichiro and his adopted family of orphans are kept as vampire fodder in an underground city until the day Mikaela, Yuichiro's best friend, plots an ill-fated escape for the orphans. Only Yuichiro survives and reaches the surface.

Four years later, Yuichiro enters into the Moon Demon Company, a Vampire Extermination Unit in the Japanese Imperial Demon Army, to enact his revenge. There he gains Asura-maru, a demon-possessed weapon capable of killing vampires. Along with his squad mates Yoichi, Shinoa, Kimizuki and Mitsuba, Yuichiro deploys to Shinjuku with orders to thwart a vampire attack.

In a battle against the vampires, Yuichiro discovers that not only is his friend Mikaela alive, but he also has been turned into a vampire. After misunderstandings and near-misses, Yuichiro and Mikaela finally meet each other in Nagoya.

Kureto Hiragi begins an experiment on the Seraph of the End at Nagoya Airport. Caught up in the cruel procedure, the Moon Demon Company suffers extreme losses. Even worse, Guren appears to betray his friends, participating in the experiment and gravely wounding Yuichiro. To further complicate things, vampires appear to stop the experiment and Ferid stages a coup, capturing the Vampire Queen and throwing everything into chaos.

Declaring enough is enough, Shinoa Squad deserts the Demon Army and escapes Nagoya to hide away in a small seaside town. Ferid tracks them down and tells them that Guren was the one who caused the Catastrophe eight years ago, and that all the answers are in Osaka...

Seraph of the End
—VAMPIRE REIGN—

13

CONTENTS

Chapter 48
The Making of an Angel

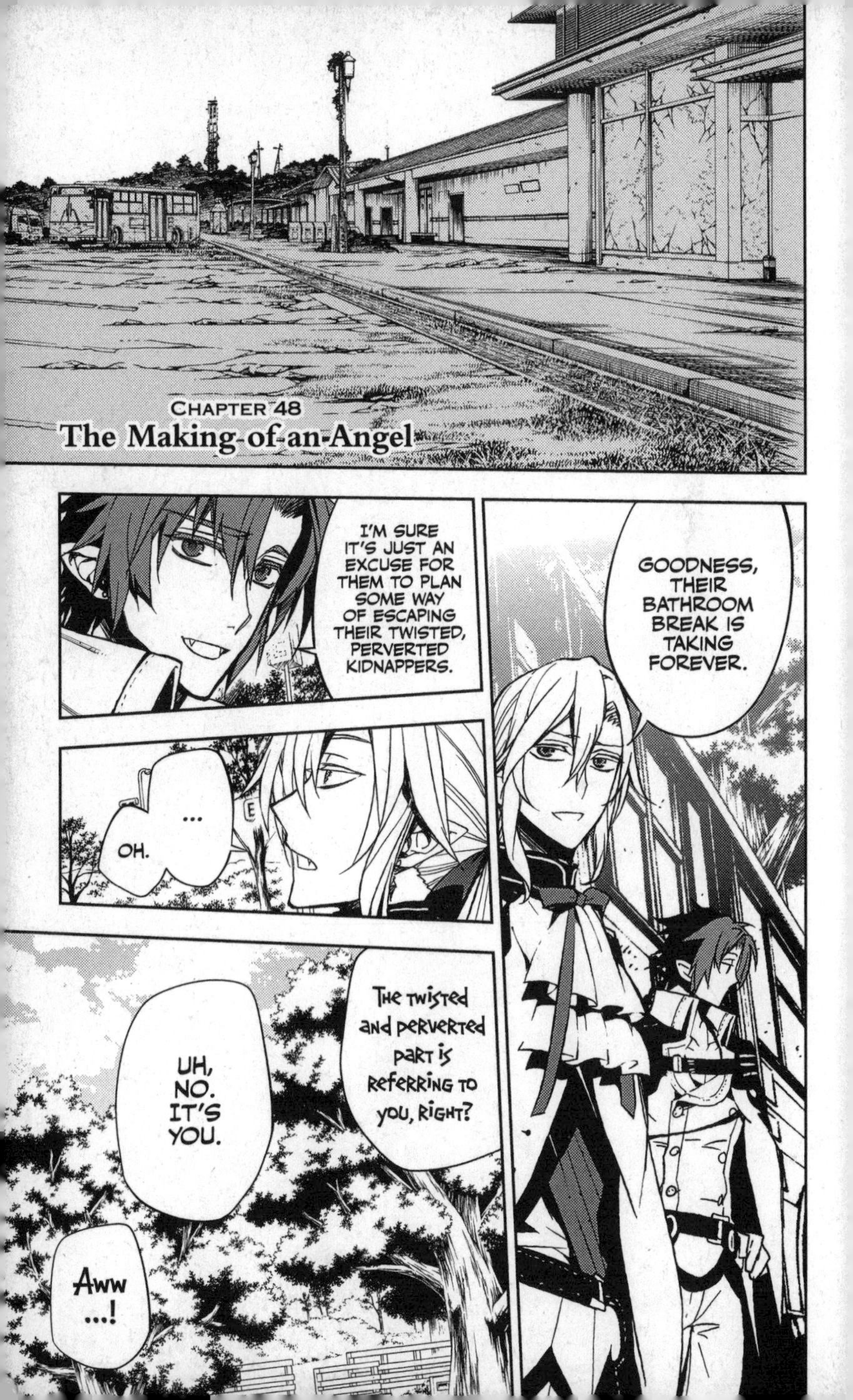
GOODNESS, THEIR BATHROOM BREAK IS TAKING FOREVER.
I'M SURE IT'S JUST AN EXCUSE FOR THEM TO PLAN SOME WAY OF ESCAPING THEIR TWISTED, PERVERTED KIDNAPPERS.
... OH.
The twisted and perverted part is referring to you, right?
UH, NO. IT'S YOU.
Aww ...!

CHAPTER 48
The Making of an Angel

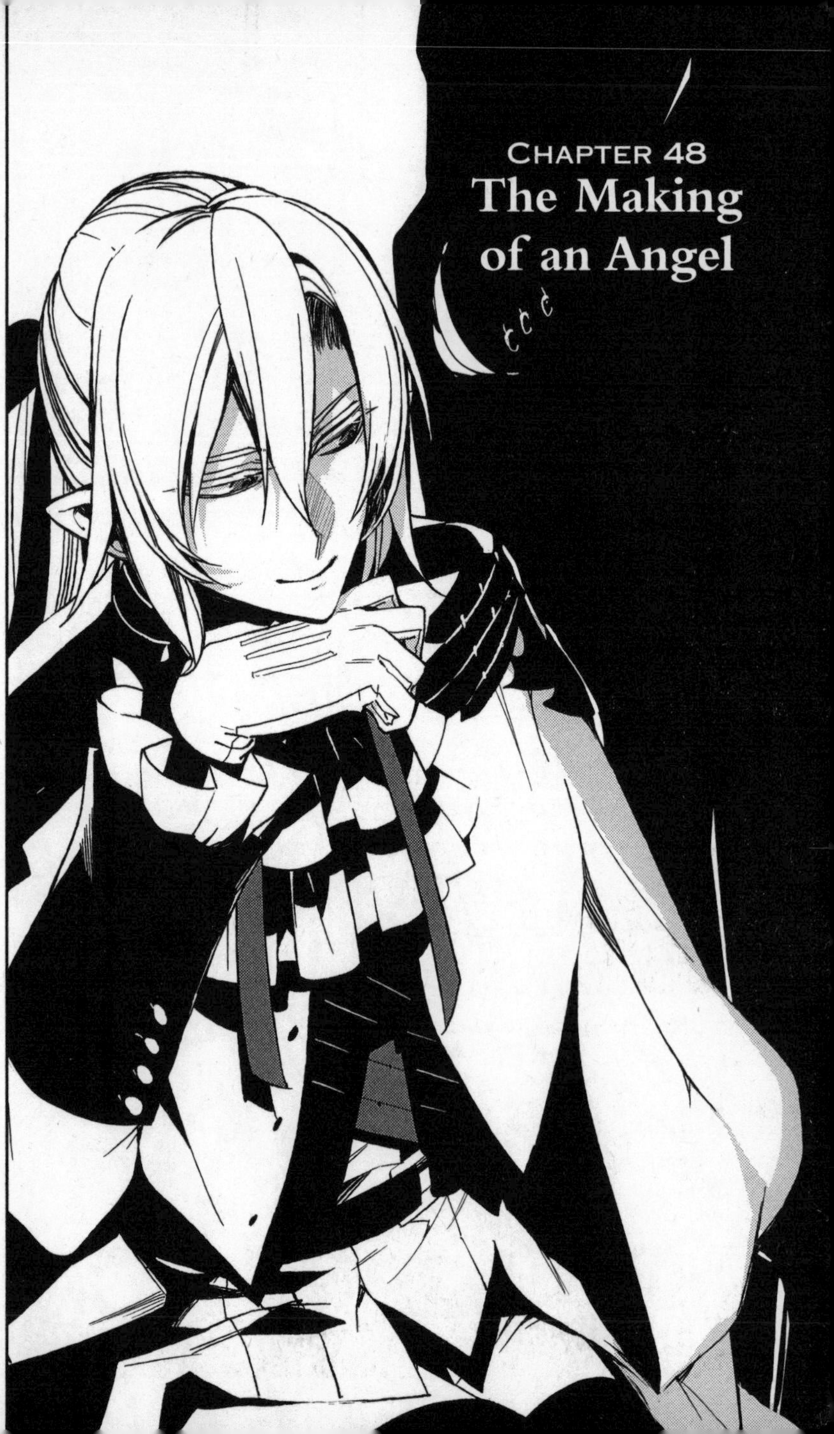

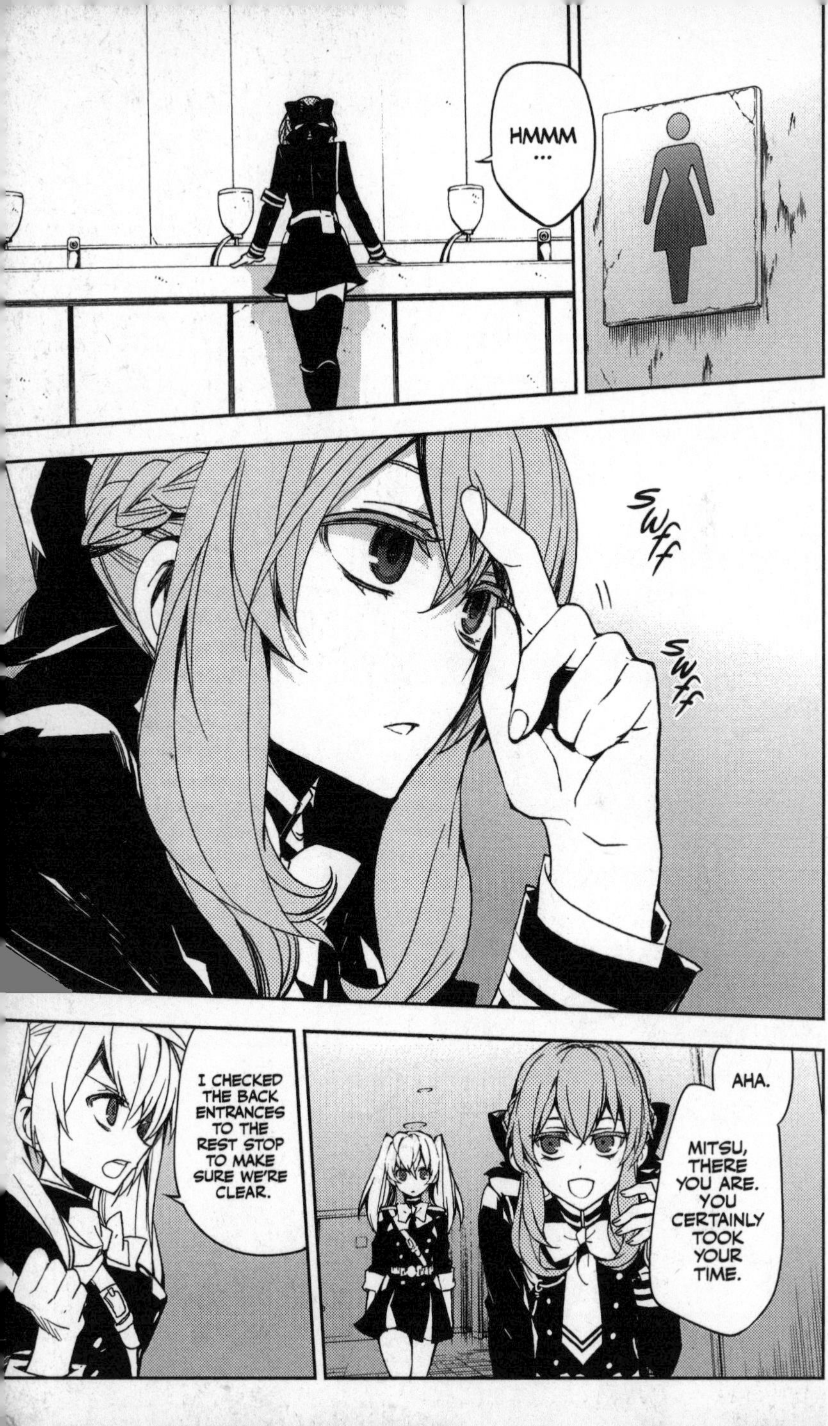
HMMM ...
SWFF
SWFF
AHA.
MITSU, THERE YOU ARE. YOU CERTAINLY TOOK YOUR TIME.
I CHECKED THE BACK ENTRANCES TO THE REST STOP TO MAKE SURE WE'RE CLEAR.

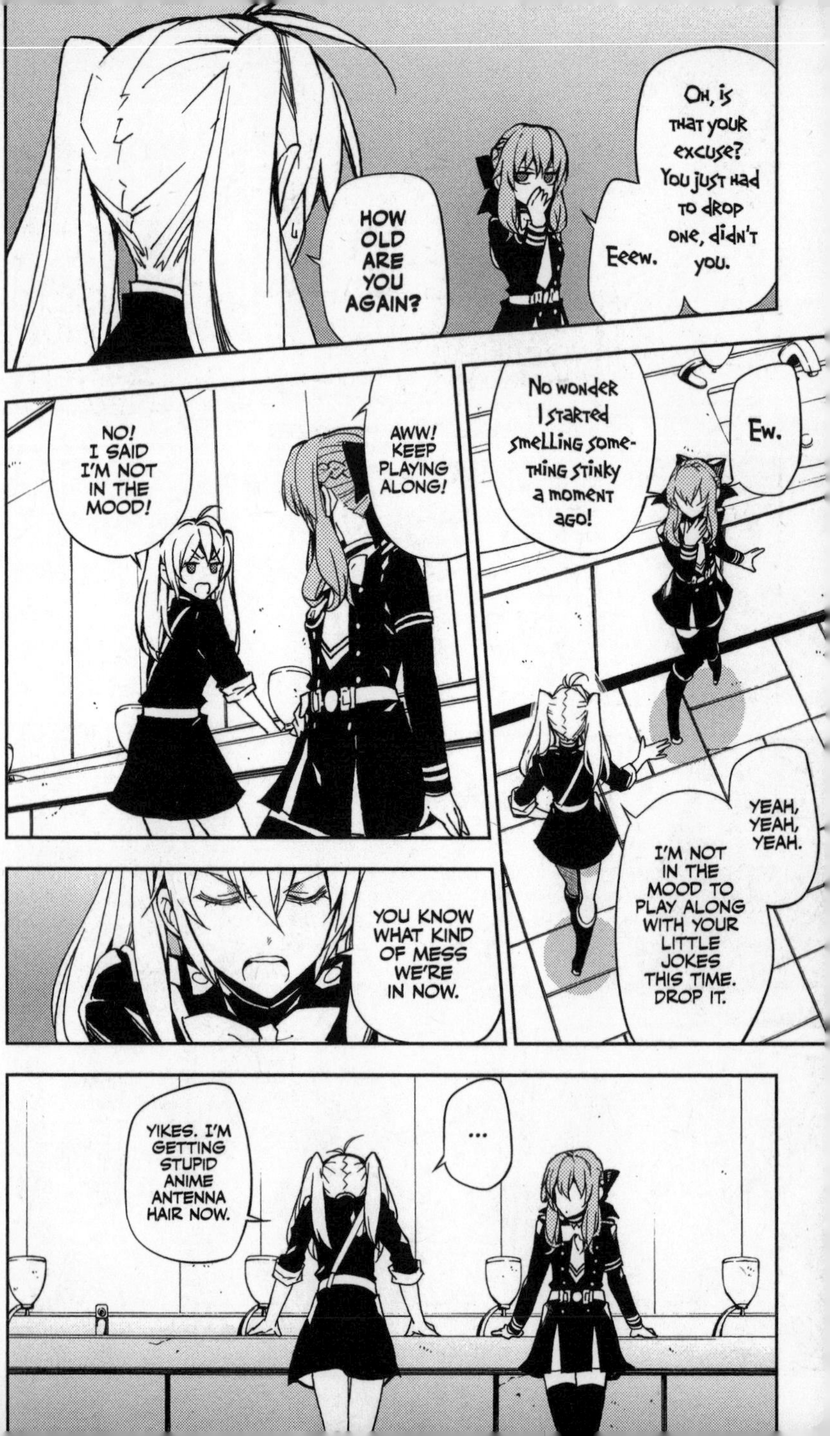
Oh, is that your excuse? You just had to drop one, didn't you.
Eeew.
HOW OLD ARE YOU AGAIN?
Ew.
No wonder I started smelling something stinky a moment ago!
YEAH, YEAH, YEAH.
I'M NOT IN THE MOOD TO PLAY ALONG WITH YOUR LITTLE JOKES THIS TIME. DROP IT.
AWW! KEEP PLAYING ALONG!
NO! I SAID I'M NOT IN THE MOOD!
YOU KNOW WHAT KIND OF MESS WE'RE IN NOW.
...
YIKES. I'M GETTING STUPID ANIME ANTENNA HAIR NOW.

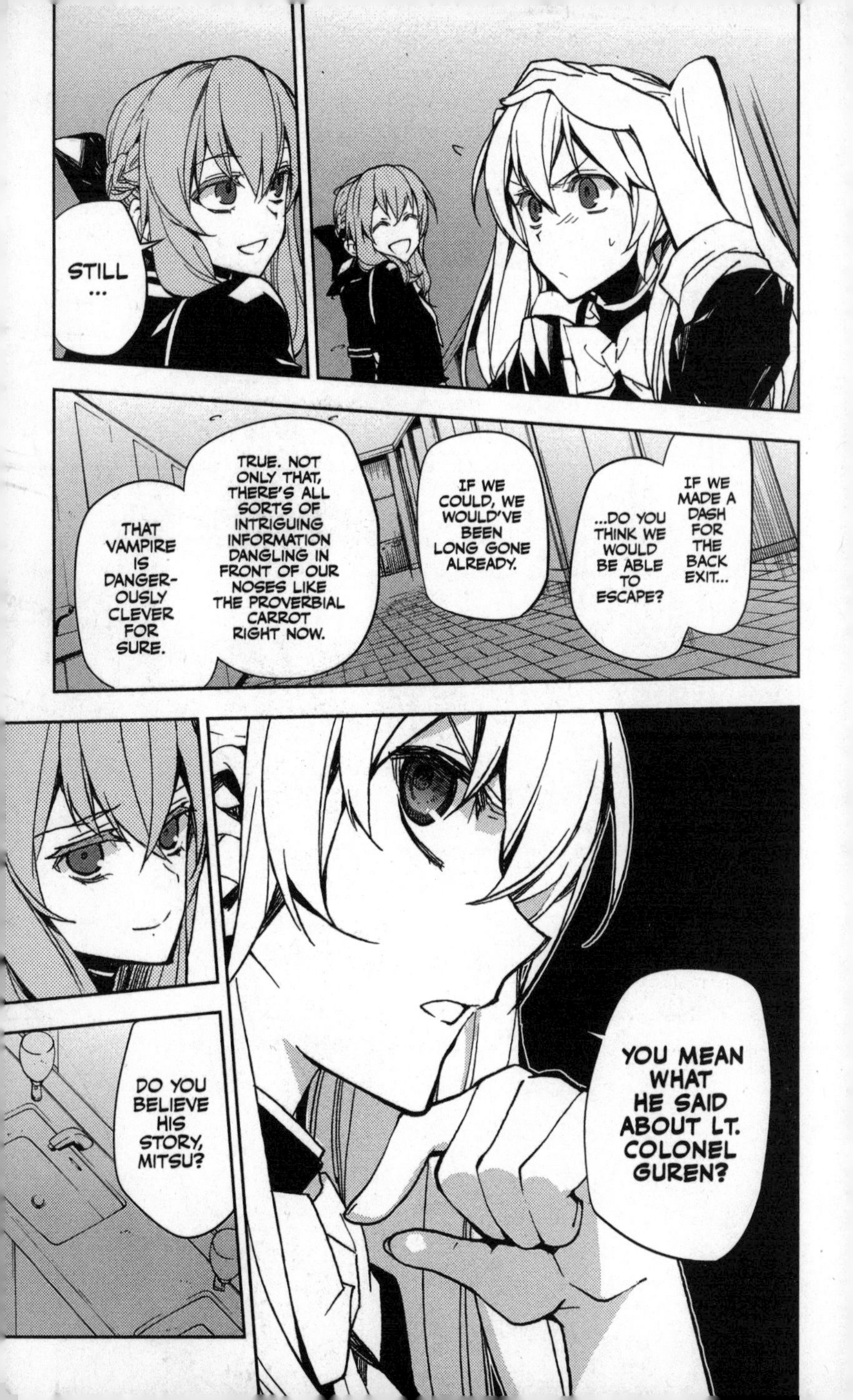
STILL ...
IF WE MADE A DASH FOR THE BACK EXIT...
...DO YOU THINK WE WOULD BE ABLE TO ESCAPE?
IF WE COULD, WE WOULD'VE BEEN LONG GONE ALREADY.
TRUE. NOT ONLY THAT, THERE'S ALL SORTS OF INTRIGUING INFORMATION DANGLING IN FRONT OF OUR NOSES LIKE THE PROVERBIAL CARROT RIGHT NOW.
THAT VAMPIRE IS DANGER-OUSLY CLEVER FOR SURE.
DO YOU BELIEVE HIS STORY, MITSU?
YOU MEAN WHAT HE SAID ABOUT LT. COLONEL GUREN?

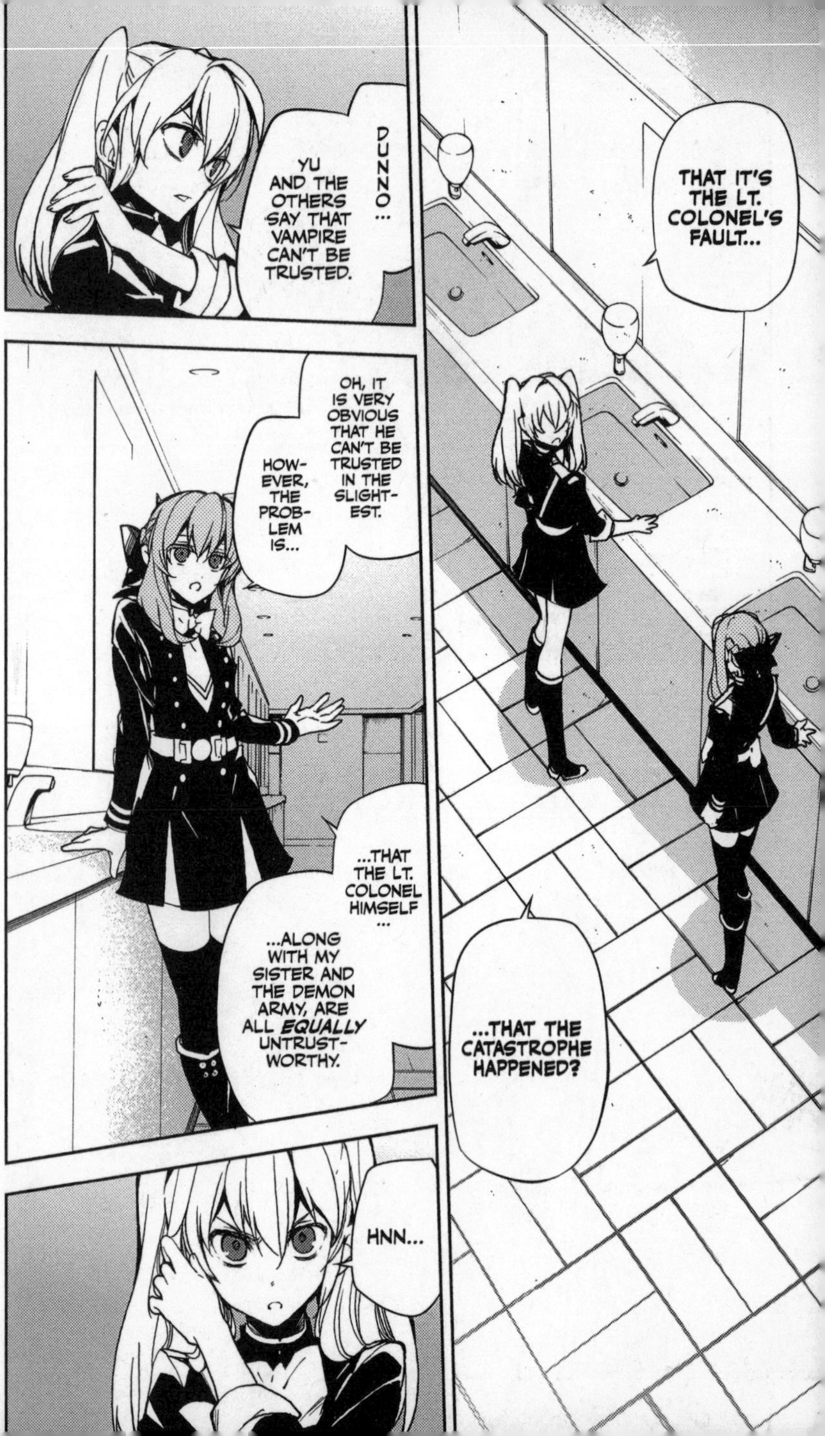
THAT IT'S THE LT. COLONEL'S FAULT...
...THAT THE CATASTROPHE HAPPENED?
DUNNO...
YU AND THE OTHERS SAY THAT VAMPIRE CAN'T BE TRUSTED.
OH, IT IS VERY OBVIOUS THAT HE CAN'T BE TRUSTED IN THE SLIGHT-EST.
HOW-EVER, THE PROB-LEM IS...
...THAT THE LT. COLONEL HIMSELF...
...ALONG WITH MY SISTER AND THE DEMON ARMY, ARE ALL *EQUALLY* UNTRUST-WORTHY.
HNN...

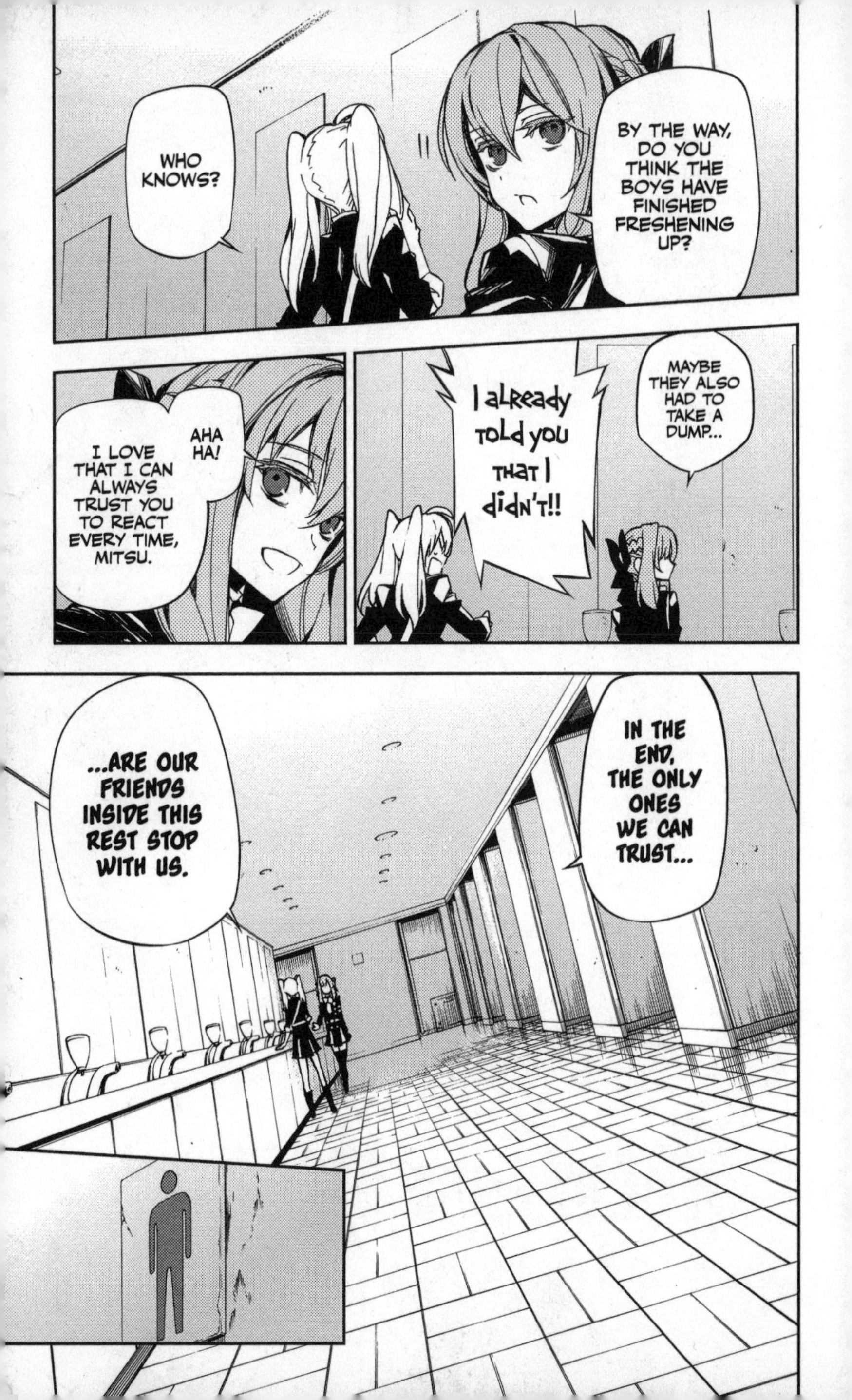
BY THE WAY, DO YOU THINK THE BOYS HAVE FINISHED FRESHENING UP?
WHO KNOWS?
MAYBE THEY ALSO HAD TO TAKE A DUMP...
I already told you that I didn't!!
AHA HA!
I LOVE THAT I CAN ALWAYS TRUST YOU TO REACT EVERY TIME, MITSU.
IN THE END, THE ONLY ONES WE CAN TRUST...
...ARE OUR FRIENDS INSIDE THIS REST STOP WITH US.

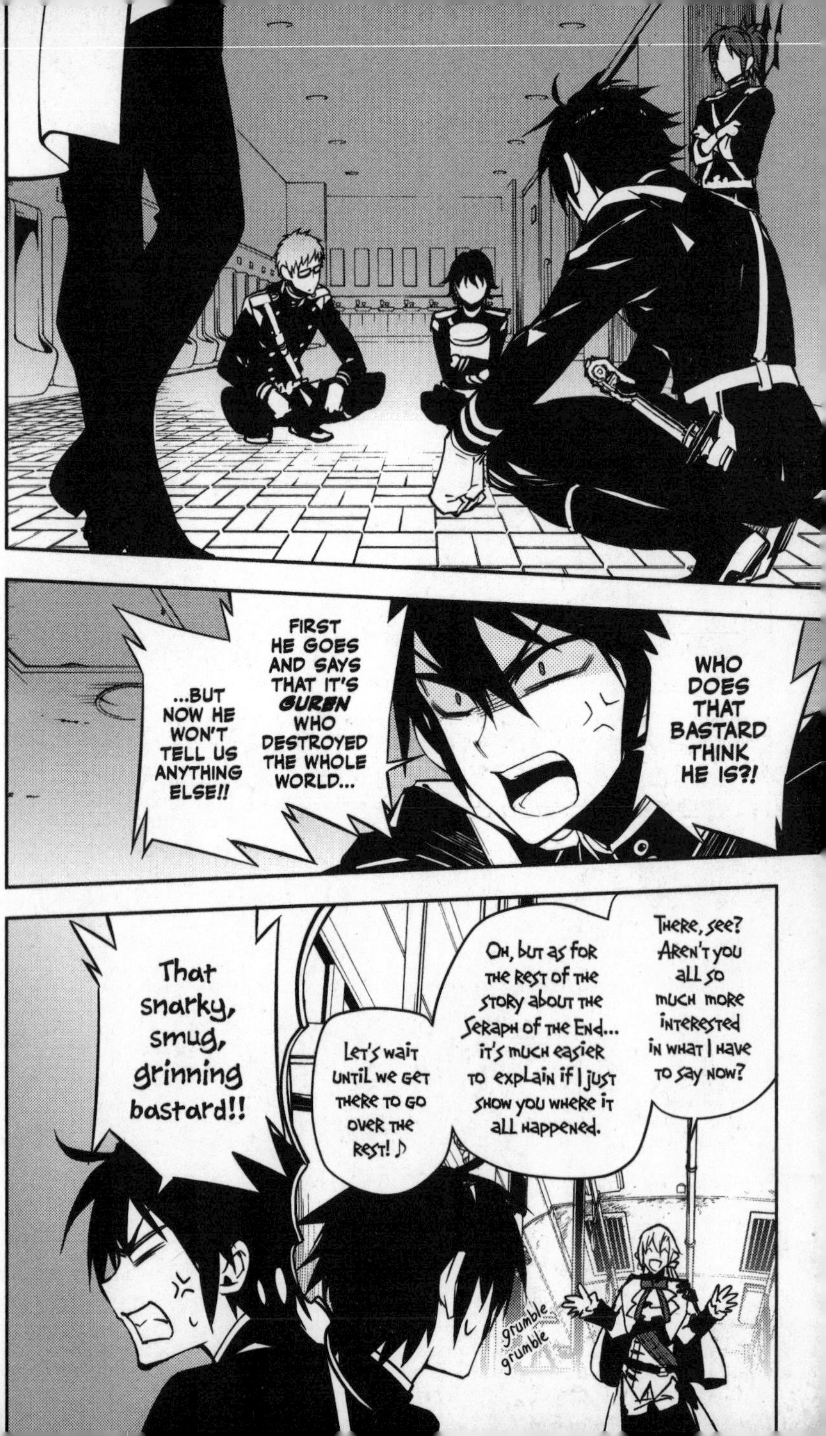
WHO DOES THAT BASTARD THINK HE IS?!
FIRST HE GOES AND SAYS THAT IT'S *GUREN* WHO DESTROYED THE WHOLE WORLD...
...BUT NOW HE WON'T TELL US ANYTHING ELSE!!
There, see? Aren't you all so much more interested in what I have to say now?
Oh, but as for the rest of the story about the Seraph of the End... it's much easier to explain if I just show you where it all happened.
Let's wait until we get there to go over the rest! ♪
That snarky, smug, grinning bastard!!
grumble grumble

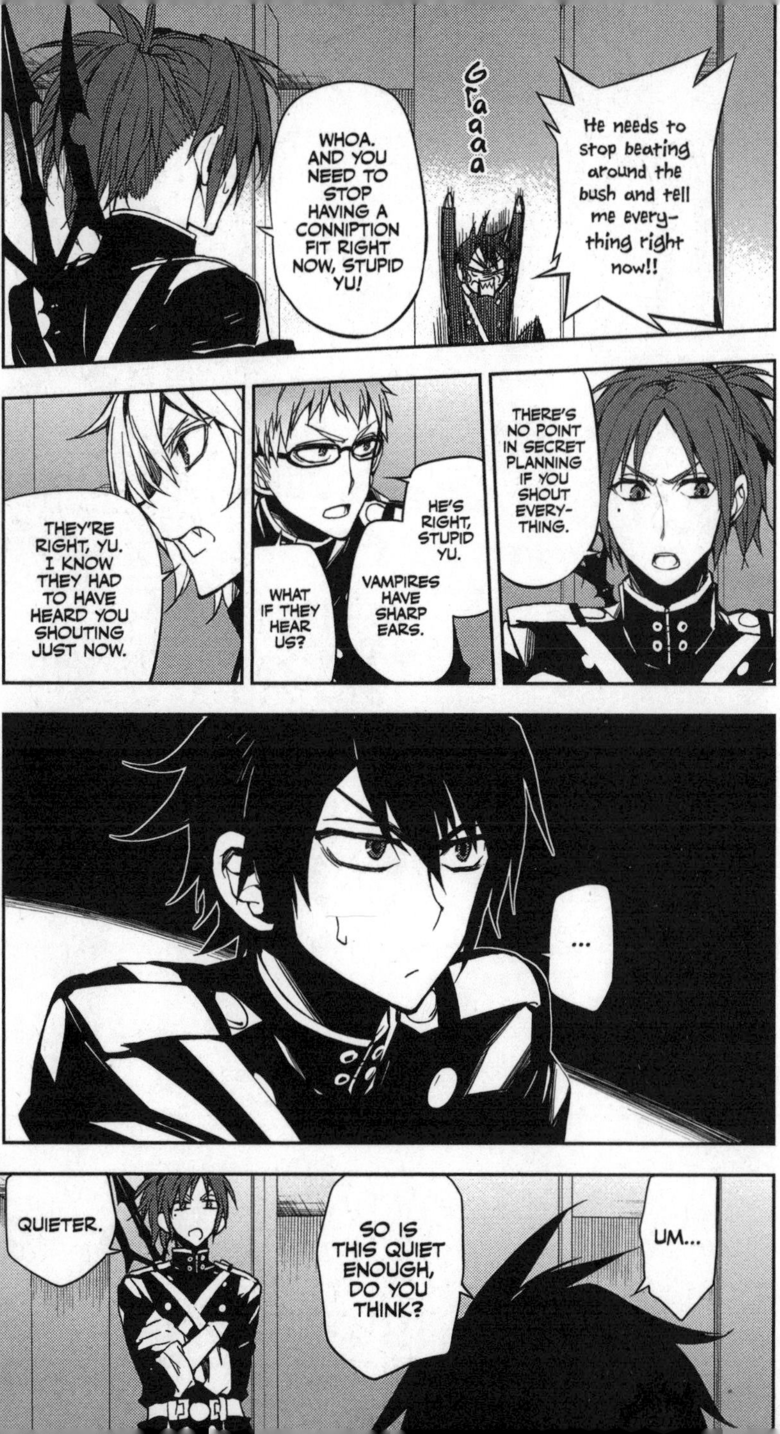
He needs to stop beating around the bush and tell me every-thing right now!!
Graaaa
WHOA. AND YOU NEED TO STOP HAVING A CONNIPTION FIT RIGHT NOW, STUPID YU!
THERE'S NO POINT IN SECRET PLANNING IF YOU SHOUT EVERY-THING.
HE'S RIGHT, STUPID YU.
VAMPIRES HAVE SHARP EARS.
WHAT IF THEY HEAR US?
THEY'RE RIGHT, YU. I KNOW THEY HAD TO HAVE HEARD YOU SHOUTING JUST NOW.
...
UM...
SO IS THIS QUIET ENOUGH, DO YOU THINK?
QUIETER.

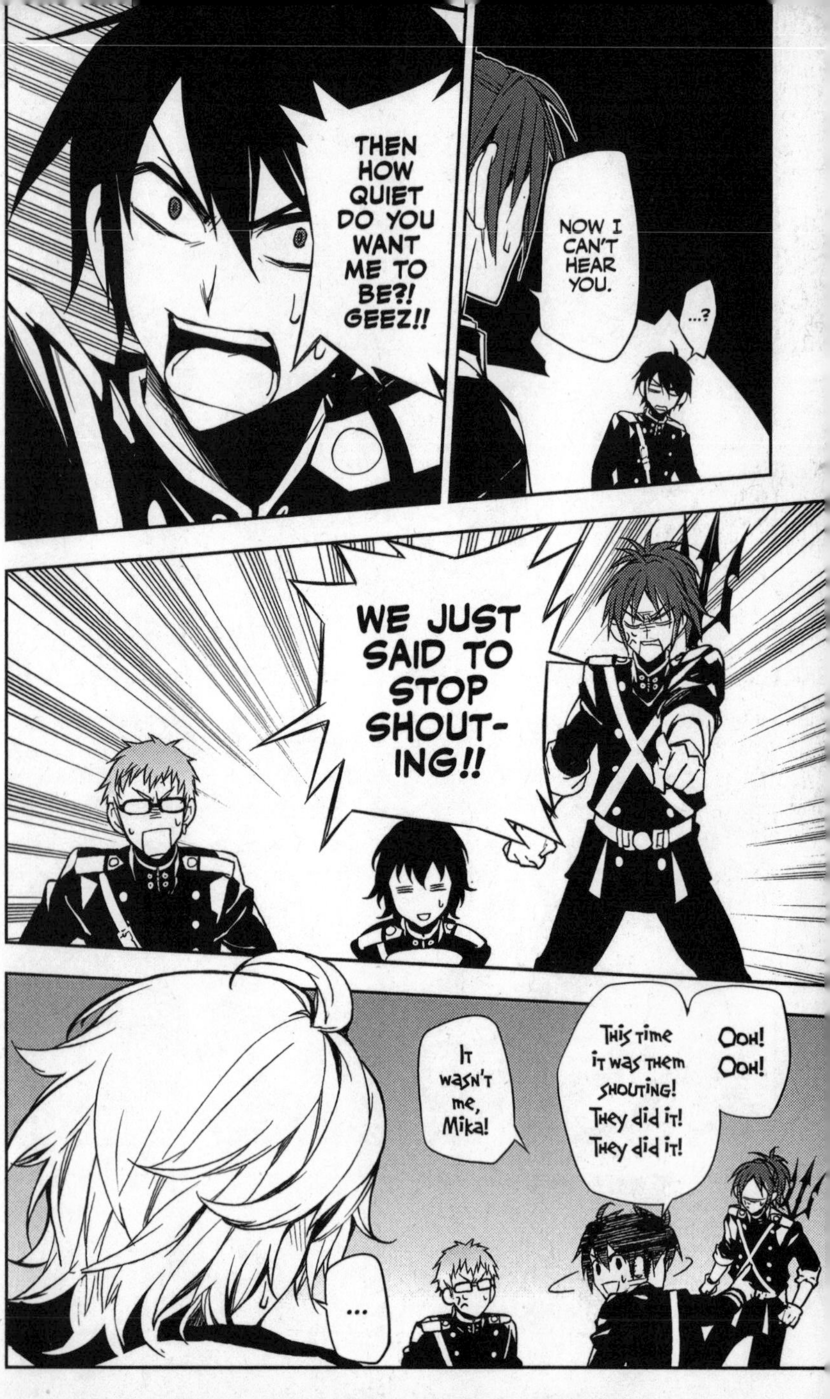
NOW I CAN'T HEAR YOU.
...?
THEN HOW QUIET DO YOU WANT ME TO BE?! GEEZ!!
WE JUST SAID TO STOP SHOUTING!!
OOH! OOH!
THIS TIME IT WAS THEM SHOUTING! THEY DID IT! THEY DID IT!
IT WASN'T ME, MIKA!
...

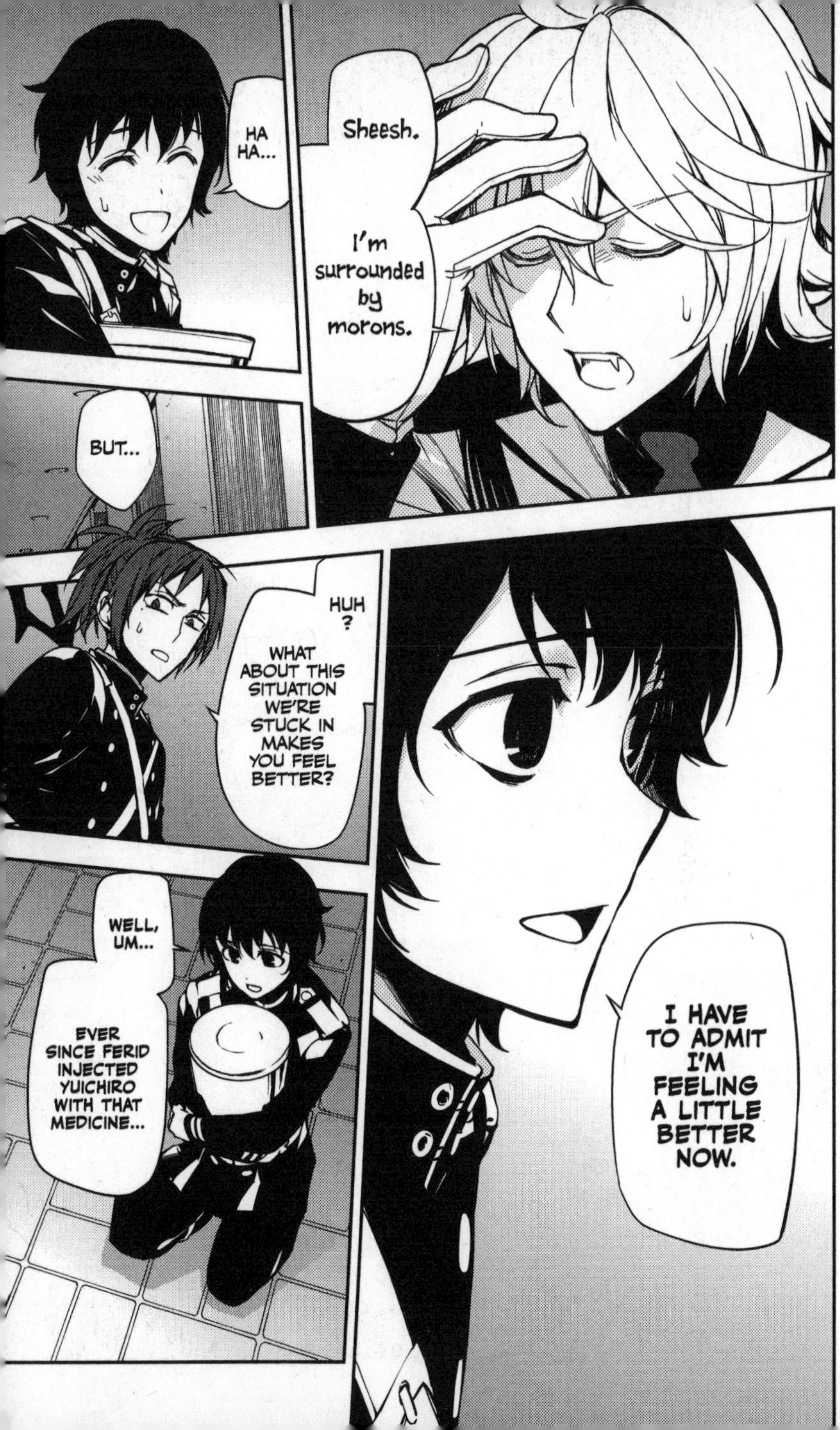
Sheesh.
I'm surrounded by morons.
HA HA...
BUT...
I HAVE TO ADMIT I'M FEELING A LITTLE BETTER NOW.
HUH?
WHAT ABOUT THIS SITUATION WE'RE STUCK IN MAKES YOU FEEL BETTER?
WELL, UM...
EVER SINCE FERID INJECTED YUICHIRO WITH THAT MEDICINE...

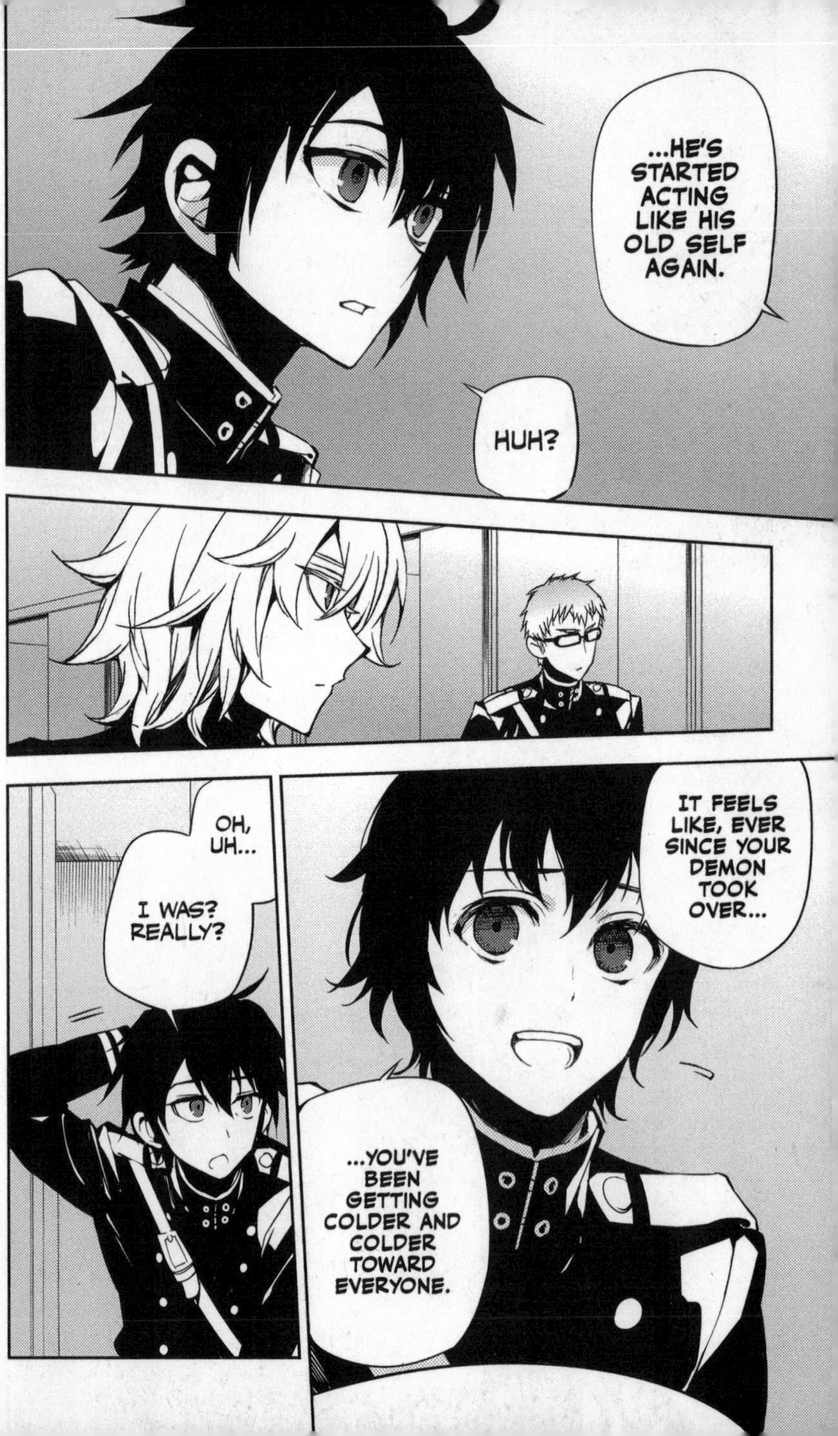
...HE'S STARTED ACTING LIKE HIS OLD SELF AGAIN.
HUH?
IT FEELS LIKE, EVER SINCE YOUR DEMON TOOK OVER...
...YOU'VE BEEN GETTING COLDER AND COLDER TOWARD EVERYONE.
OH, UH...
I WAS? REALLY?

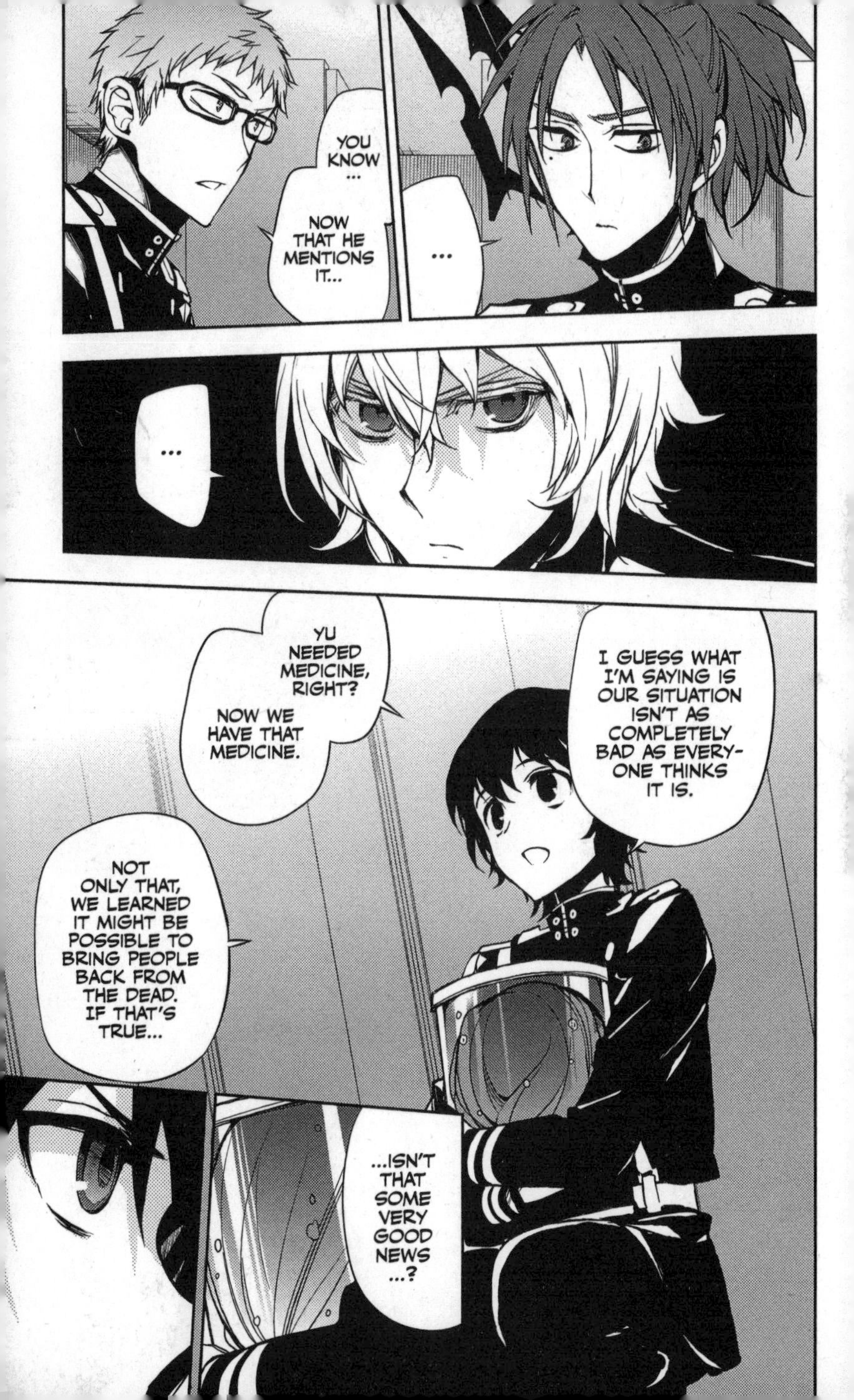
...
YOU KNOW...
NOW THAT HE MENTIONS IT...
...
I GUESS WHAT I'M SAYING IS OUR SITUATION ISN'T AS COMPLETELY BAD AS EVERYONE THINKS IT IS.
YU NEEDED MEDICINE, RIGHT?
NOW WE HAVE THAT MEDICINE.
NOT ONLY THAT, WE LEARNED IT MIGHT BE POSSIBLE TO BRING PEOPLE BACK FROM THE DEAD. IF THAT'S TRUE...
...ISN'T THAT SOME VERY GOOD NEWS...?

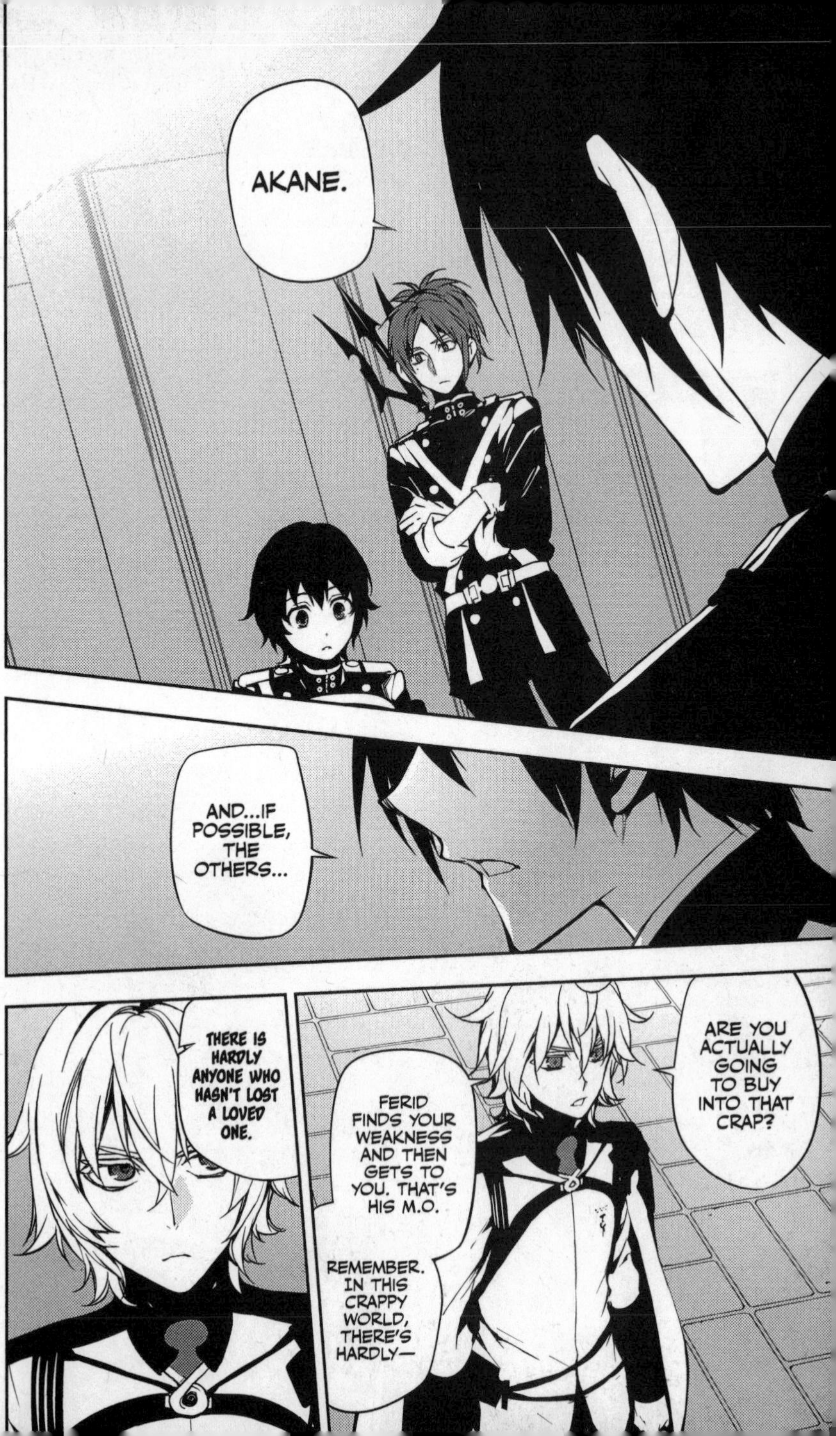
AKANE.
AND...IF POSSIBLE, THE OTHERS...
ARE YOU ACTUALLY GOING TO BUY INTO THAT CRAP?
FERID FINDS YOUR WEAKNESS AND THEN GETS TO YOU. THAT'S HIS M.O.
REMEMBER. IN THIS CRAPPY WORLD, THERE'S HARDLY—
THERE IS HARDLY ANYONE WHO HASN'T LOST A LOVED ONE.

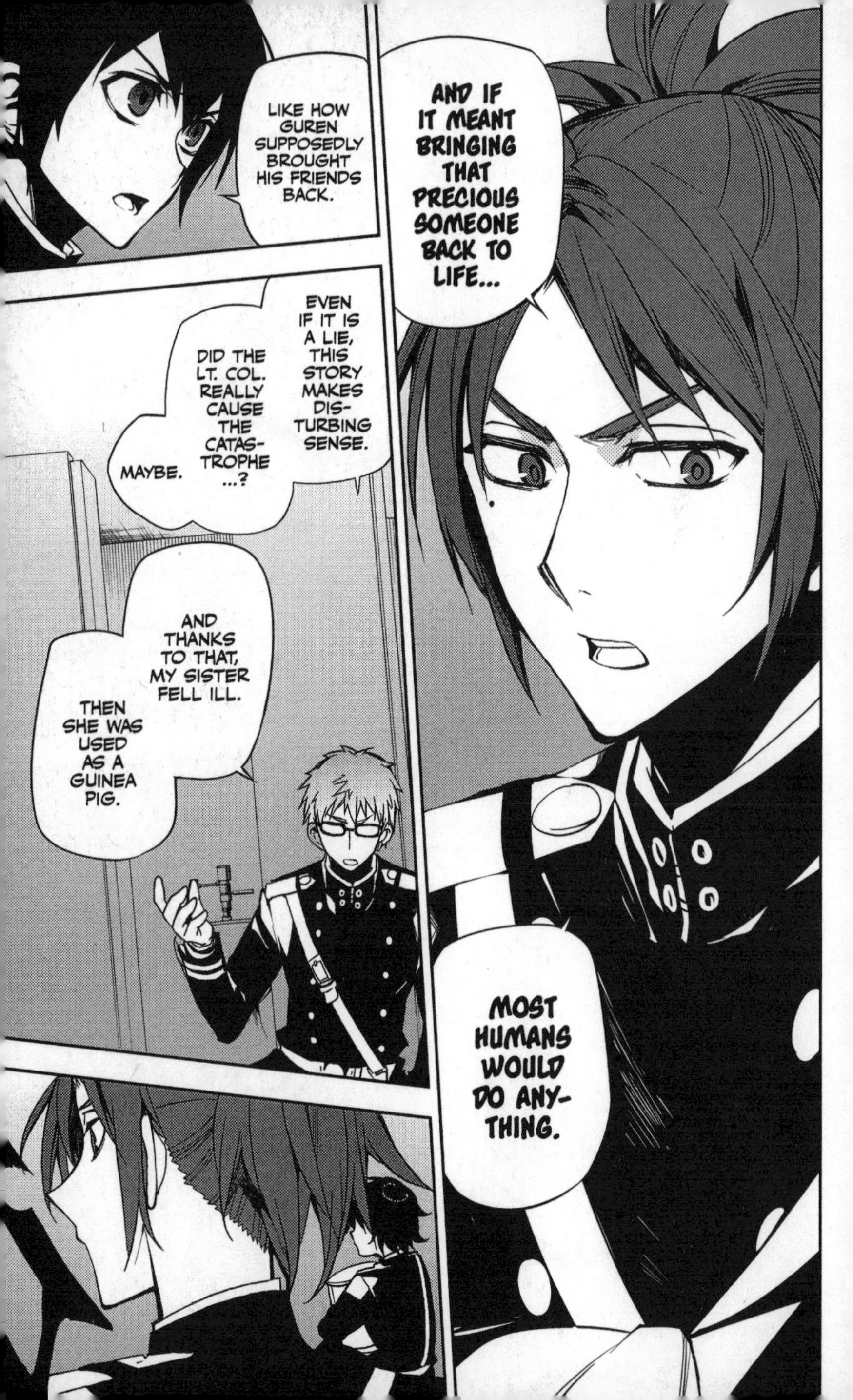
AND IF IT MEANT BRINGING THAT PRECIOUS SOMEONE BACK TO LIFE...
MOST HUMANS WOULD DO ANY-THING.
LIKE HOW GUREN SUPPOSEDLY BROUGHT HIS FRIENDS BACK.
EVEN IF IT IS A LIE, THIS STORY MAKES DIS-TURBING SENSE.
DID THE LT. COL. REALLY CAUSE THE CATAS-TROPHE ...?
MAYBE.
AND THANKS TO THAT, MY SISTER FELL ILL.
THEN SHE WAS USED AS A GUINEA PIG.

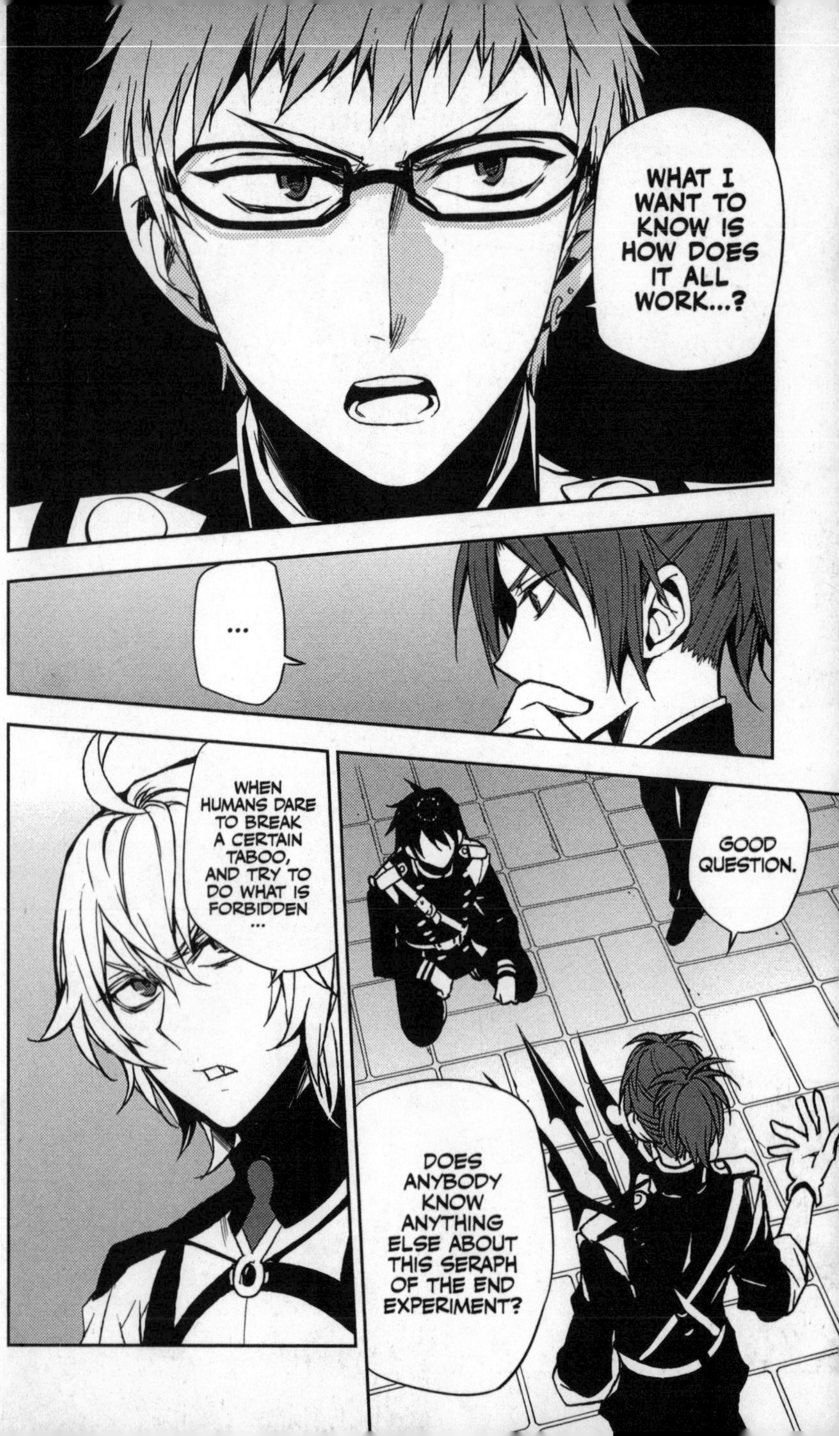
WHAT I WANT TO KNOW IS HOW DOES IT ALL WORK...?
...
GOOD QUESTION.
DOES ANYBODY KNOW ANYTHING ELSE ABOUT THIS SERAPH OF THE END EXPERIMENT?
WHEN HUMANS DARE TO BREAK A CERTAIN TABOO, AND TRY TO DO WHAT IS FORBIDDEN...

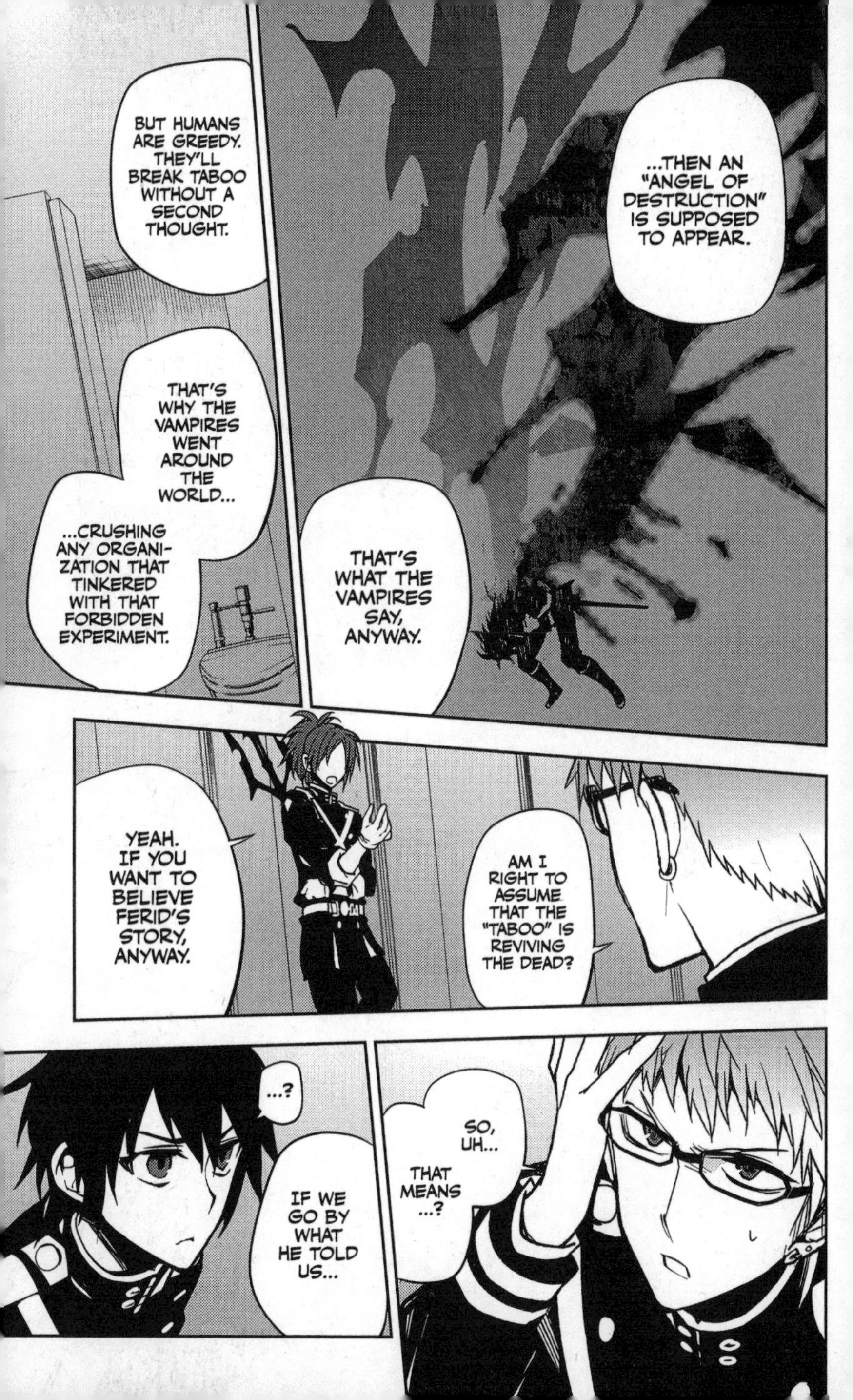
...THEN AN "ANGEL OF DESTRUCTION" IS SUPPOSED TO APPEAR.
THAT'S WHAT THE VAMPIRES SAY, ANYWAY.
BUT HUMANS ARE GREEDY. THEY'LL BREAK TABOO WITHOUT A SECOND THOUGHT.
THAT'S WHY THE VAMPIRES WENT AROUND THE WORLD...
...CRUSHING ANY ORGANIZATION THAT TINKERED WITH THAT FORBIDDEN EXPERIMENT.
AM I RIGHT TO ASSUME THAT THE "TABOO" IS REVIVING THE DEAD?
YEAH. IF YOU WANT TO BELIEVE FERID'S STORY, ANYWAY.
SO, UH...
THAT MEANS ...?
...?
IF WE GO BY WHAT HE TOLD US...

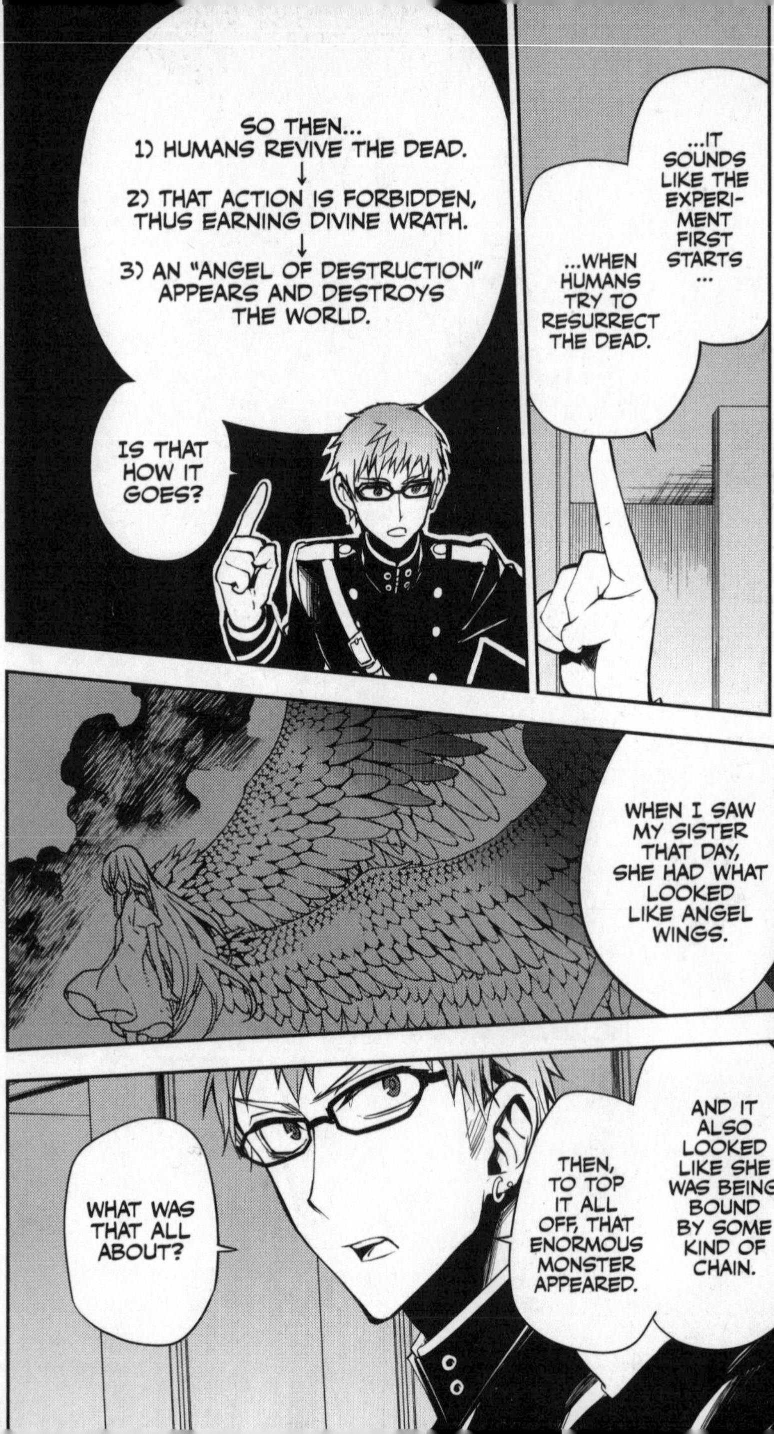
...IT SOUNDS LIKE THE EXPERIMENT FIRST STARTS...
...WHEN HUMANS TRY TO RESURRECT THE DEAD.
SO THEN... 1) HUMANS REVIVE THE DEAD. ↓ 2) THAT ACTION IS FORBIDDEN, THUS EARNING DIVINE WRATH. ↓ 3) AN "ANGEL OF DESTRUCTION" APPEARS AND DESTROYS THE WORLD.
IS THAT HOW IT GOES?
WHEN I SAW MY SISTER THAT DAY, SHE HAD WHAT LOOKED LIKE ANGEL WINGS.
AND IT ALSO LOOKED LIKE SHE WAS BEING BOUND BY SOME KIND OF CHAIN.
THEN, TO TOP IT ALL OFF, THAT ENORMOUS MONSTER APPEARED.
WHAT WAS THAT ALL ABOUT?

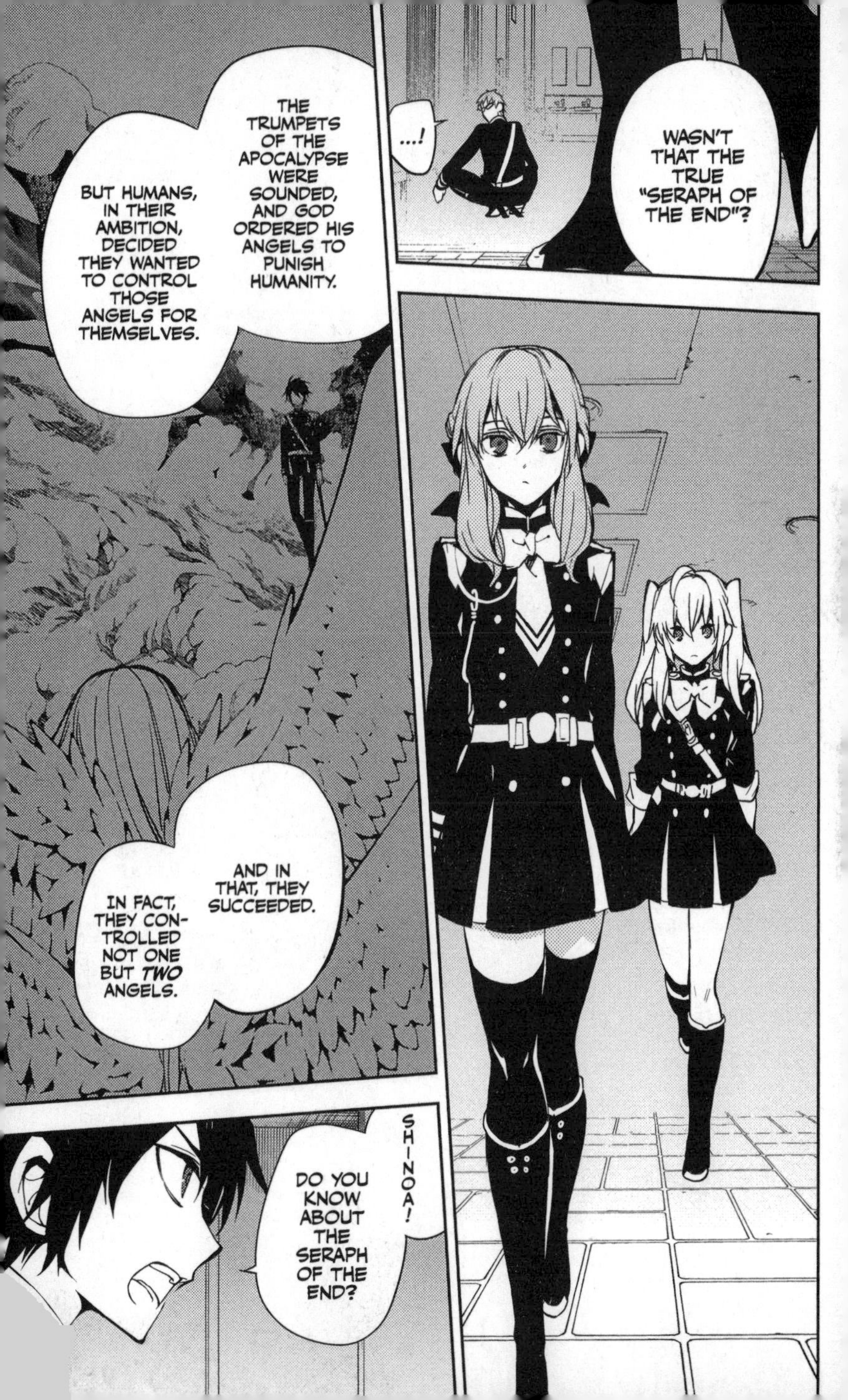
WASN'T THAT THE TRUE "SERAPH OF THE END"?
...!
THE TRUMPETS OF THE APOCALYPSE WERE SOUNDED, AND GOD ORDERED HIS ANGELS TO PUNISH HUMANITY.
BUT HUMANS, IN THEIR AMBITION, DECIDED THEY WANTED TO CONTROL THOSE ANGELS FOR THEMSELVES.
AND IN THAT, THEY SUCCEEDED.
IN FACT, THEY CONTROLLED NOT ONE BUT *TWO* ANGELS.
SHINOA!
DO YOU KNOW ABOUT THE SERAPH OF THE END?

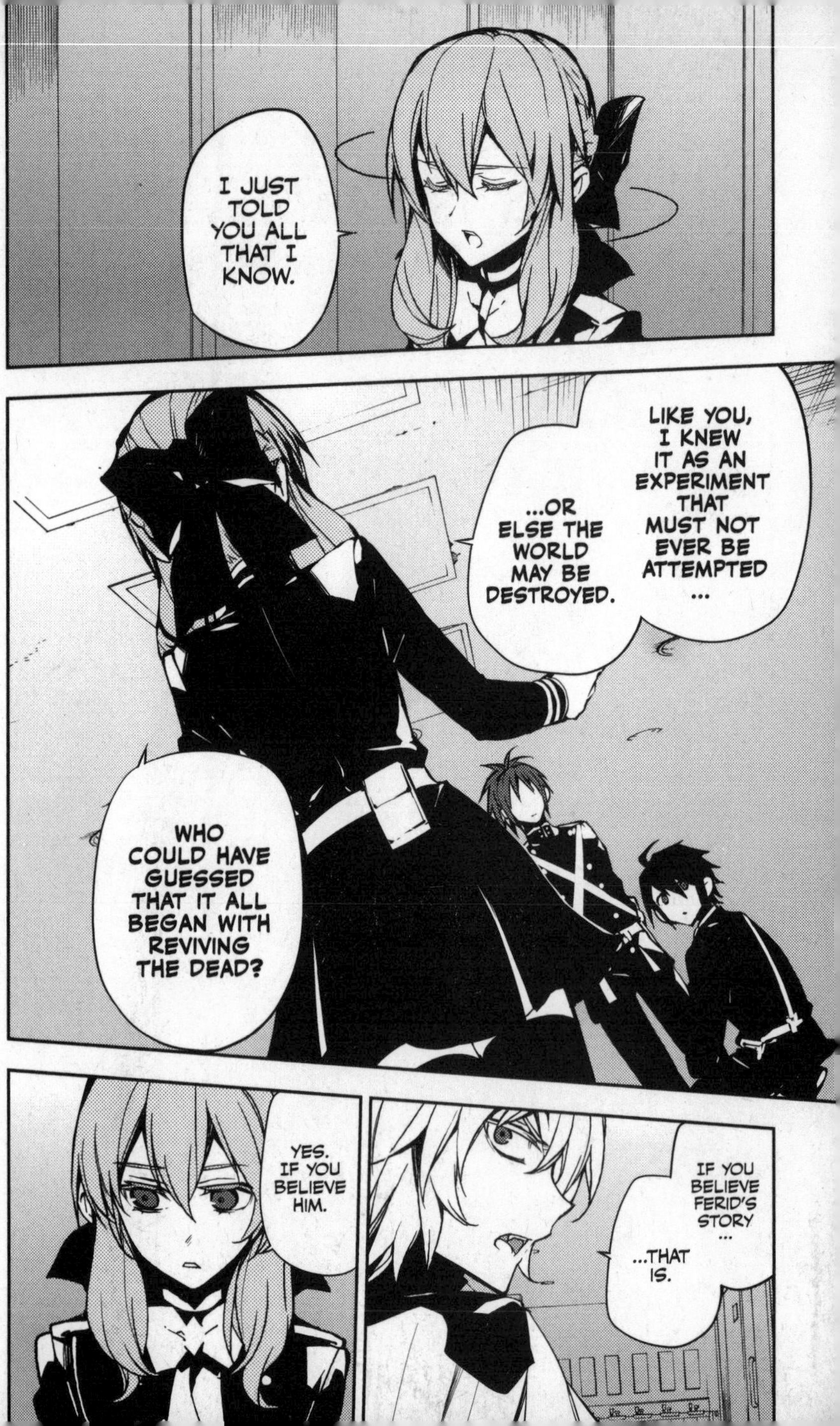
I JUST TOLD YOU ALL THAT I KNOW.
LIKE YOU, I KNEW IT AS AN EXPERIMENT THAT MUST NOT EVER BE ATTEMPTED ...
...OR ELSE THE WORLD MAY BE DESTROYED.
WHO COULD HAVE GUESSED THAT IT ALL BEGAN WITH REVIVING THE DEAD?
IF YOU BELIEVE FERID'S STORY ...
...THAT IS.
YES. IF YOU BELIEVE HIM.

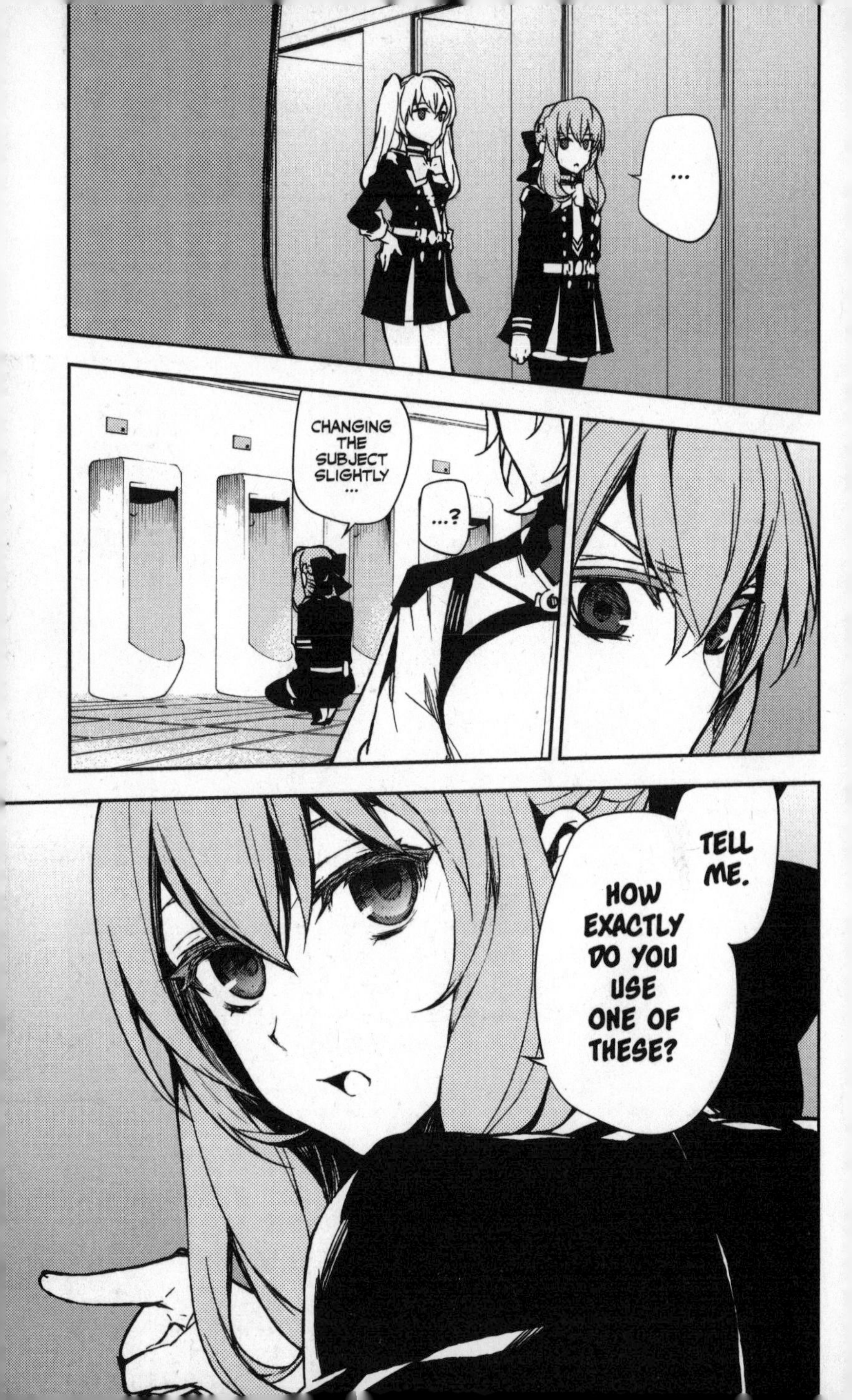
...
CHANGING THE SUBJECT SLIGHTLY ...
...?
TELL ME.
HOW EXACTLY DO YOU USE ONE OF THESE?

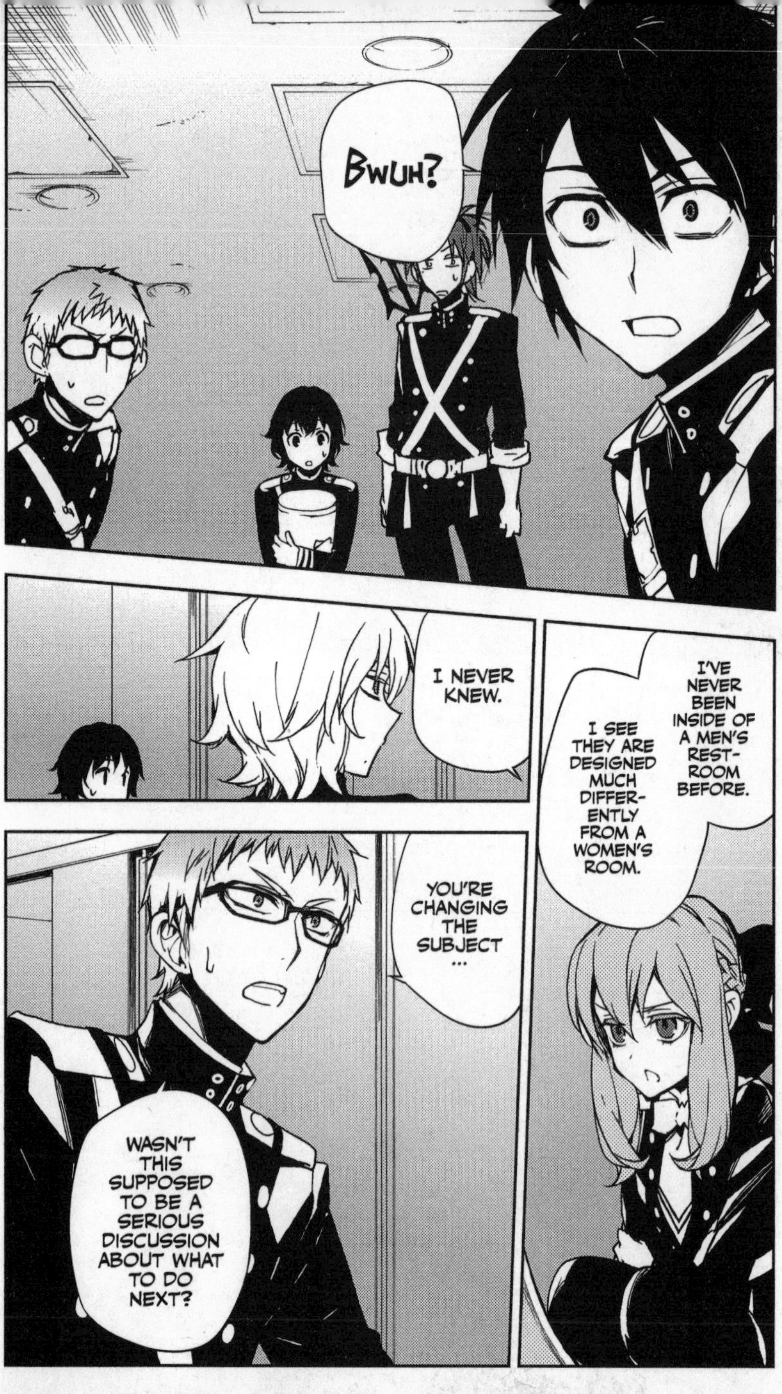
BWUH?
I'VE NEVER BEEN INSIDE OF A MEN'S REST-ROOM BEFORE.
I SEE THEY ARE DESIGNED MUCH DIFFER-ENTLY FROM A WOMEN'S ROOM.
I NEVER KNEW.
YOU'RE CHANGING THE SUBJECT ...
WASN'T THIS SUPPOSED TO BE A SERIOUS DISCUSSION ABOUT WHAT TO DO NEXT?

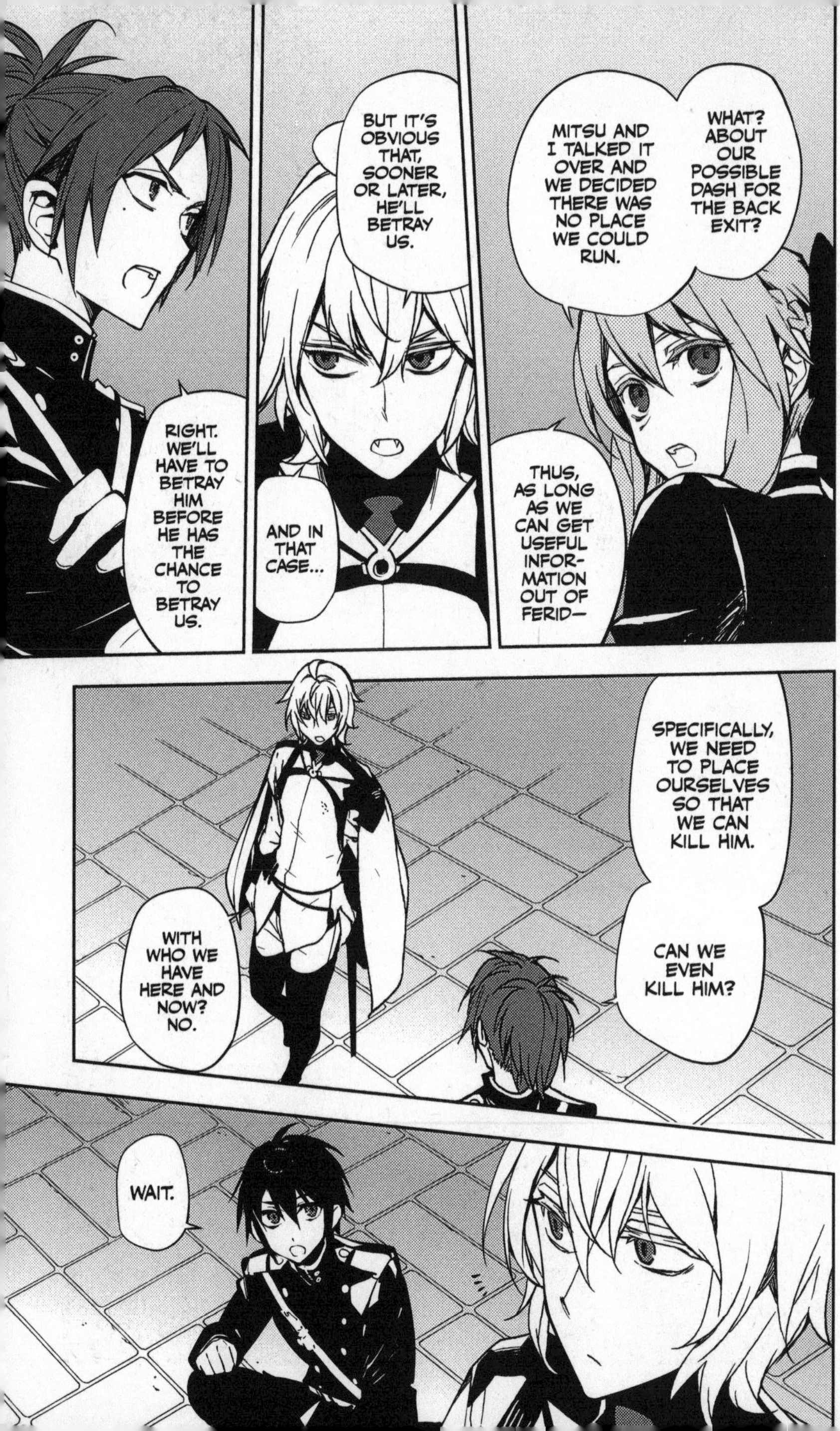
WHAT? ABOUT OUR POSSIBLE DASH FOR THE BACK EXIT?
MITSU AND I TALKED IT OVER AND WE DECIDED THERE WAS NO PLACE WE COULD RUN.
THUS, AS LONG AS WE CAN GET USEFUL INFORMATION OUT OF FERID—
BUT IT'S OBVIOUS THAT, SOONER OR LATER, HE'LL BETRAY US.
AND IN THAT CASE...
RIGHT. WE'LL HAVE TO BETRAY HIM BEFORE HE HAS THE CHANCE TO BETRAY US.
SPECIFICALLY, WE NEED TO PLACE OURSELVES SO THAT WE CAN KILL HIM.
CAN WE EVEN KILL HIM?
WITH WHO WE HAVE HERE AND NOW? NO.
WAIT.

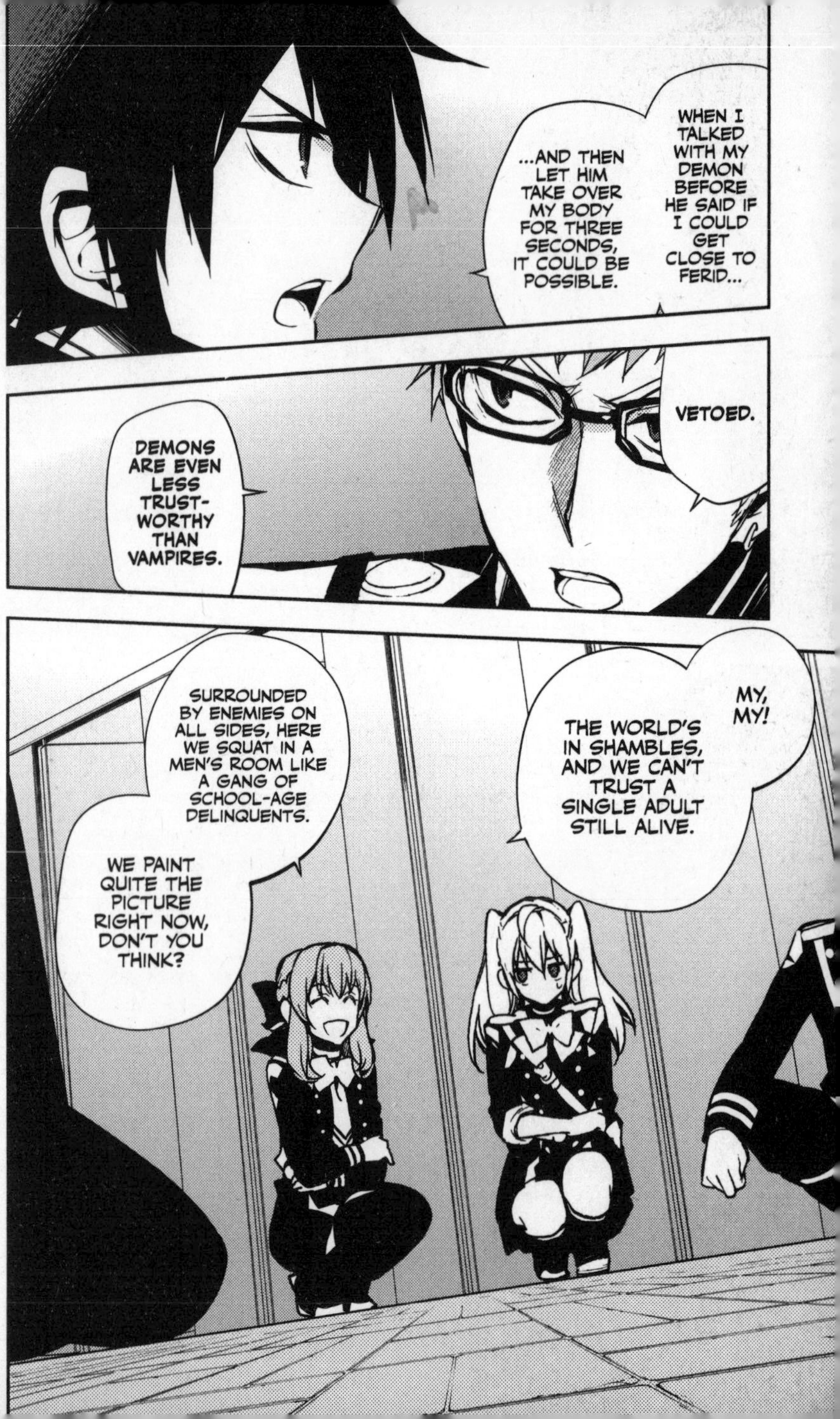
WHEN I TALKED WITH MY DEMON BEFORE HE SAID IF I COULD GET CLOSE TO FERID...
...AND THEN LET HIM TAKE OVER MY BODY FOR THREE SECONDS, IT COULD BE POSSIBLE.
VETOED.
DEMONS ARE EVEN LESS TRUST-WORTHY THAN VAMPIRES.
MY, MY!
THE WORLD'S IN SHAMBLES, AND WE CAN'T TRUST A SINGLE ADULT STILL ALIVE.
SURROUNDED BY ENEMIES ON ALL SIDES, HERE WE SQUAT IN A MEN'S ROOM LIKE A GANG OF SCHOOL-AGE DELINQUENTS.
WE PAINT QUITE THE PICTURE RIGHT NOW, DON'T YOU THINK?

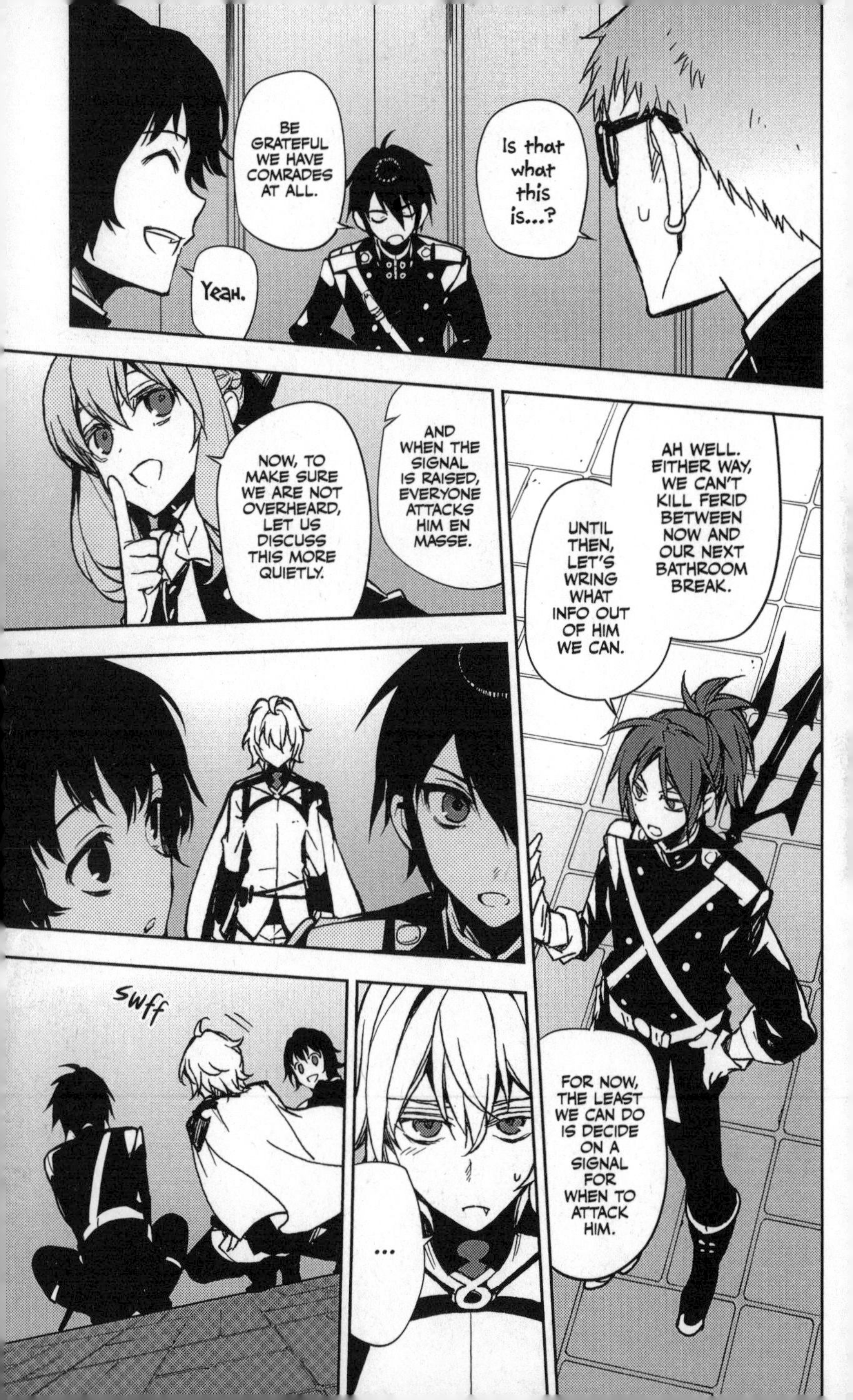
Is that what this is...?
BE GRATEFUL WE HAVE COMRADES AT ALL.
Yeah.
AH WELL. EITHER WAY, WE CAN'T KILL FERID BETWEEN NOW AND OUR NEXT BATHROOM BREAK.
UNTIL THEN, LET'S WRING WHAT INFO OUT OF HIM WE CAN.
FOR NOW, THE LEAST WE CAN DO IS DECIDE ON A SIGNAL FOR WHEN TO ATTACK HIM.
AND WHEN THE SIGNAL IS RAISED, EVERYONE ATTACKS HIM EN MASSE.
NOW, TO MAKE SURE WE ARE NOT OVERHEARD, LET US DISCUSS THIS MORE QUIETLY.
...
swff

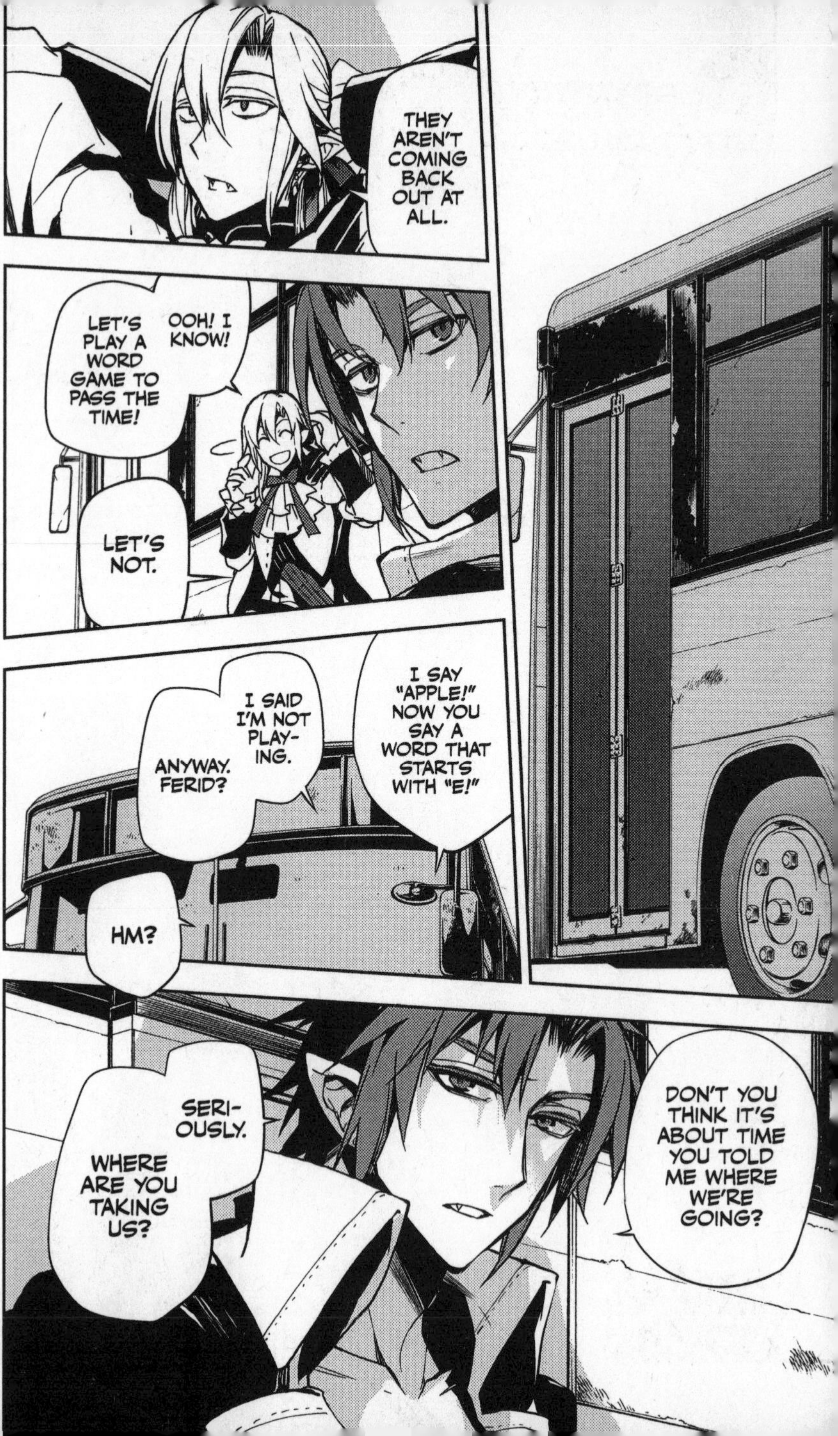
THEY AREN'T COMING BACK OUT AT ALL.
OOH! I KNOW!
LET'S PLAY A WORD GAME TO PASS THE TIME!
LET'S NOT.
I SAY "APPLE!" NOW YOU SAY A WORD THAT STARTS WITH "E!"
I SAID I'M NOT PLAY-ING.
ANYWAY. FERID?
HM?
DON'T YOU THINK IT'S ABOUT TIME YOU TOLD ME WHERE WE'RE GOING?
SERI-OUSLY.
WHERE ARE YOU TAKING US?

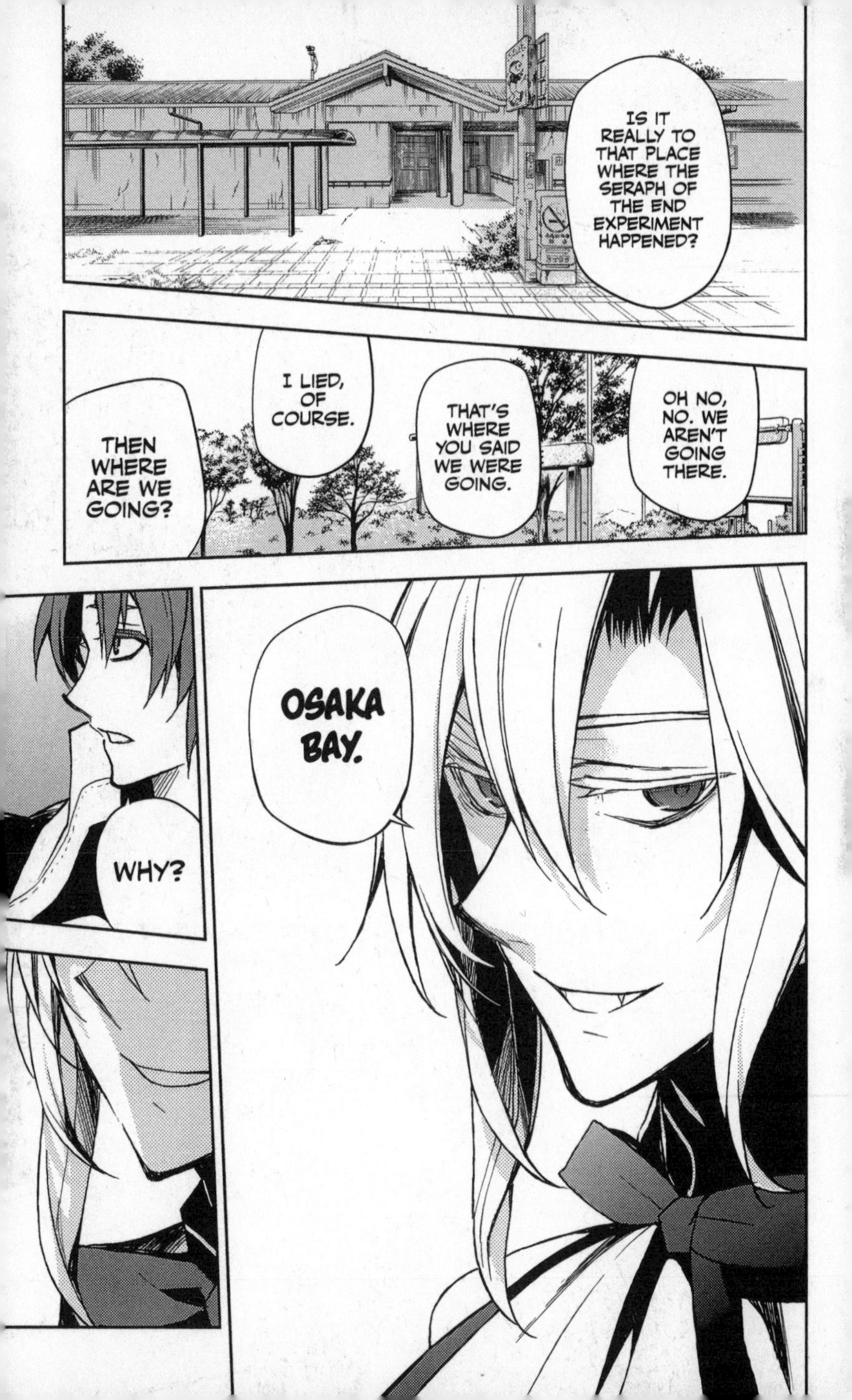
IS IT REALLY TO THAT PLACE WHERE THE SERAPH OF THE END EXPERIMENT HAPPENED?
OH NO, NO. WE AREN'T GOING THERE.
THAT'S WHERE YOU SAID WE WERE GOING.
I LIED, OF COURSE.
THEN WHERE ARE WE GOING?
OSAKA BAY.
WHY?

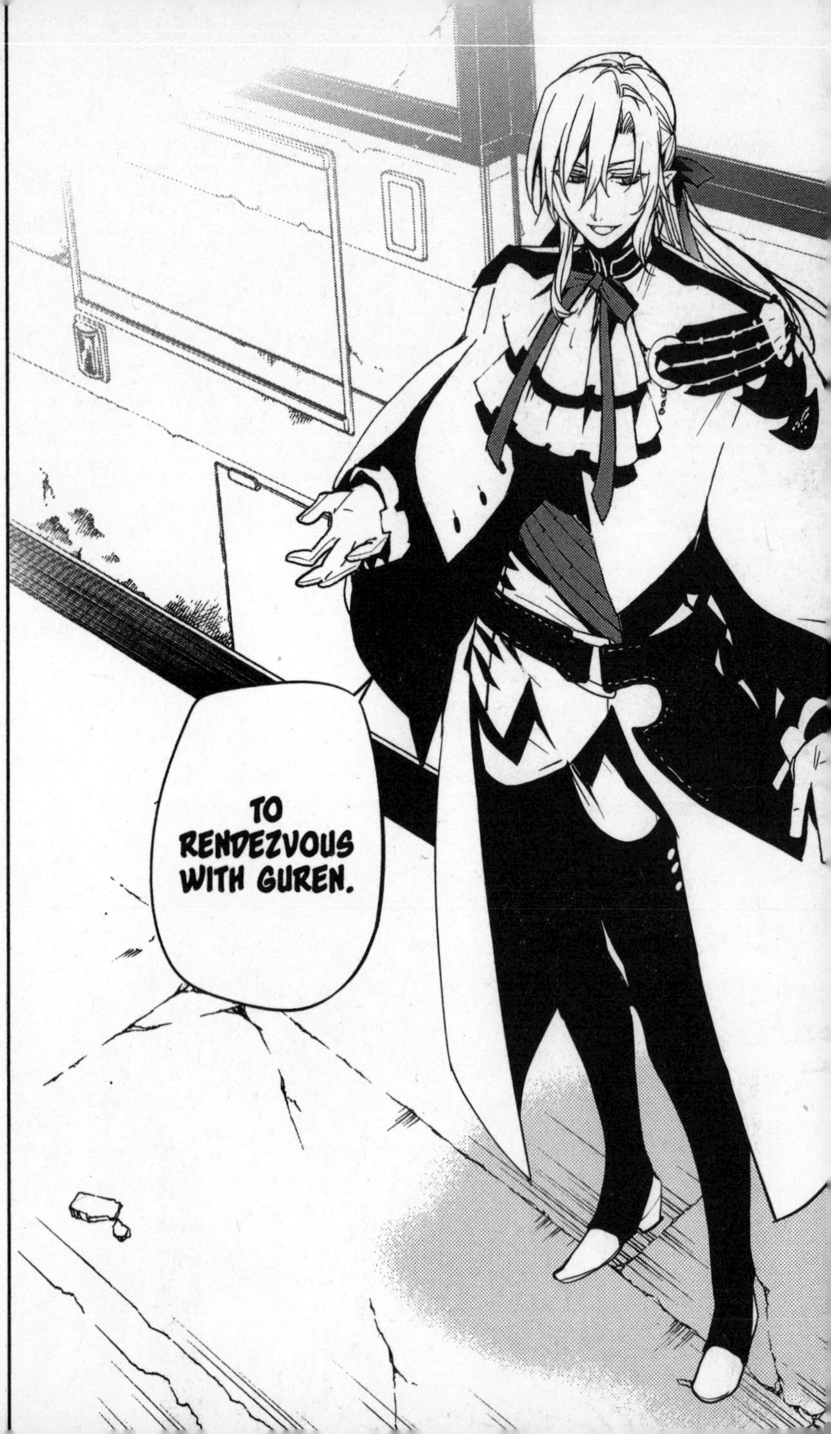
TO RENDEZVOUS WITH GUREN.

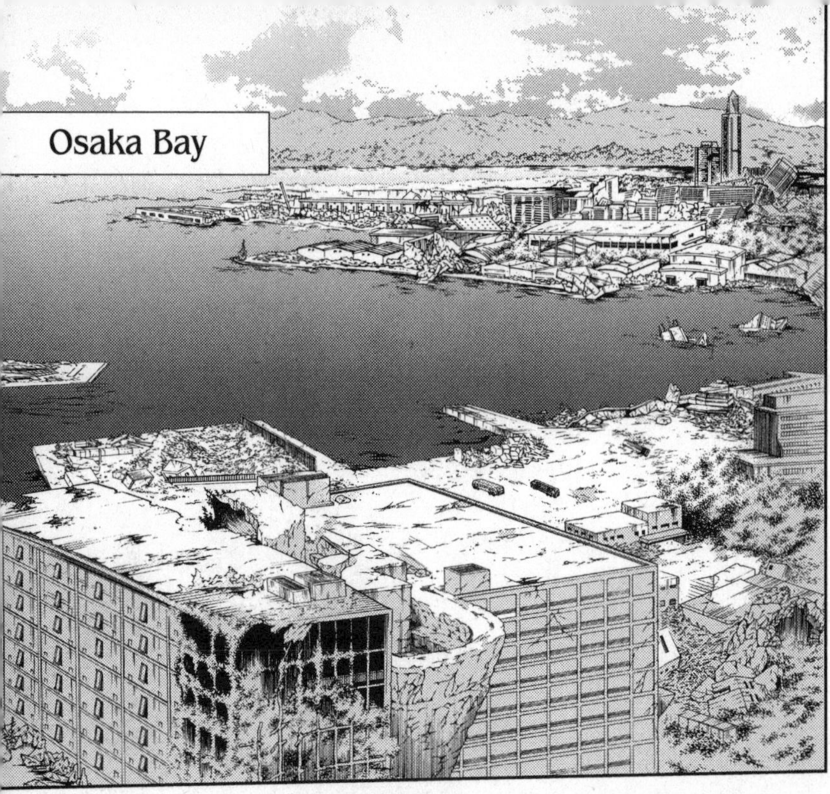
Osaka Bay

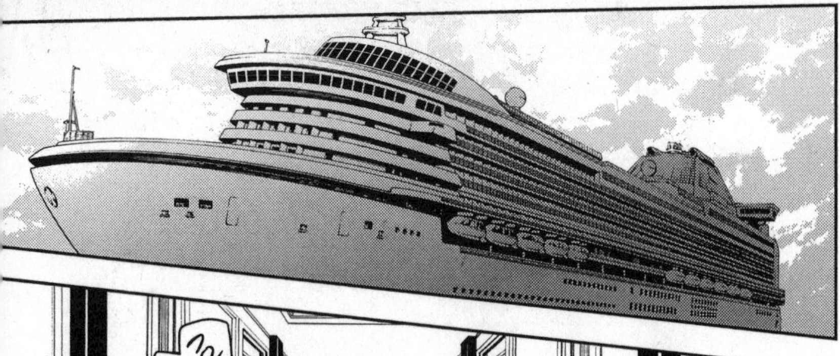

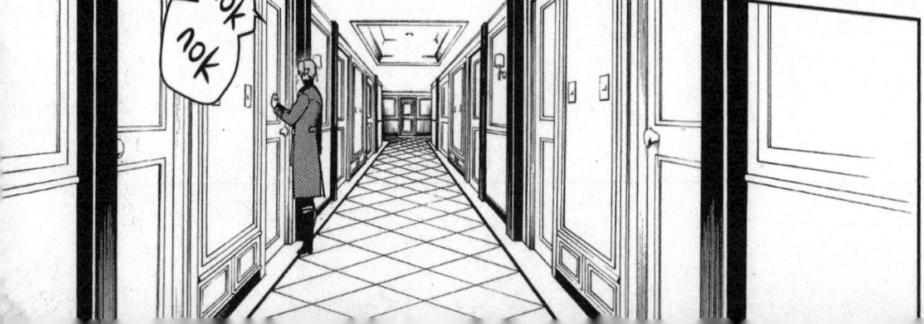
nok
nok

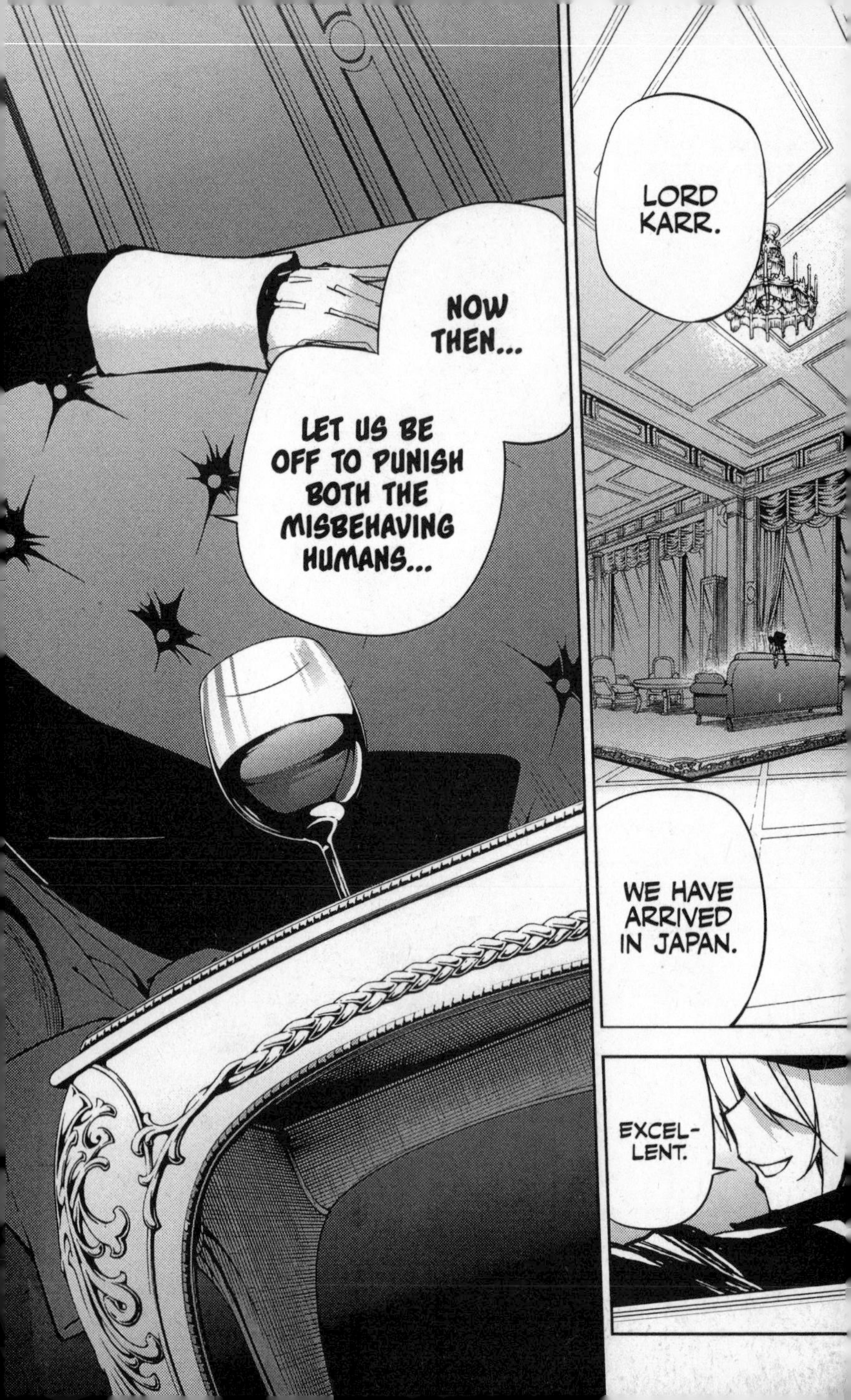
LORD KARR.
WE HAVE ARRIVED IN JAPAN.
EXCEL-LENT.
NOW THEN...
LET US BE OFF TO PUNISH BOTH THE MISBEHAVING HUMANS...

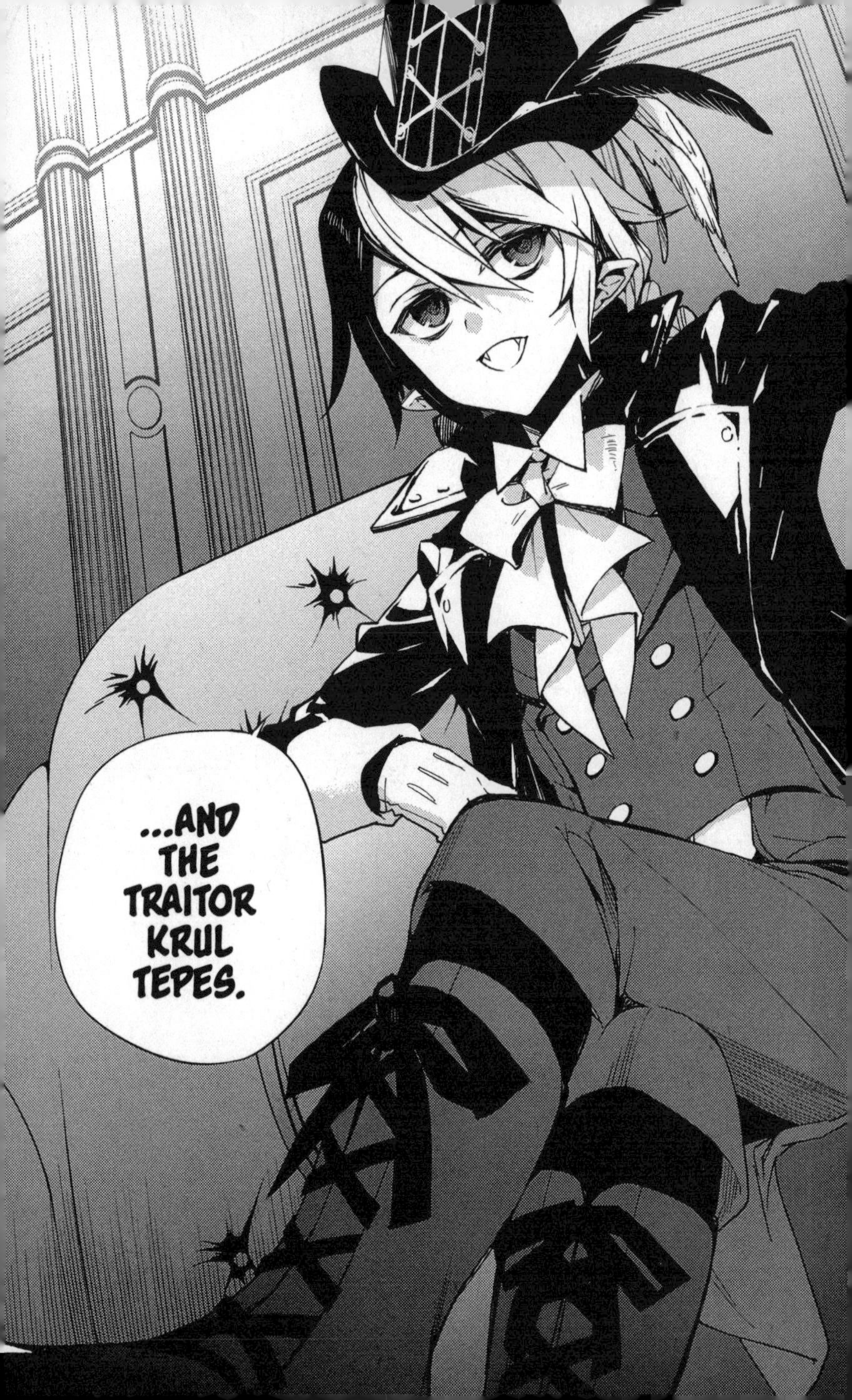
...AND THE TRAITOR KRUL TEPES.

Seraph of the End
—VAMPIRE REIGN—

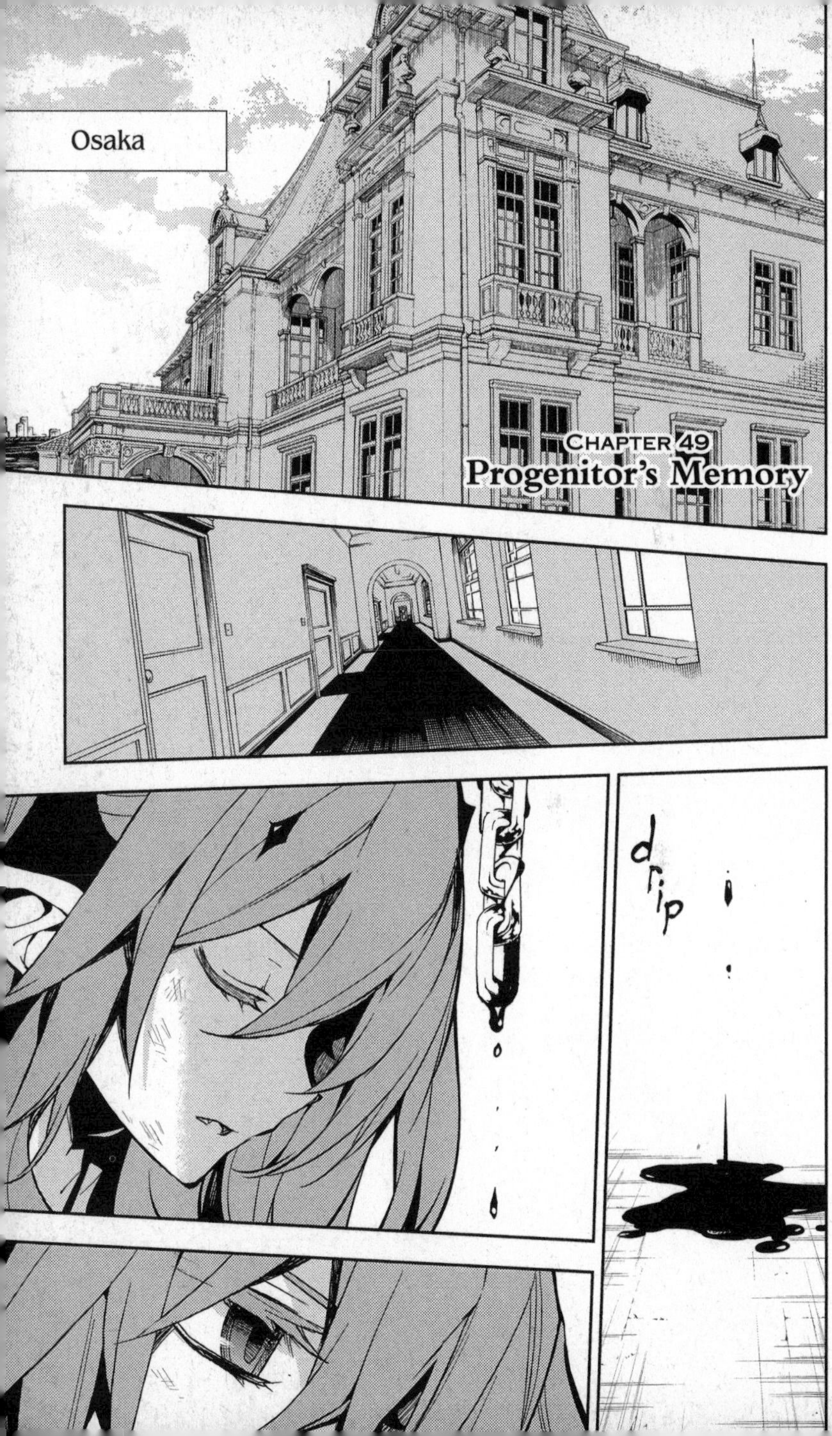
Osaka
Chapter 49
Progenitor's Memory
drip

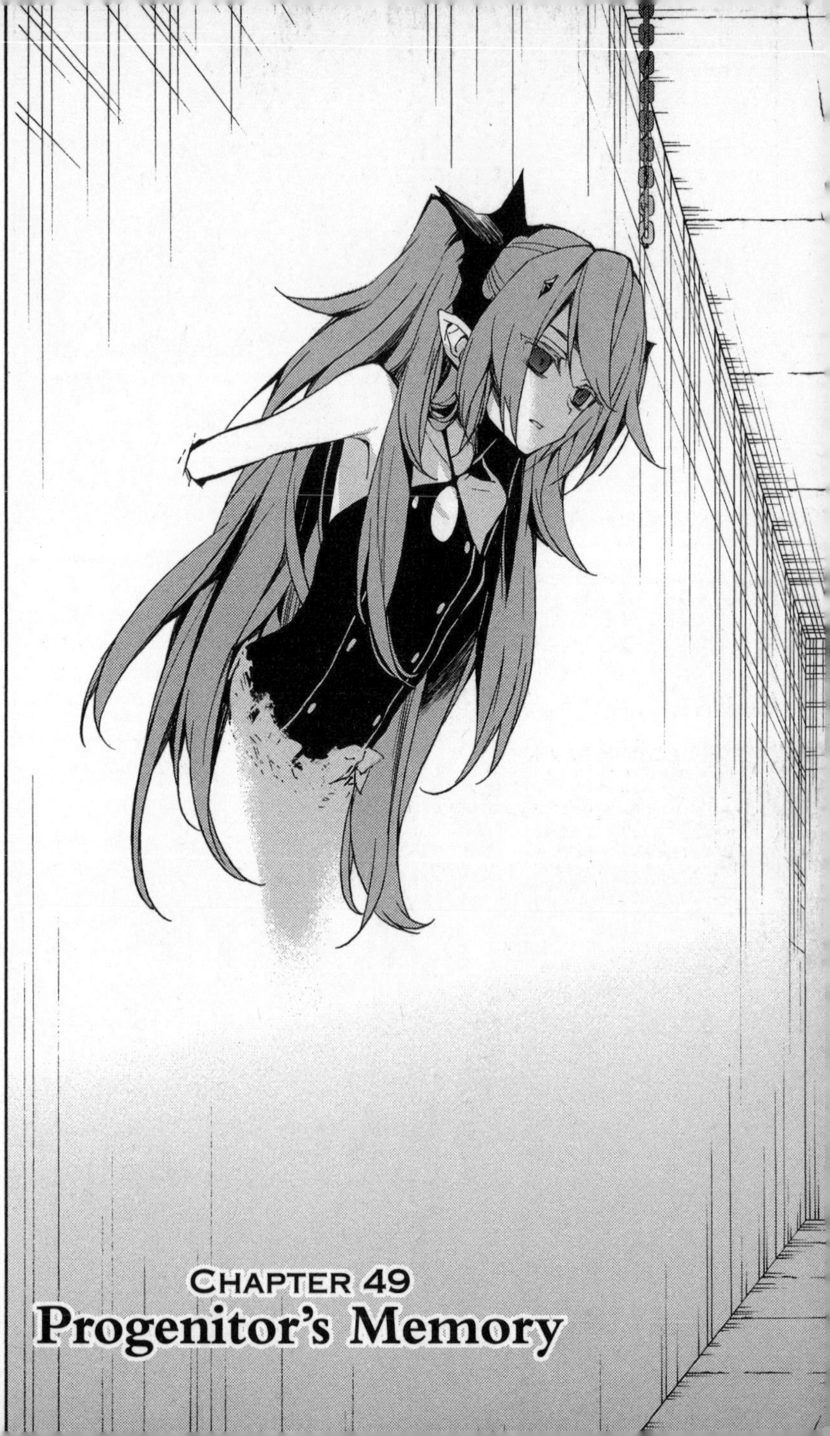

CHAPTER 49
Progenitor's Memory

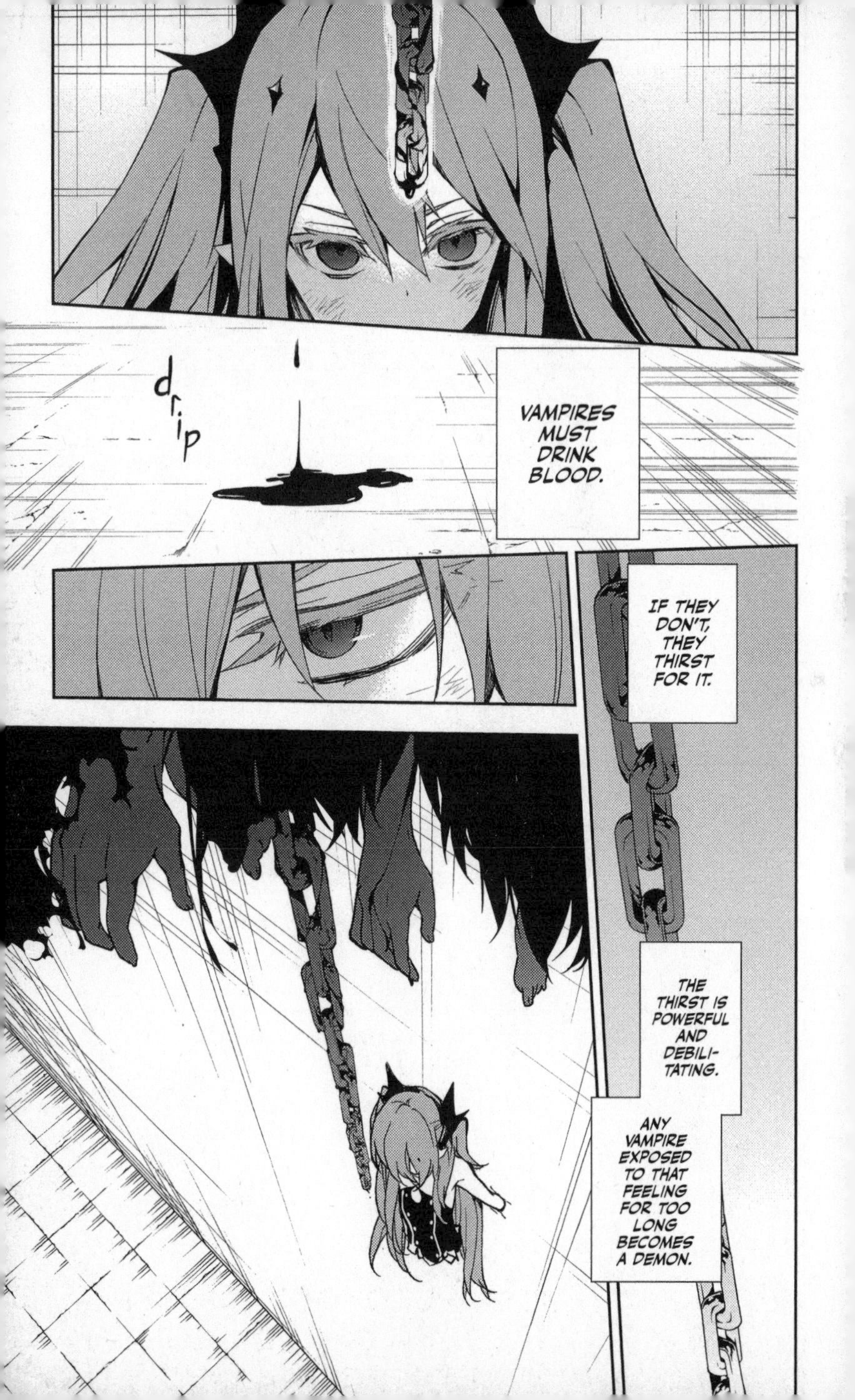
VAMPIRES MUST DRINK BLOOD.
drip
IF THEY DON'T, THEY THIRST FOR IT.
THE THIRST IS POWERFUL AND DEBILI-TATING.
ANY VAMPIRE EXPOSED TO THAT FEELING FOR TOO LONG BECOMES A DEMON.

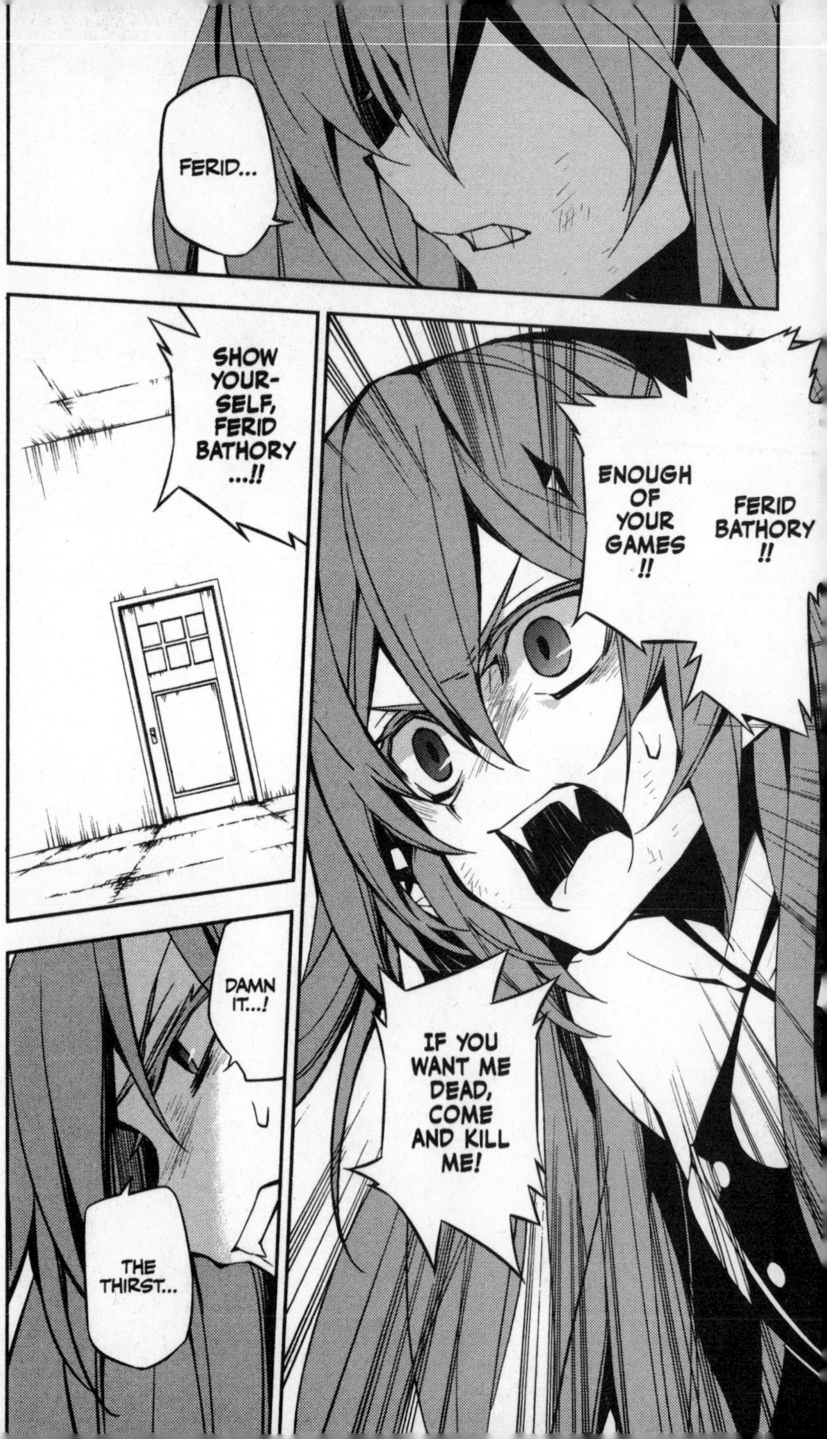
FERID...
FERID BATHORY!!
ENOUGH OF YOUR GAMES!!
IF YOU WANT ME DEAD, COME AND KILL ME!
SHOW YOUR-SELF, FERID BATHORY...!!
DAMN IT...!
THE THIRST...

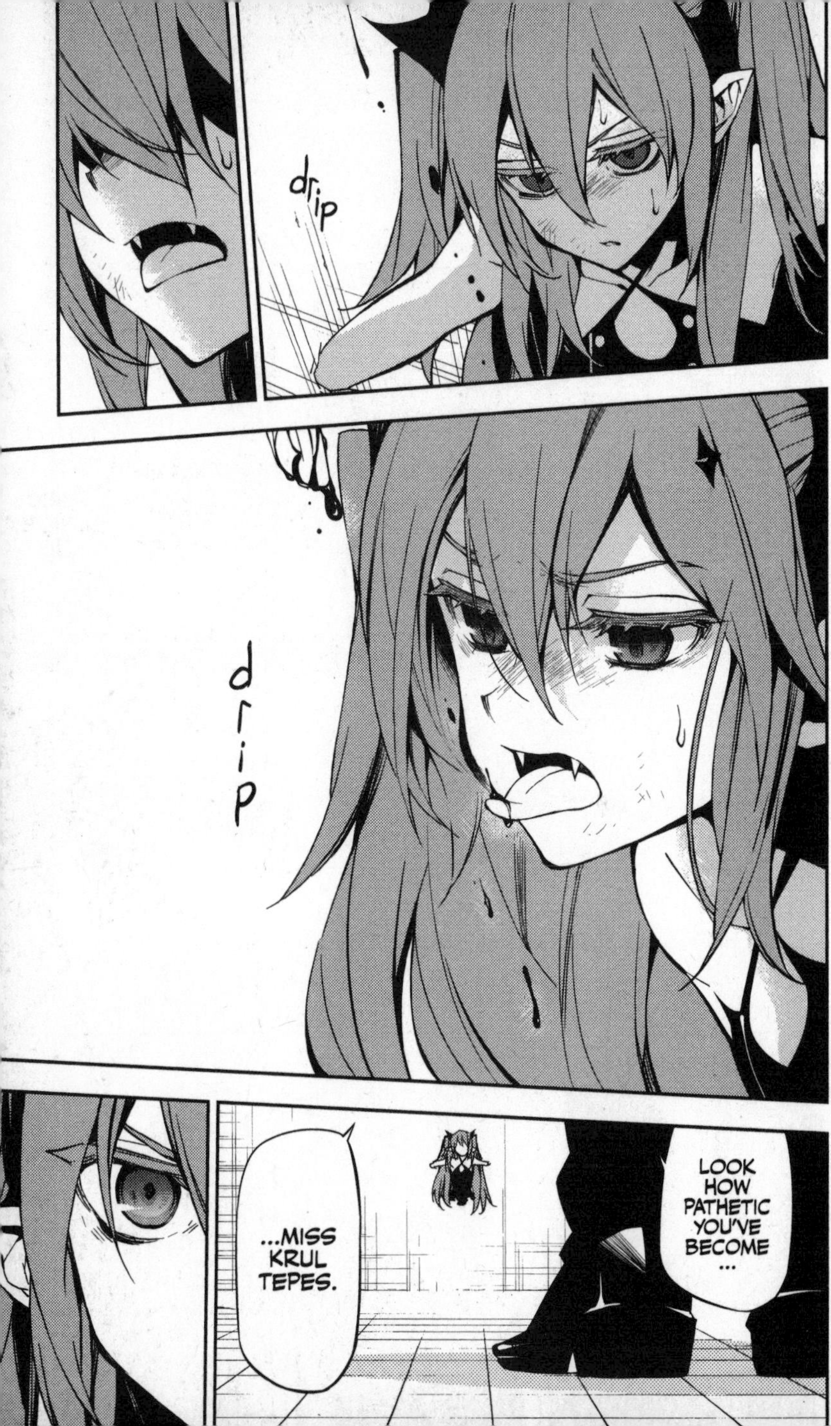

drip
drip
LOOK HOW PATHETIC YOU'VE BECOME ...
...MISS KRUL TEPES.

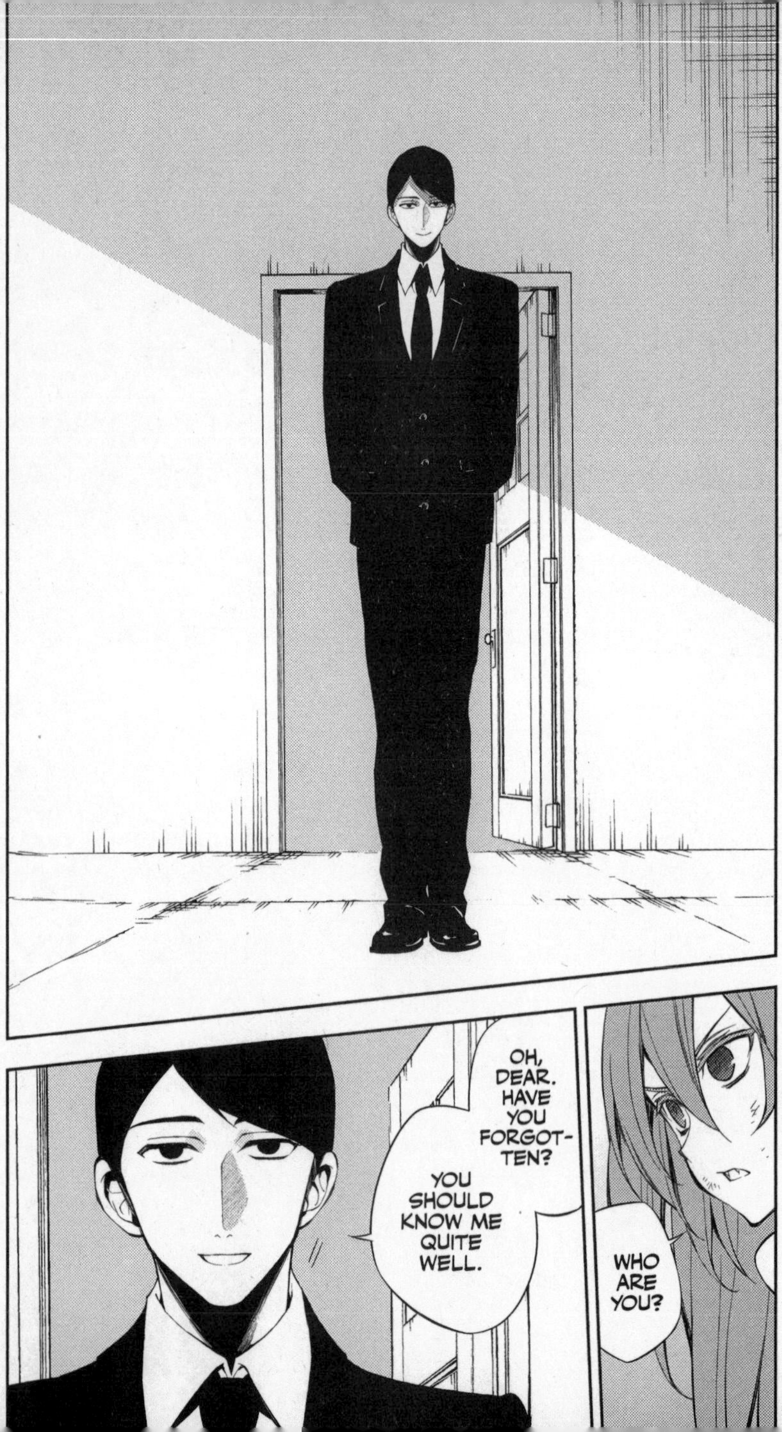
OH, DEAR. HAVE YOU FORGOTTEN?
YOU SHOULD KNOW ME QUITE WELL.
WHO ARE YOU?

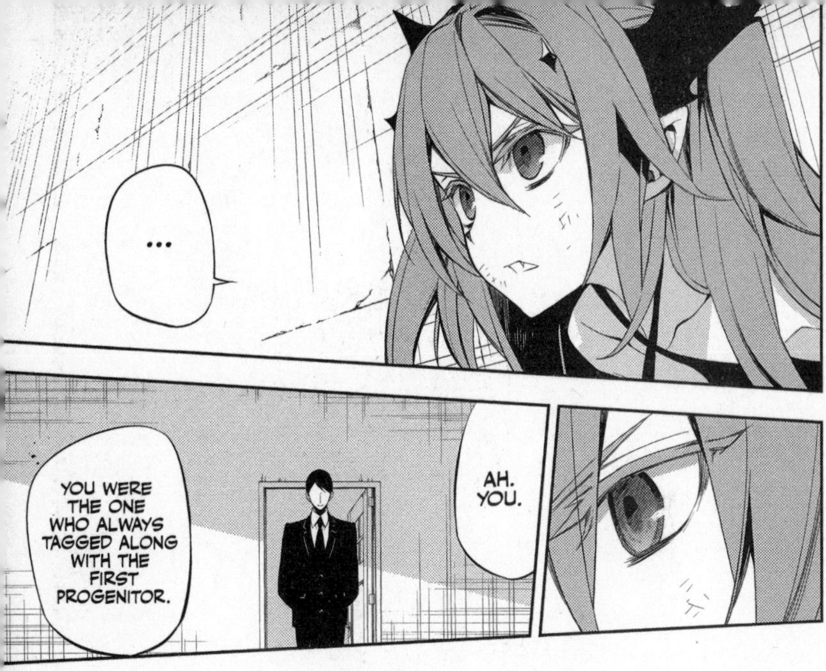
...
AH. YOU.
YOU WERE THE ONE WHO ALWAYS TAGGED ALONG WITH THE FIRST PROGENITOR.

1,000 Years Ago

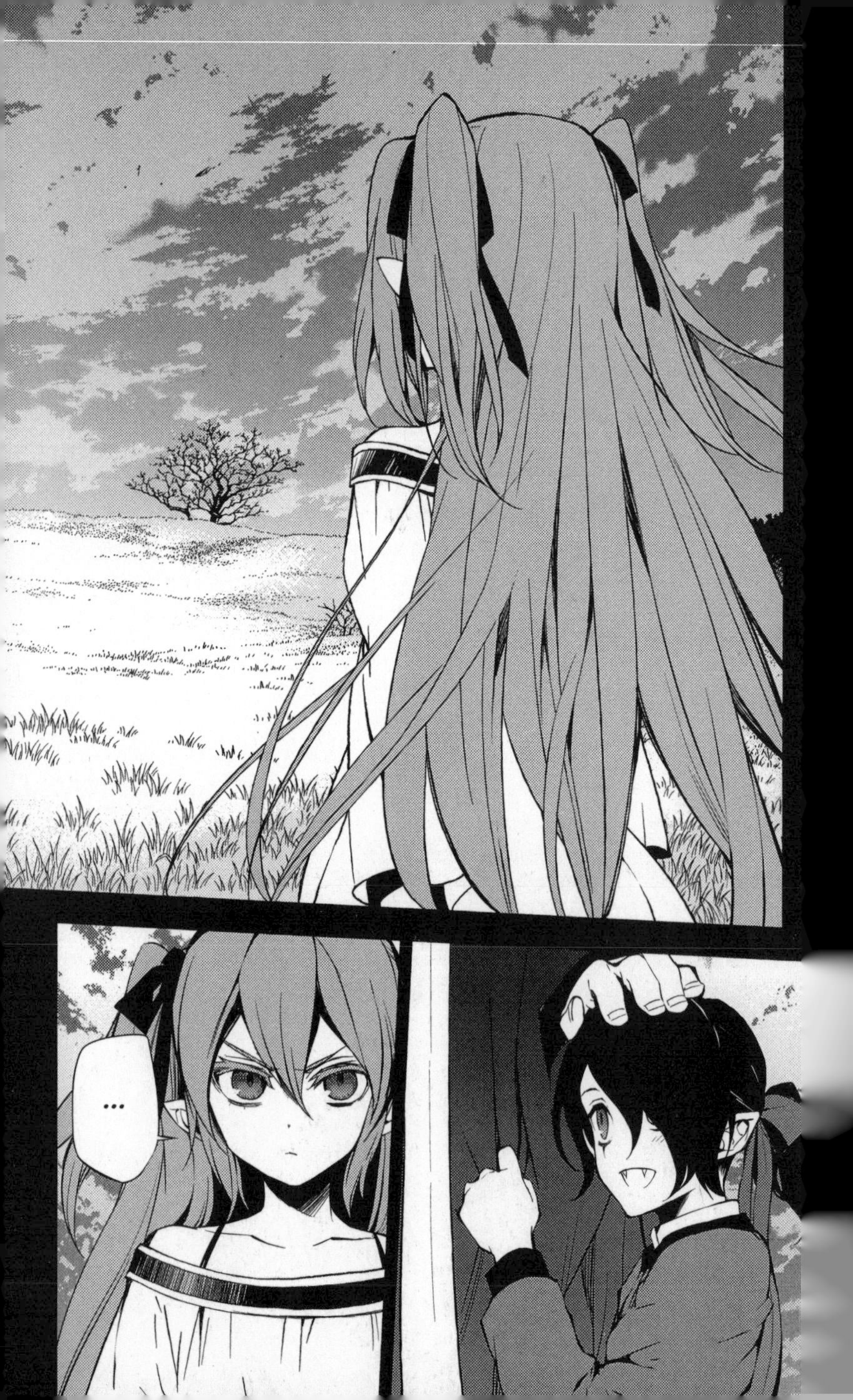
...

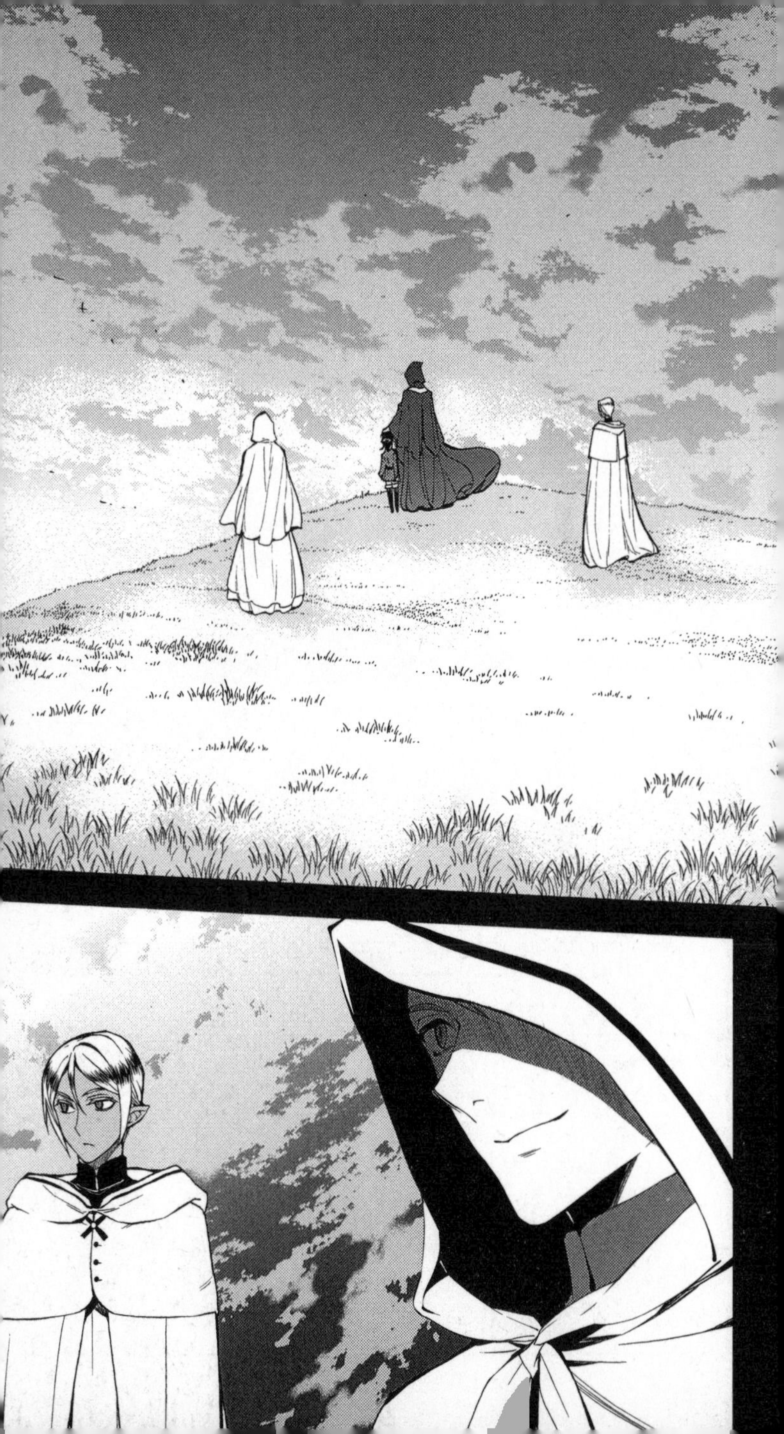

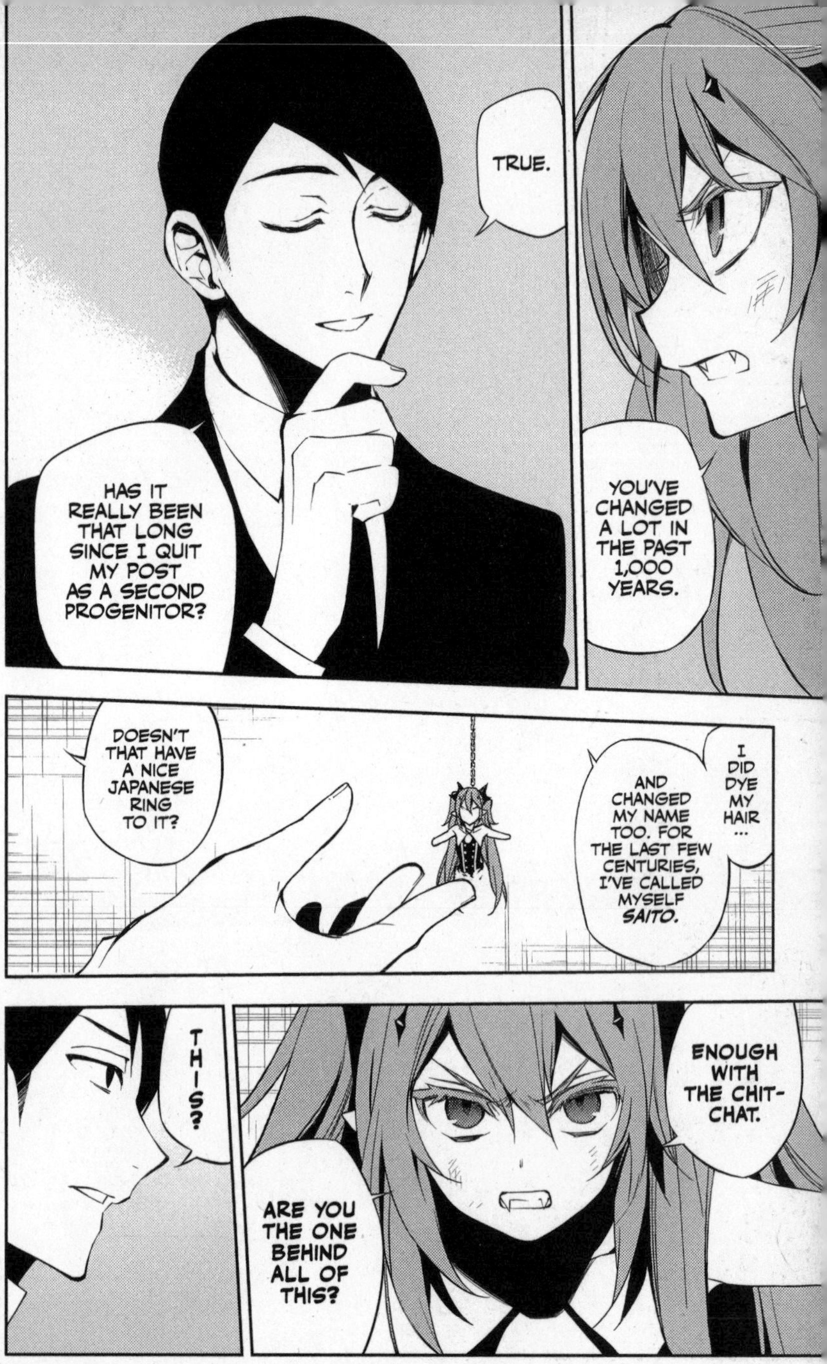
YOU'VE CHANGED A LOT IN THE PAST 1,000 YEARS.
TRUE.
HAS IT REALLY BEEN THAT LONG SINCE I QUIT MY POST AS A SECOND PROGENITOR?
I DID DYE MY HAIR...
AND CHANGED MY NAME TOO. FOR THE LAST FEW CENTURIES, I'VE CALLED MYSELF *SAITO*.
DOESN'T THAT HAVE A NICE JAPANESE RING TO IT?
ENOUGH WITH THE CHIT-CHAT.
ARE YOU THE ONE BEHIND ALL OF THIS?
THIS?

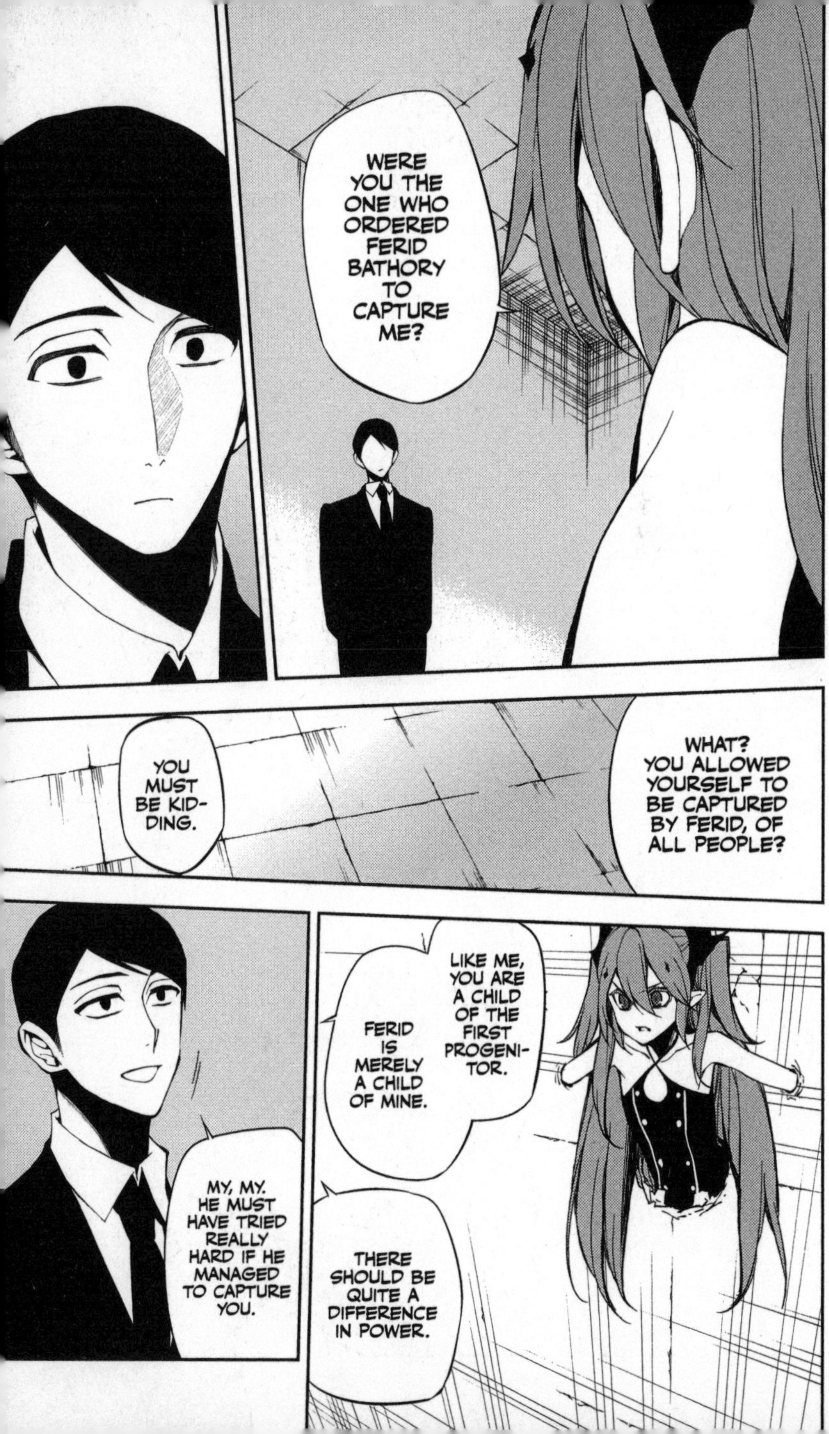
WERE YOU THE ONE WHO ORDERED FERID BATHORY TO CAPTURE ME?
WHAT? YOU ALLOWED YOURSELF TO BE CAPTURED BY FERID, OF ALL PEOPLE?
YOU MUST BE KID-DING.
LIKE ME, YOU ARE A CHILD OF THE FIRST PROGENI-TOR.
FERID IS MERELY A CHILD OF MINE.
THERE SHOULD BE QUITE A DIFFERENCE IN POWER.
MY, MY. HE MUST HAVE TRIED REALLY HARD IF HE MANAGED TO CAPTURE YOU.

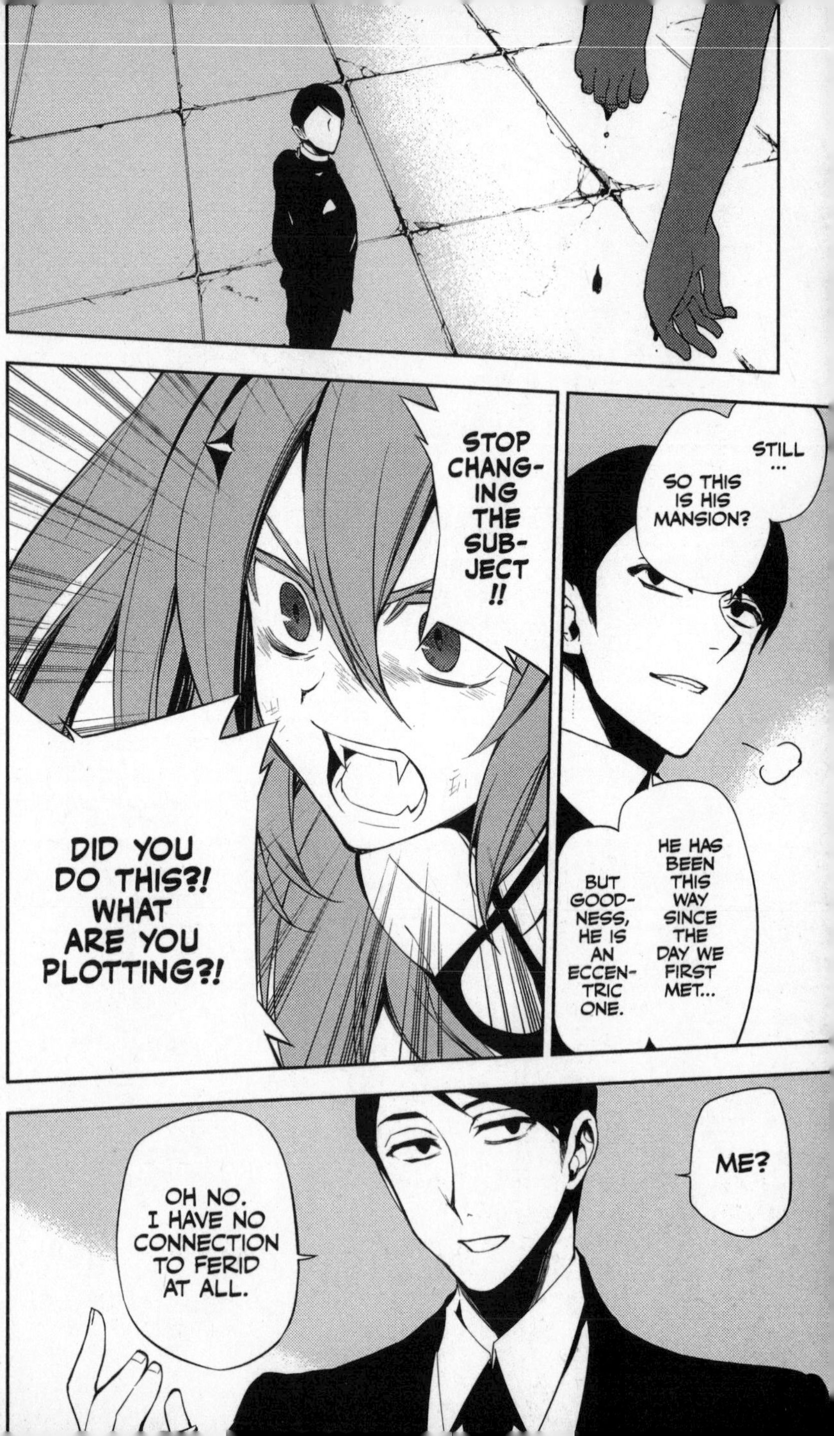
STILL... SO THIS IS HIS MANSION?
HE HAS BEEN THIS WAY SINCE THE DAY WE FIRST MET...
BUT GOODNESS, HE IS AN ECCENTRIC ONE.
STOP CHANGING THE SUBJECT!!
DID YOU DO THIS?! WHAT ARE YOU PLOTTING?!
ME?
OH NO. I HAVE NO CONNECTION TO FERID AT ALL.

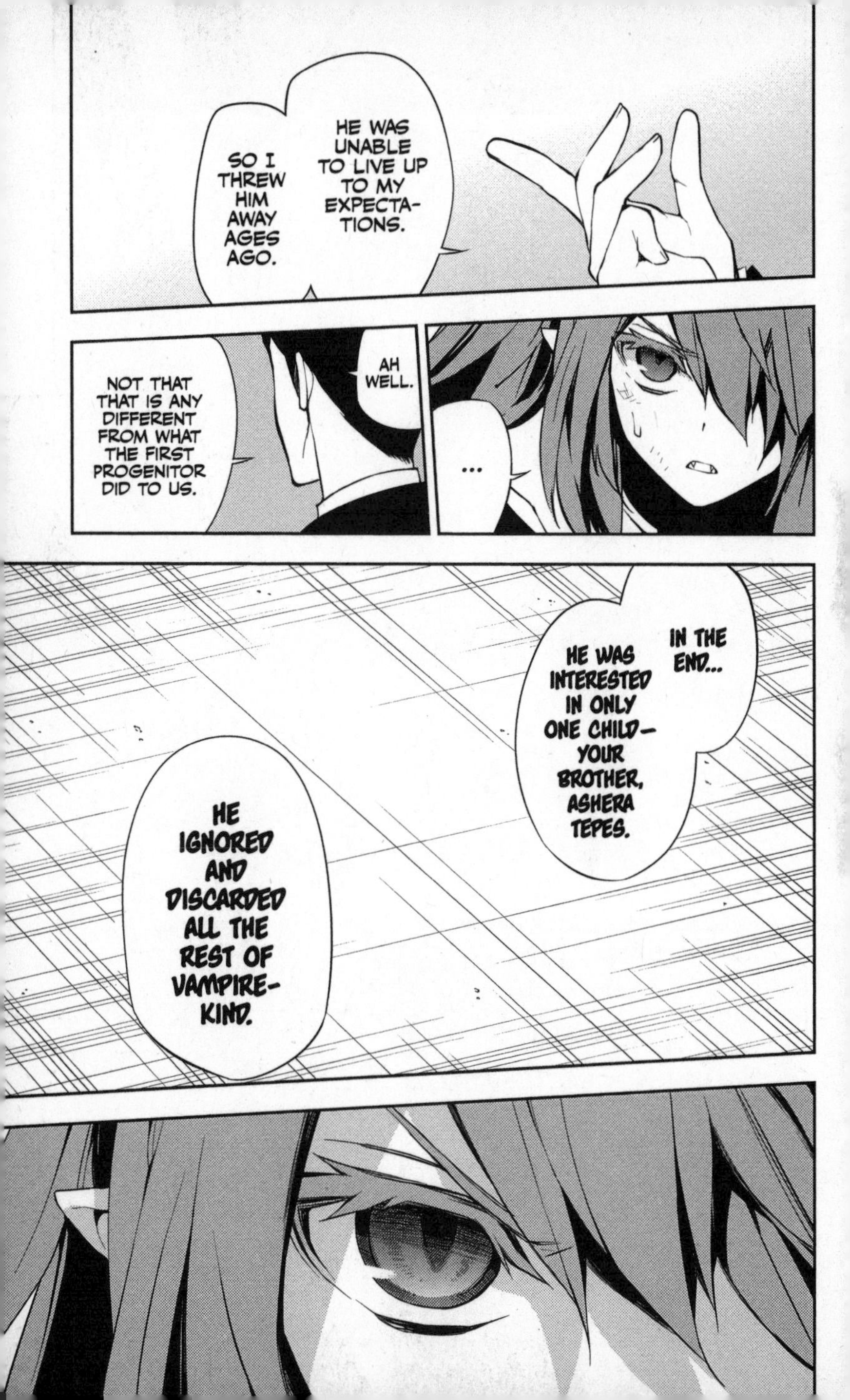
HE WAS UNABLE TO LIVE UP TO MY EXPECTATIONS.
SO I THREW HIM AWAY AGES AGO.
...
AH WELL.
NOT THAT THAT IS ANY DIFFERENT FROM WHAT THE FIRST PROGENITOR DID TO US.
IN THE END...
HE WAS INTERESTED IN ONLY ONE CHILD—YOUR BROTHER, ASHERA TEPES.
HE IGNORED AND DISCARDED ALL THE REST OF VAMPIRE-KIND.

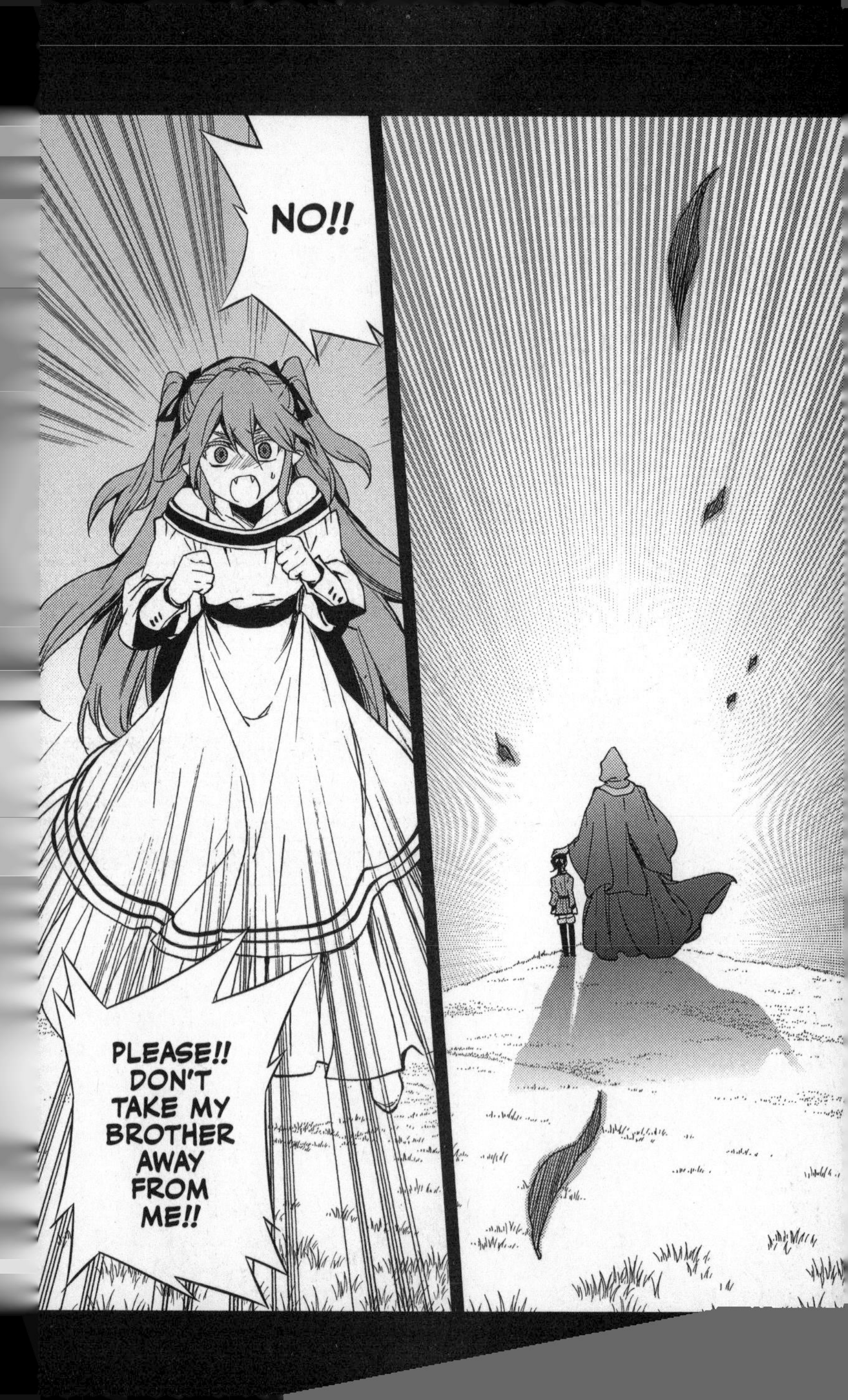
NO!!
PLEASE!! DON'T TAKE MY BROTHER AWAY FROM ME!!

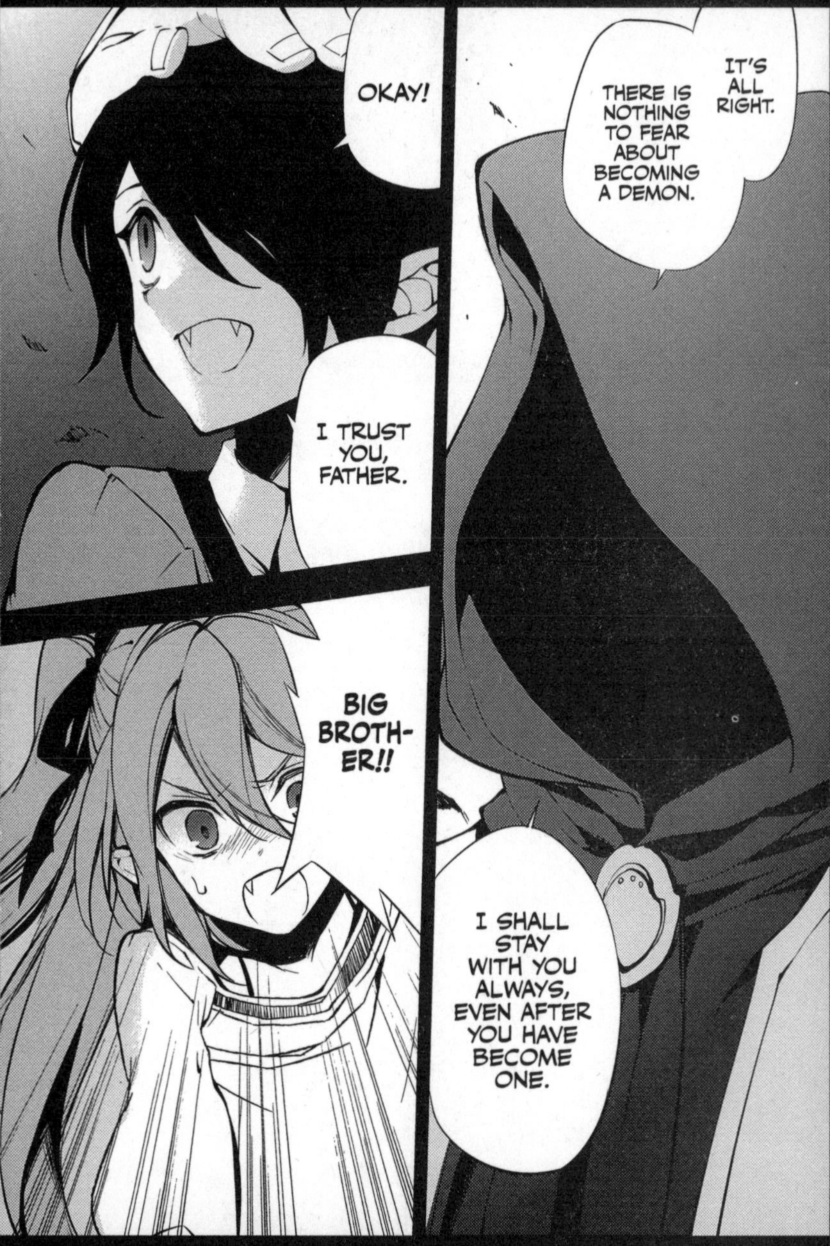
IT'S ALL RIGHT.
THERE IS NOTHING TO FEAR ABOUT BECOMING A DEMON.
I SHALL STAY WITH YOU ALWAYS, EVEN AFTER YOU HAVE BECOME ONE.
OKAY!
I TRUST YOU, FATHER.
BIG BROTH-ER!!

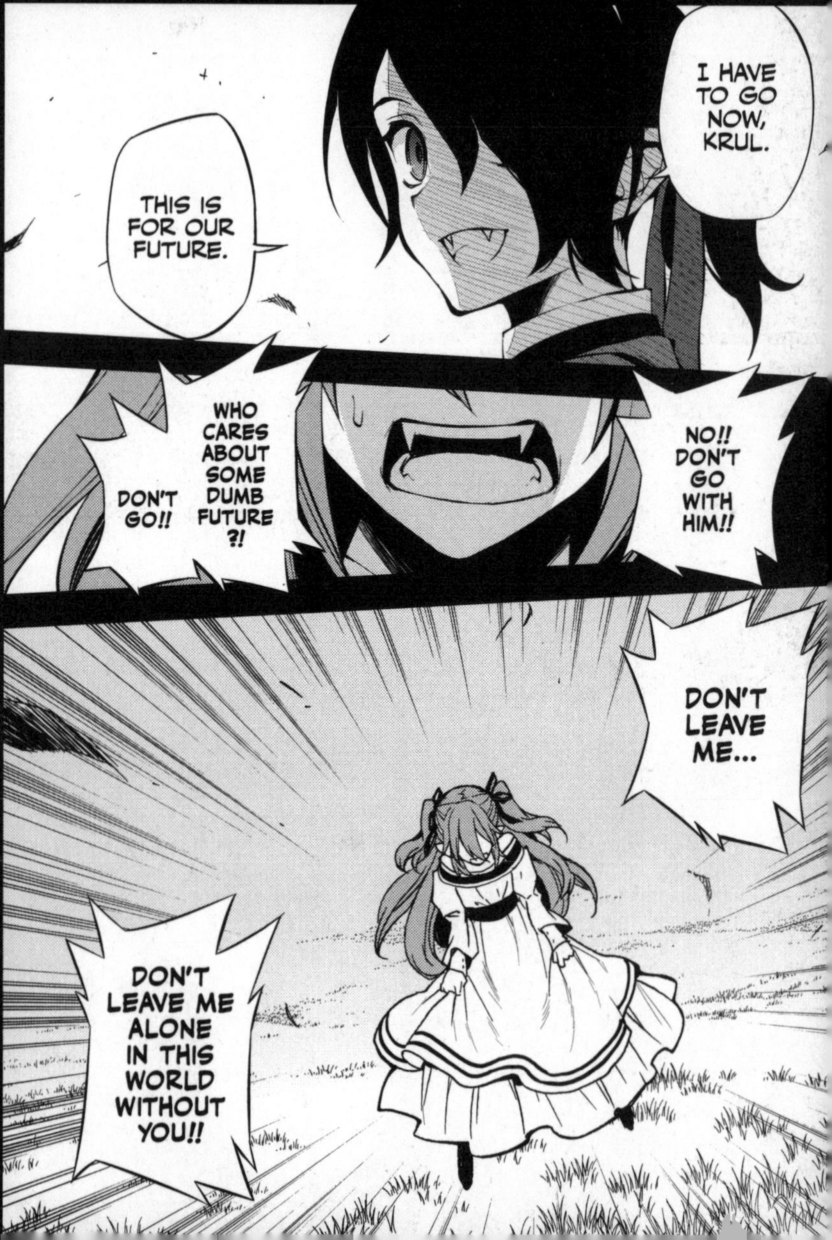
I HAVE TO GO NOW, KRUL.
THIS IS FOR OUR FUTURE.
NO!! DON'T GO WITH HIM!!
WHO CARES ABOUT SOME DUMB FUTURE ?!
DON'T GO!!
DON'T LEAVE ME...
DON'T LEAVE ME ALONE IN THIS WORLD WITHOUT YOU!!

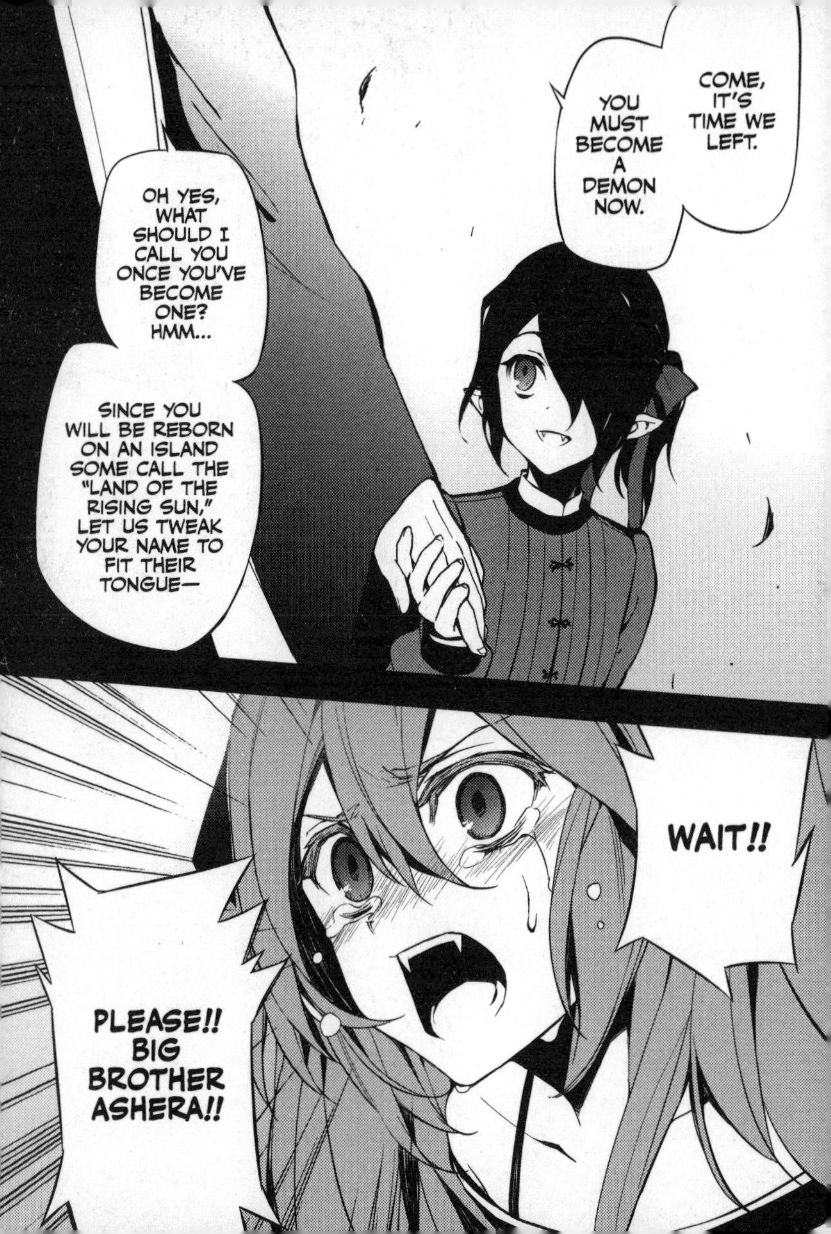
COME, IT'S TIME WE LEFT.
YOU MUST BECOME A DEMON NOW.
OH YES, WHAT SHOULD I CALL YOU ONCE YOU'VE BECOME ONE? HMM...
SINCE YOU WILL BE REBORN ON AN ISLAND SOME CALL THE "LAND OF THE RISING SUN," LET US TWEAK YOUR NAME TO FIT THEIR TONGUE—
WAIT!!
PLEASE!! BIG BROTHER ASHERA!!

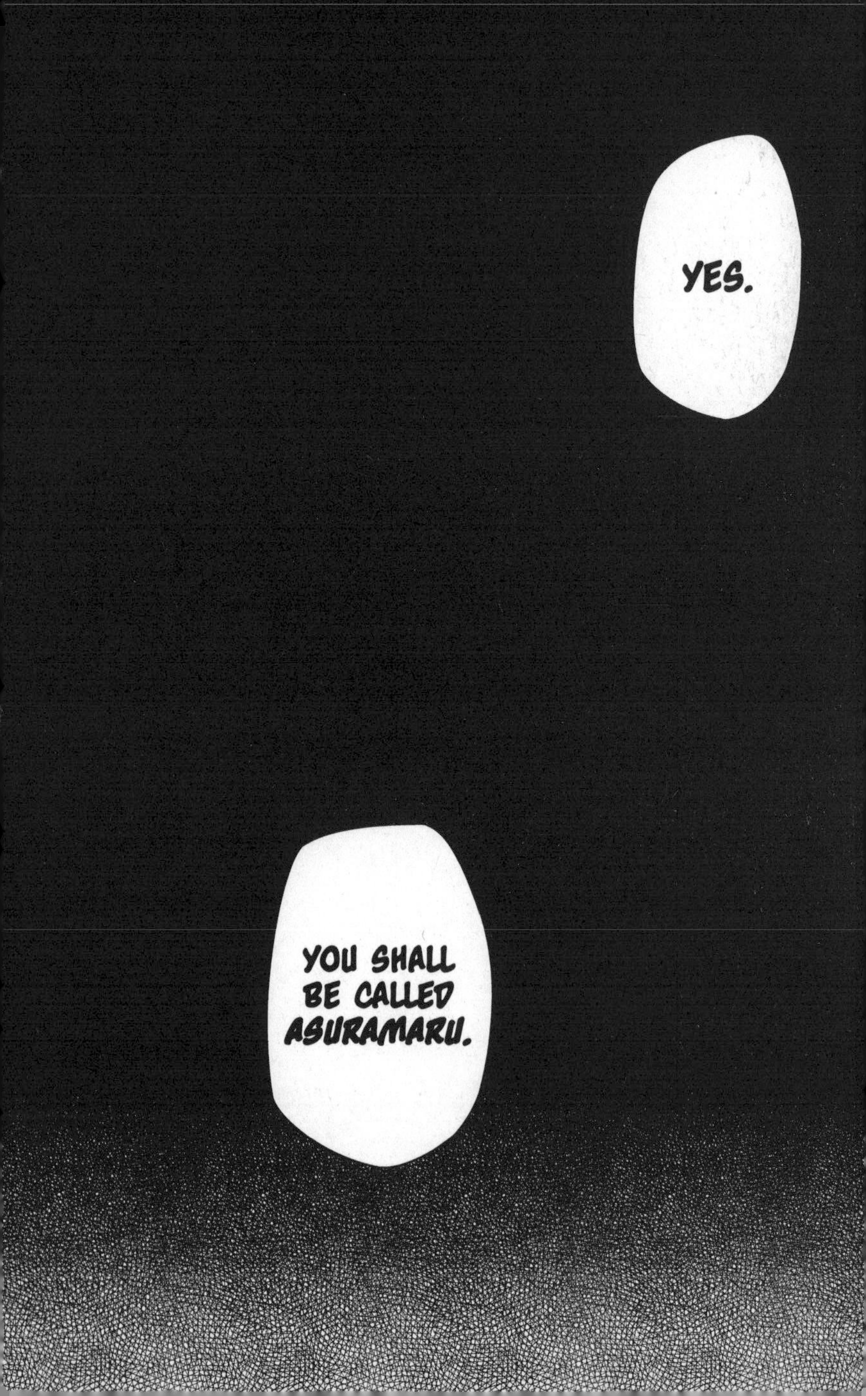
YES.
YOU SHALL BE CALLED ASURAMARU.

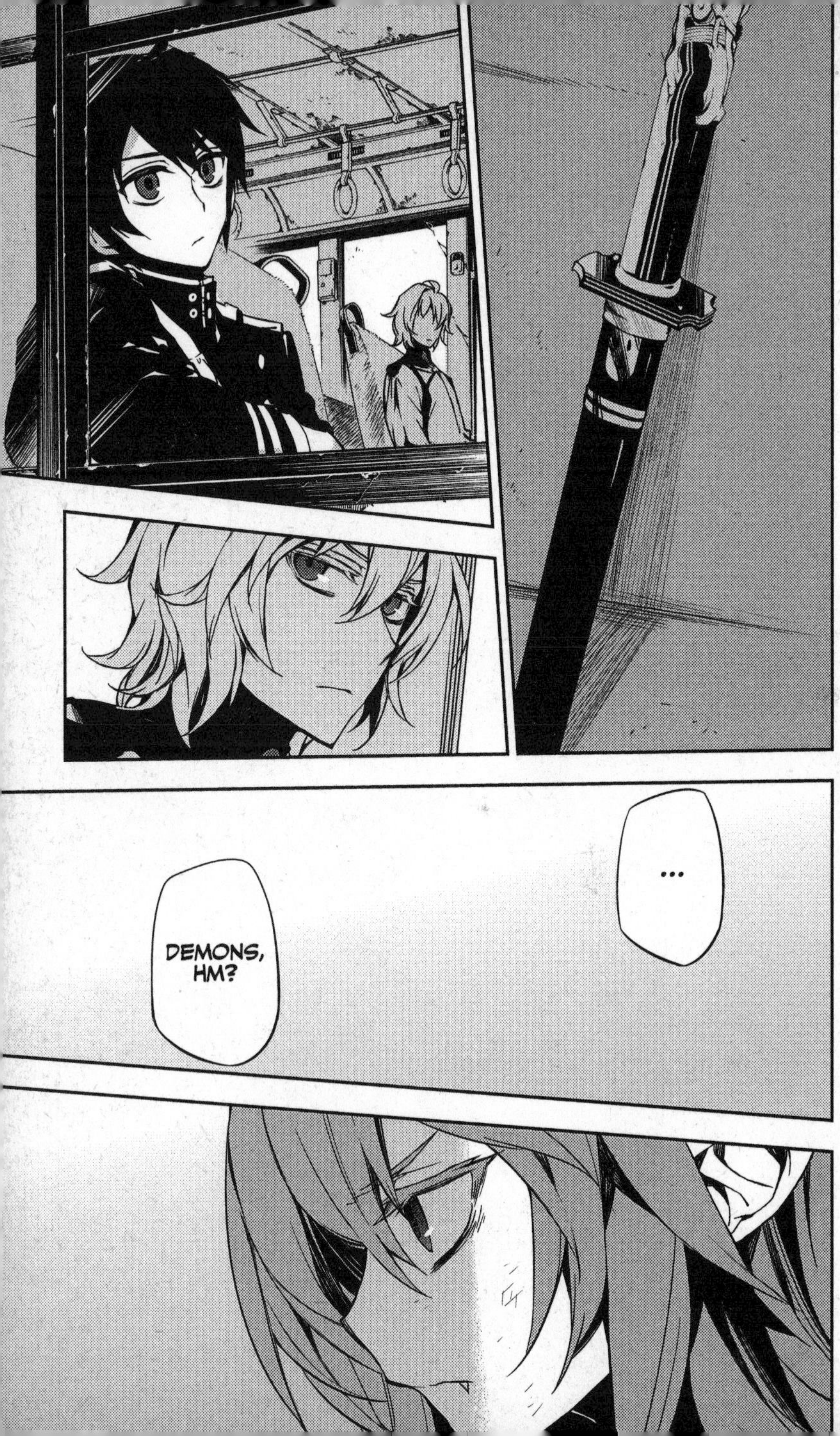
...
DEMONS, HM?

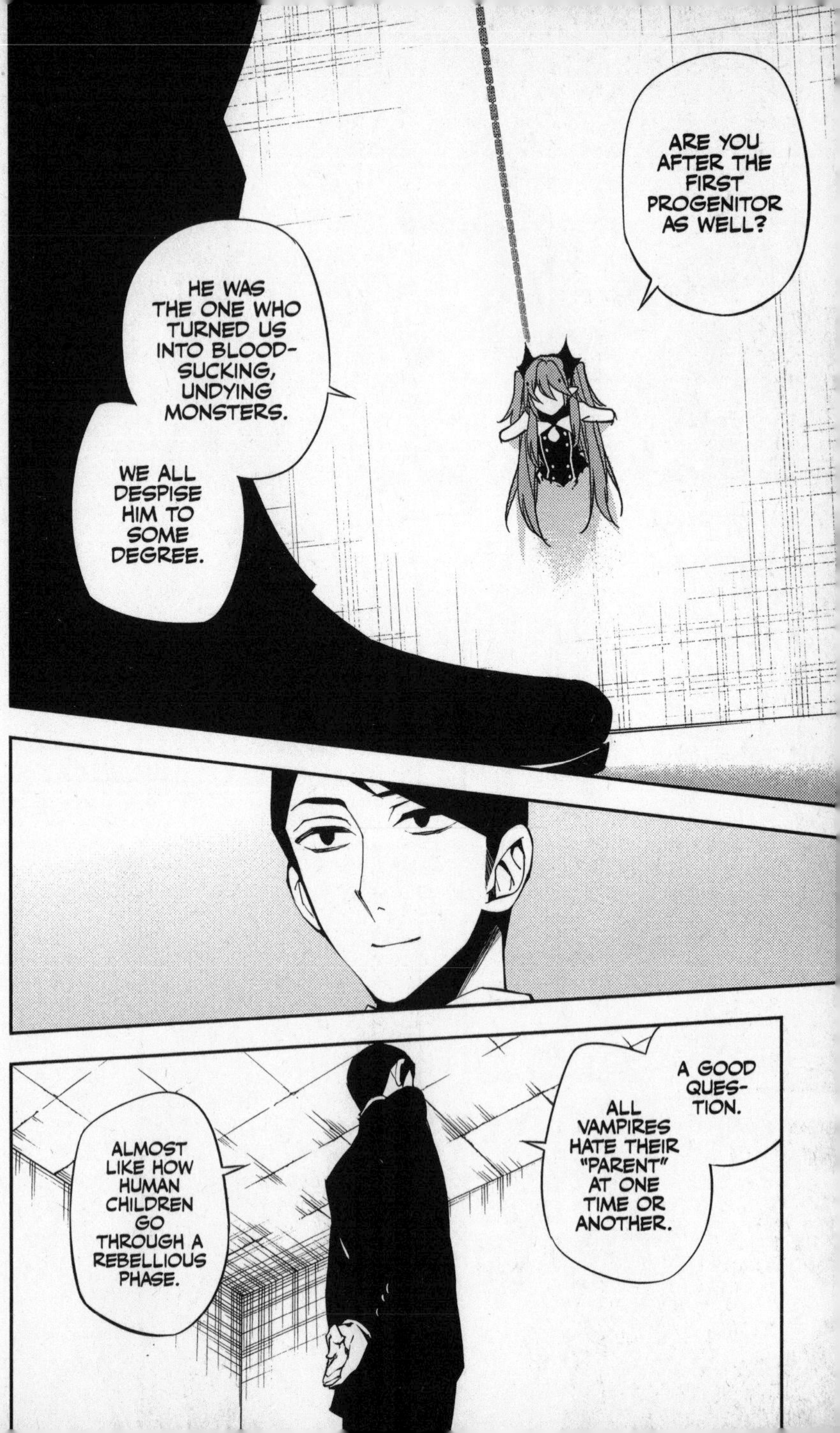
ARE YOU AFTER THE FIRST PROGENITOR AS WELL?
HE WAS THE ONE WHO TURNED US INTO BLOOD-SUCKING, UNDYING MONSTERS.
WE ALL DESPISE HIM TO SOME DEGREE.
A GOOD QUES-TION.
ALL VAMPIRES HATE THEIR "PARENT" AT ONE TIME OR ANOTHER.
ALMOST LIKE HOW HUMAN CHILDREN GO THROUGH A REBELLIOUS PHASE.

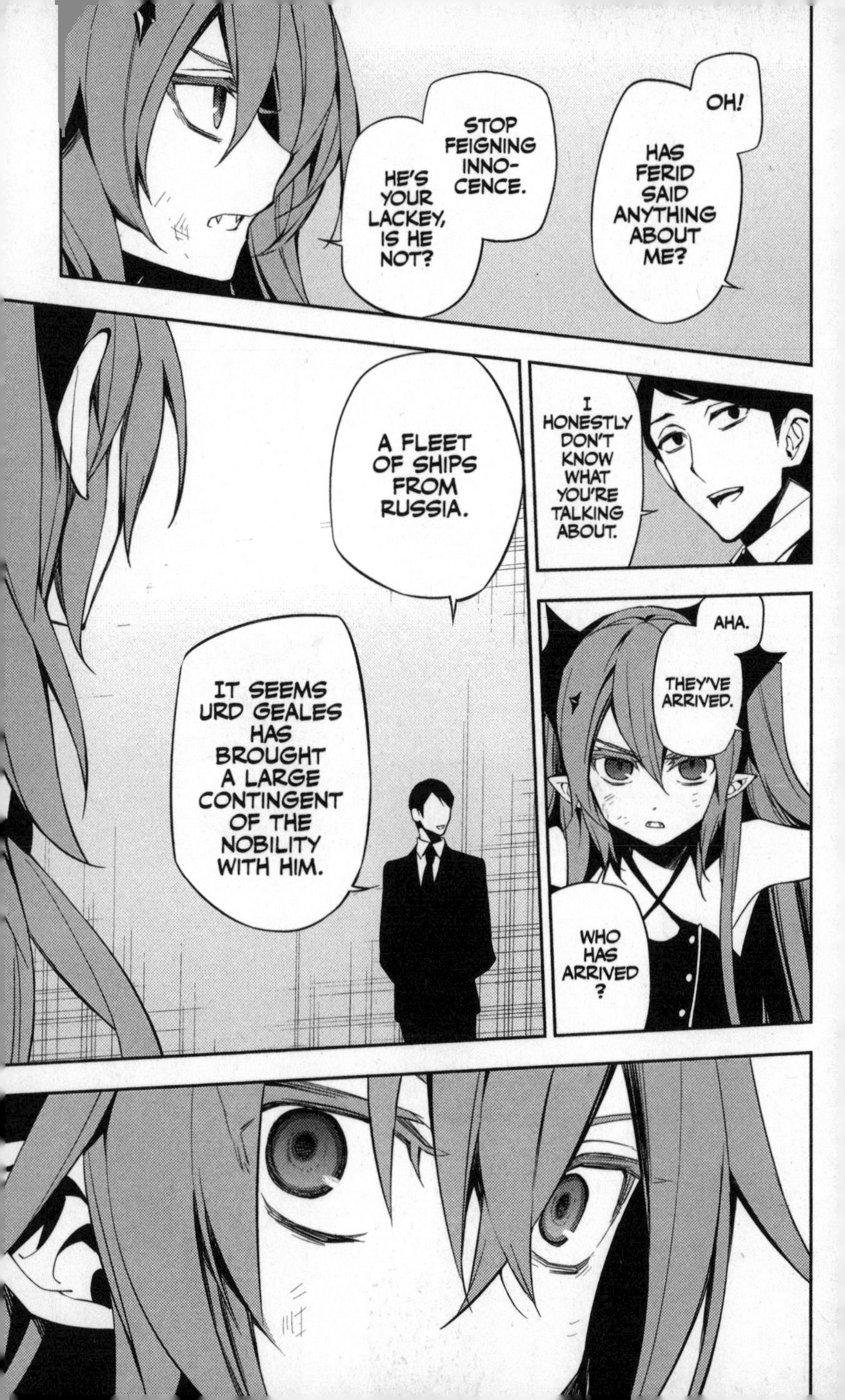
OH!
HAS FERID SAID ANYTHING ABOUT ME?
STOP FEIGNING INNO-CENCE.
HE'S YOUR LACKEY, IS HE NOT?
I HONESTLY DON'T KNOW WHAT YOU'RE TALKING ABOUT.
AHA.
THEY'VE ARRIVED.
WHO HAS ARRIVED?
A FLEET OF SHIPS FROM RUSSIA.
IT SEEMS URD GEALES HAS BROUGHT A LARGE CONTINGENT OF THE NOBILITY WITH HIM.

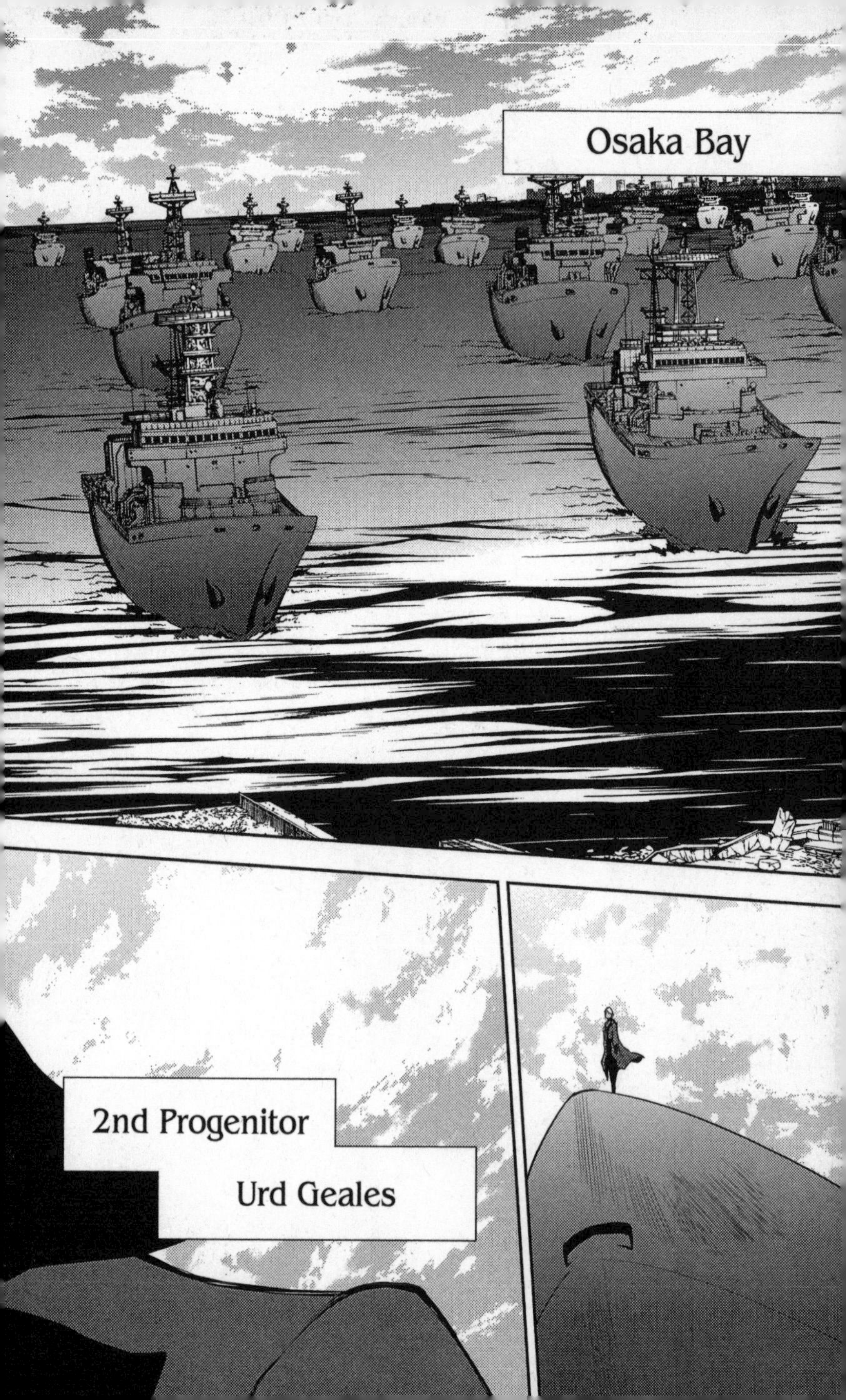
Osaka Bay
2nd Progenitor
Urd Geales

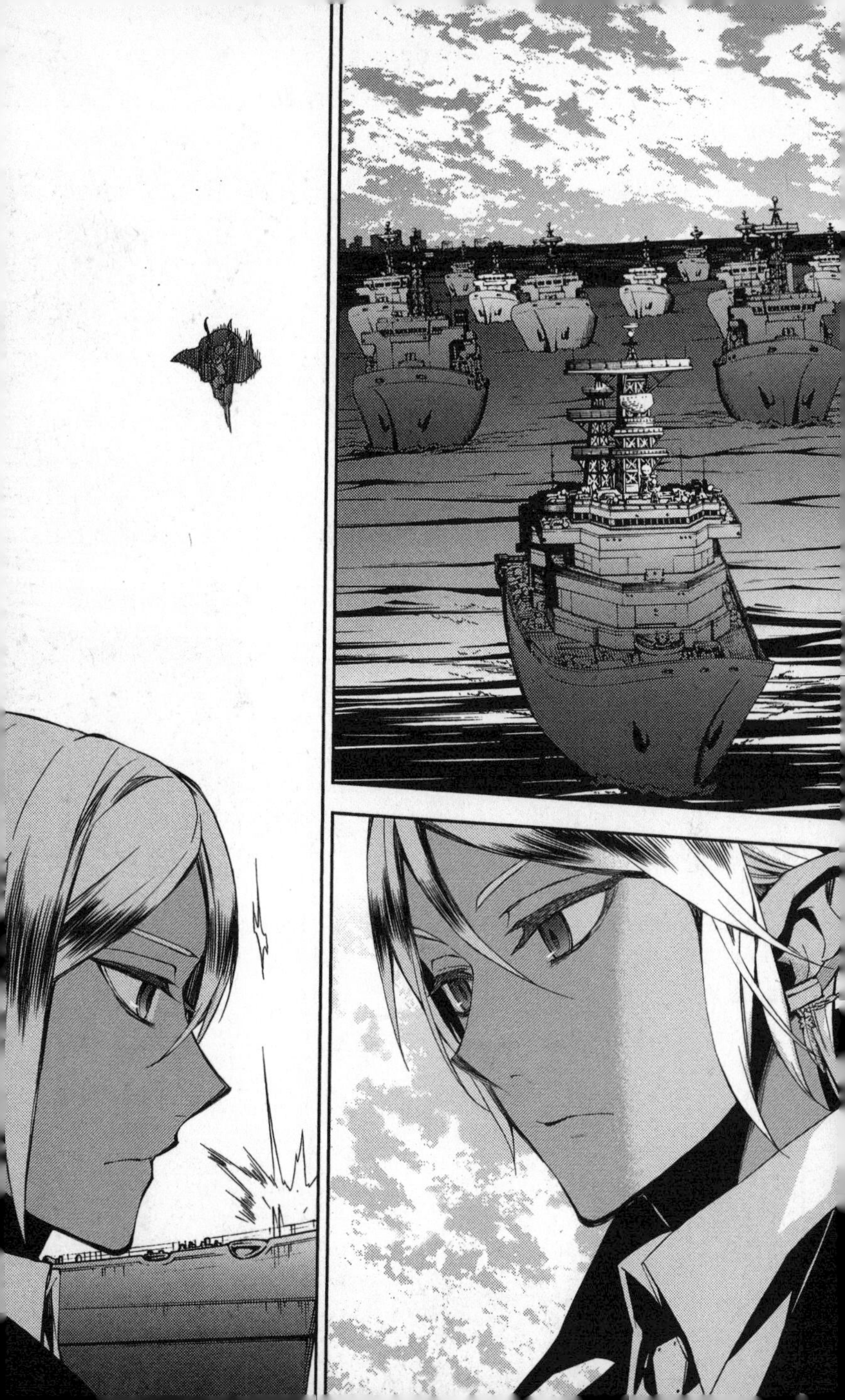

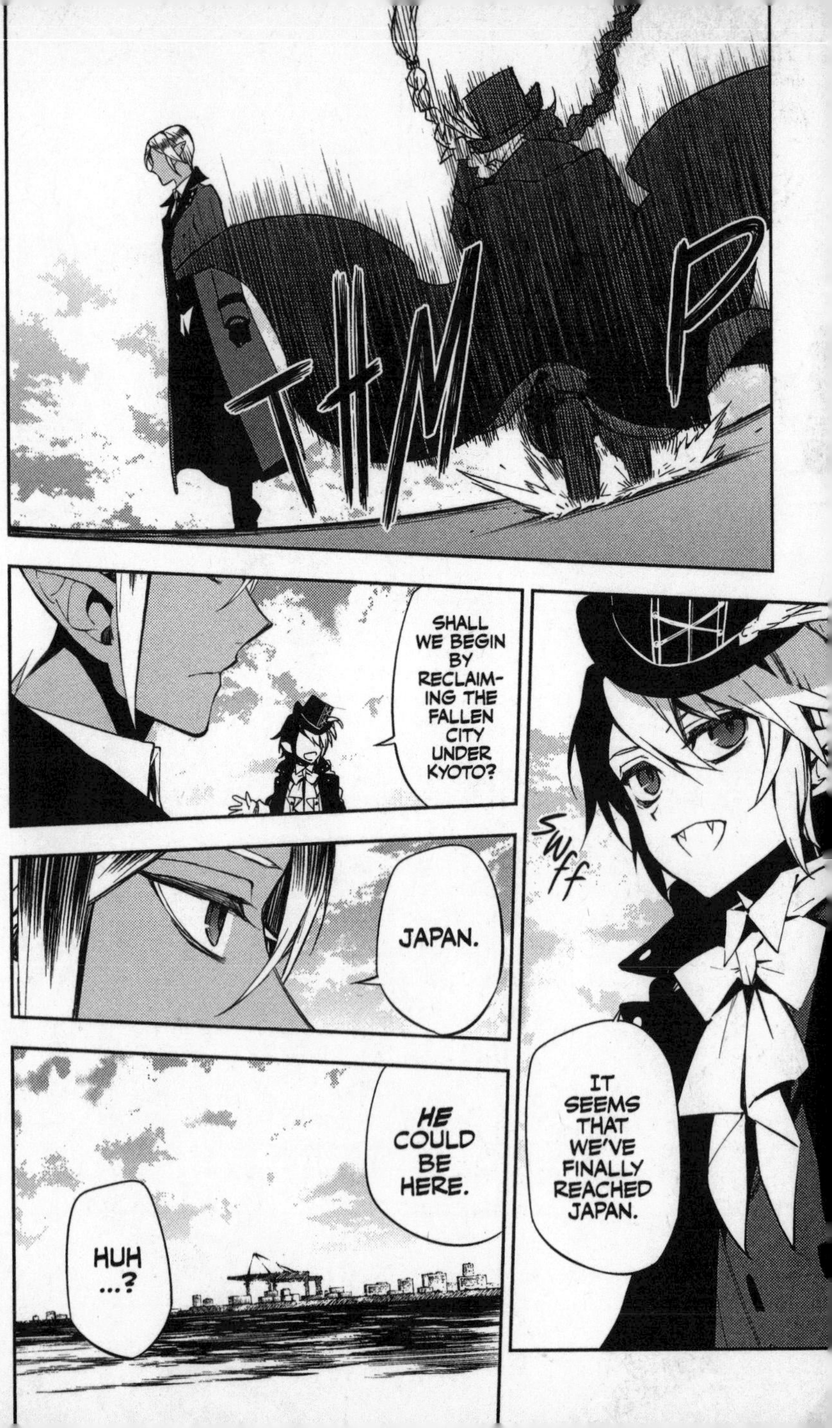
THMP
SWFF
IT SEEMS THAT WE'VE FINALLY REACHED JAPAN.
SHALL WE BEGIN BY RECLAIMING THE FALLEN CITY UNDER KYOTO?
JAPAN.
HE COULD BE HERE.
HUH ...?

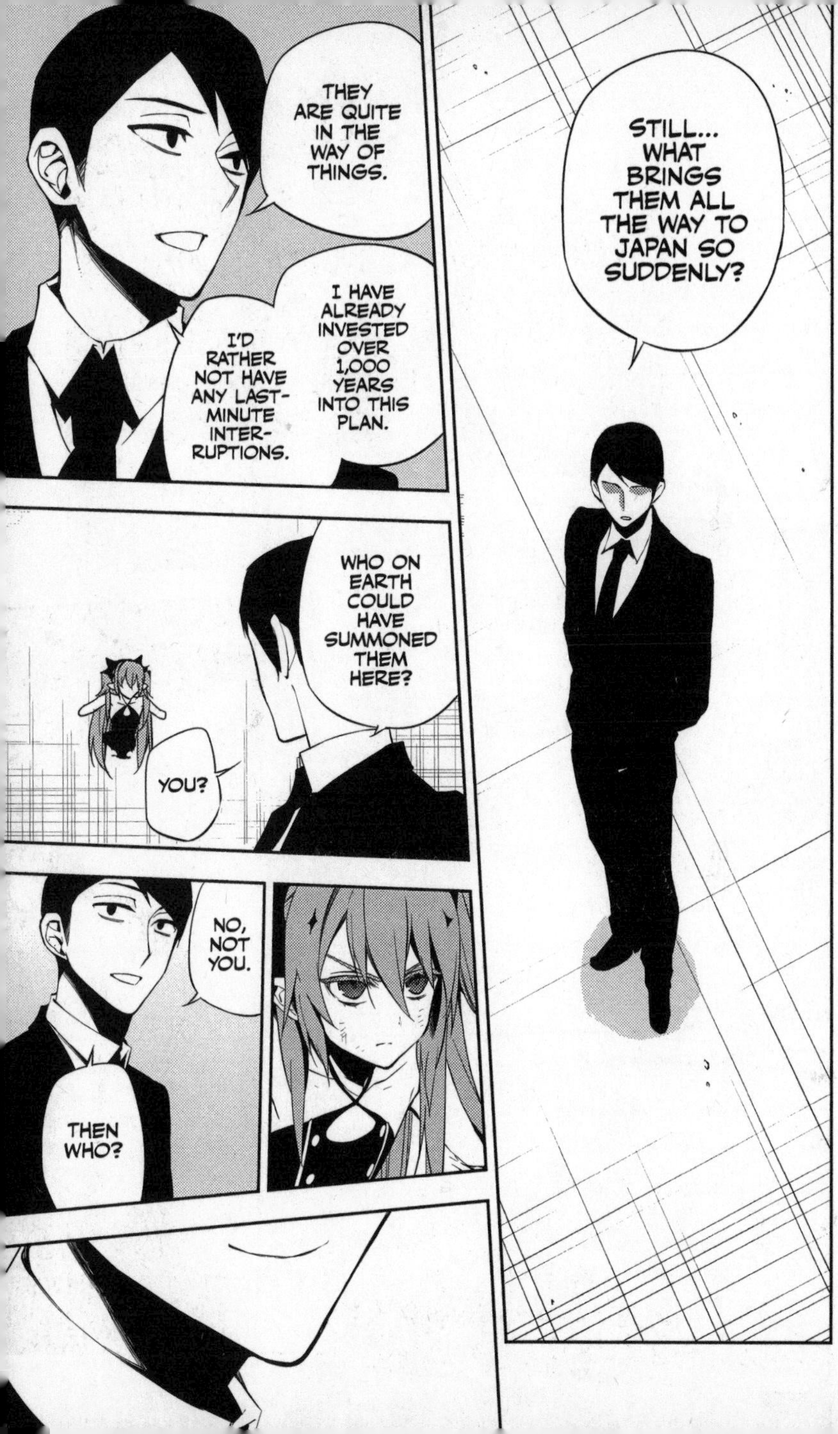
STILL... WHAT BRINGS THEM ALL THE WAY TO JAPAN SO SUDDENLY?
THEY ARE QUITE IN THE WAY OF THINGS.
I HAVE ALREADY INVESTED OVER 1,000 YEARS INTO THIS PLAN.
I'D RATHER NOT HAVE ANY LAST-MINUTE INTER-RUPTIONS.
WHO ON EARTH COULD HAVE SUMMONED THEM HERE?
YOU?
NO, NOT YOU.
THEN WHO?

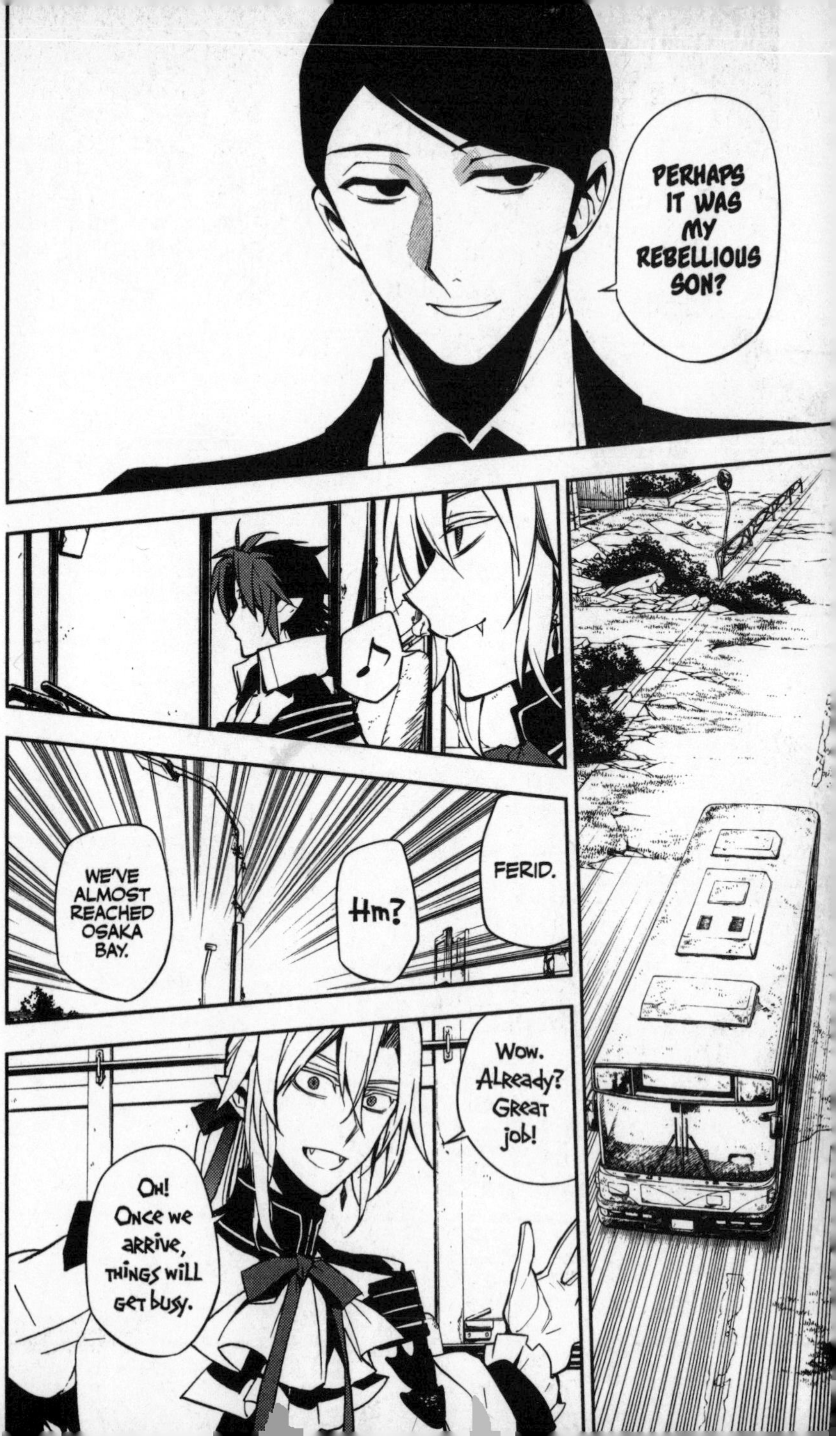
PERHAPS IT WAS MY REBELLIOUS SON?
FERID.
Hm?
WE'VE ALMOST REACHED OSAKA BAY.
Wow. Already? Great job!
Oh! Once we arrive, things will get busy.

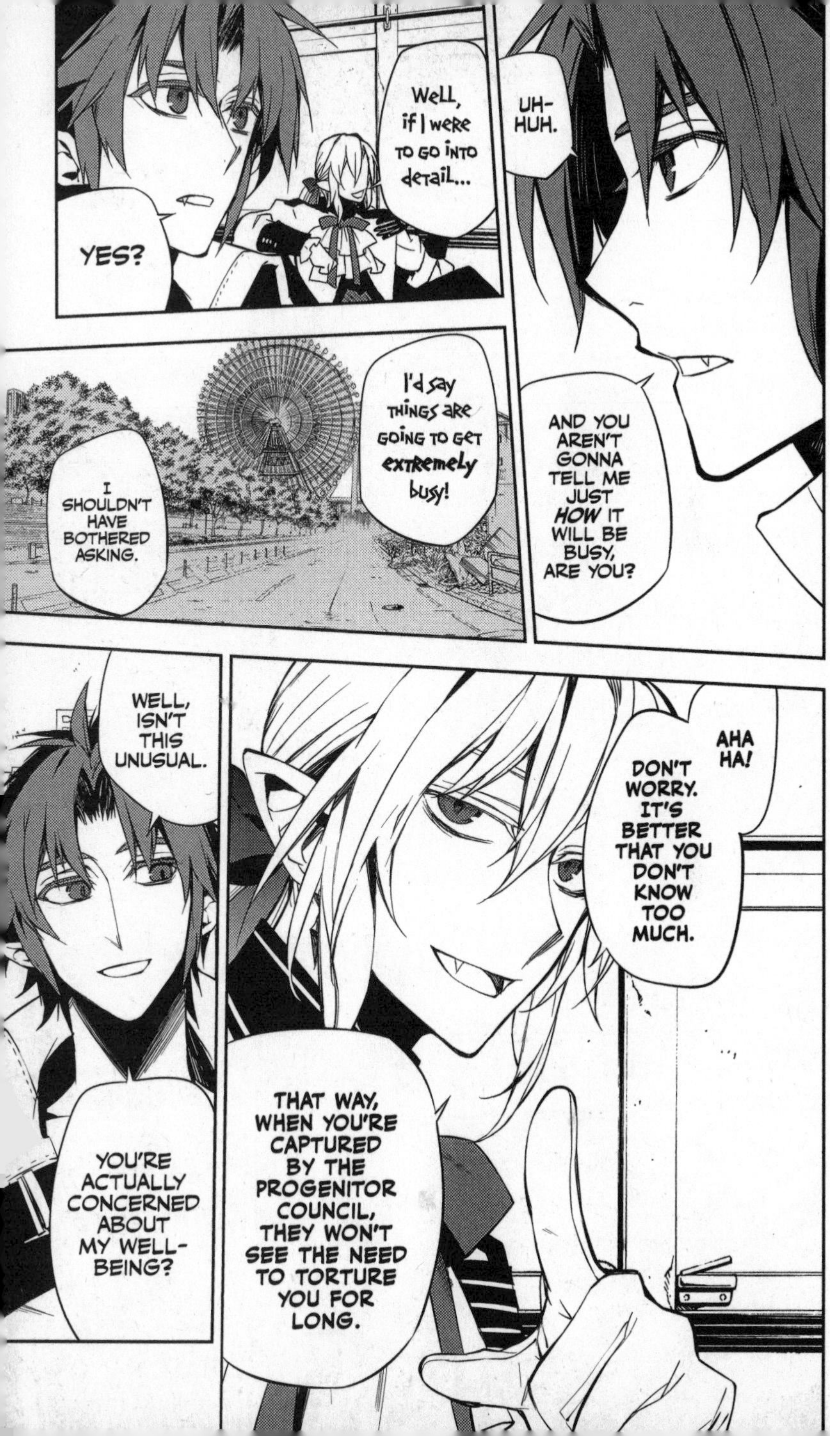
UH-HUH.
AND YOU AREN'T GONNA TELL ME JUST HOW IT WILL BE BUSY, ARE YOU?
Well, if I were to go into detail...
YES?
I'd say things are going to get extremely busy!
I SHOULDN'T HAVE BOTHERED ASKING.
AHA HA!
DON'T WORRY. IT'S BETTER THAT YOU DON'T KNOW TOO MUCH.
THAT WAY, WHEN YOU'RE CAPTURED BY THE PROGENITOR COUNCIL, THEY WON'T SEE THE NEED TO TORTURE YOU FOR LONG.
WELL, ISN'T THIS UNUSUAL.
YOU'RE ACTUALLY CONCERNED ABOUT MY WELL-BEING?

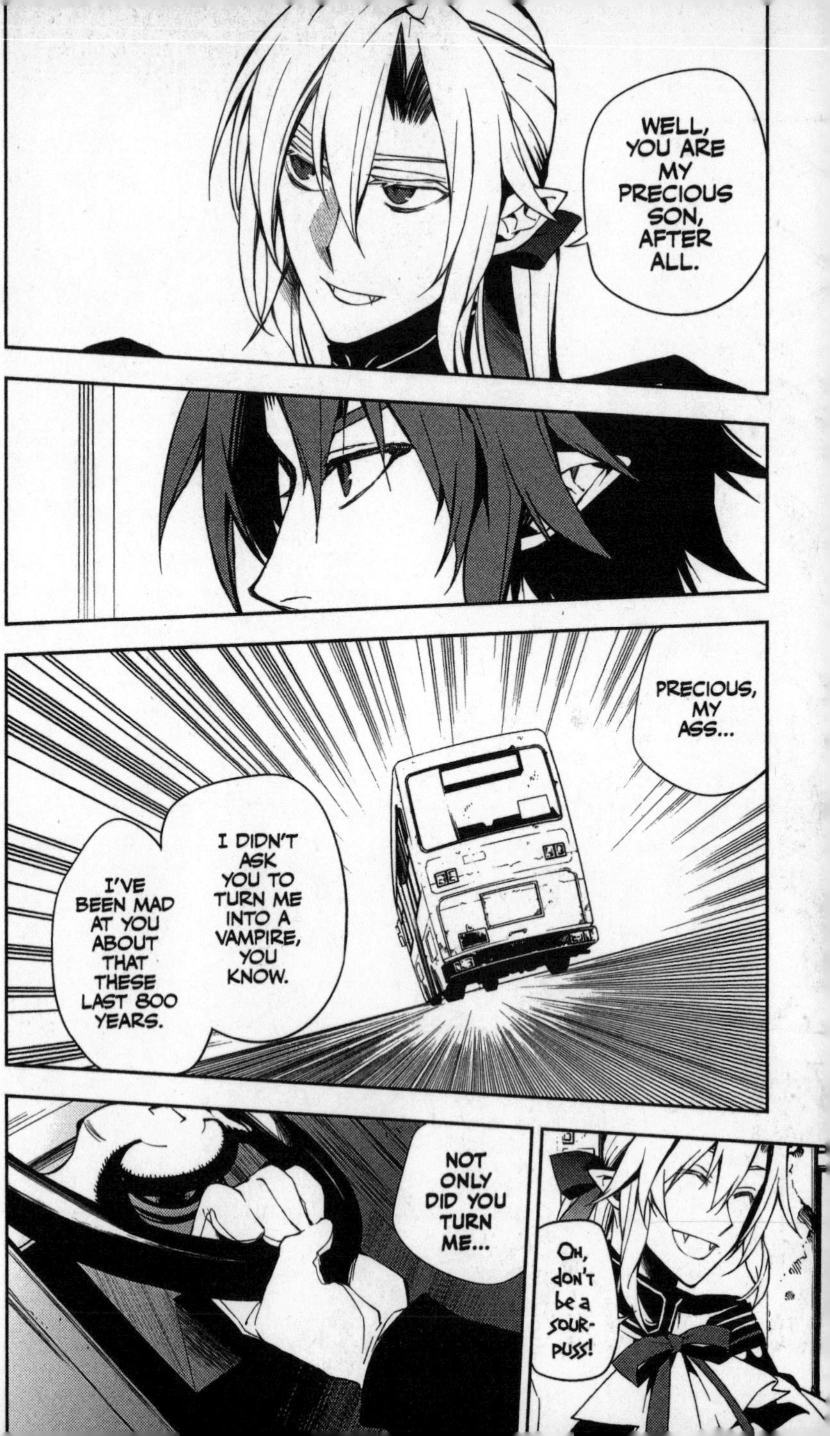
WELL, YOU ARE MY PRECIOUS SON, AFTER ALL.
PRECIOUS, MY ASS...
I DIDN'T ASK YOU TO TURN ME INTO A VAMPIRE, YOU KNOW.
I'VE BEEN MAD AT YOU ABOUT THAT THESE LAST 800 YEARS.
OH, DON'T BE A SOUR-PUSS!
NOT ONLY DID YOU TURN ME...

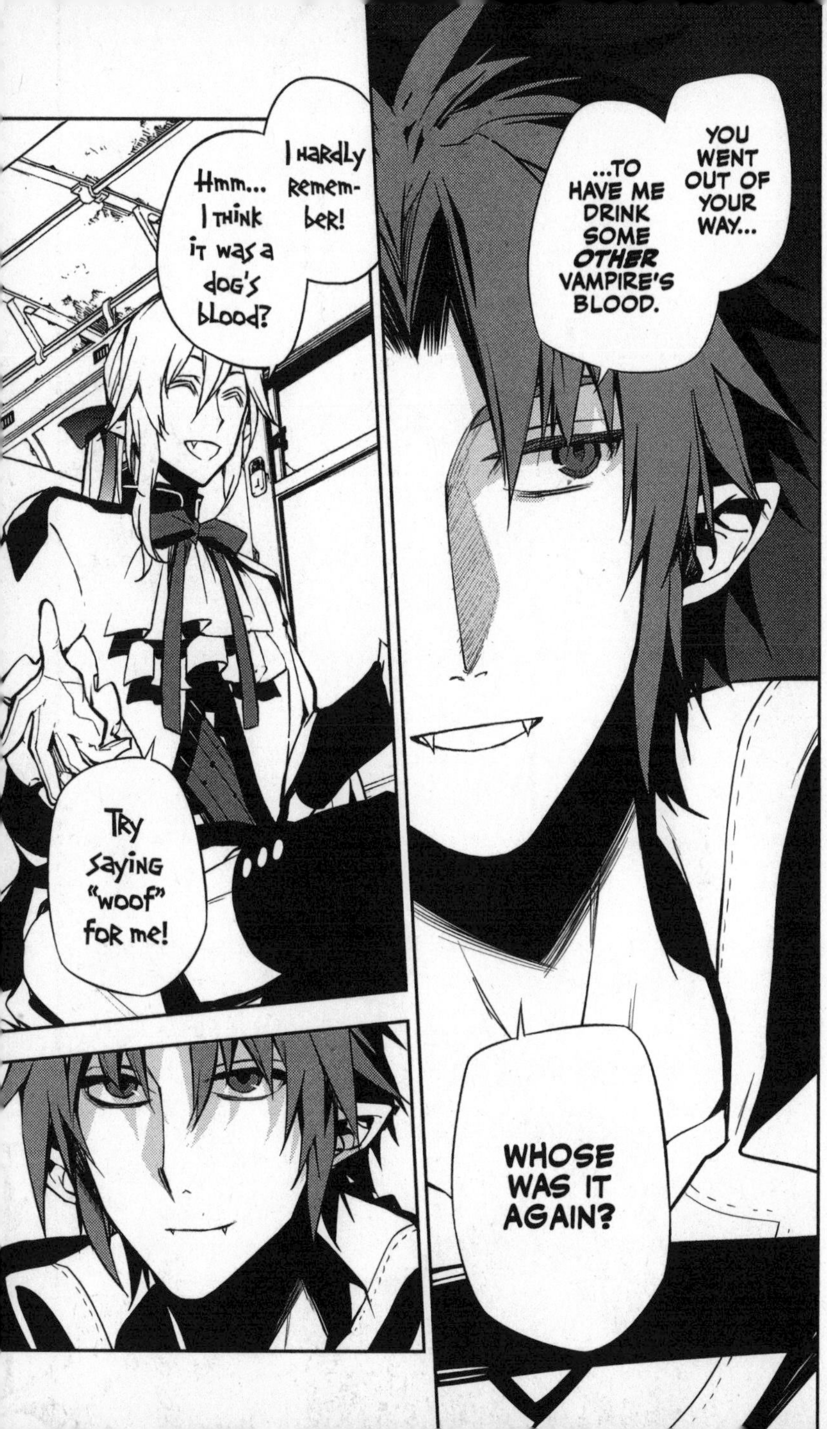
YOU WENT OUT OF YOUR WAY...
...TO HAVE ME DRINK SOME *OTHER* VAMPIRE'S BLOOD.
WHOSE WAS IT AGAIN?
I hardly remember!
Hmm... I think it was a dog's blood?
Try saying "woof" for me!

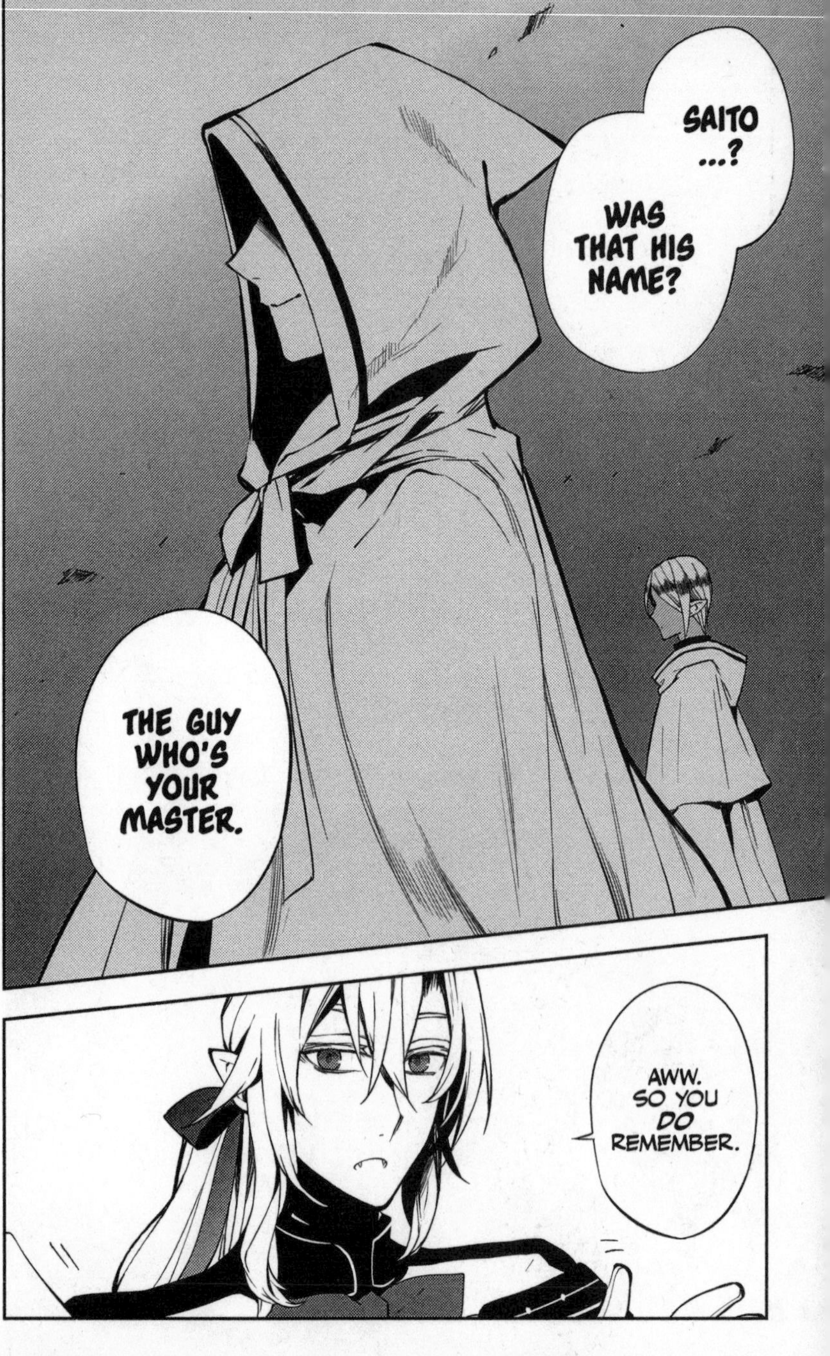
SAITO ...?
WAS THAT HIS NAME?
THE GUY WHO'S YOUR MASTER.
AWW. SO YOU *DO* REMEMBER.

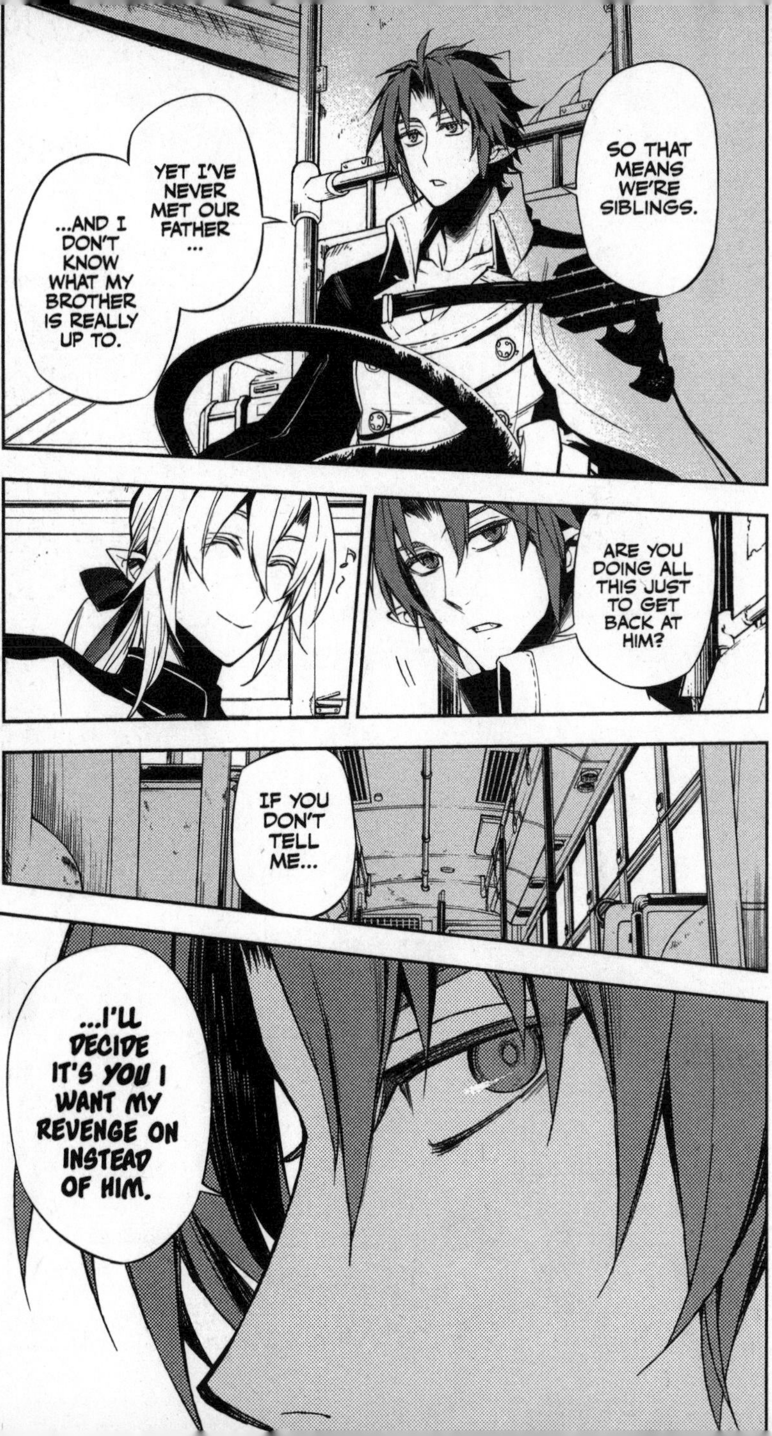
SO THAT MEANS WE'RE SIBLINGS.
YET I'VE NEVER MET OUR FATHER ...
...AND I DON'T KNOW WHAT MY BROTHER IS REALLY UP TO.
ARE YOU DOING ALL THIS JUST TO GET BACK AT HIM?
IF YOU DON'T TELL ME...
...I'LL DECIDE IT'S YOU I WANT MY REVENGE ON INSTEAD OF HIM.

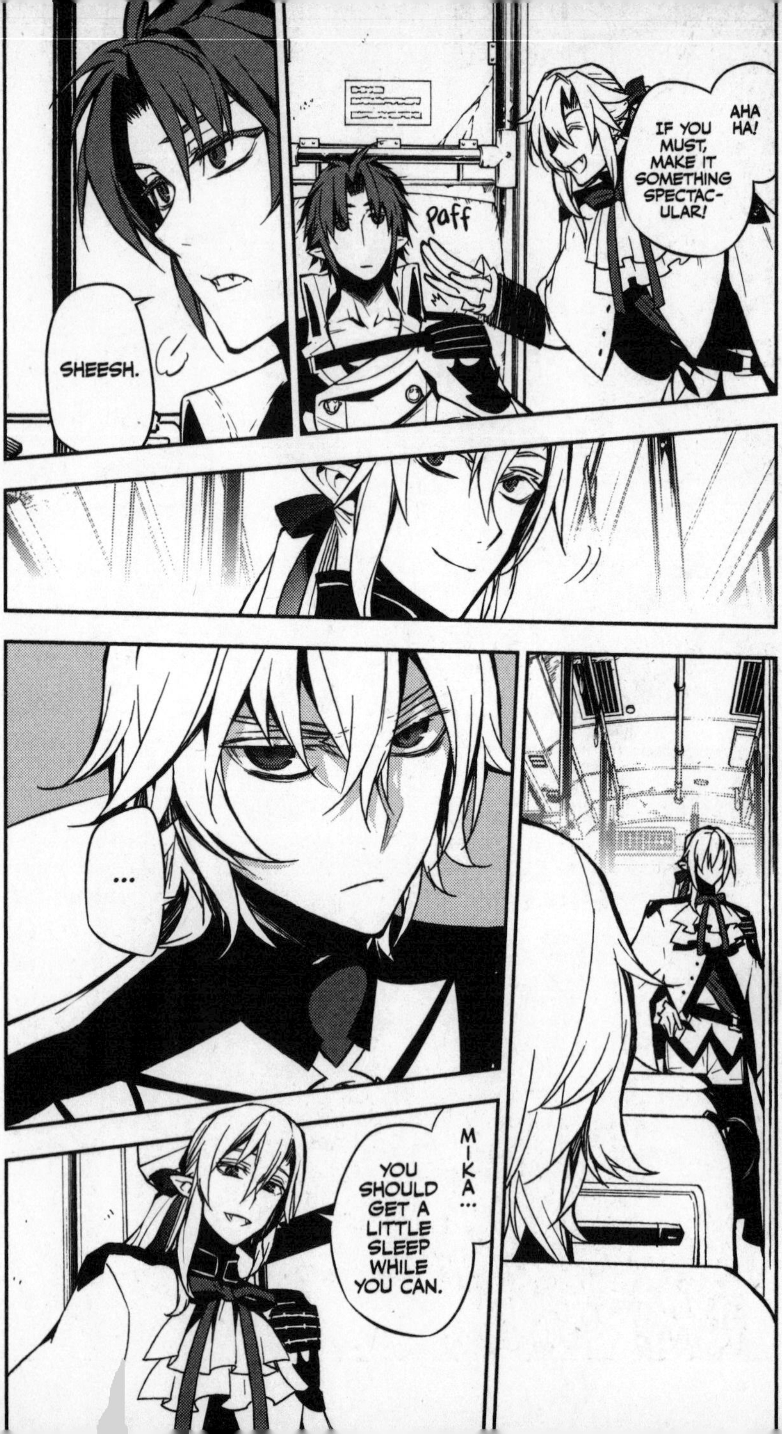
AHA HA!
IF YOU MUST, MAKE IT SOMETHING SPECTACULAR!
paff
SHEESH.
...
MIKA...
YOU SHOULD GET A LITTLE SLEEP WHILE YOU CAN.

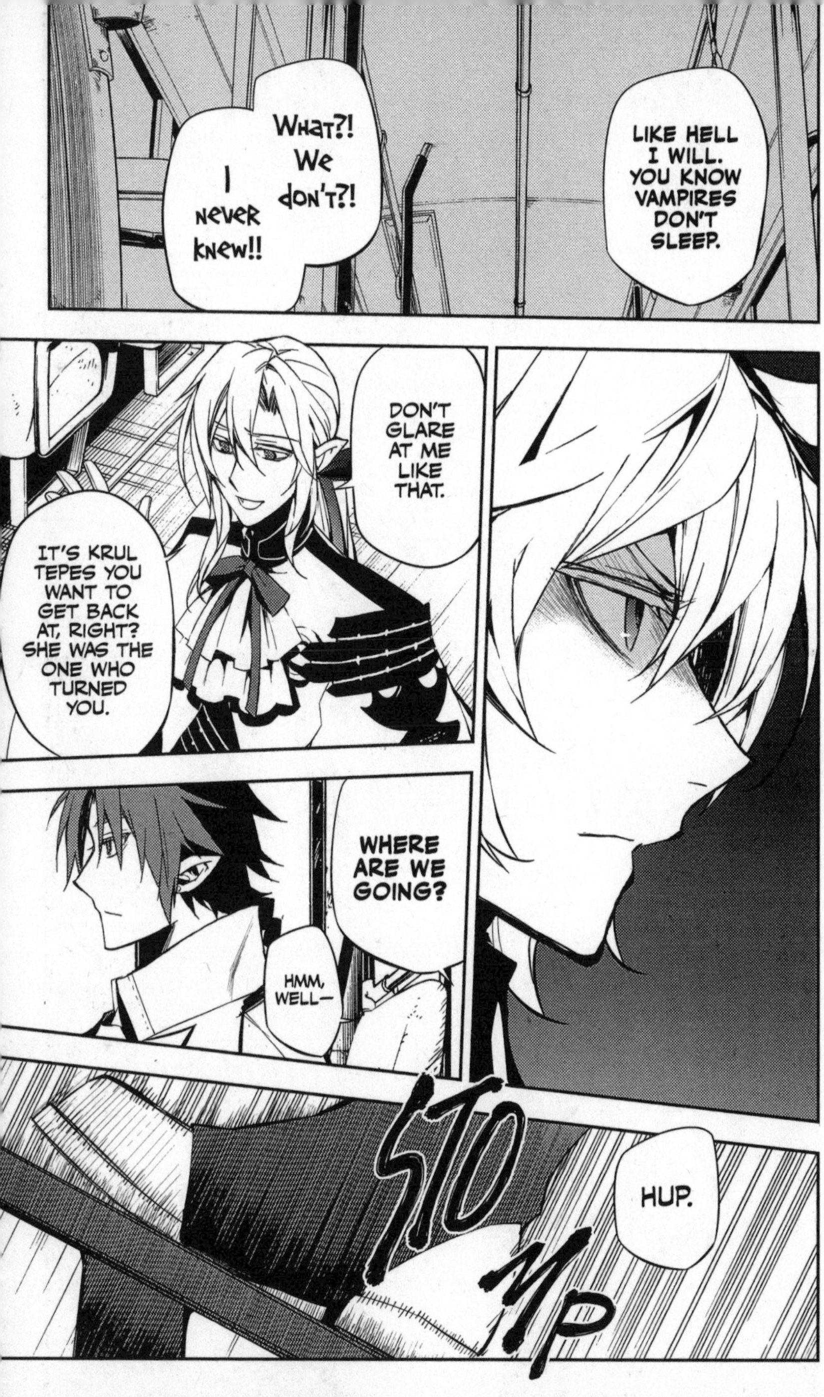
LIKE HELL I WILL. YOU KNOW VAMPIRES DON'T SLEEP.
WHAT?! We don't?!
I never knew!!
DON'T GLARE AT ME LIKE THAT.
IT'S KRUL TEPES YOU WANT TO GET BACK AT, RIGHT? SHE WAS THE ONE WHO TURNED YOU.
WHERE ARE WE GOING?
HMM, WELL—
HUP.
STOMP

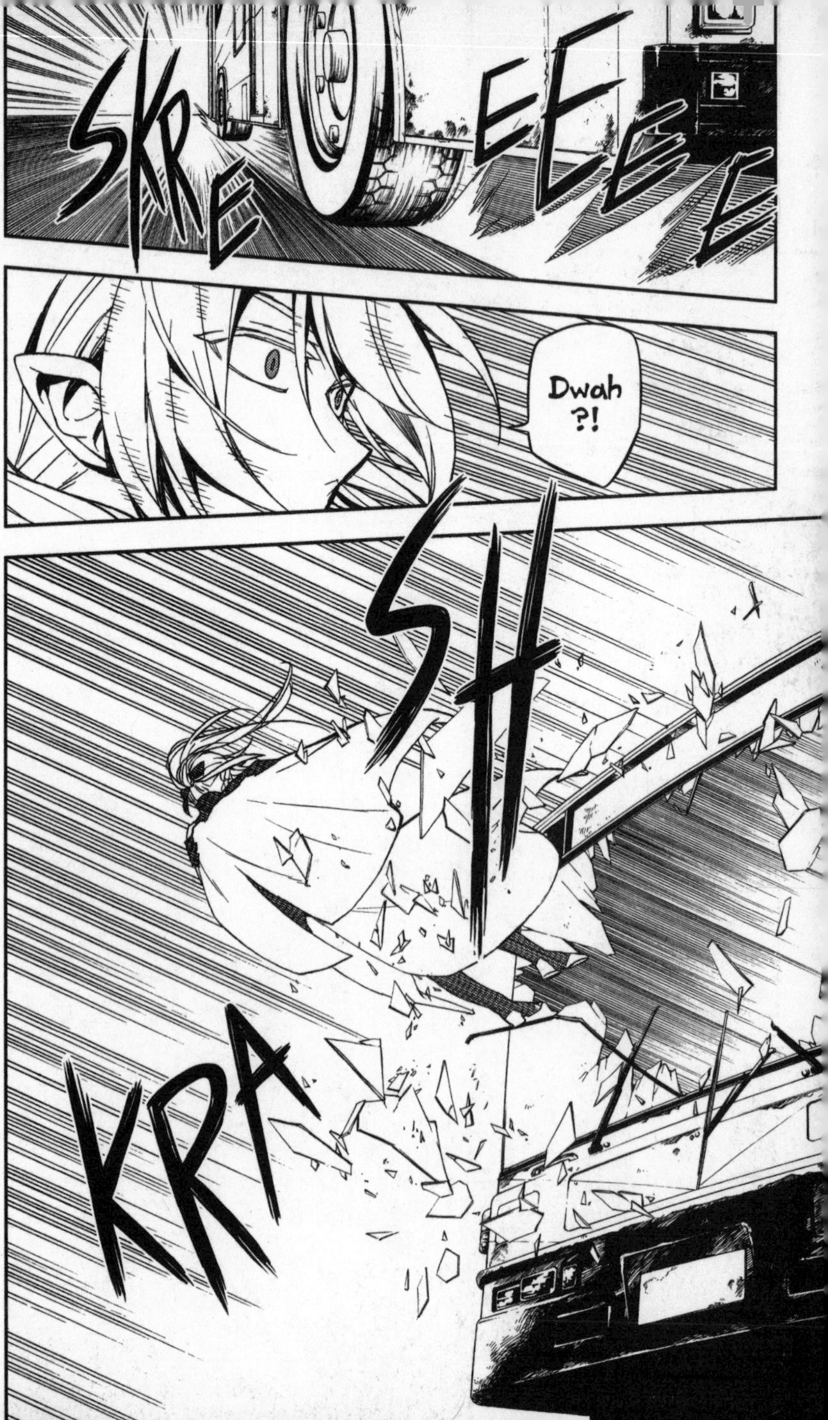
SKREEEEEE
Dwah ?!
SH
KRA

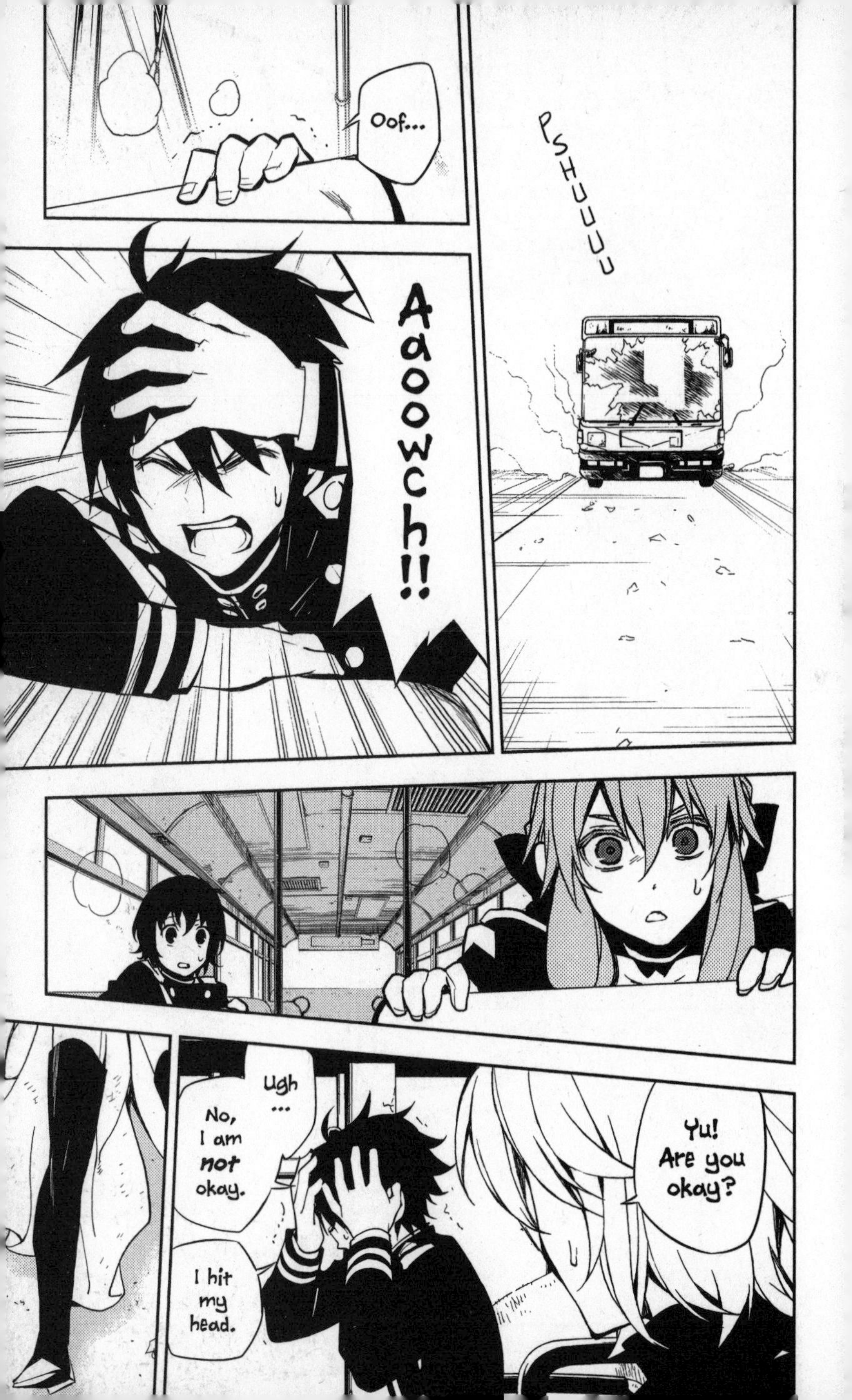
PSHUUUUU
Oof...
Aaooowch!!
Yu! Are you okay?
Ugh...
No, I am *not* okay.
I hit my head.

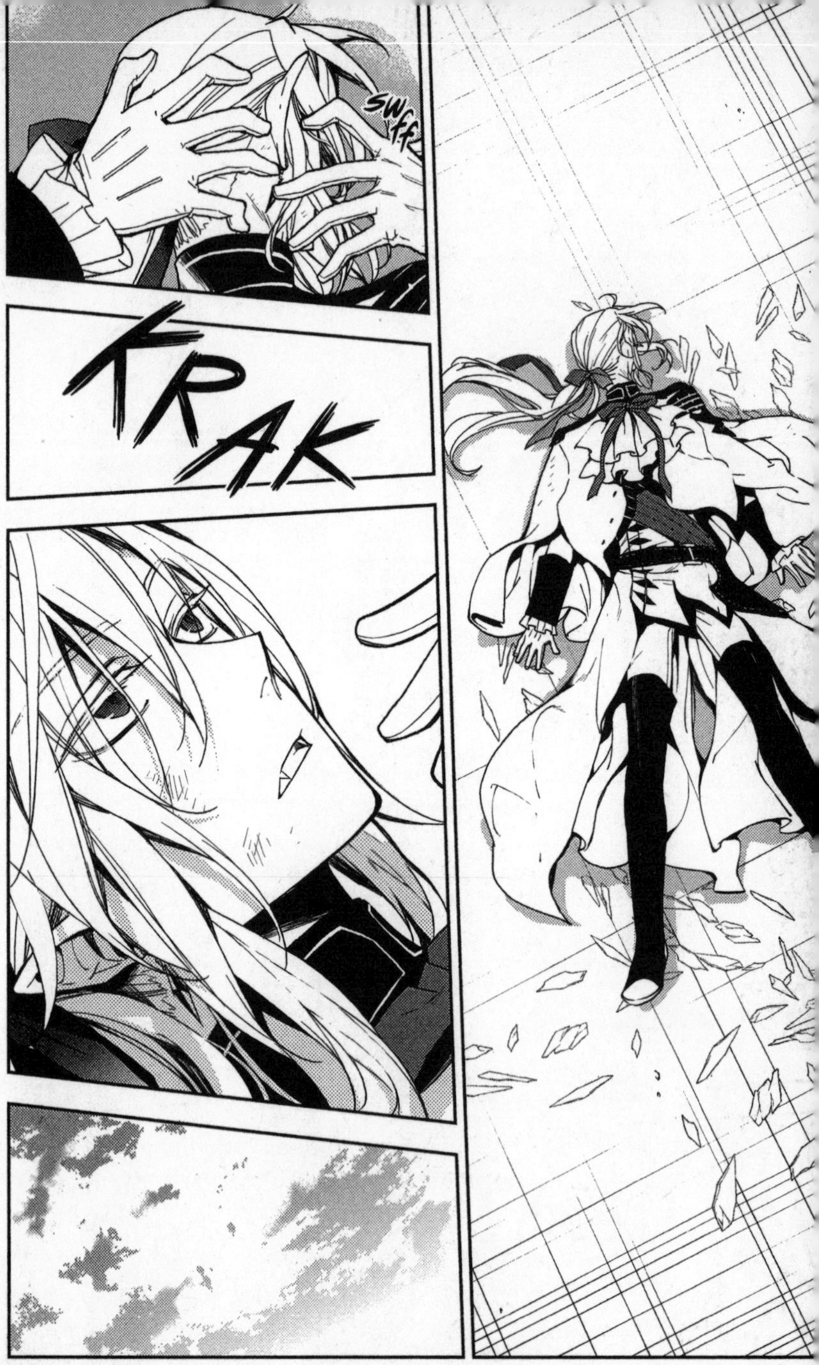
SWFF
KRAK

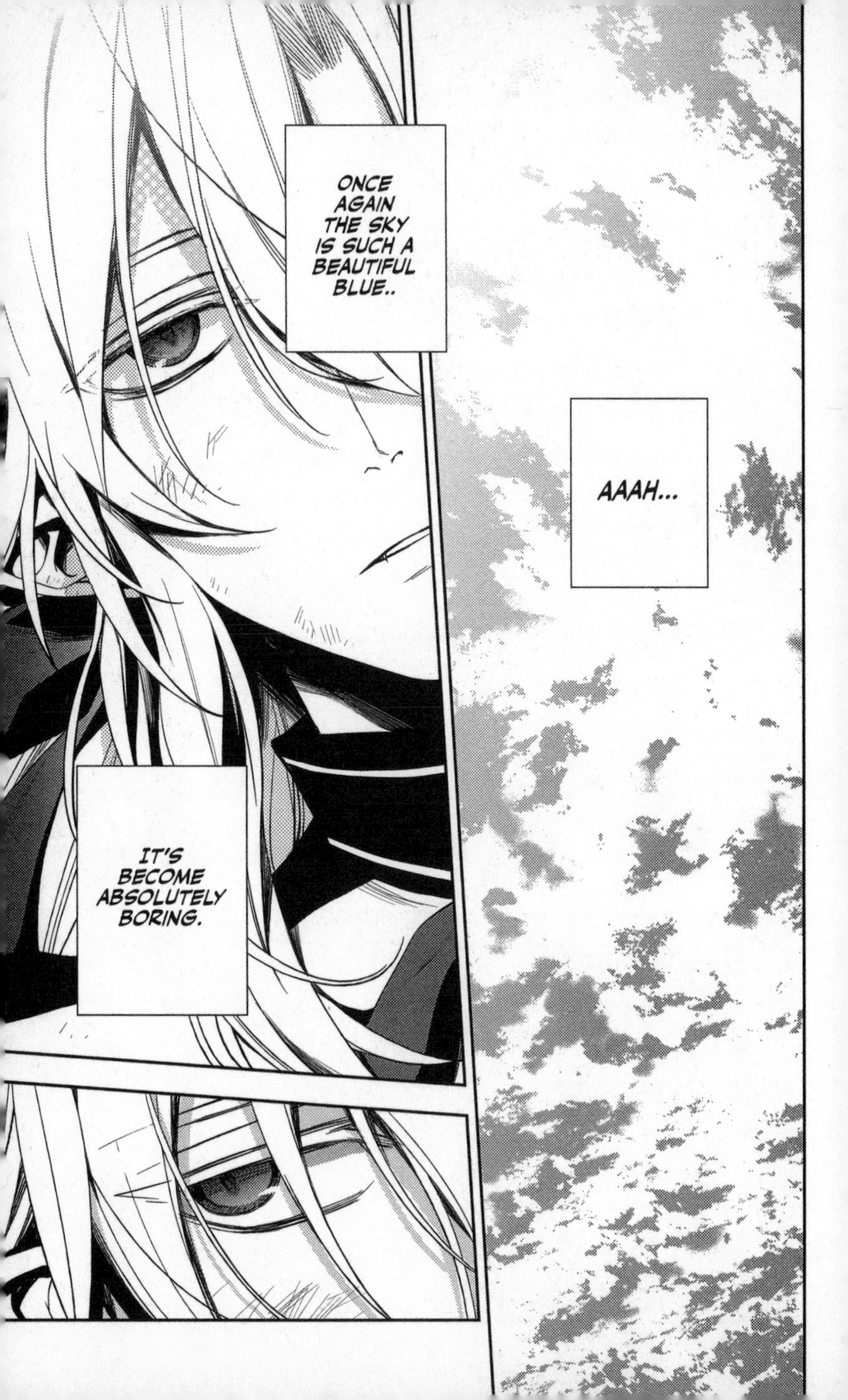
AAAH...
ONCE AGAIN THE SKY IS SUCH A BEAUTIFUL BLUE..
IT'S BECOME ABSOLUTELY BORING.

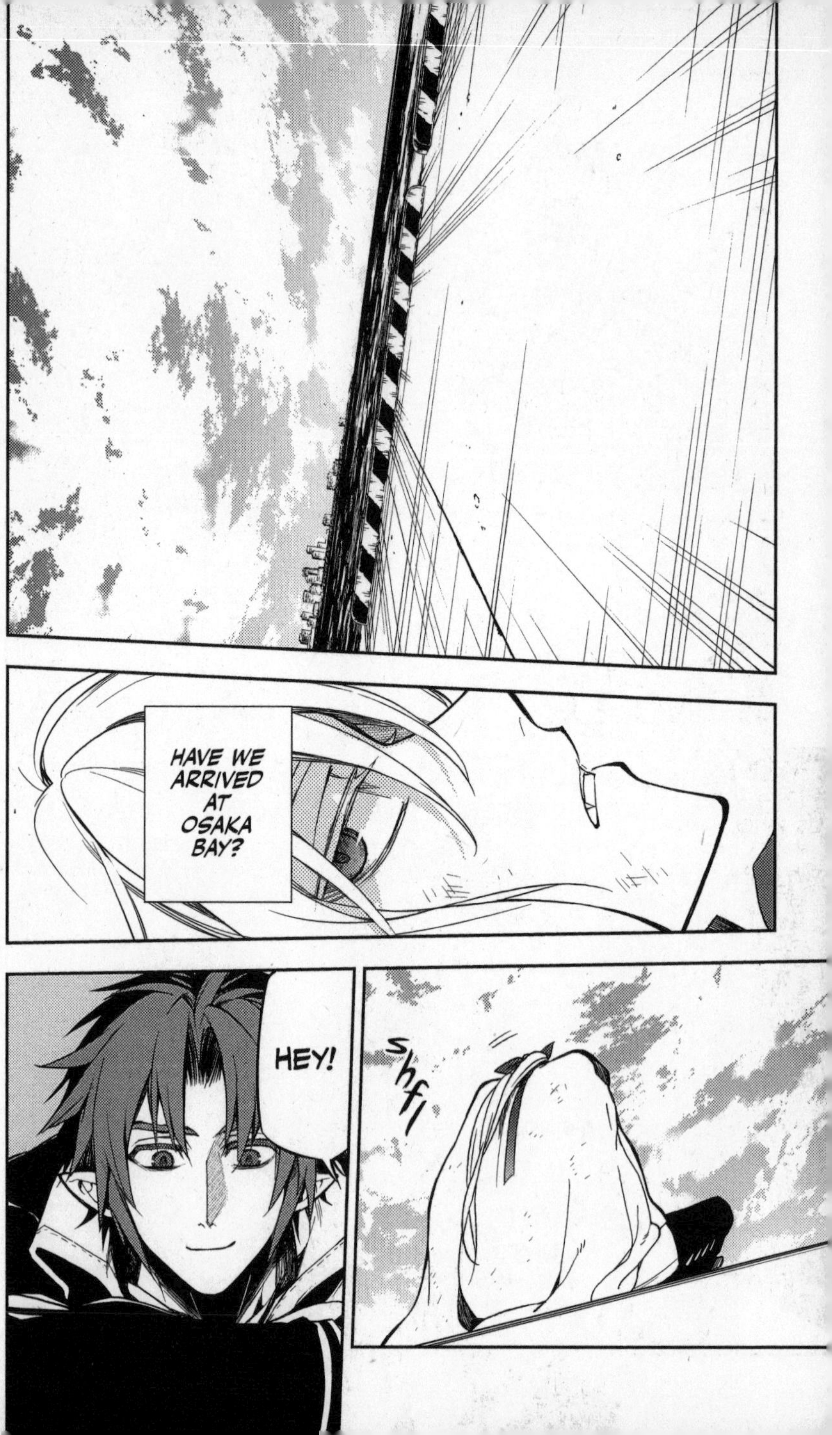
HAVE WE ARRIVED AT OSAKA BAY?
shfl
HEY!

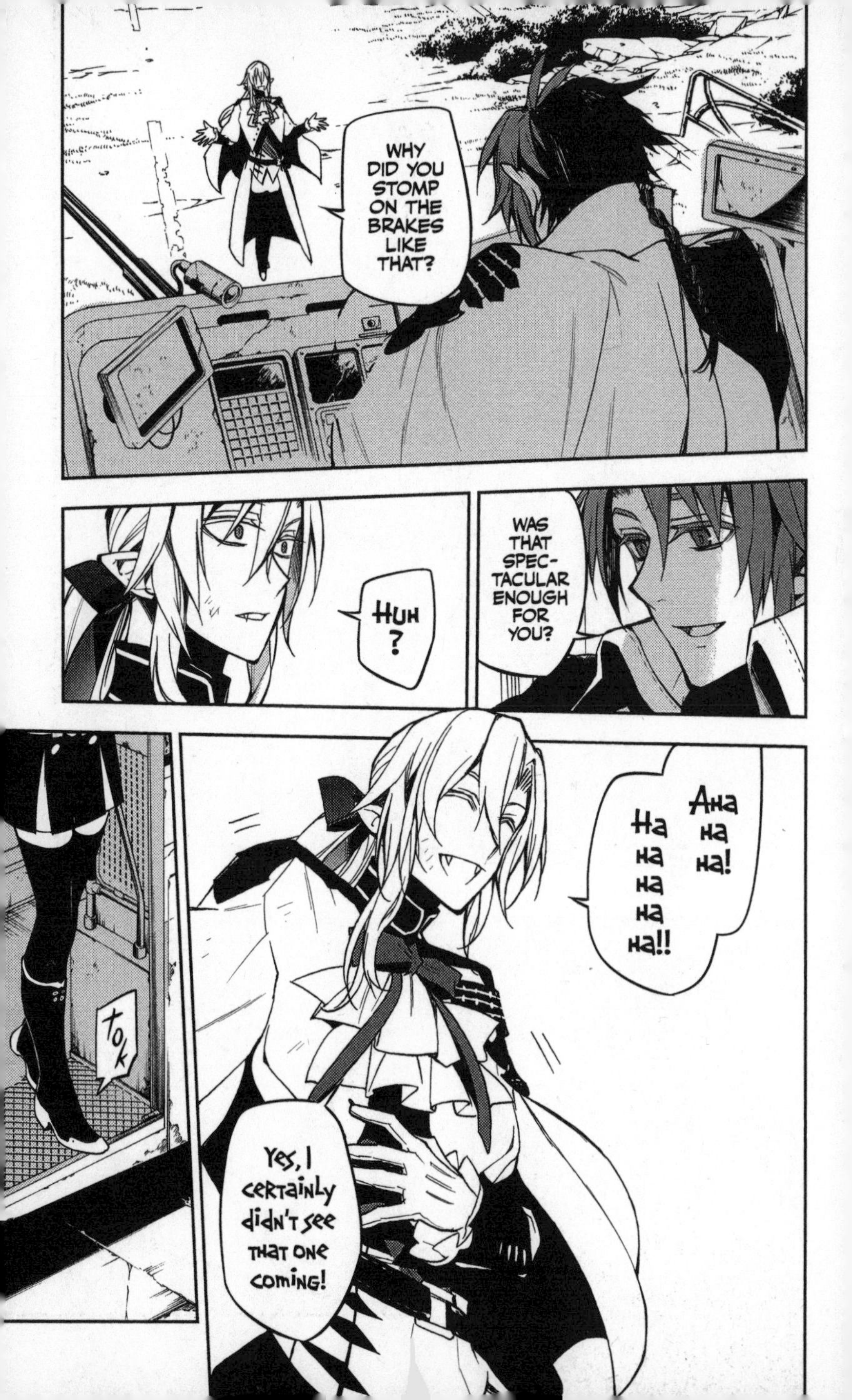
WHY DID YOU STOMP ON THE BRAKES LIKE THAT?
WAS THAT SPEC-TACULAR ENOUGH FOR YOU?
HUH?
AHA HA HA!
HA HA HA HA HA!!
TOK
YES, I CERTAINLY DIDN'T SEE THAT ONE COMING!

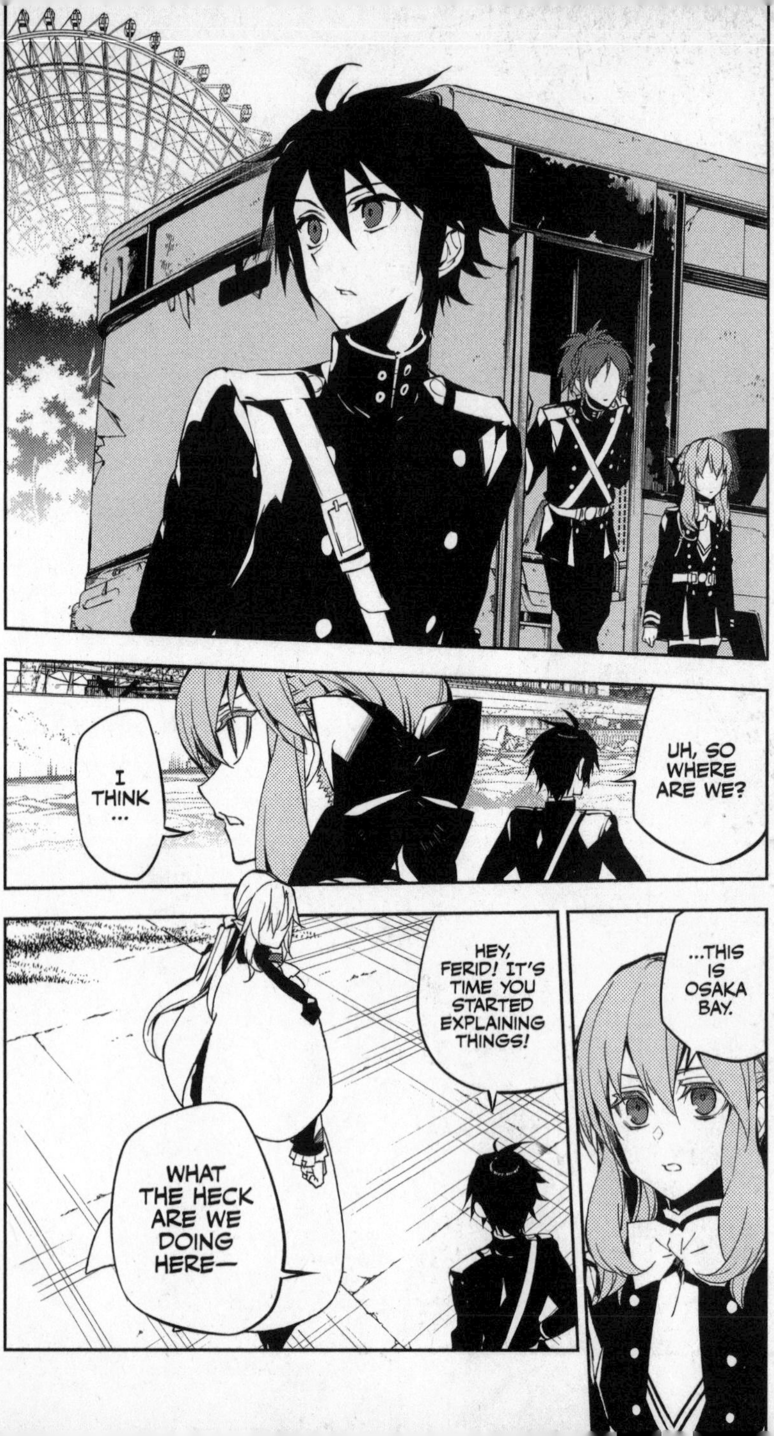
UH, SO WHERE ARE WE?
I THINK...
...THIS IS OSAKA BAY.
HEY, FERID! IT'S TIME YOU STARTED EXPLAINING THINGS!
WHAT THE HECK ARE WE DOING HERE—

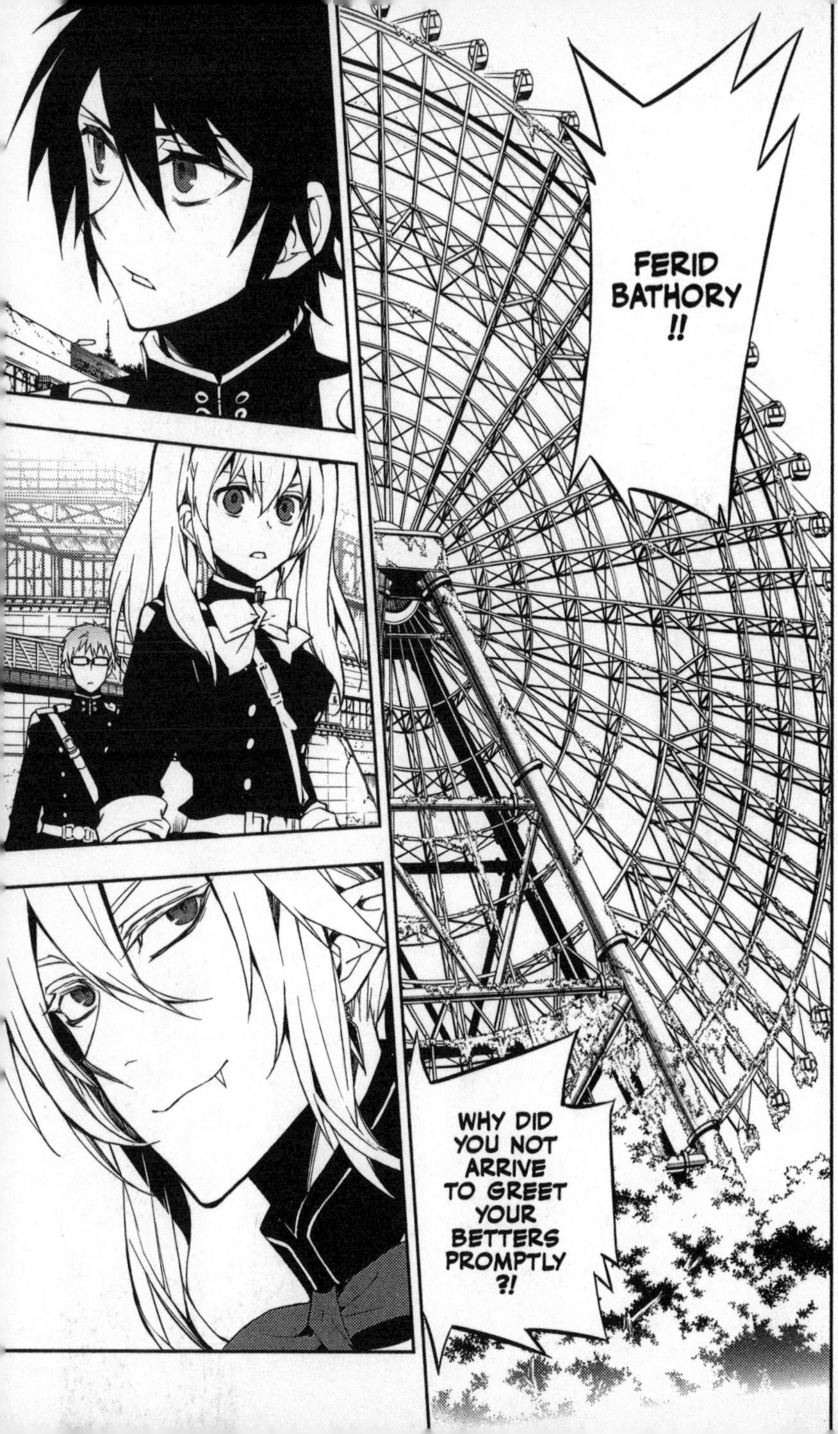
FERID BATHORY !!
WHY DID YOU NOT ARRIVE TO GREET YOUR BETTERS PROMPTLY ?!

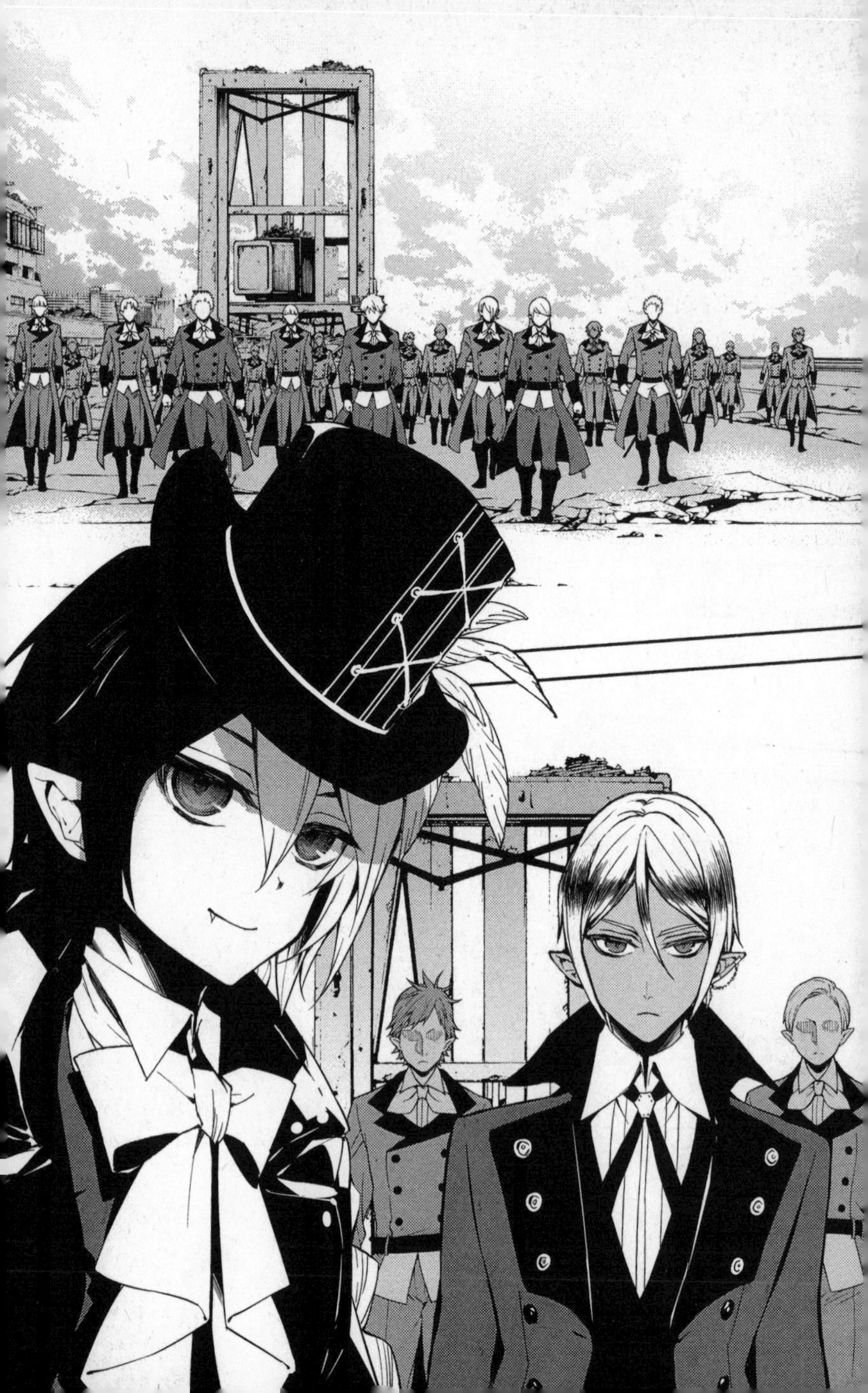

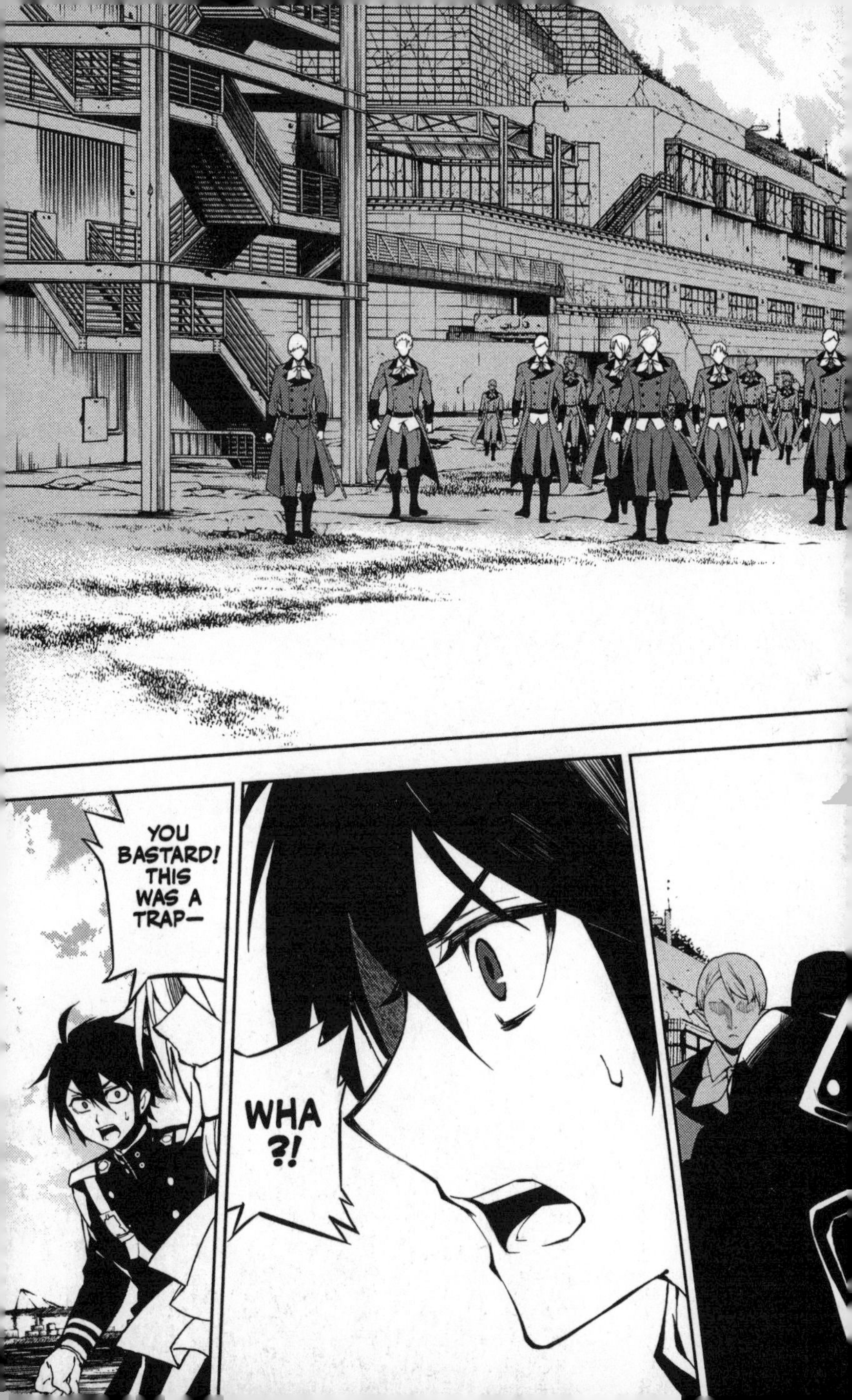
WHA ?!
YOU BASTARD! THIS WAS A TRAP—

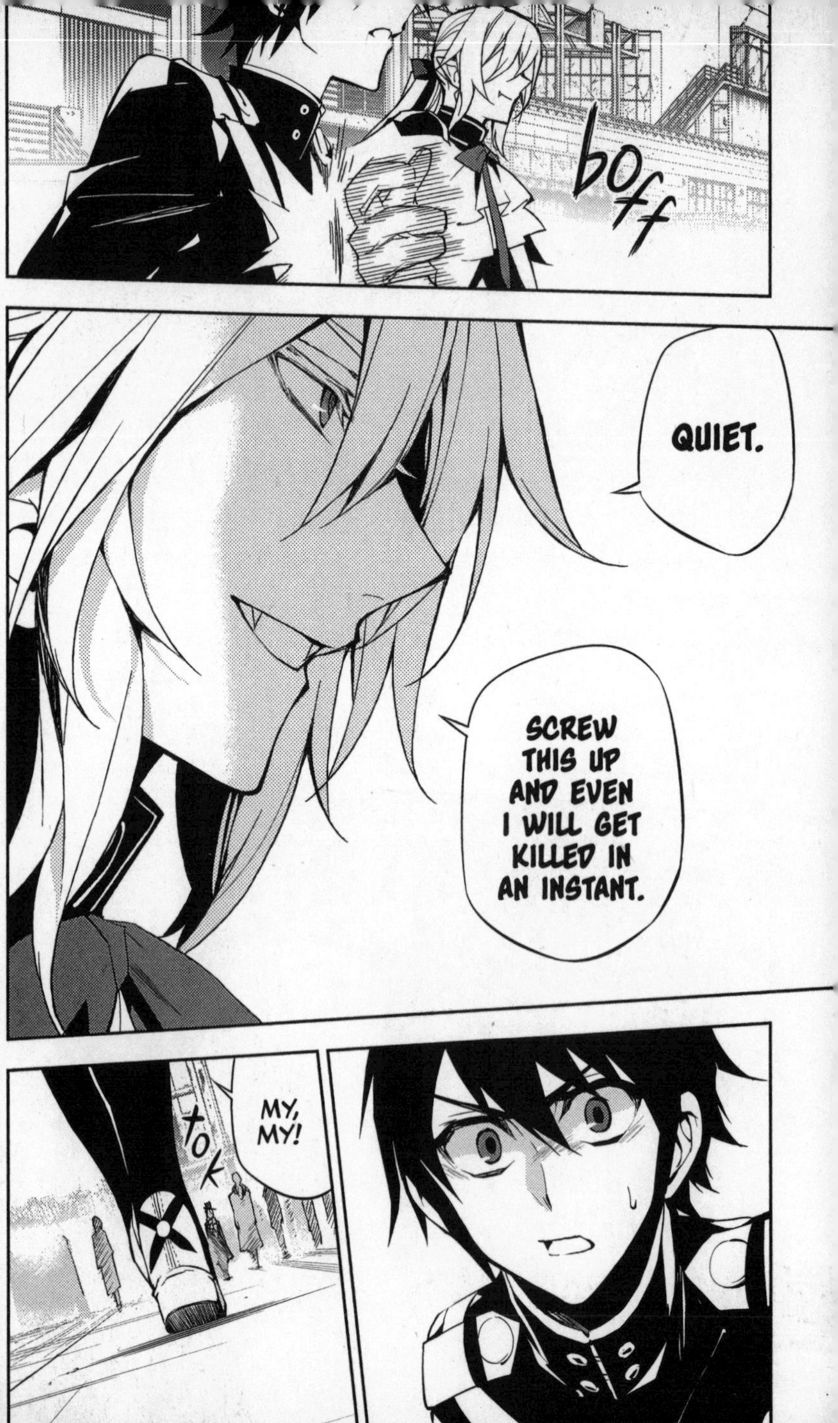
boff
QUIET.
SCREW THIS UP AND EVEN I WILL GET KILLED IN AN INSTANT.
MY, MY!
TOK

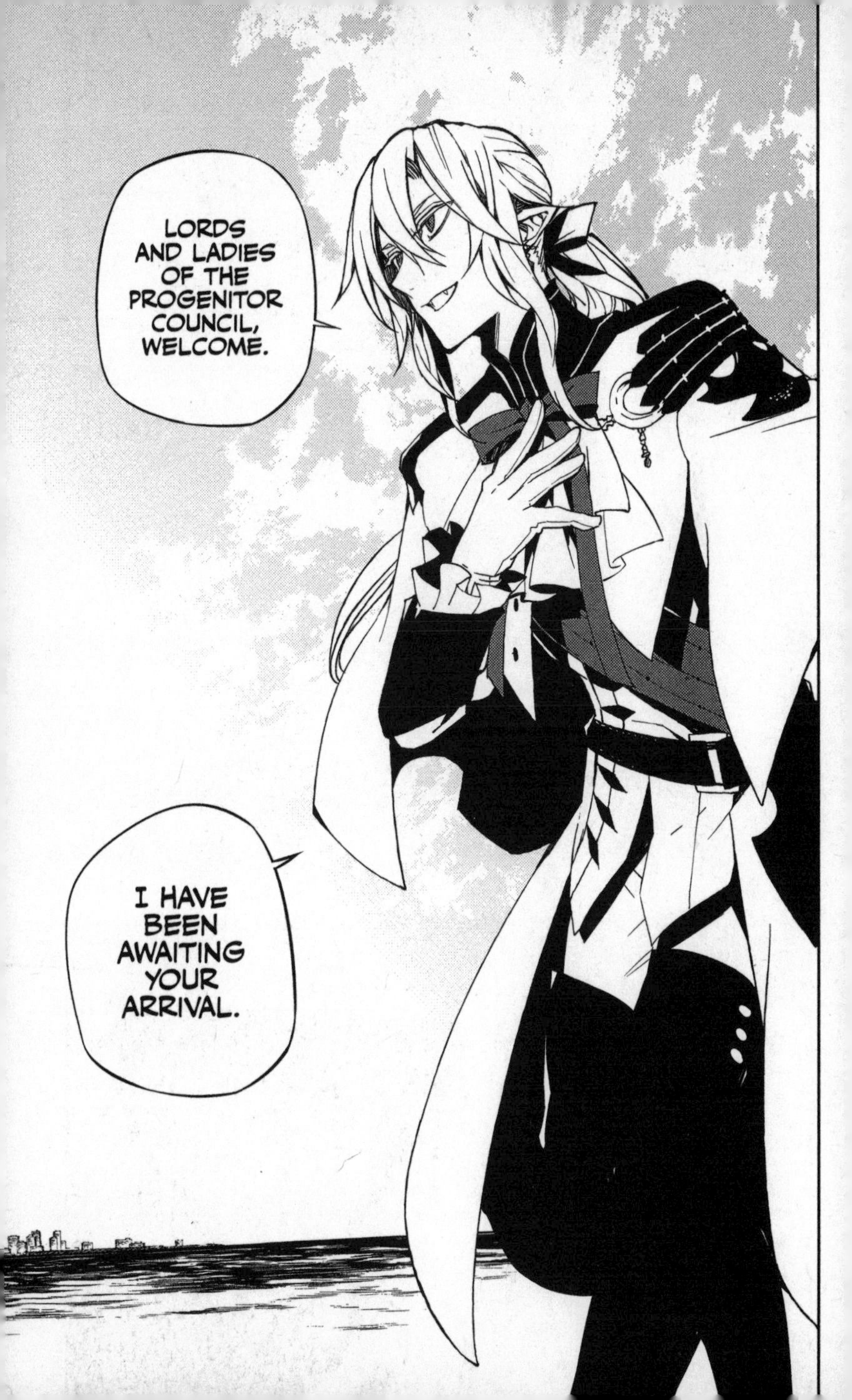
LORDS AND LADIES OF THE PROGENITOR COUNCIL, WELCOME.
I HAVE BEEN AWAITING YOUR ARRIVAL.

Seraph of the End
—VAMPIRE REIGN—

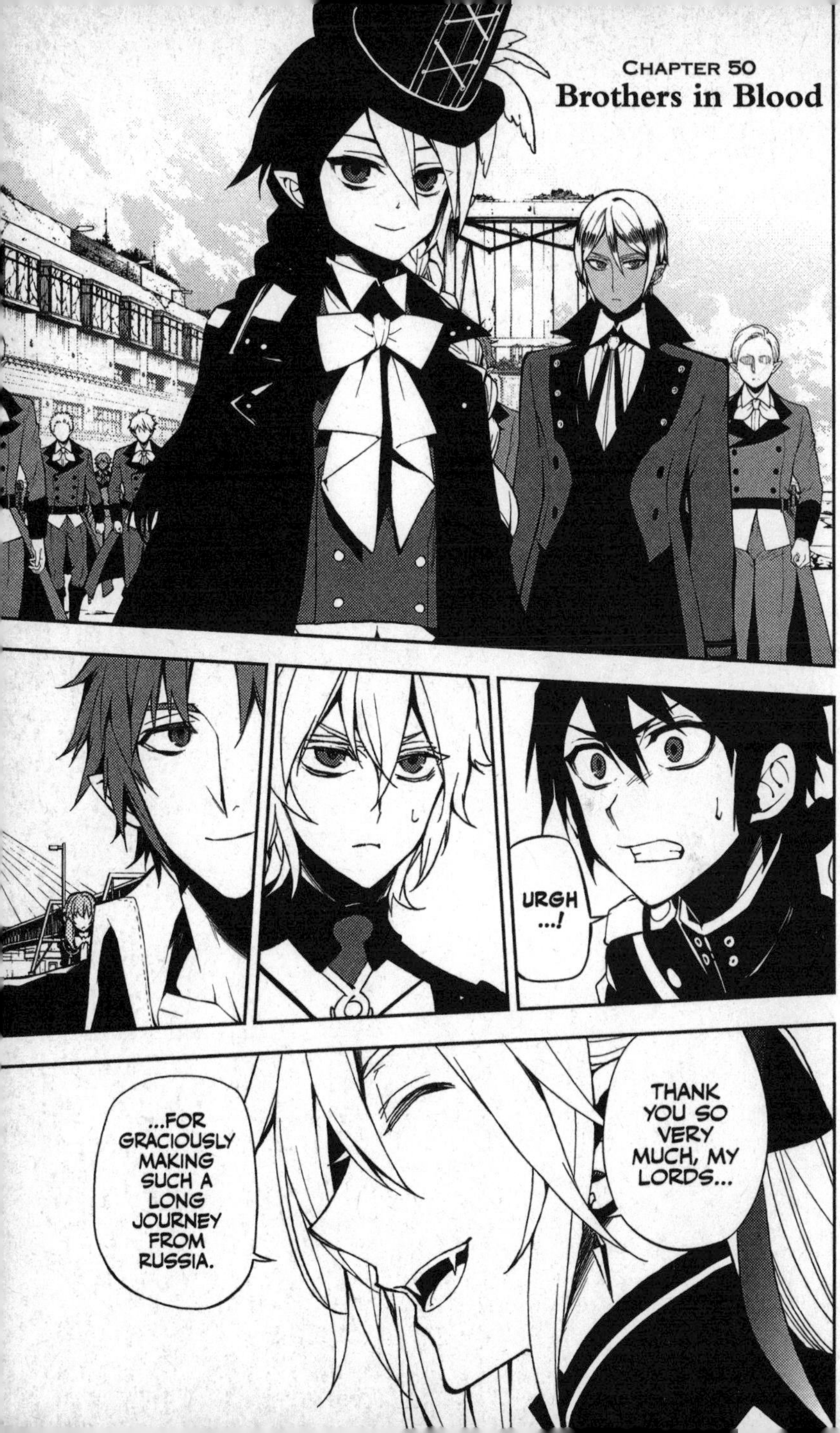
CHAPTER 50
Brothers in Blood
URGH ...!
THANK YOU SO VERY MUCH, MY LORDS...
...FOR GRACIOUSLY MAKING SUCH A LONG JOURNEY FROM RUSSIA.

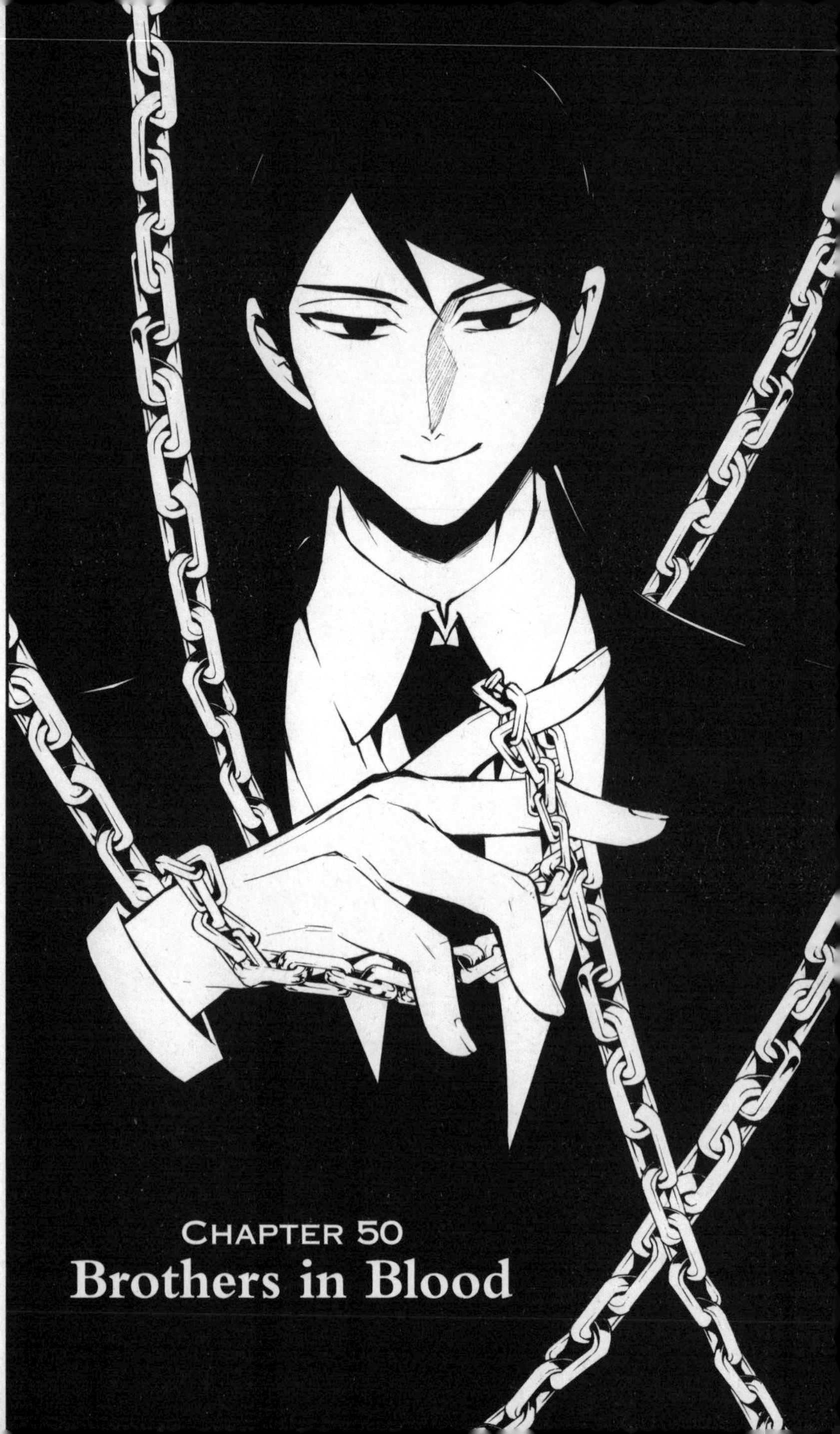

Chapter 50
Brothers in Blood

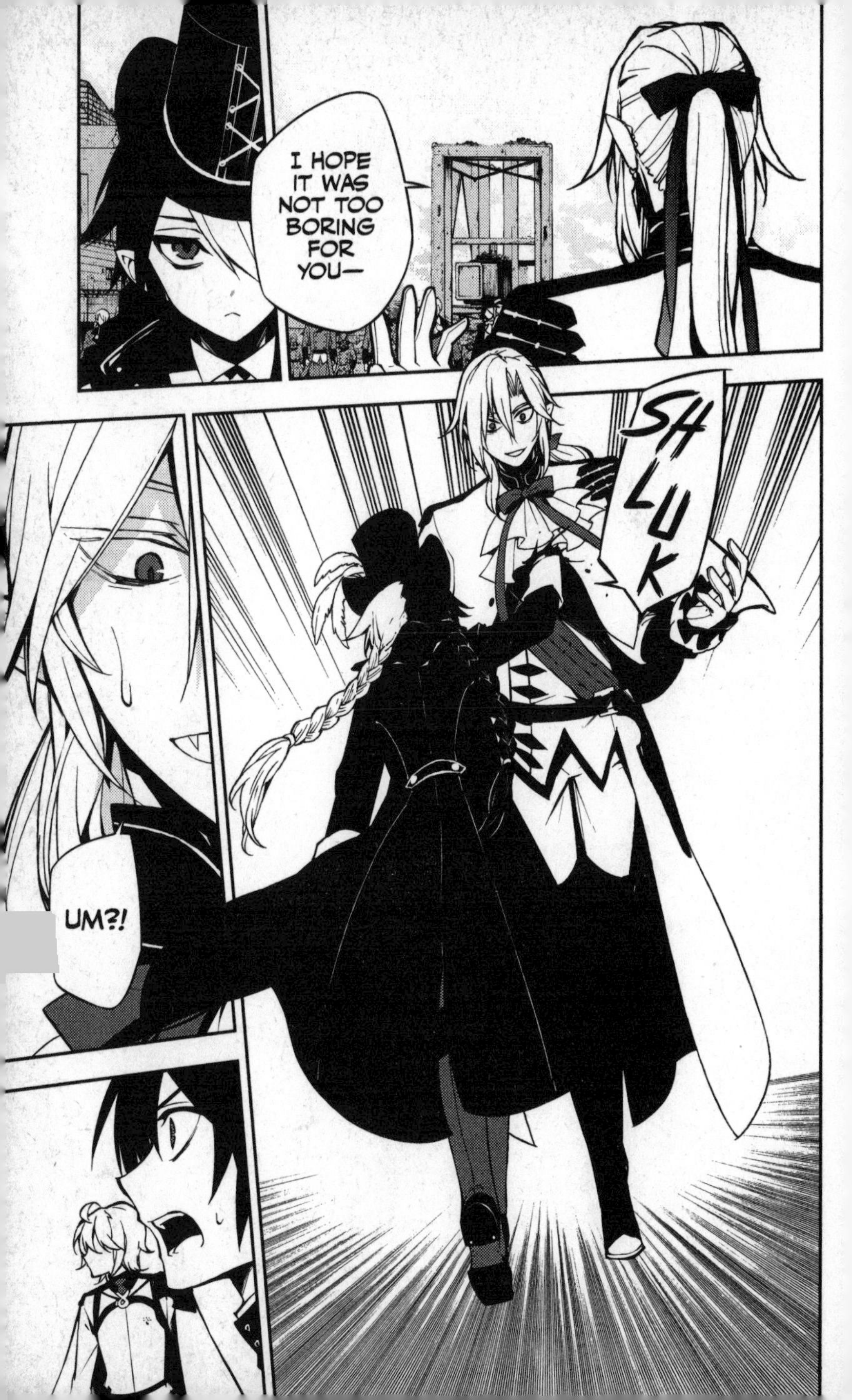
I HOPE IT WAS NOT TOO BORING FOR YOU—
SHLUK
UM?!

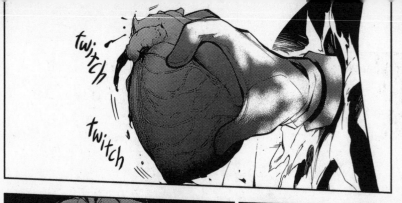

twitch

twitch

THIS IS JUST A GAME HE PLAYS.

WHA ?!

DON'T MOVE.

SLUMP

...?!

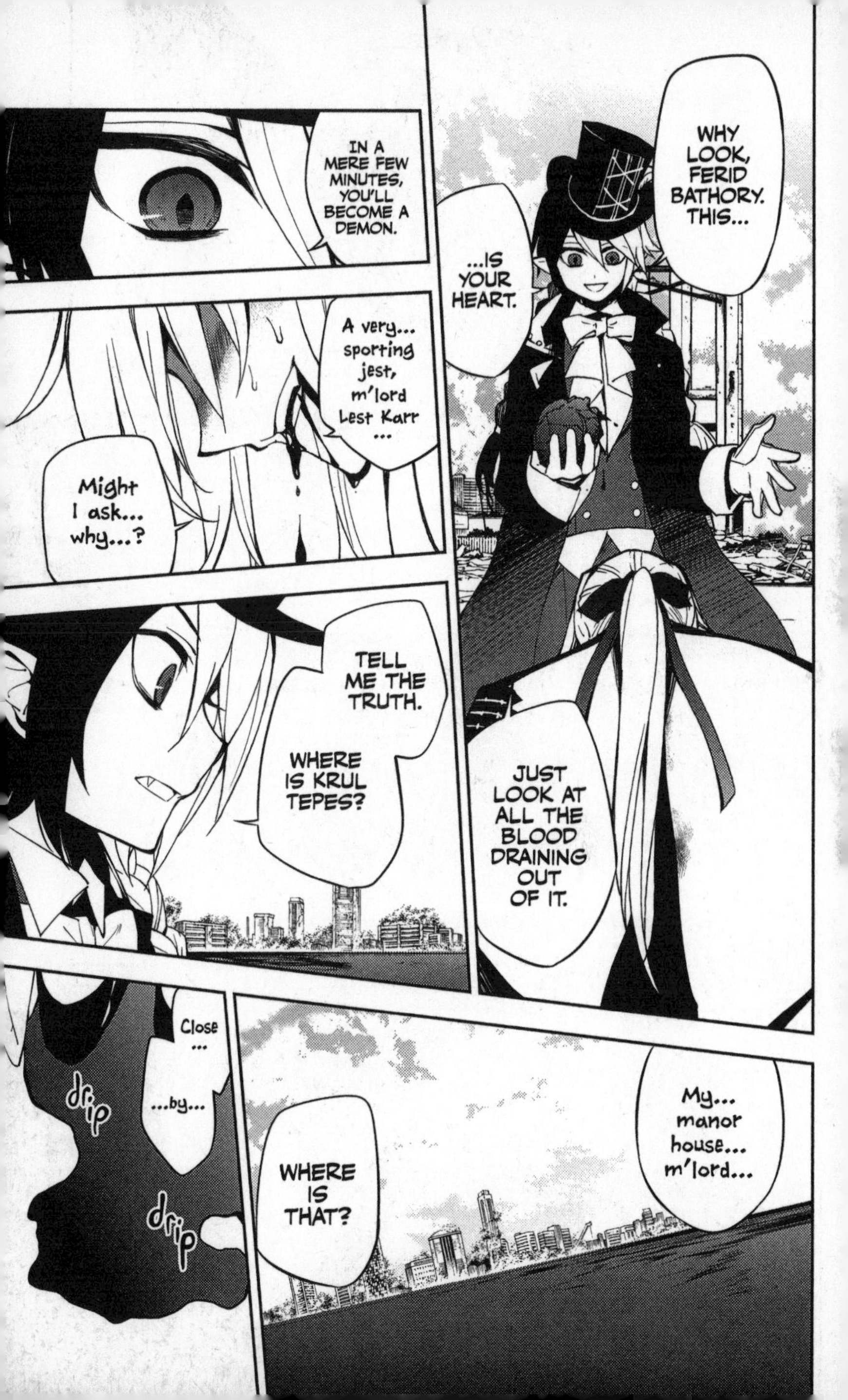
WHY LOOK, FERID BATHORY. THIS...
...IS YOUR HEART.
JUST LOOK AT ALL THE BLOOD DRAINING OUT OF IT.
IN A MERE FEW MINUTES, YOU'LL BECOME A DEMON.
A very... sporting jest, m'lord Lest Karr...
Might I ask... why...?
TELL ME THE TRUTH.
WHERE IS KRUL TEPES?
My... manor house... m'lord...
WHERE IS THAT?
Close...
...by...
drip
drip

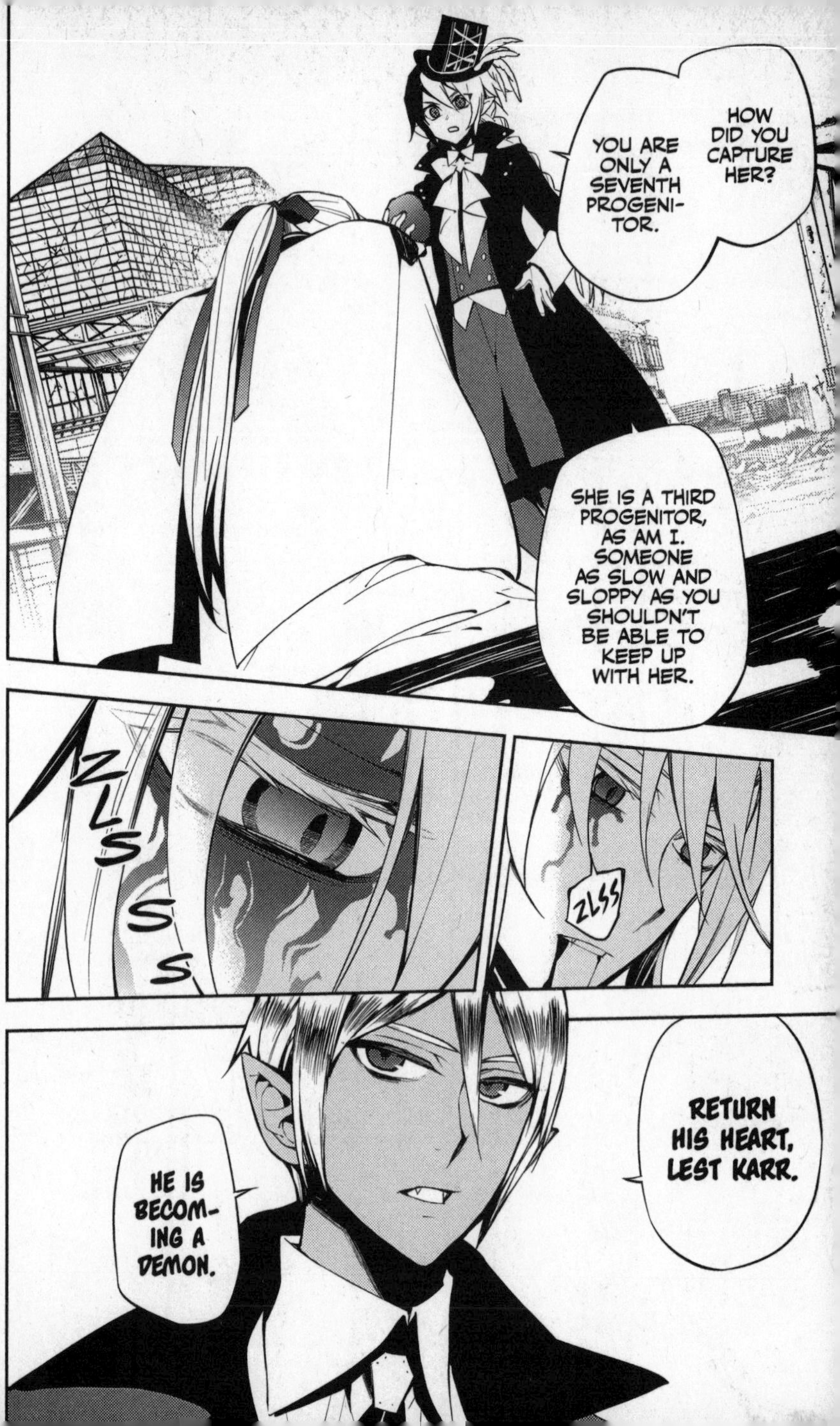
HOW DID YOU CAPTURE HER?
YOU ARE ONLY A SEVENTH PROGENI-TOR.
SHE IS A THIRD PROGENITOR, AS AM I. SOMEONE AS SLOW AND SLOPPY AS YOU SHOULDN'T BE ABLE TO KEEP UP WITH HER.
ZLSS
ZLSSSS
RETURN HIS HEART, LEST KARR.
HE IS BECOM-ING A DEMON.

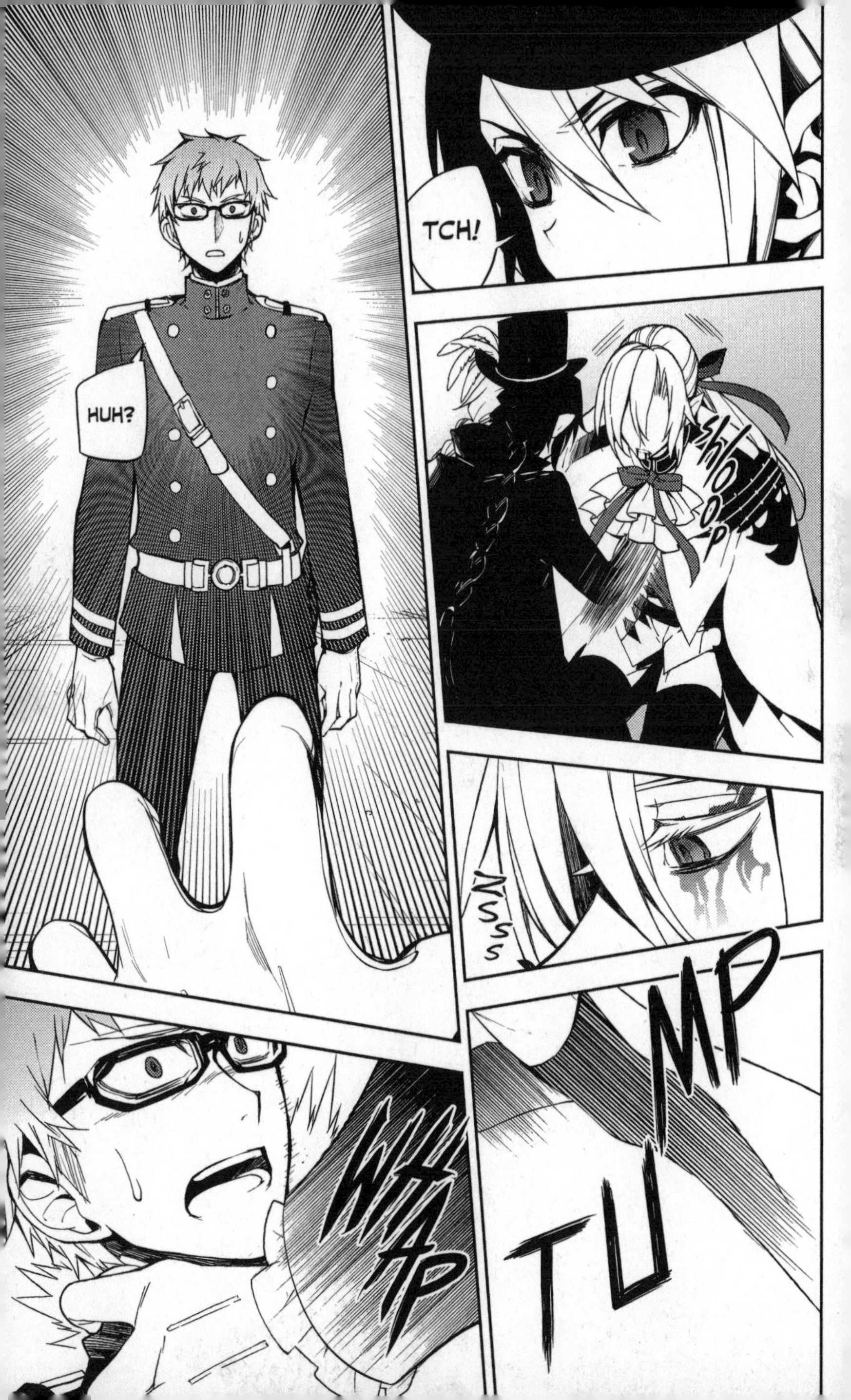
TCH!
SHLOOOP
ZSSS
HUH?
TUMP
WHAP

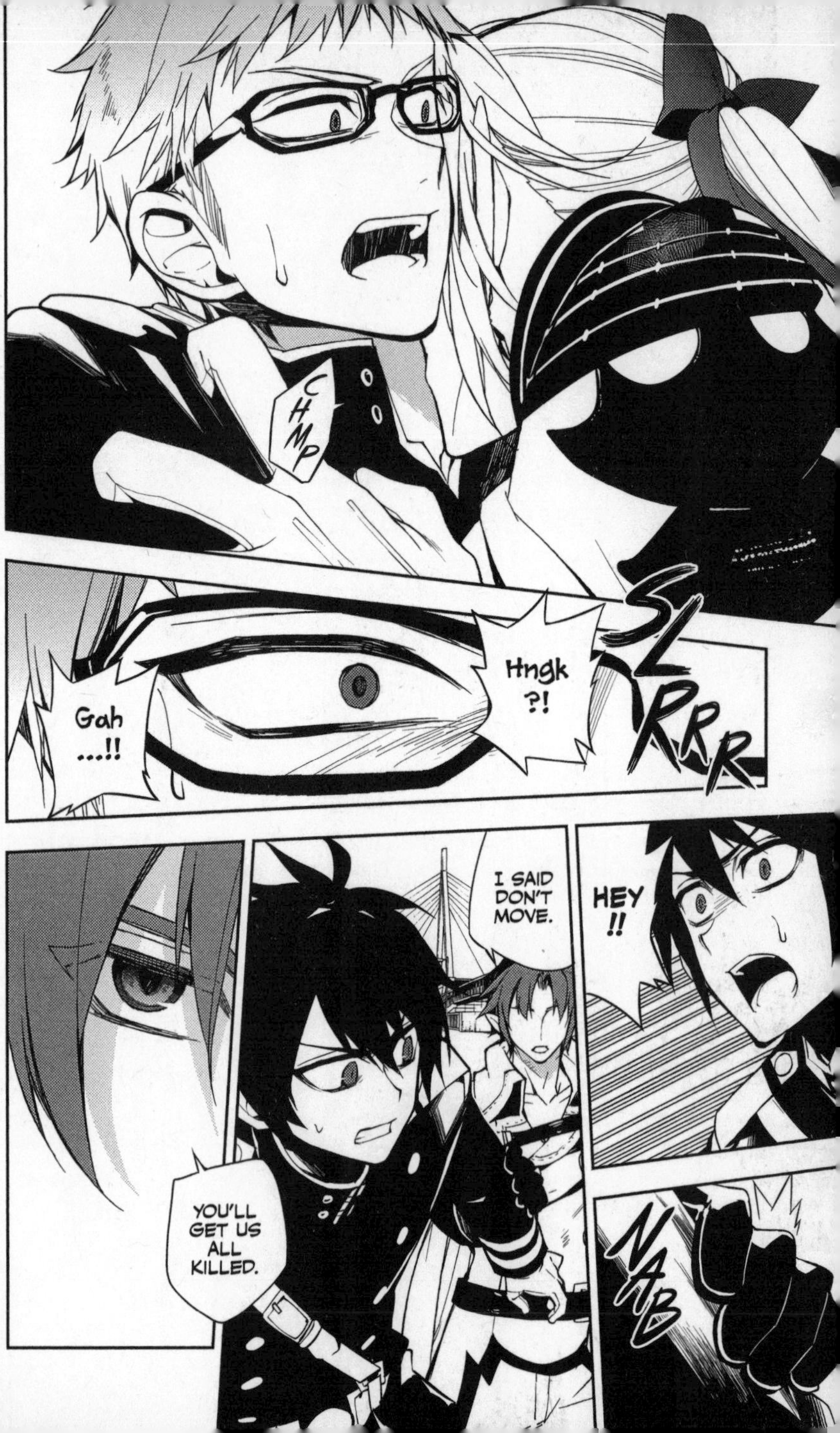
CHMP
SLRRR
Hngk ?!
Gah ...!!
HEY !!
NAB
I SAID DON'T MOVE.
YOU'LL GET US ALL KILLED.

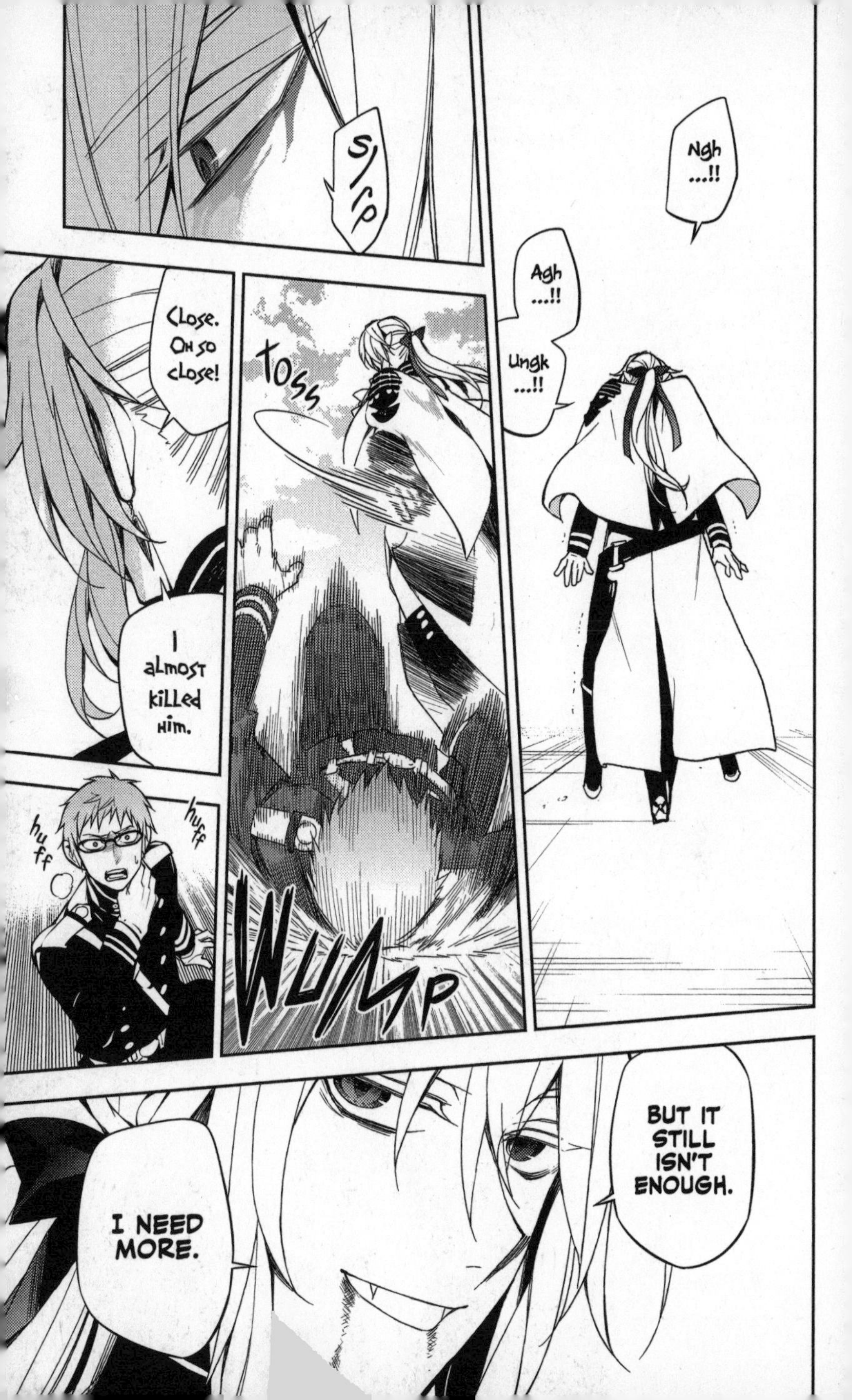
Ngh ...!!
Agh ...!!
Ungk ...!!
Slrp
TOSS
WUMP
Close. Oh so close!
I almost killed him.
huff
huff
BUT IT STILL ISN'T ENOUGH.
I NEED MORE.

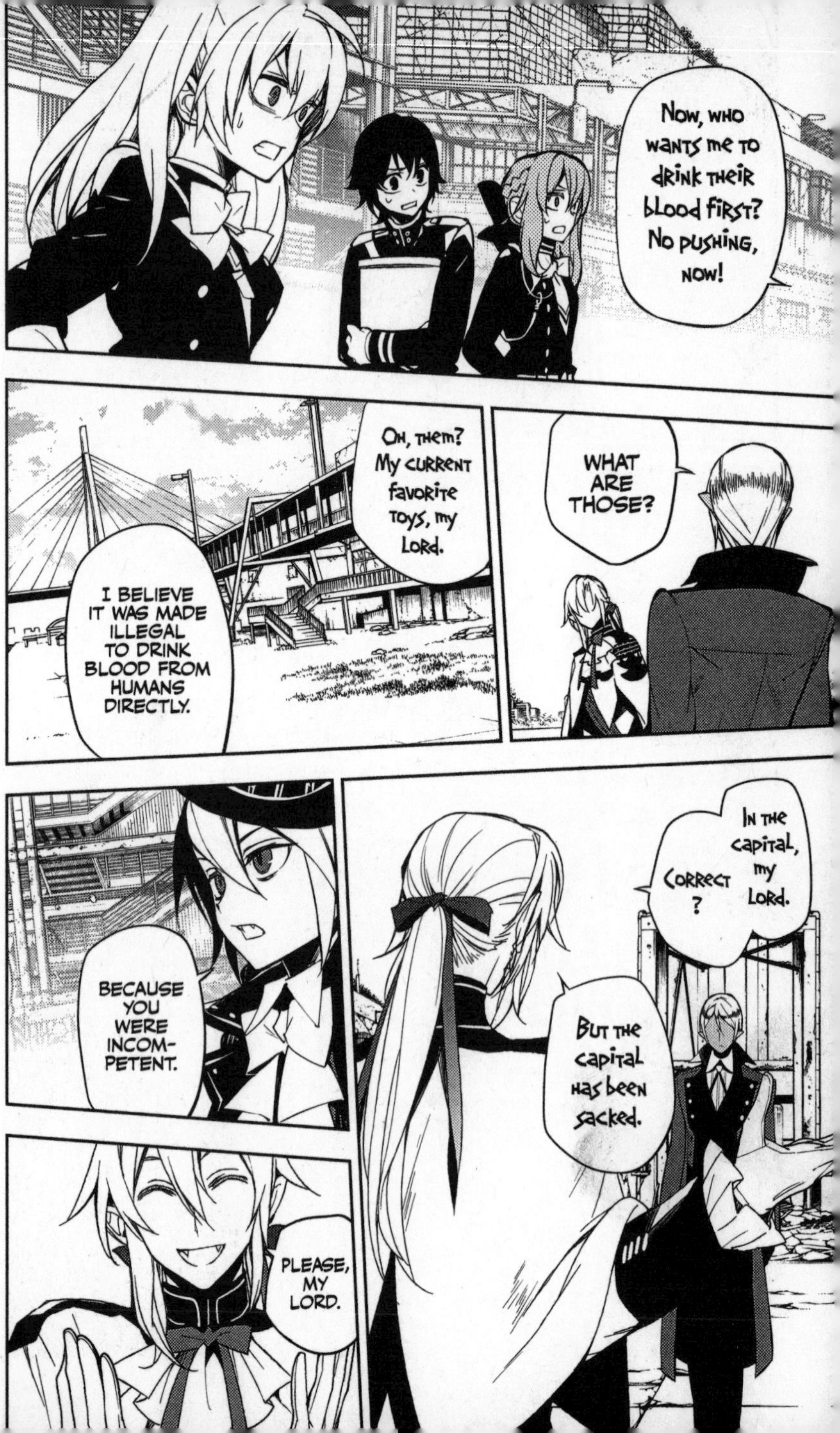
Now, who wants me to drink their blood first? No pushing, now!
WHAT ARE THOSE?
Oh, them? My current favorite toys, my Lord.
I BELIEVE IT WAS MADE ILLEGAL TO DRINK BLOOD FROM HUMANS DIRECTLY.
In the capital, my Lord.
Correct?
But the capital has been sacked.
BECAUSE YOU WERE INCOMPETENT.
PLEASE, MY LORD.

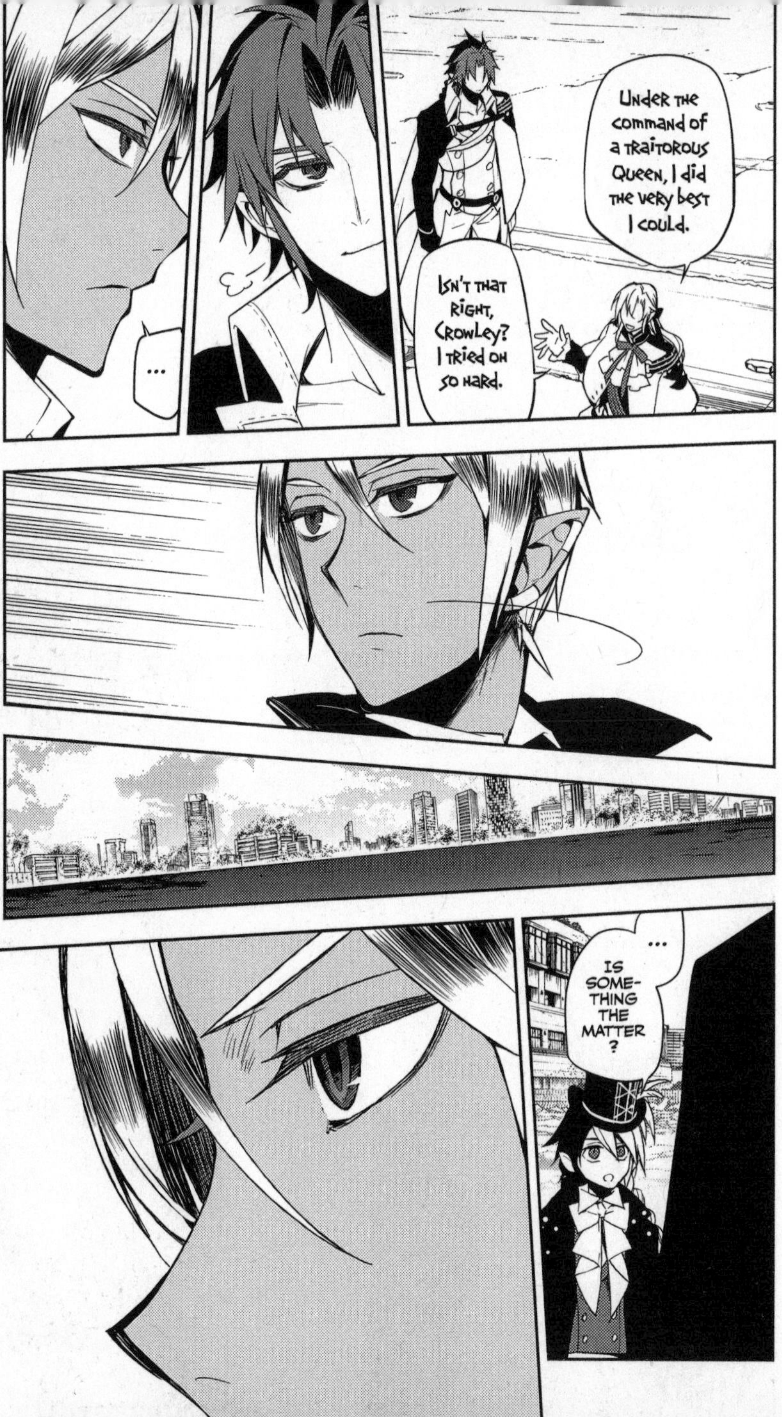
Under the command of a traitorous Queen, I did the very best I could.
Isn't that right, Crowley? I tried oh so hard.
...
...
Is something the matter?

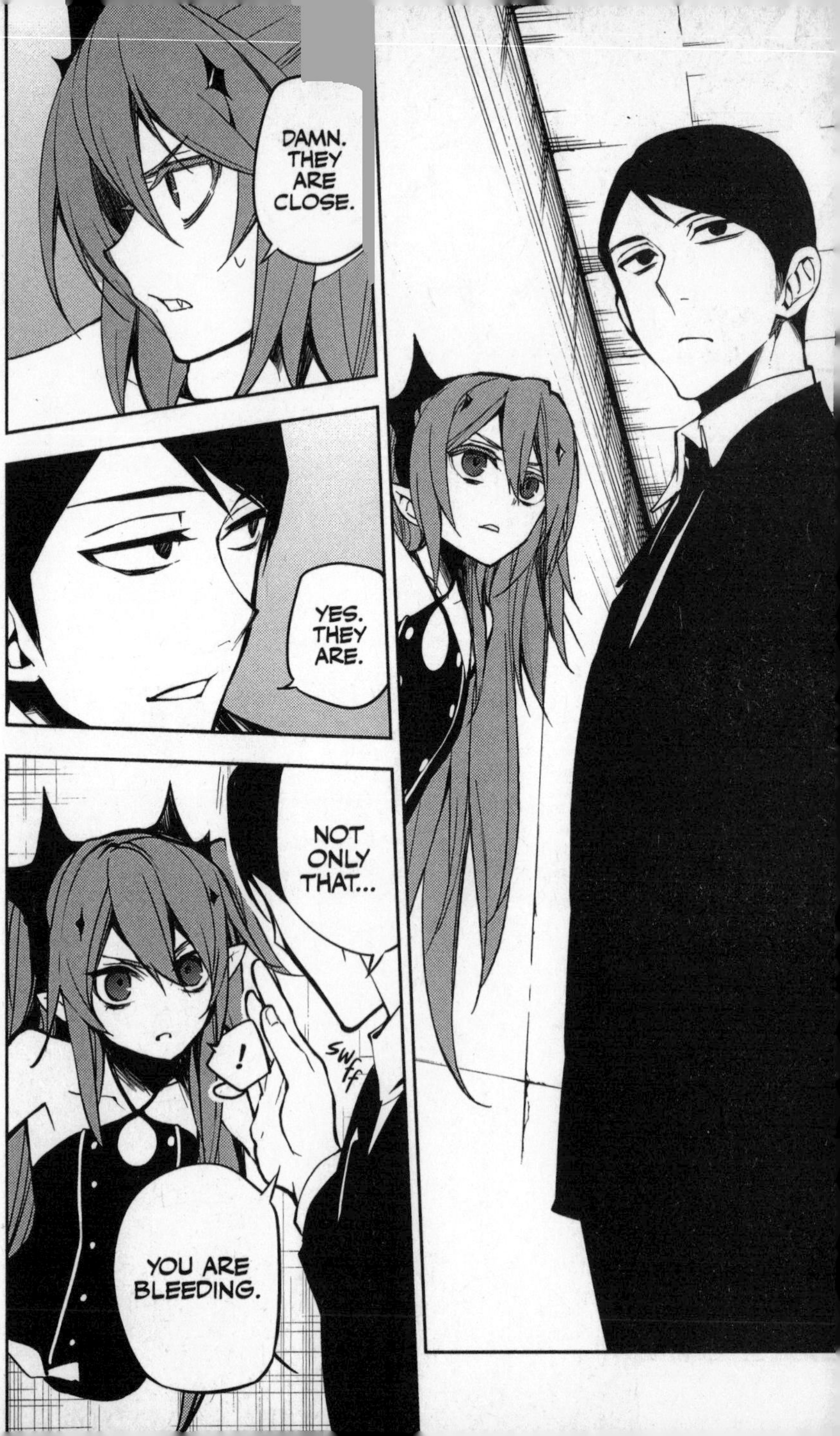
DAMN. THEY ARE CLOSE.
YES. THEY ARE.
NOT ONLY THAT...
!
SWFF
YOU ARE BLEEDING.

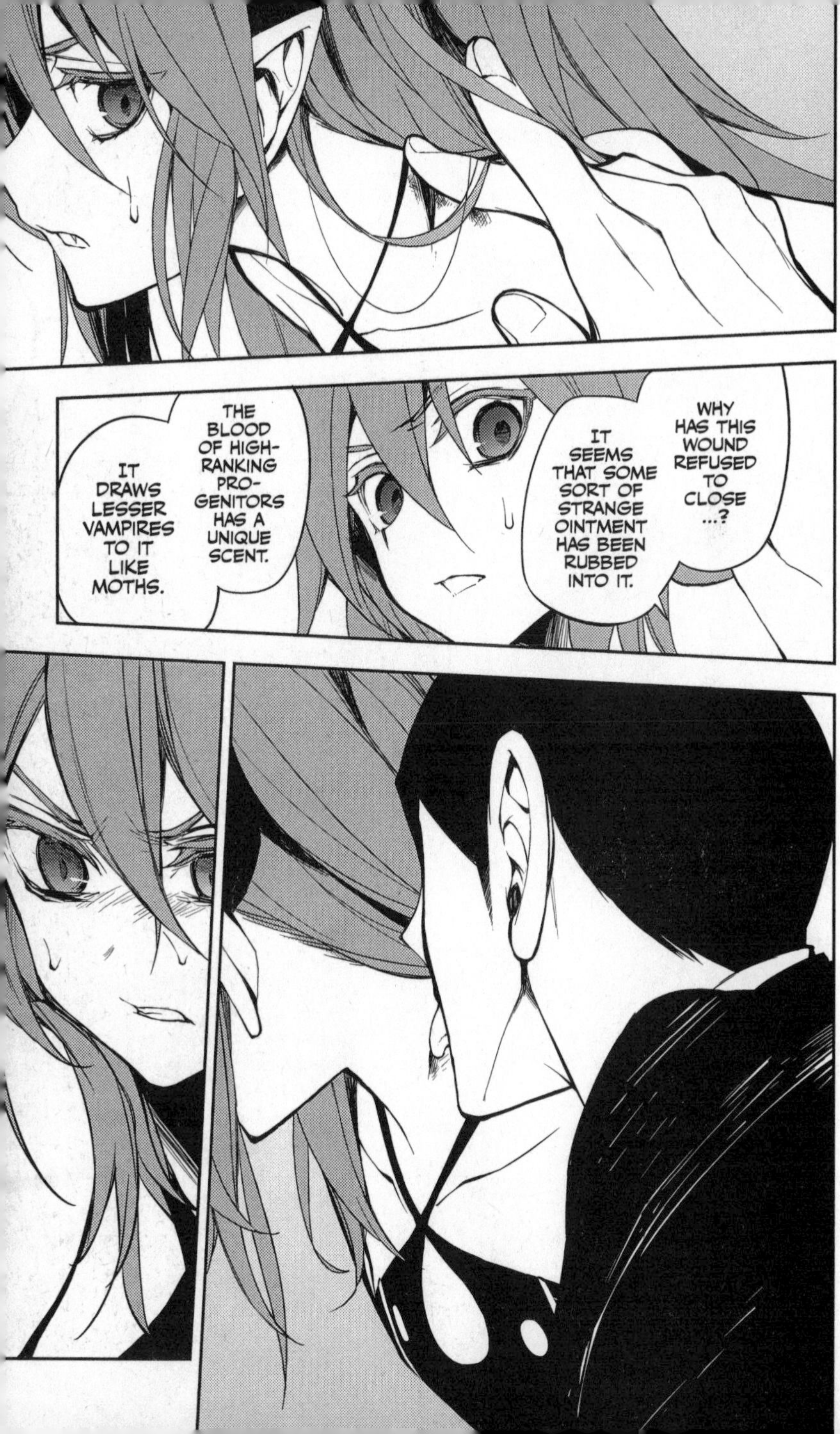
WHY HAS THIS WOUND REFUSED TO CLOSE ...?
IT SEEMS THAT SOME SORT OF STRANGE OINTMENT HAS BEEN RUBBED INTO IT.
THE BLOOD OF HIGH-RANKING PRO-GENITORS HAS A UNIQUE SCENT.
IT DRAWS LESSER VAMPIRES TO IT LIKE MOTHS.

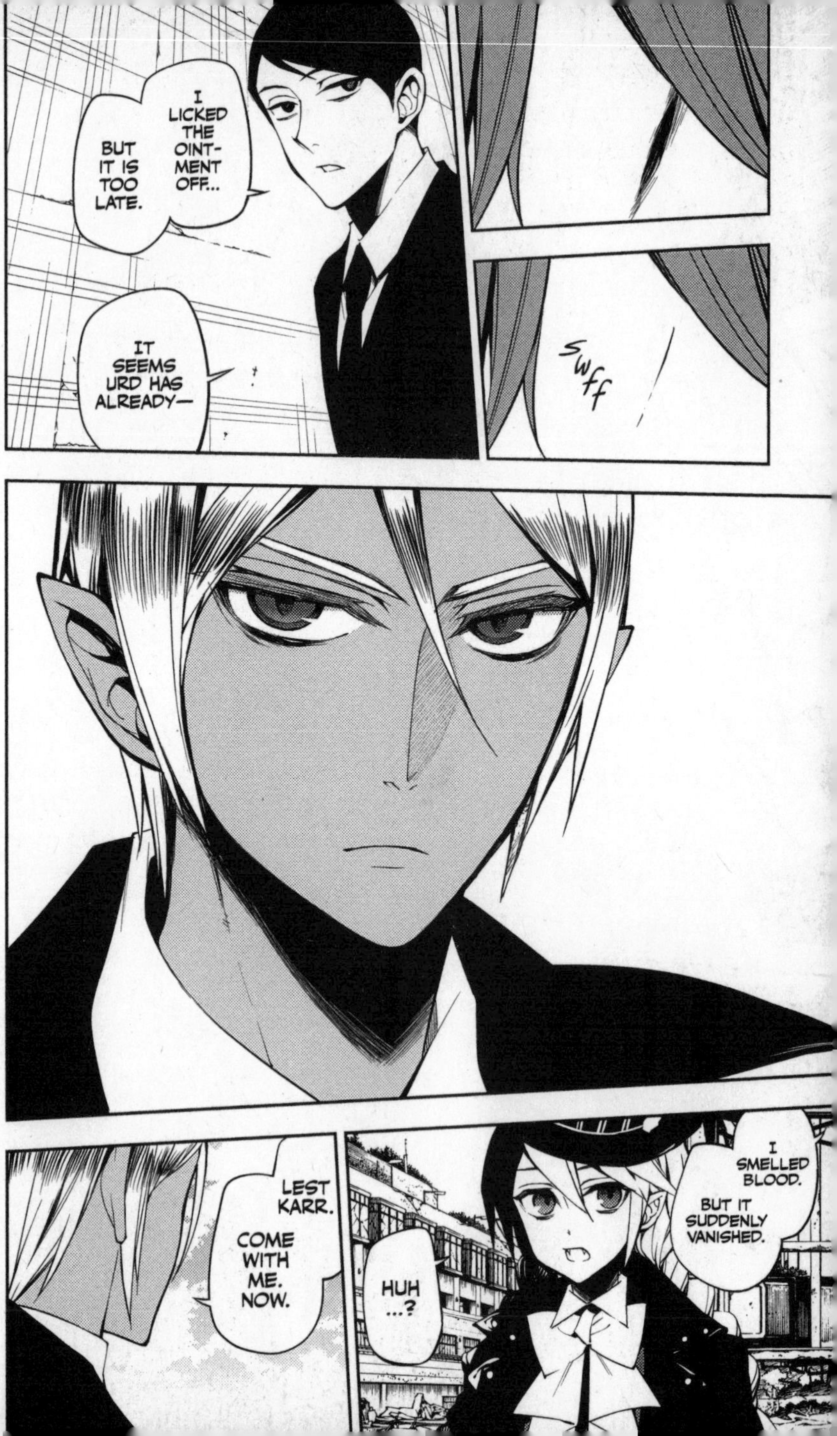
swff
I licked the ointment off...
But it is too late.
It seems Urd has already—
I smelled blood.
But it suddenly vanished.
Huh ...?
Lest Karr.
Come with me. Now.

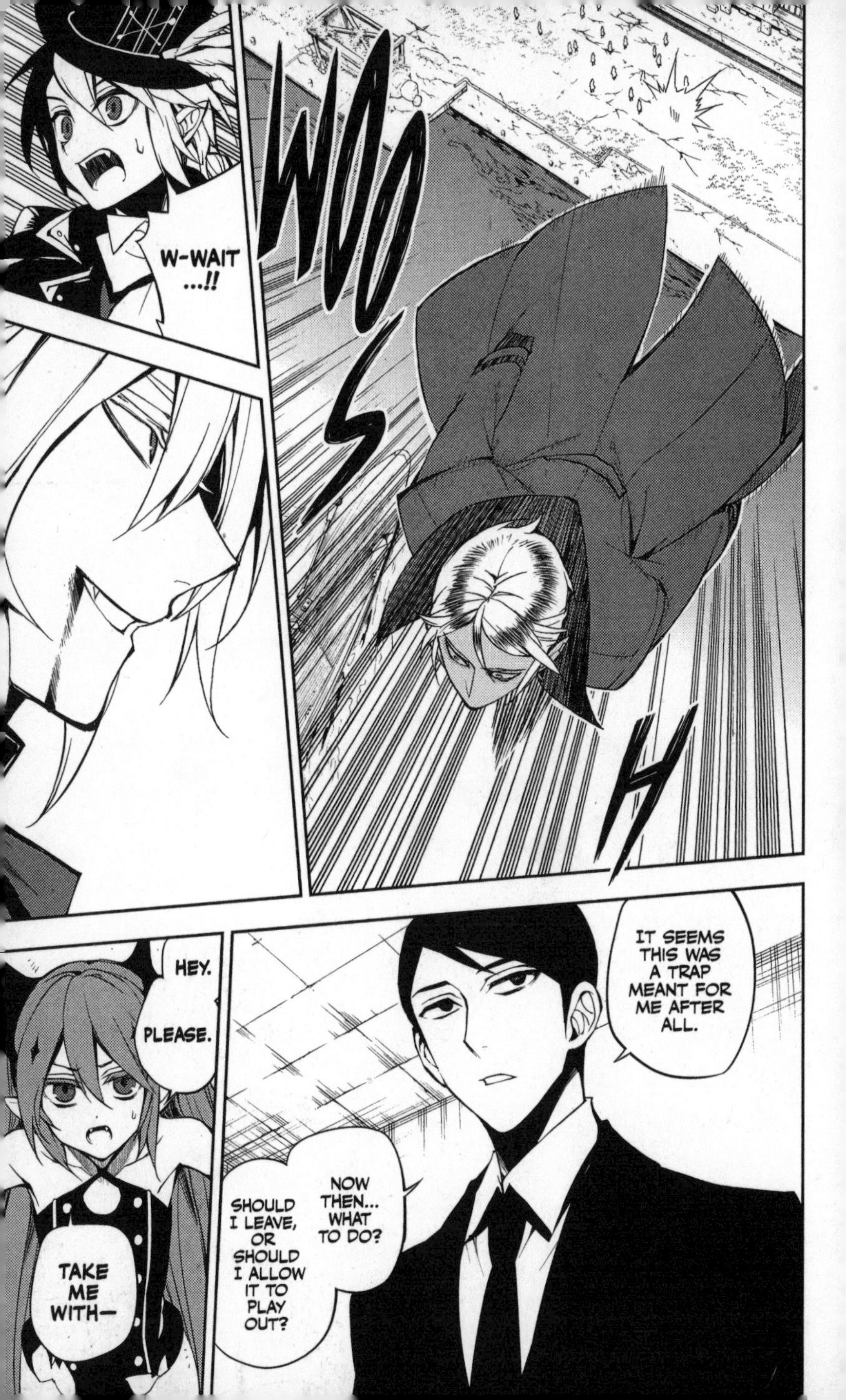
WOOSH
W-WAIT ...!!
IT SEEMS THIS WAS A TRAP MEANT FOR ME AFTER ALL.
NOW THEN... WHAT TO DO?
SHOULD I LEAVE, OR SHOULD I ALLOW IT TO PLAY OUT?
HEY.
PLEASE.
TAKE ME WITH—

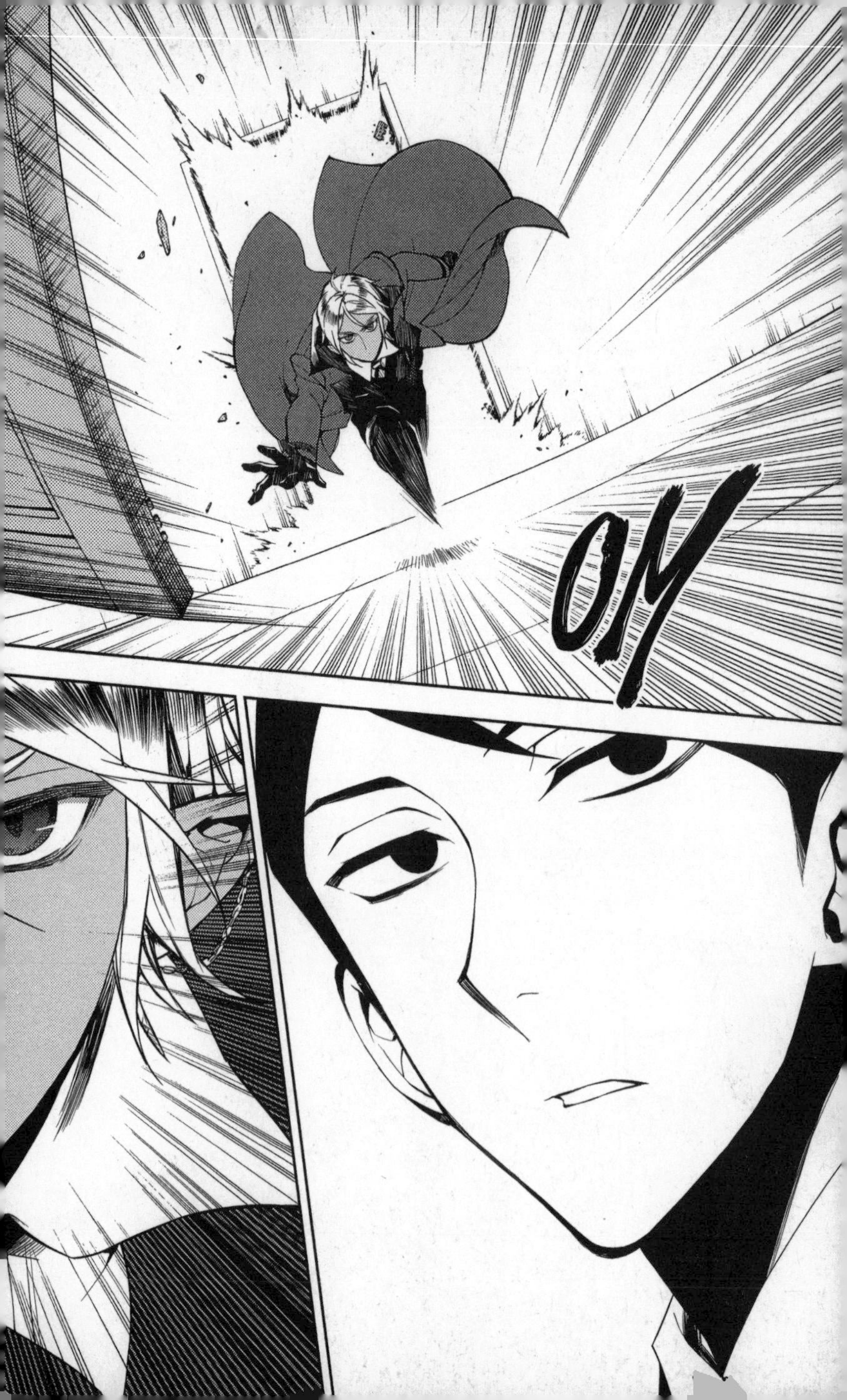
OM

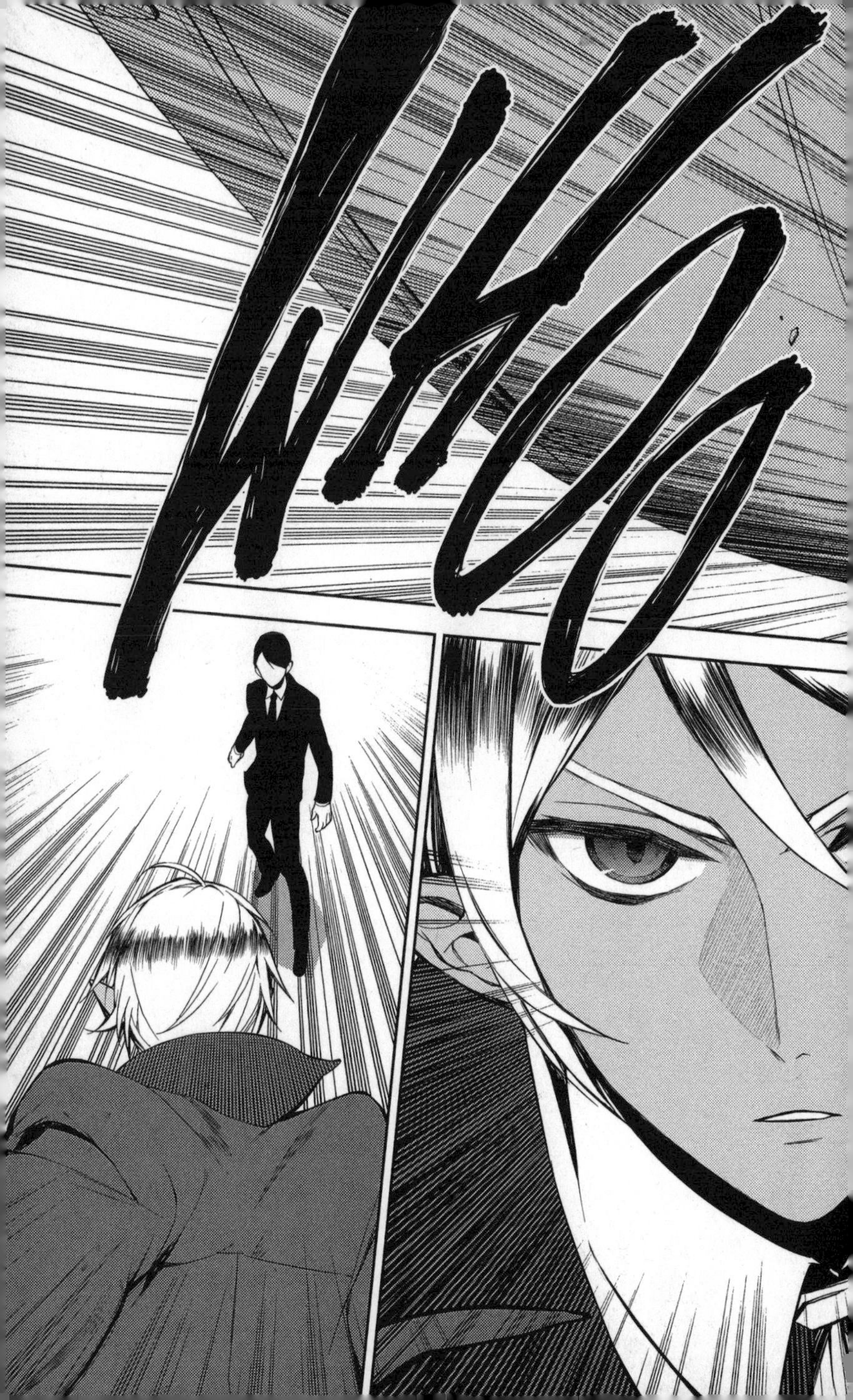
WHOO

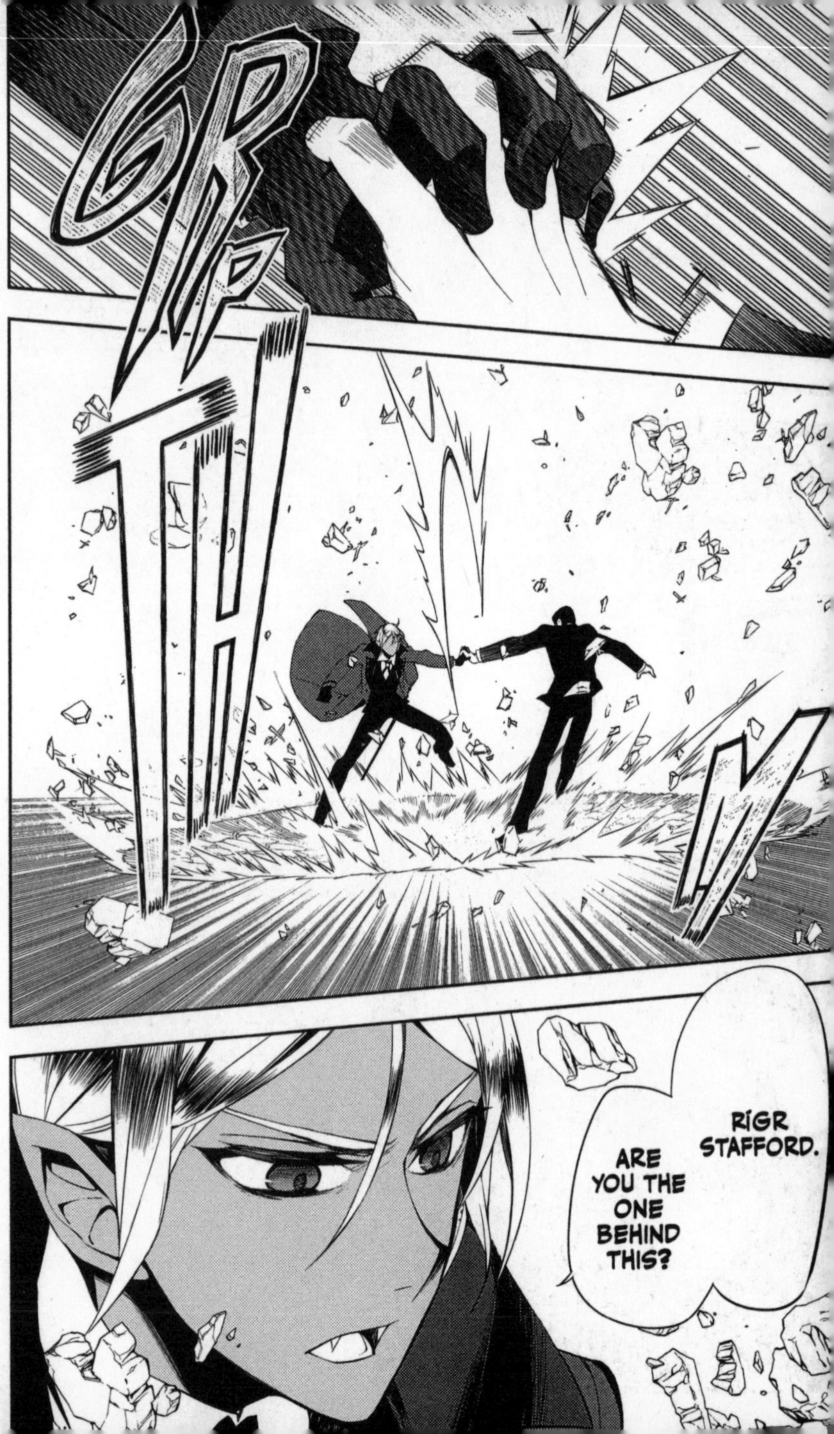
GRP
THM
RIGR STAFFORD.
ARE YOU THE ONE BEHIND THIS?

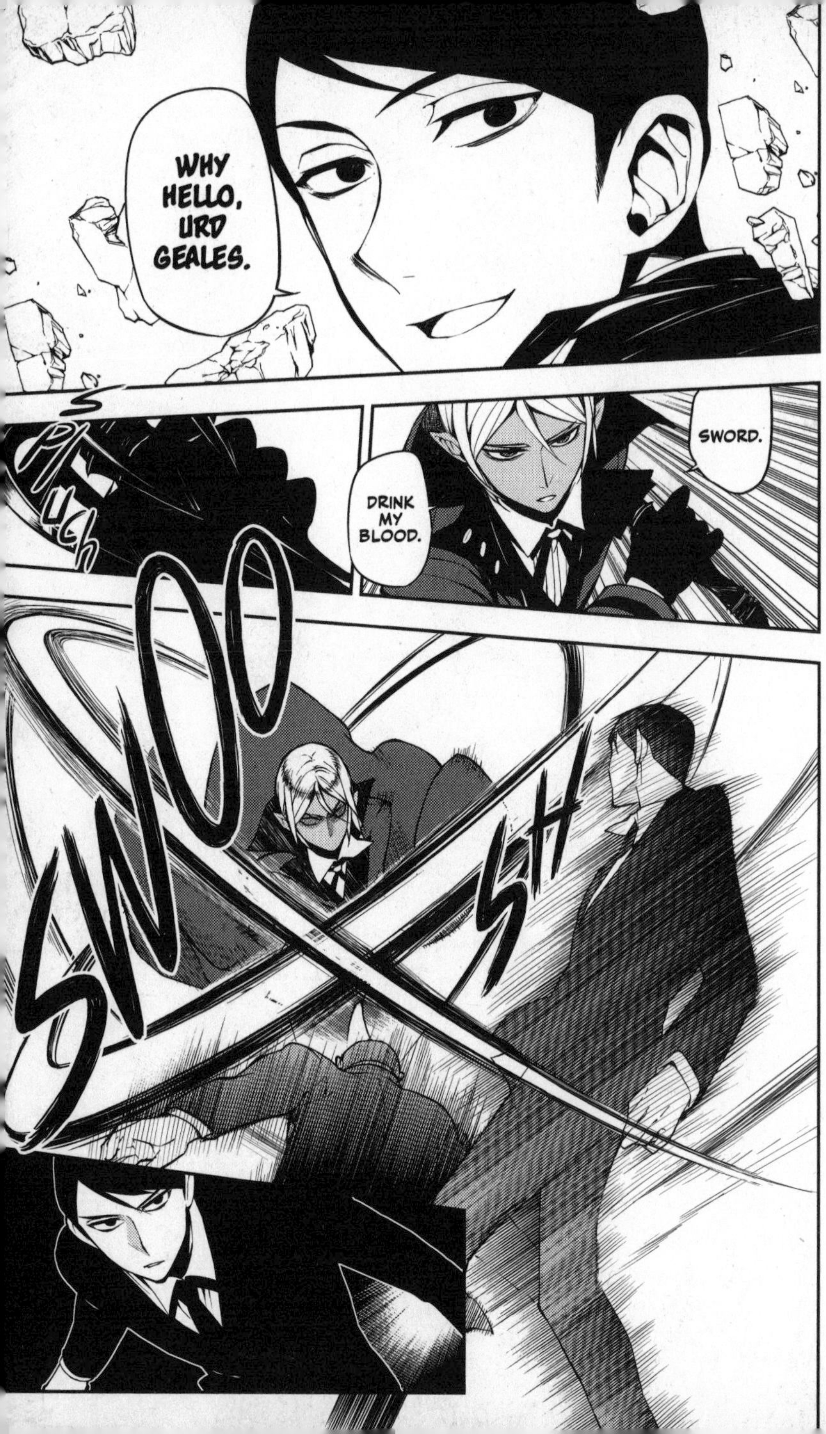
WHY HELLO, URD GEALES.
SWORD.
DRINK MY BLOOD.
SPLUCH
SWOOSH

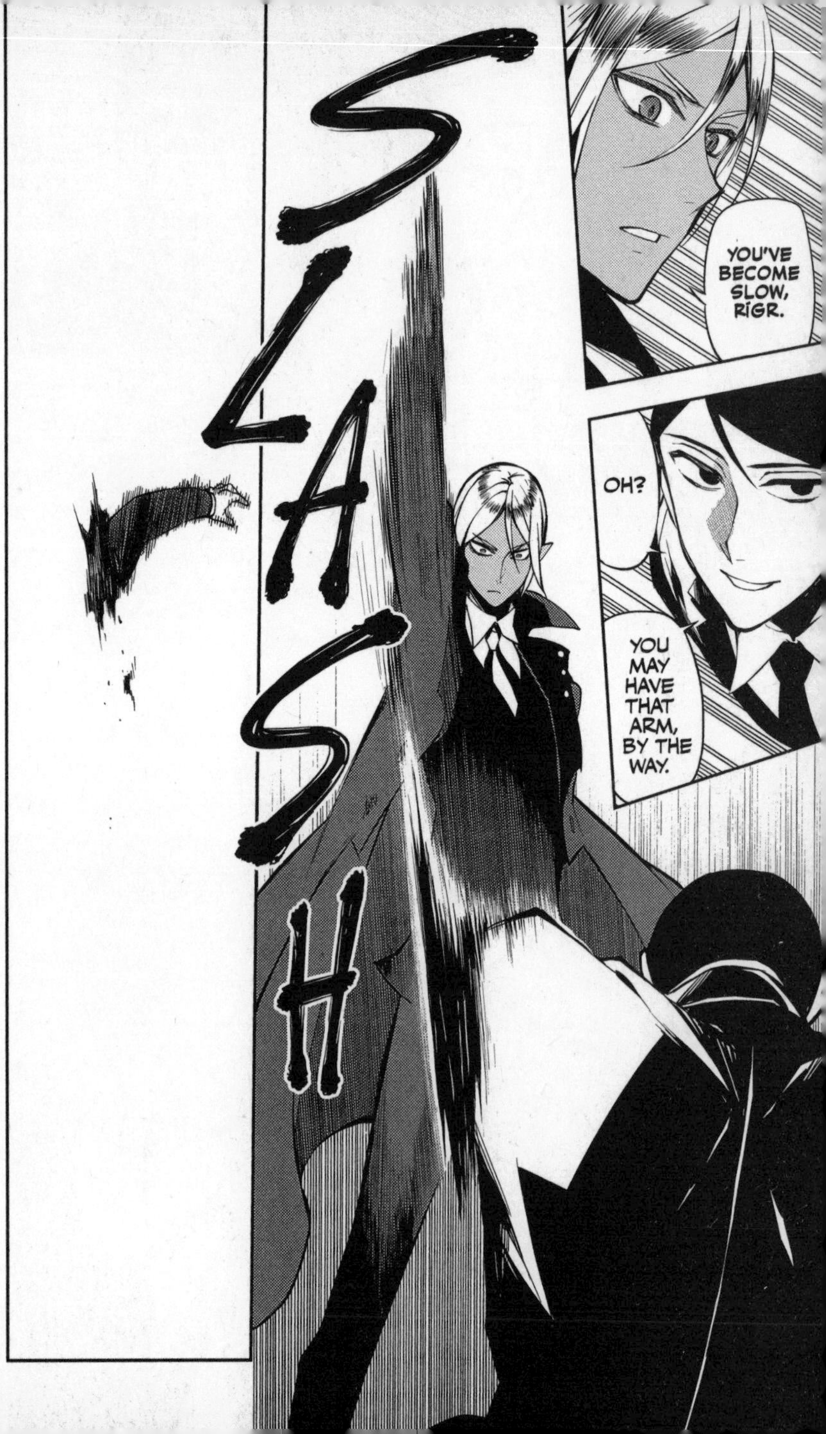
YOU'VE BECOME SLOW, RIGR.
OH?
YOU MAY HAVE THAT ARM, BY THE WAY.
SLASSH

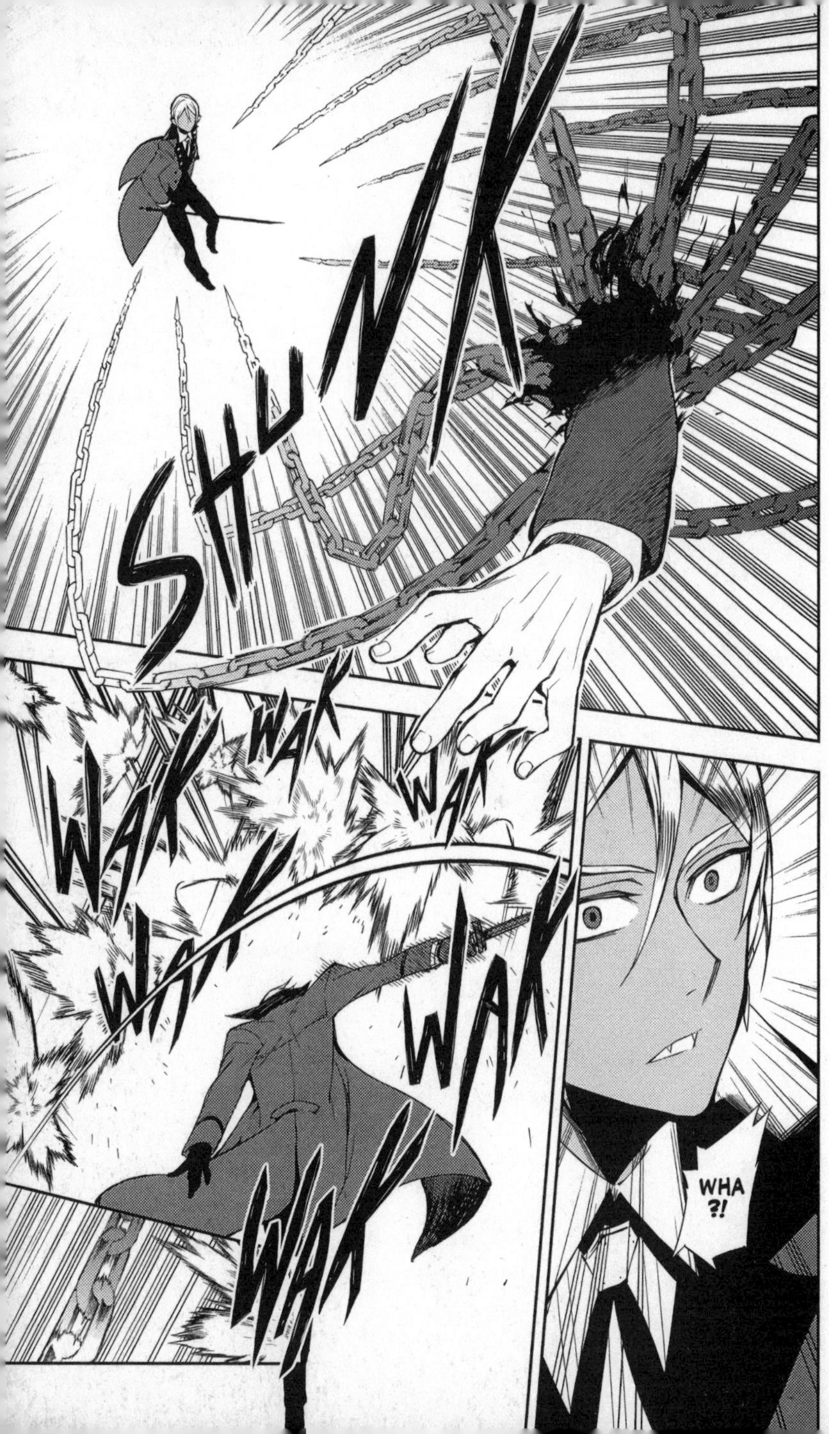
SHUNK
WHA ?!
WAK
WAK
WAK
WAK
WAK
WAK

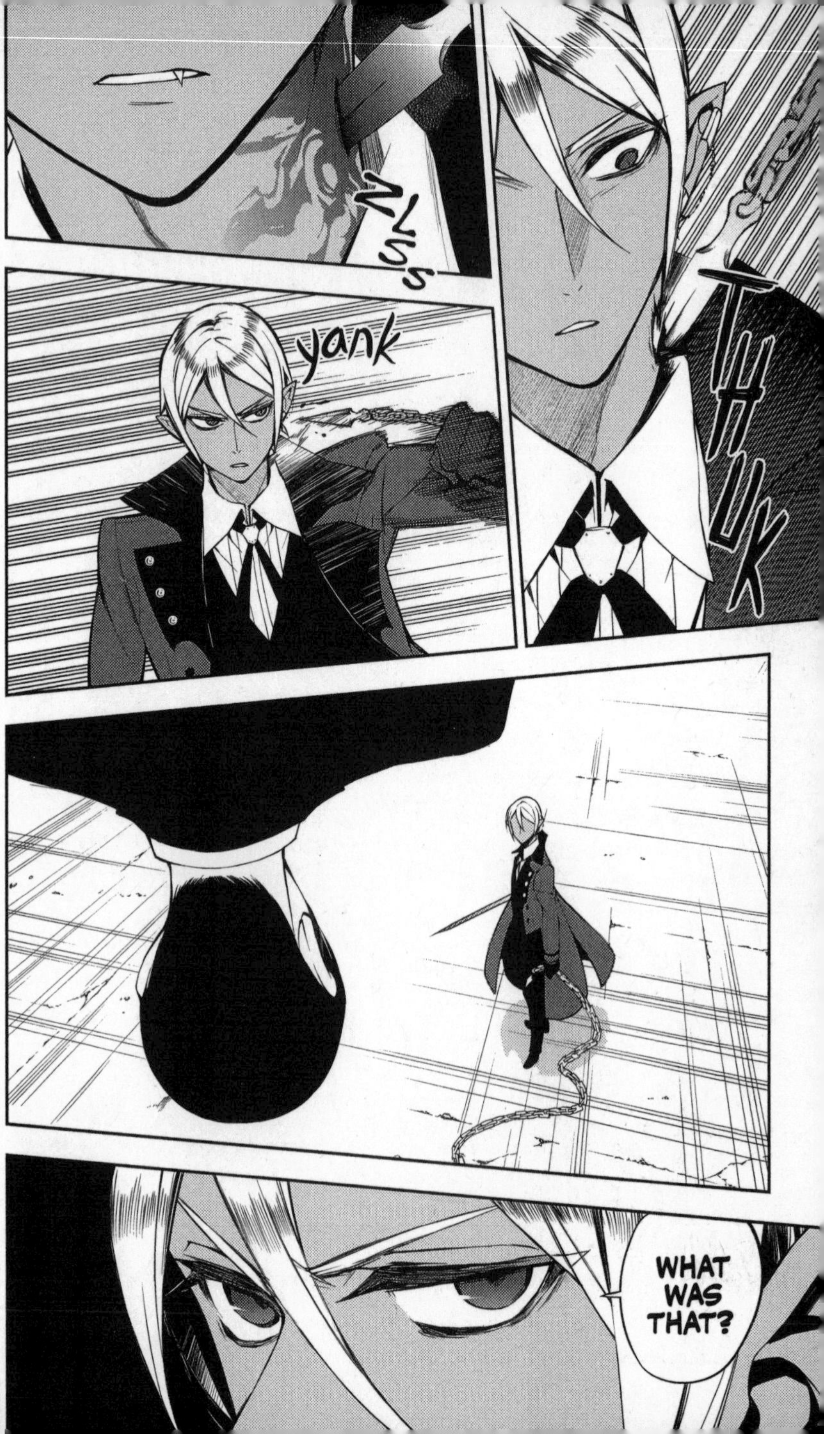
THUNK
ZLSS
yank
WHAT WAS THAT?

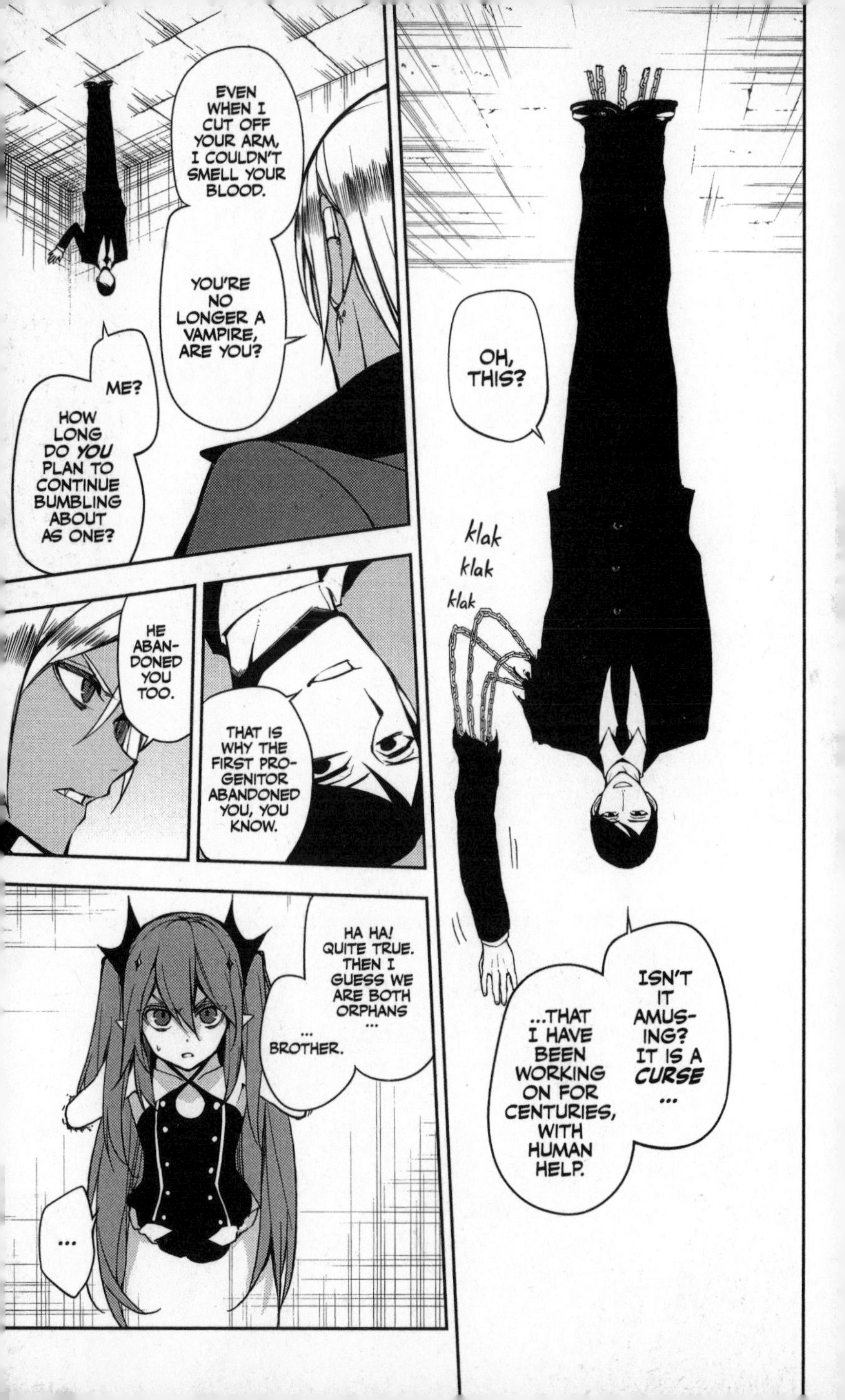
OH, THIS?
klak klak klak
ISN'T IT AMUSING? IT IS A *CURSE*...
...THAT I HAVE BEEN WORKING ON FOR CENTURIES, WITH HUMAN HELP.
EVEN WHEN I CUT OFF YOUR ARM, I COULDN'T SMELL YOUR BLOOD.
YOU'RE NO LONGER A VAMPIRE, ARE YOU?
ME? HOW LONG DO *YOU* PLAN TO CONTINUE BUMBLING ABOUT AS ONE?
THAT IS WHY THE FIRST PROGENITOR ABANDONED YOU, YOU KNOW.
HE ABANDONED YOU TOO.
HA HA! QUITE TRUE. THEN I GUESS WE ARE BOTH ORPHANS... ...BROTHER.
...

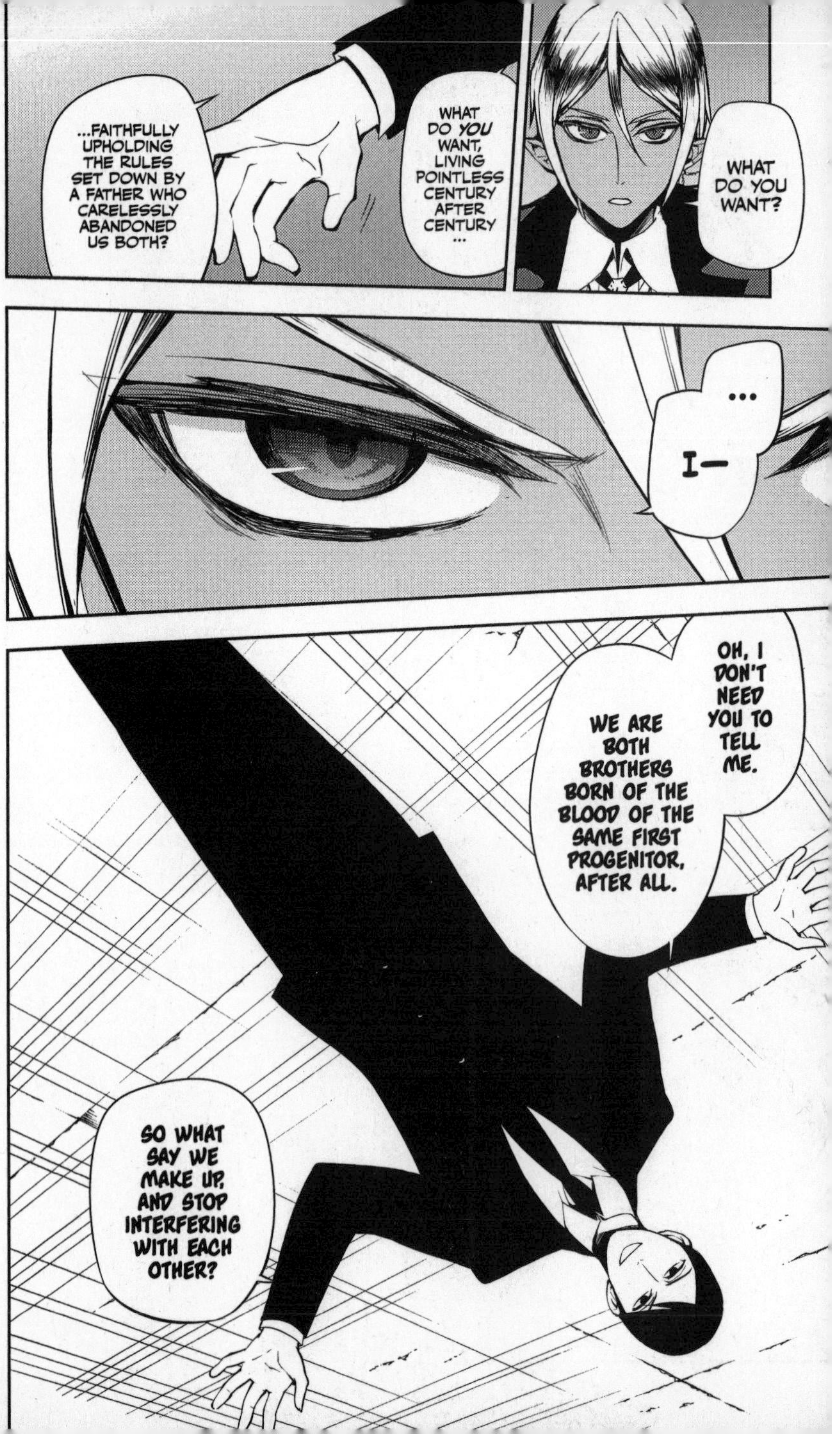
WHAT DO YOU WANT?
WHAT DO YOU WANT, LIVING POINTLESS CENTURY AFTER CENTURY...
...FAITHFULLY UPHOLDING THE RULES SET DOWN BY A FATHER WHO CARELESSLY ABANDONED US BOTH?
... I—
OH, I DON'T NEED YOU TO TELL ME.
WE ARE BOTH BROTHERS BORN OF THE BLOOD OF THE SAME FIRST PROGENITOR, AFTER ALL.
SO WHAT SAY WE MAKE UP, AND STOP INTERFERING WITH EACH OTHER?

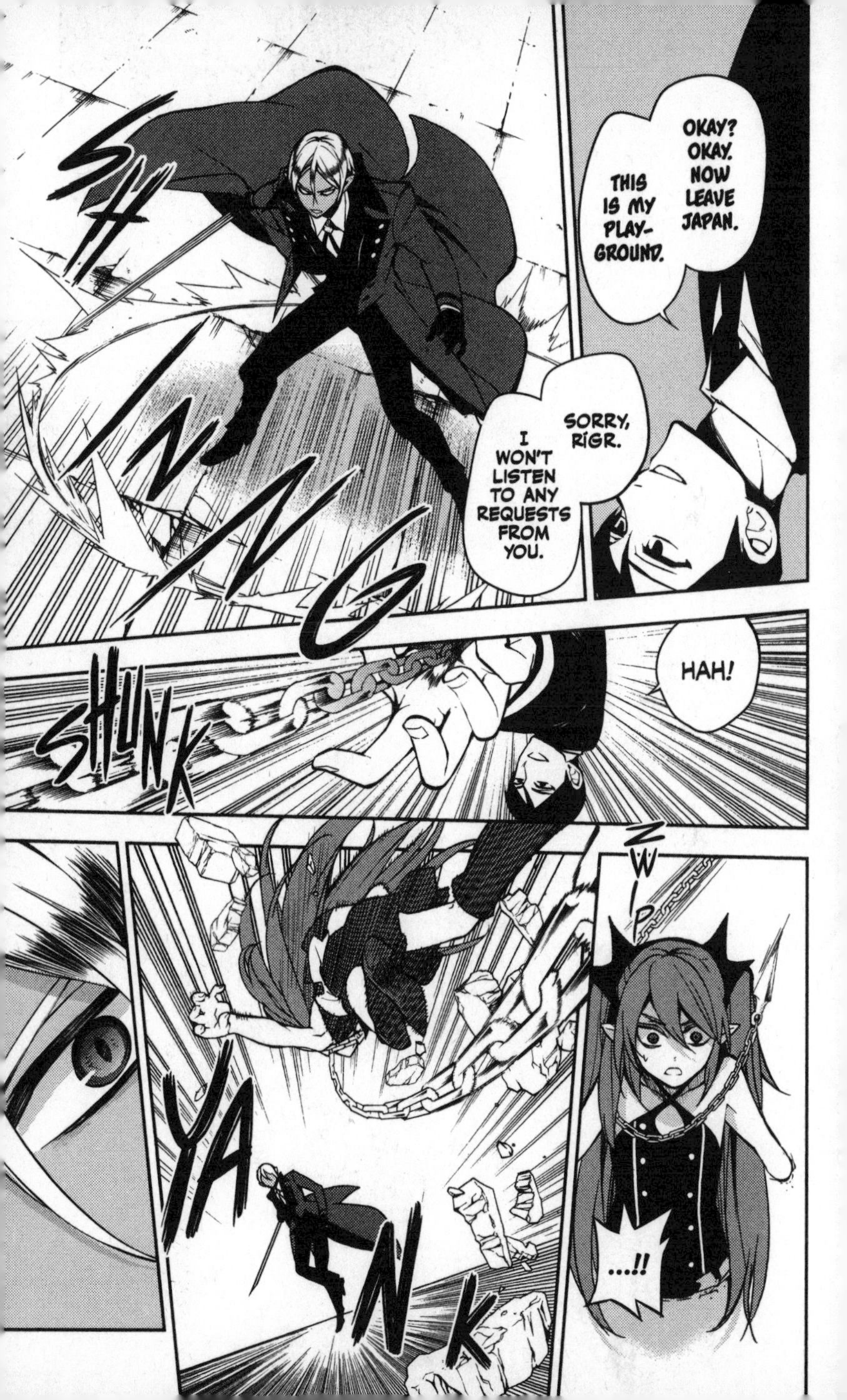
OKAY? OKAY. NOW LEAVE JAPAN.
THIS IS MY PLAY-GROUND.
SORRY, RIGR.
I WON'T LISTEN TO ANY REQUESTS FROM YOU.
SHING
HAH!
SHUNK
ZWIP
...!!
YANK

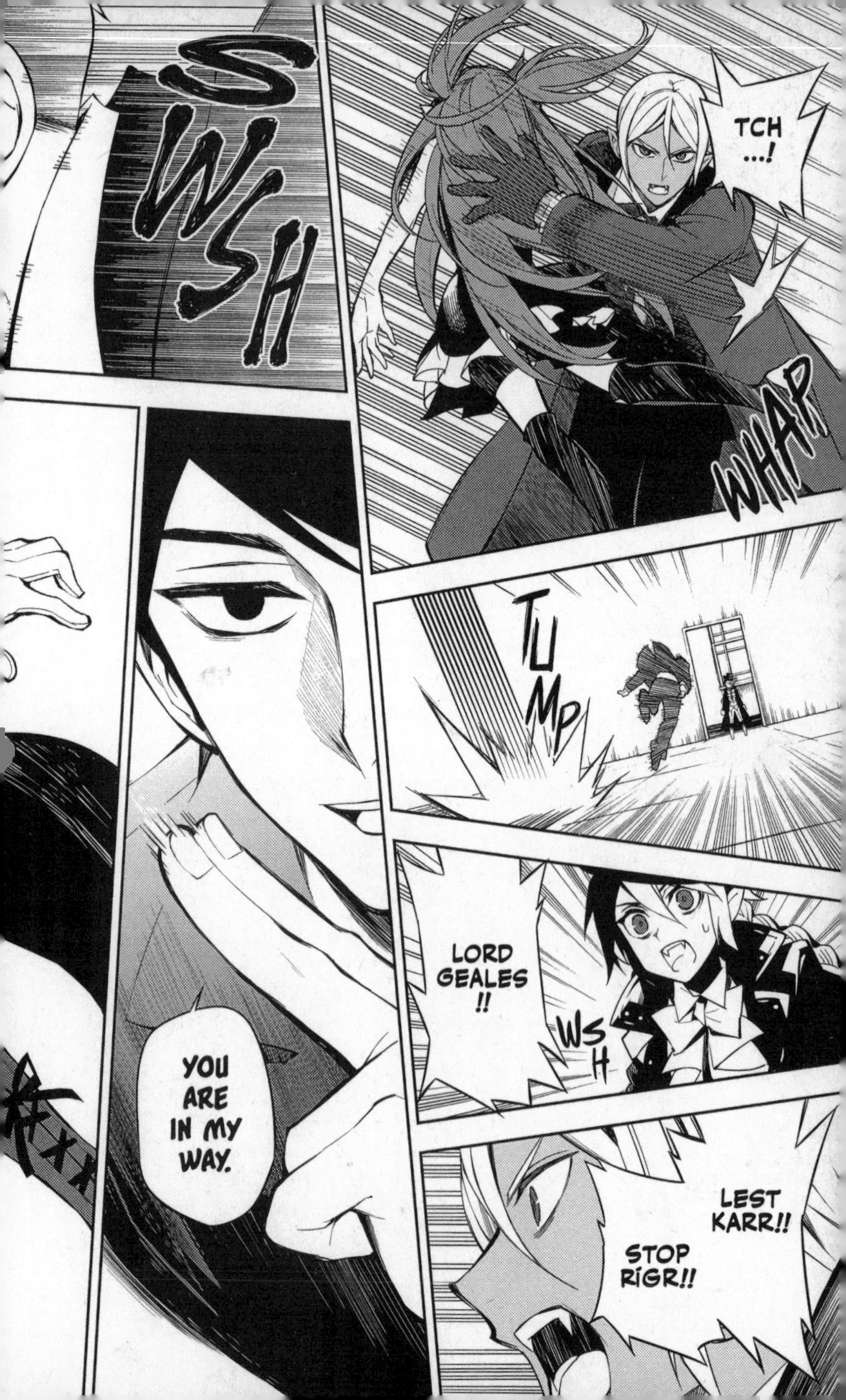
TCH ...!
WHAP
SWSH
TUMP
LORD GEALES !!
WSH
LEST KARR!!
STOP RIGR!!
YOU ARE IN MY WAY.

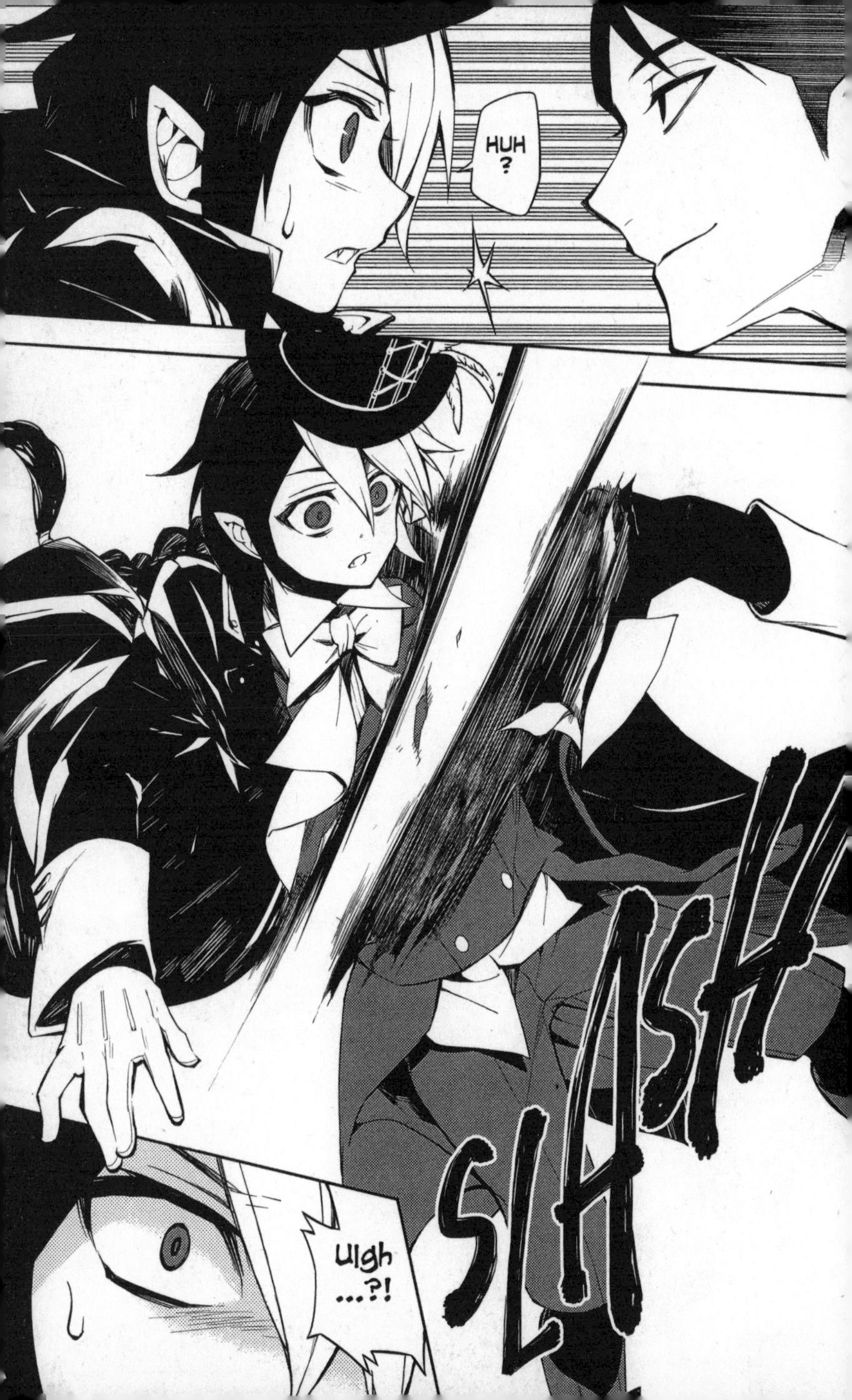
HUH?
SLASH
Ulgh...?!

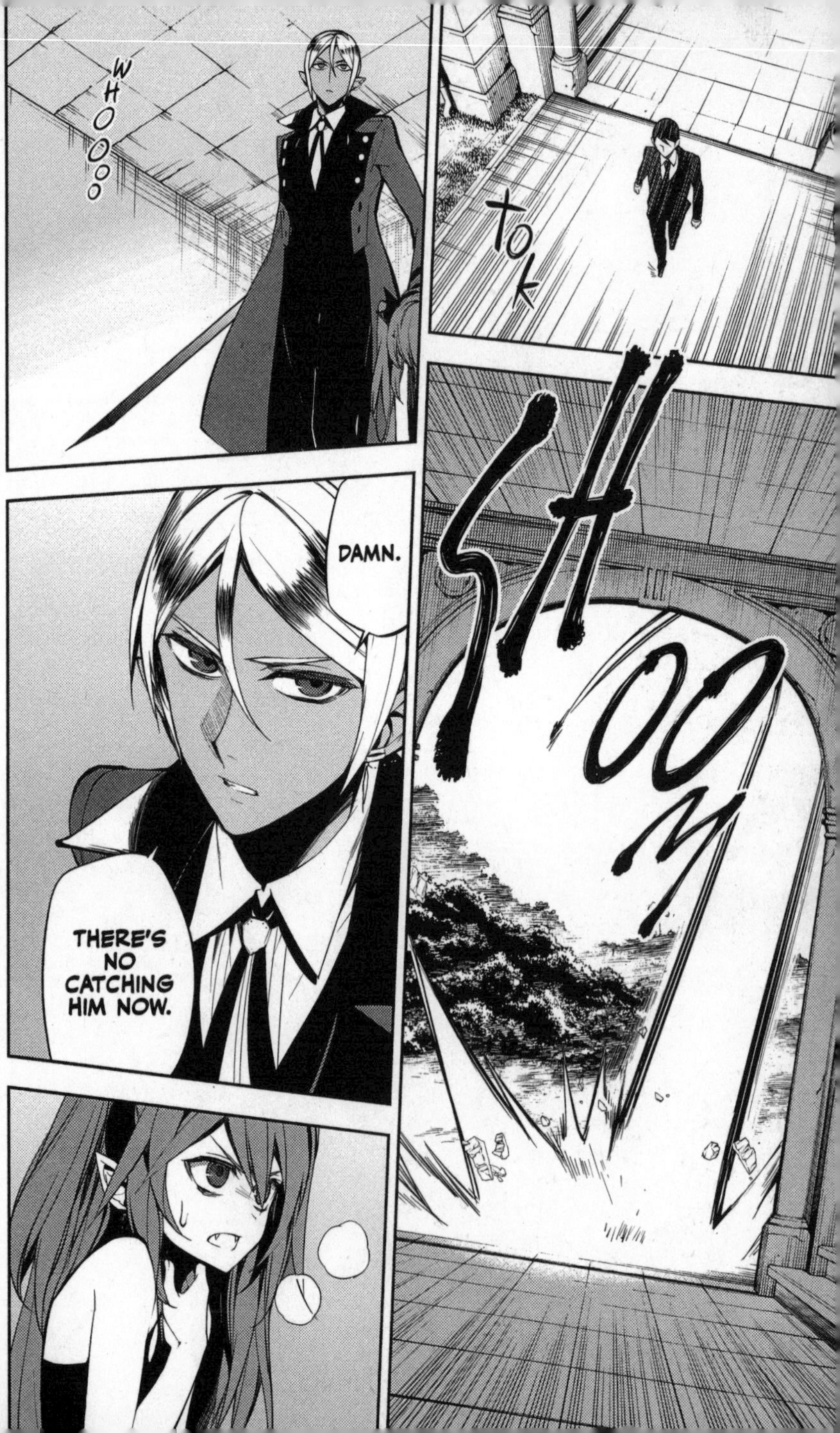
TOK
WHOOOO
SHOOOM
DAMN.
THERE'S NO CATCHING HIM NOW.

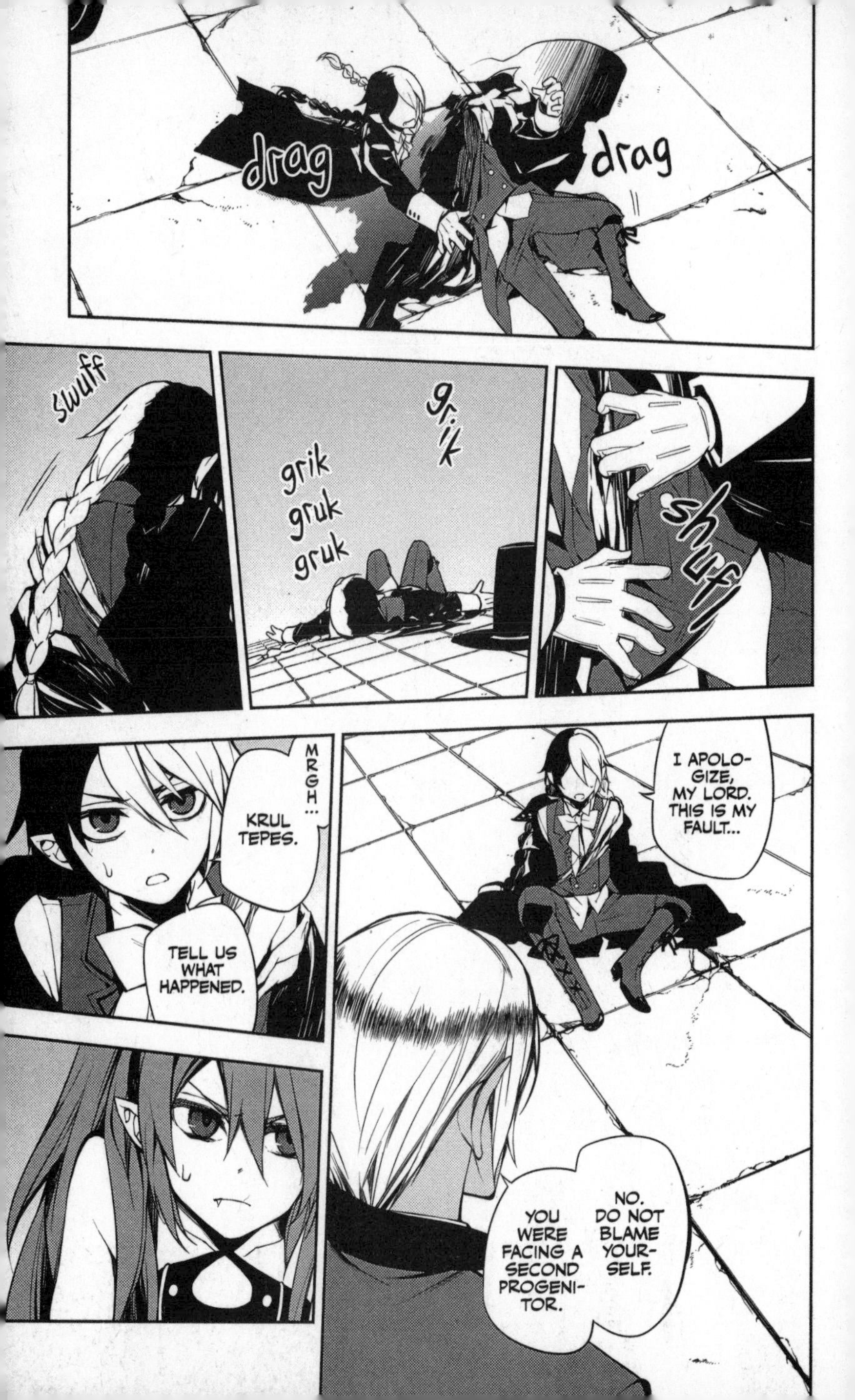
drag
drag
shuf!
grik
grik gruk gruk
swuff
I APOLOGIZE, MY LORD. THIS IS MY FAULT...
NO. DO NOT BLAME YOURSELF.
YOU WERE FACING A SECOND PROGENITOR.
MRGH...
KRUL TEPES.
TELL US WHAT HAPPENED.

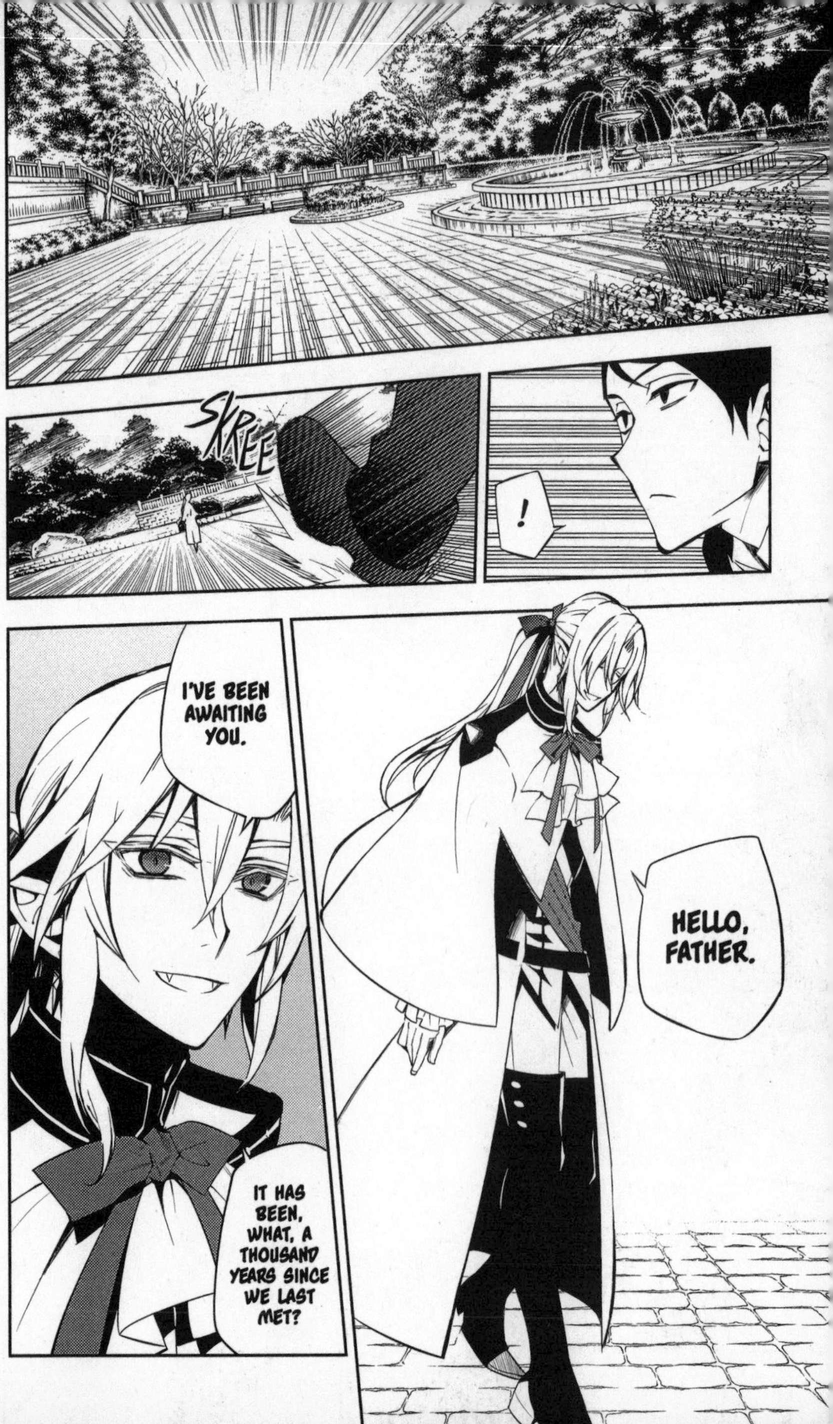
!
SKREE
HELLO, FATHER.
I'VE BEEN AWAITING YOU.
IT HAS BEEN, WHAT, A THOUSAND YEARS SINCE WE LAST MET?

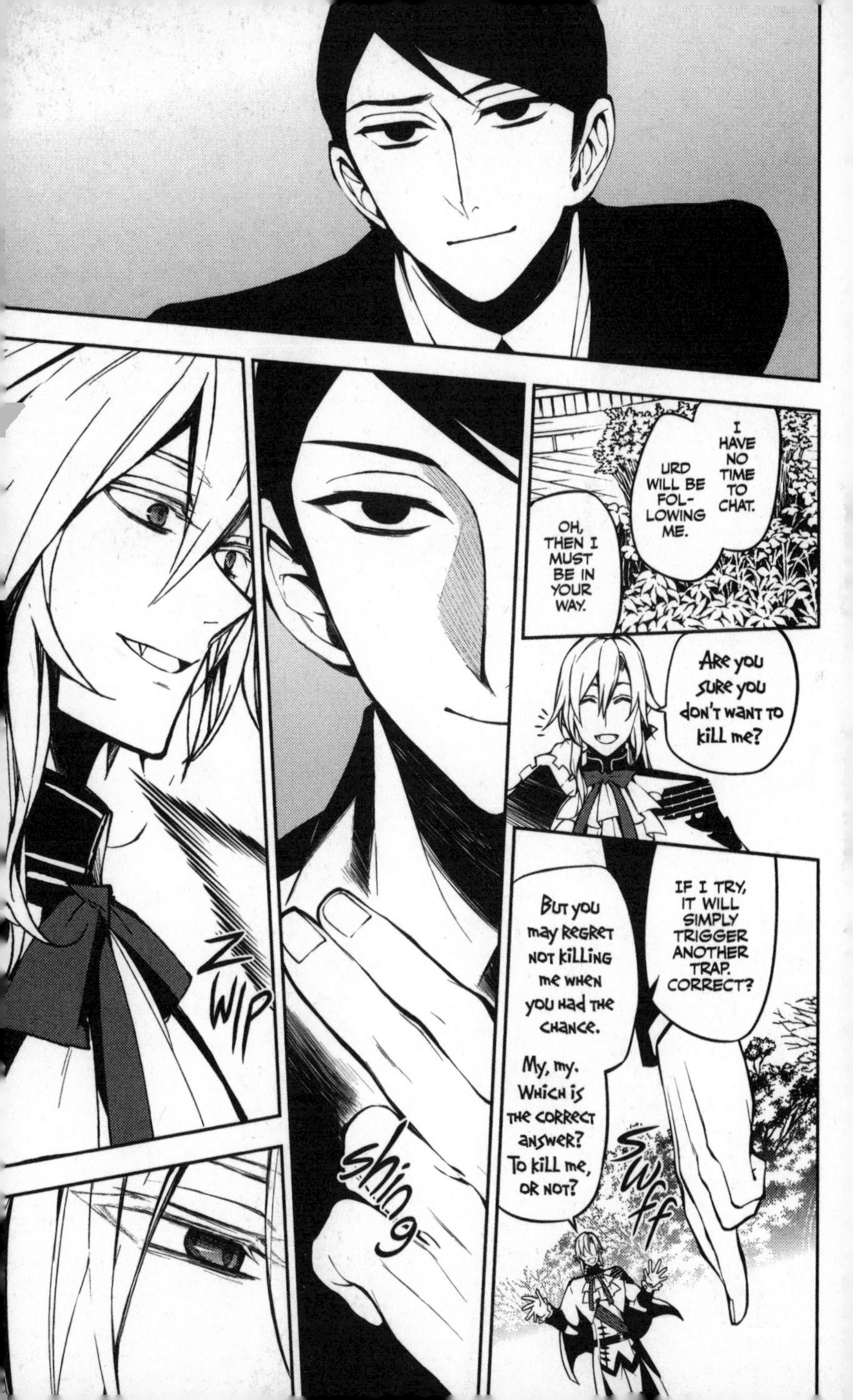
I HAVE NO TIME TO CHAT.
URD WILL BE FOL-LOWING ME.
OH, THEN I MUST BE IN YOUR WAY.
Are you sure you don't want to kill me?
IF I TRY, IT WILL SIMPLY TRIGGER ANOTHER TRAP. CORRECT?
But you may regret not killing me when you had the chance.
My, my. Which is the correct answer? To kill me, or not?
SWFF
shing
ZWIP

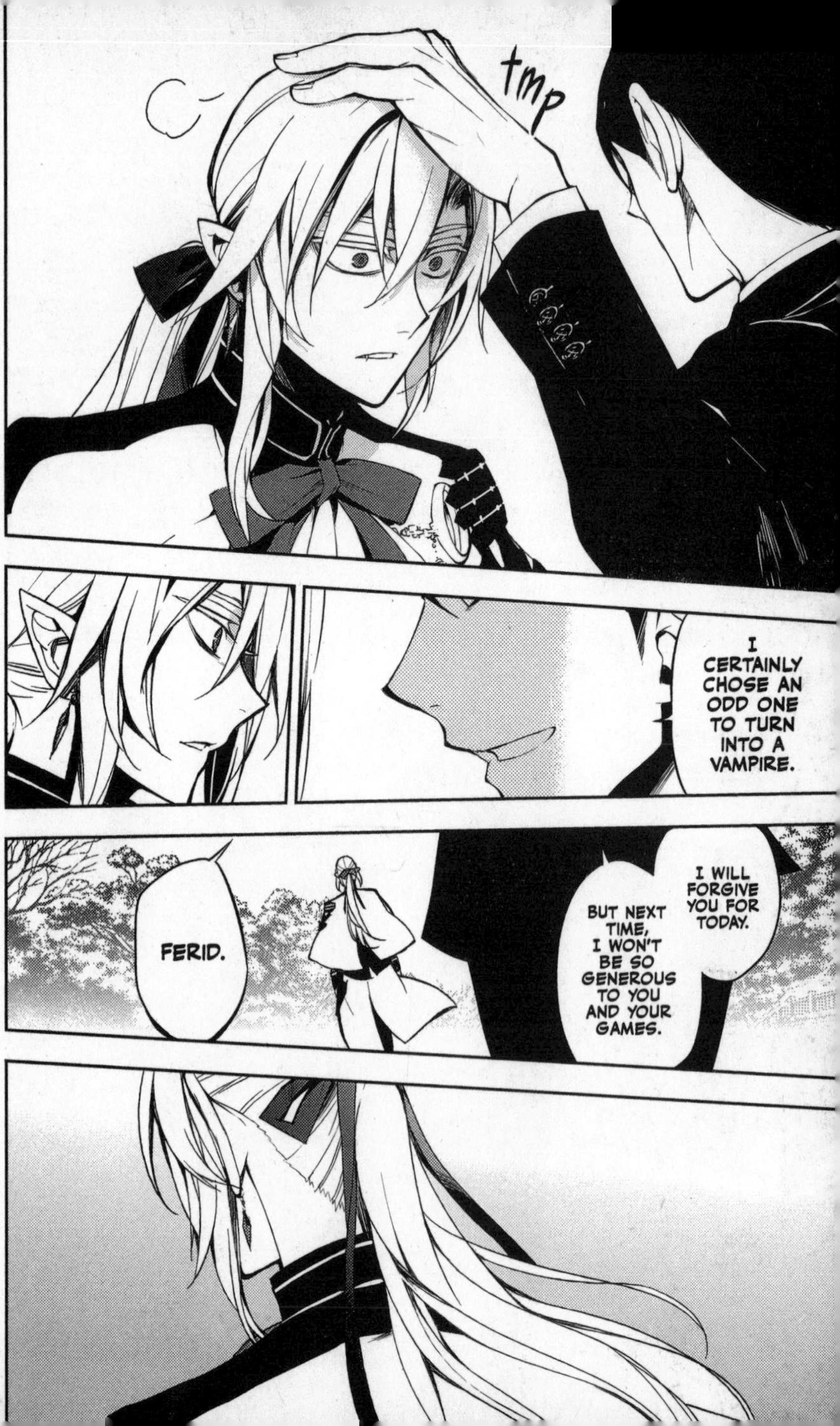
tmp
I CERTAINLY CHOSE AN ODD ONE TO TURN INTO A VAMPIRE.
I WILL FORGIVE YOU FOR TODAY.
BUT NEXT TIME, I WON'T BE SO GENEROUS TO YOU AND YOUR GAMES.
FERID.

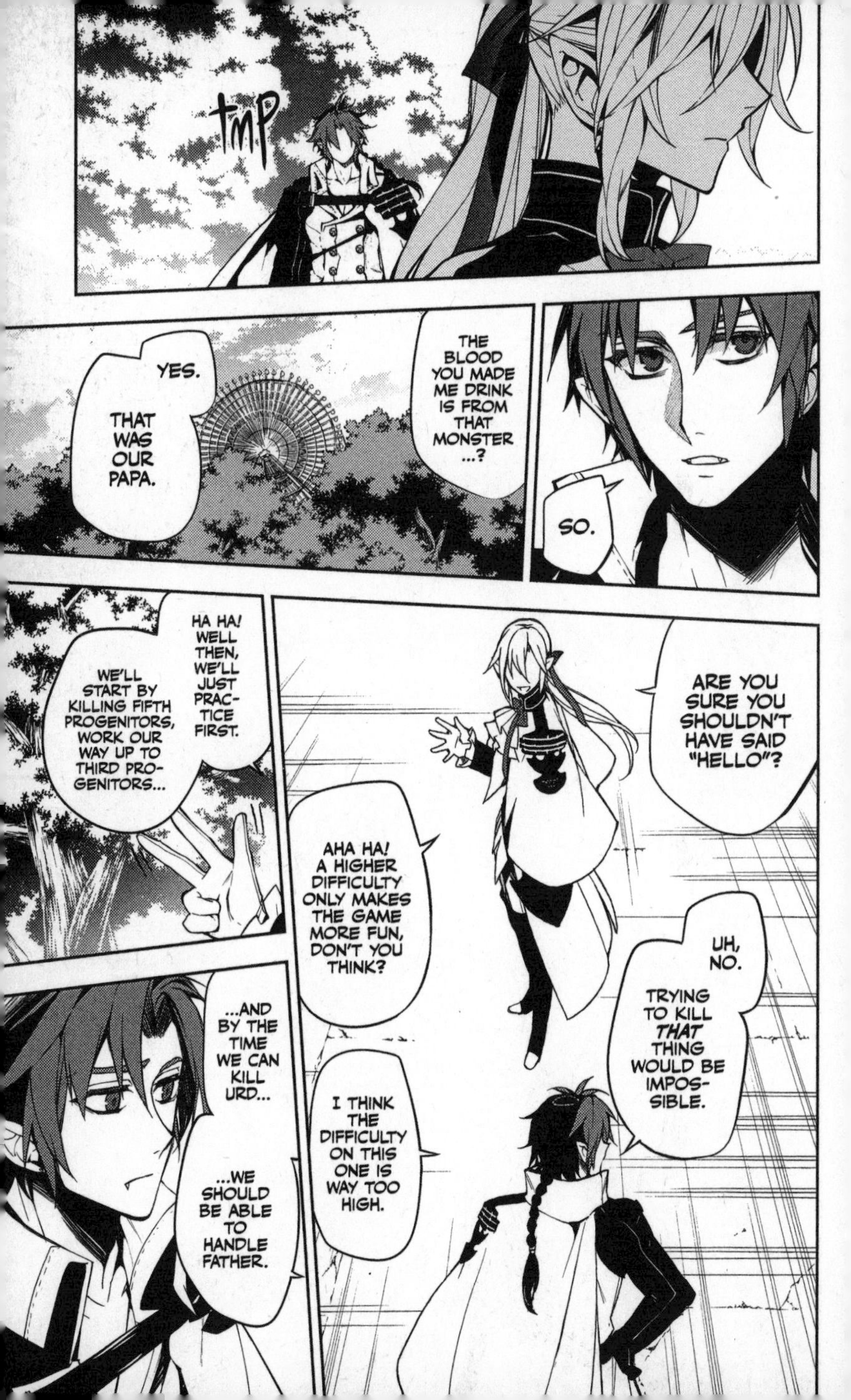
tmp
THE BLOOD YOU MADE ME DRINK IS FROM THAT MONSTER ...?
YES.
THAT WAS OUR PAPA.
SO.
ARE YOU SURE YOU SHOULDN'T HAVE SAID "HELLO"?
AHA HA! A HIGHER DIFFICULTY ONLY MAKES THE GAME MORE FUN, DON'T YOU THINK?
UH, NO.
TRYING TO KILL *THAT* THING WOULD BE IMPOSSIBLE.
I THINK THE DIFFICULTY ON THIS ONE IS WAY TOO HIGH.
HA HA! WELL THEN, WE'LL JUST PRACTICE FIRST.
WE'LL START BY KILLING FIFTH PROGENITORS, WORK OUR WAY UP TO THIRD PROGENITORS...
...AND BY THE TIME WE CAN KILL URD...
...WE SHOULD BE ABLE TO HANDLE FATHER.

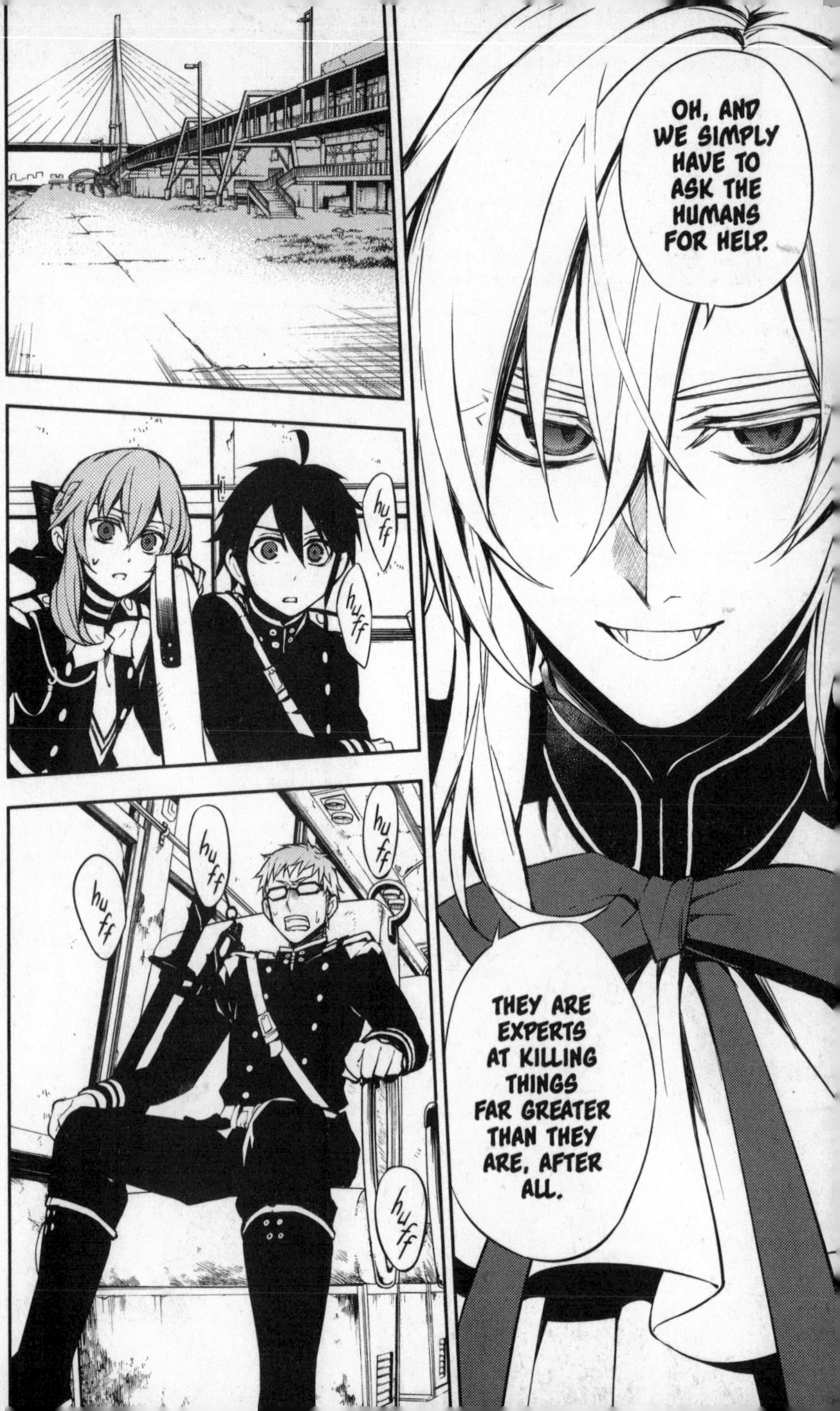
OH, AND WE SIMPLY HAVE TO ASK THE HUMANS FOR HELP.
THEY ARE EXPERTS AT KILLING THINGS FAR GREATER THAN THEY ARE, AFTER ALL.
huff
huff
huff
huff
huff
huff

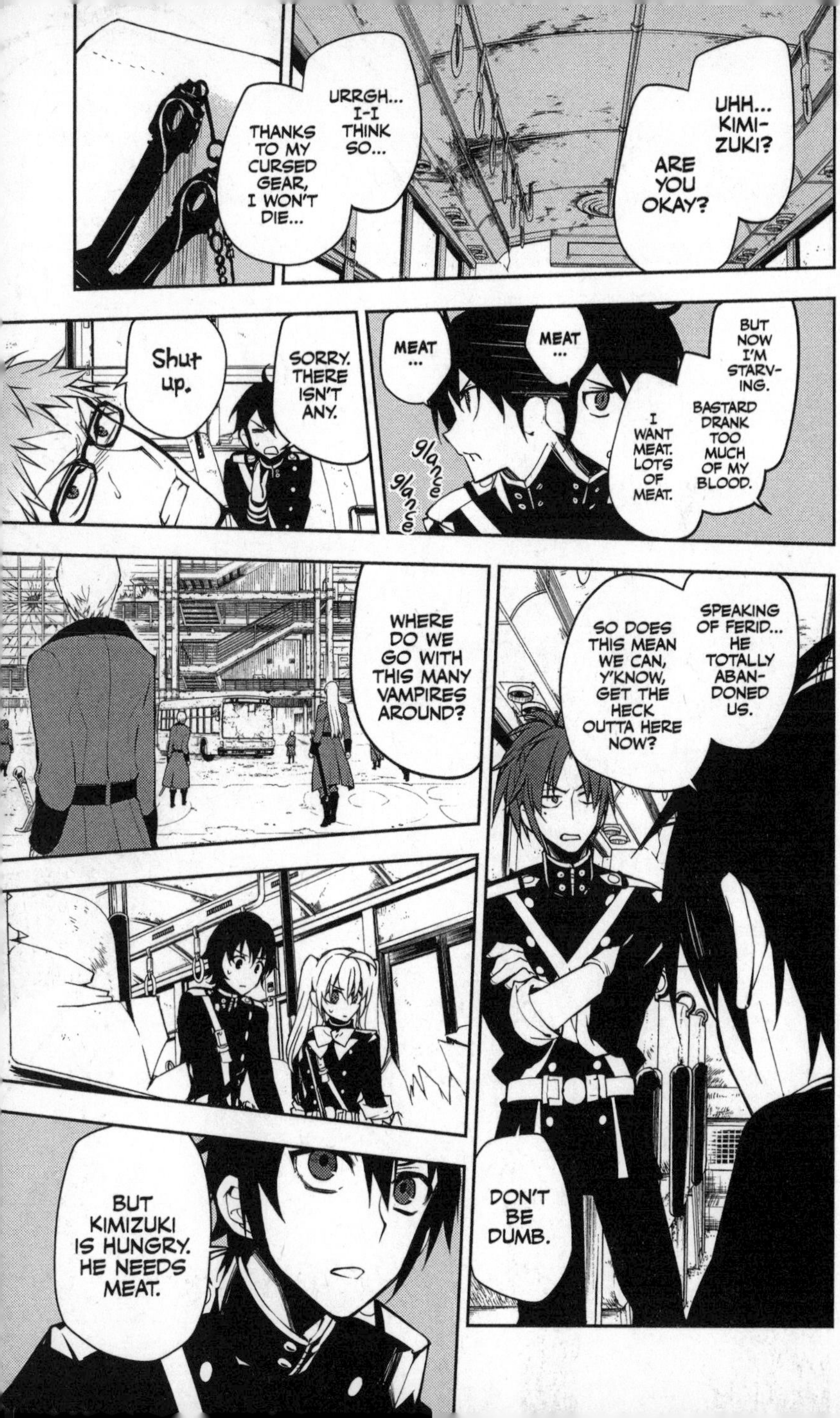
UHH... KIMIZUKI?
ARE YOU OKAY?
URRGH... I-I THINK SO...
THANKS TO MY CURSED GEAR, I WON'T DIE...
BUT NOW I'M STARVING.
BASTARD DRANK TOO MUCH OF MY BLOOD.
I WANT MEAT. LOTS OF MEAT.
MEAT...
MEAT...
glance glance
SORRY. THERE ISN'T ANY.
Shut up.
SPEAKING OF FERID... HE TOTALLY ABANDONED US.
SO DOES THIS MEAN WE CAN, Y'KNOW, GET THE HECK OUTTA HERE NOW?
WHERE DO WE GO WITH THIS MANY VAMPIRES AROUND?
BUT KIMIZUKI IS HUNGRY. HE NEEDS MEAT.
DON'T BE DUMB.

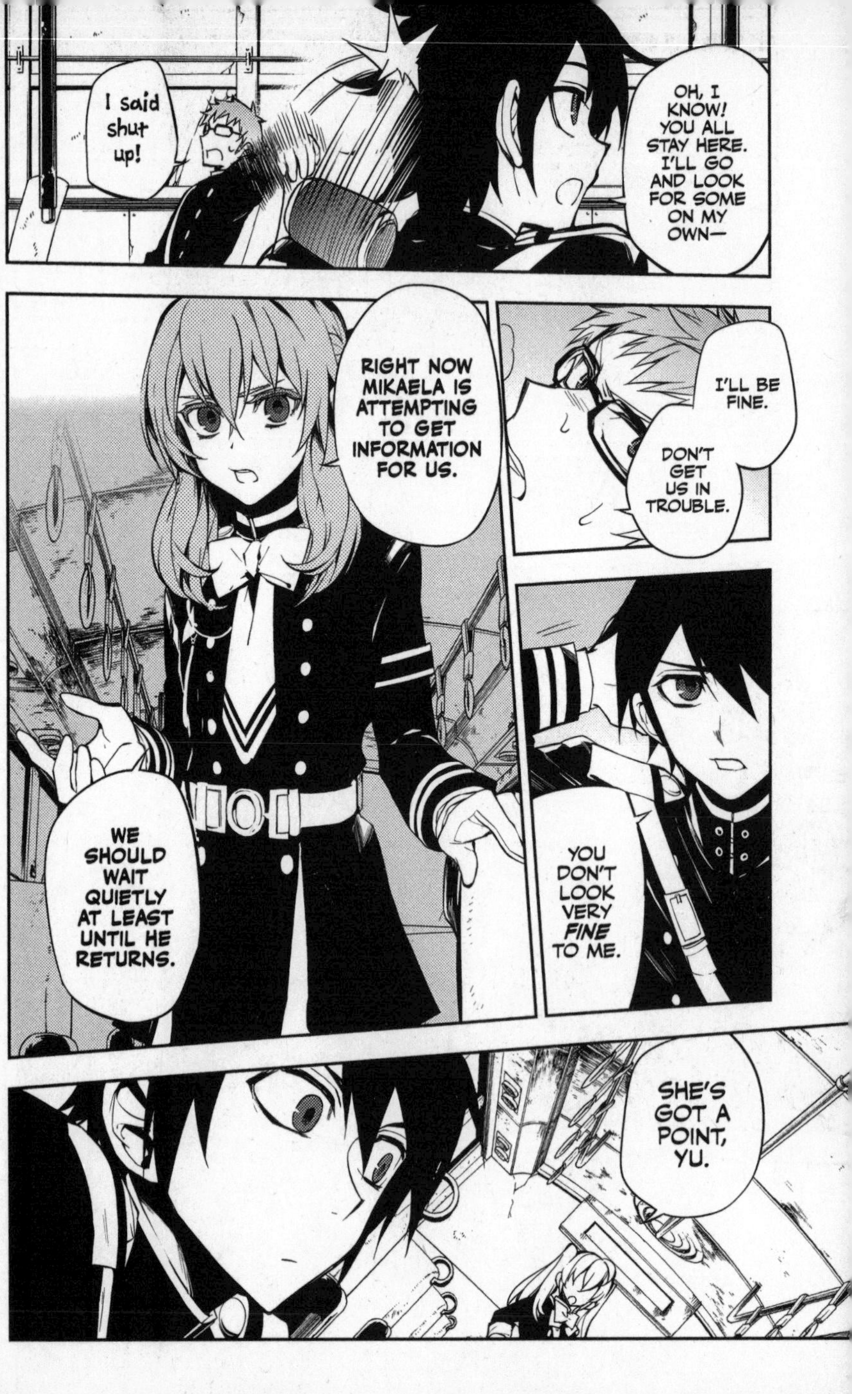
OH, I KNOW! YOU ALL STAY HERE. I'LL GO AND LOOK FOR SOME ON MY OWN—
I said shut up!
I'LL BE FINE.
DON'T GET US IN TROUBLE.
YOU DON'T LOOK VERY *FINE* TO ME.
RIGHT NOW MIKAELA IS ATTEMPTING TO GET INFORMATION FOR US.
WE SHOULD WAIT QUIETLY AT LEAST UNTIL HE RETURNS.
SHE'S GOT A POINT, YU.

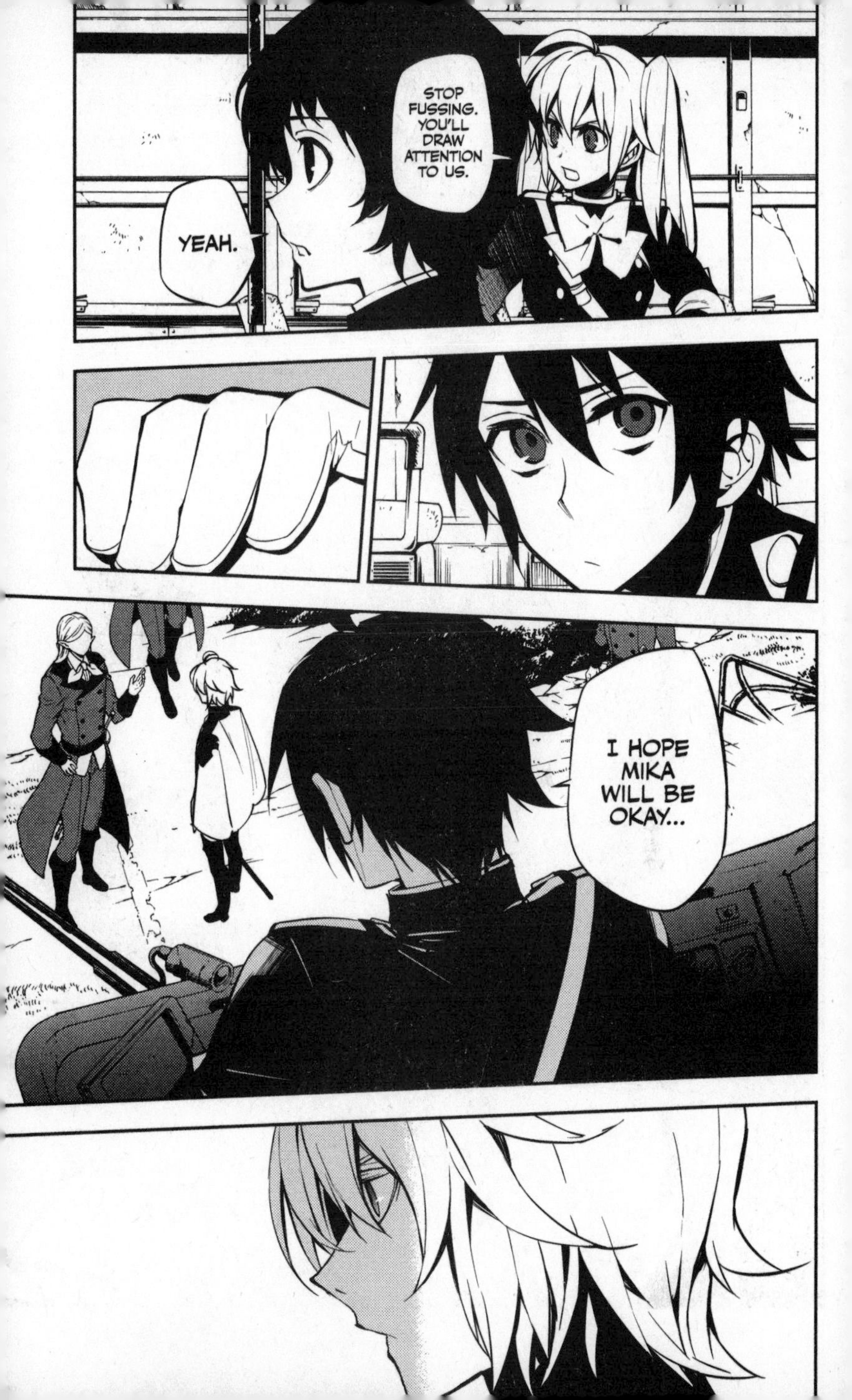
STOP FUSSING. YOU'LL DRAW ATTENTION TO US.
YEAH.
I HOPE MIKA WILL BE OKAY...

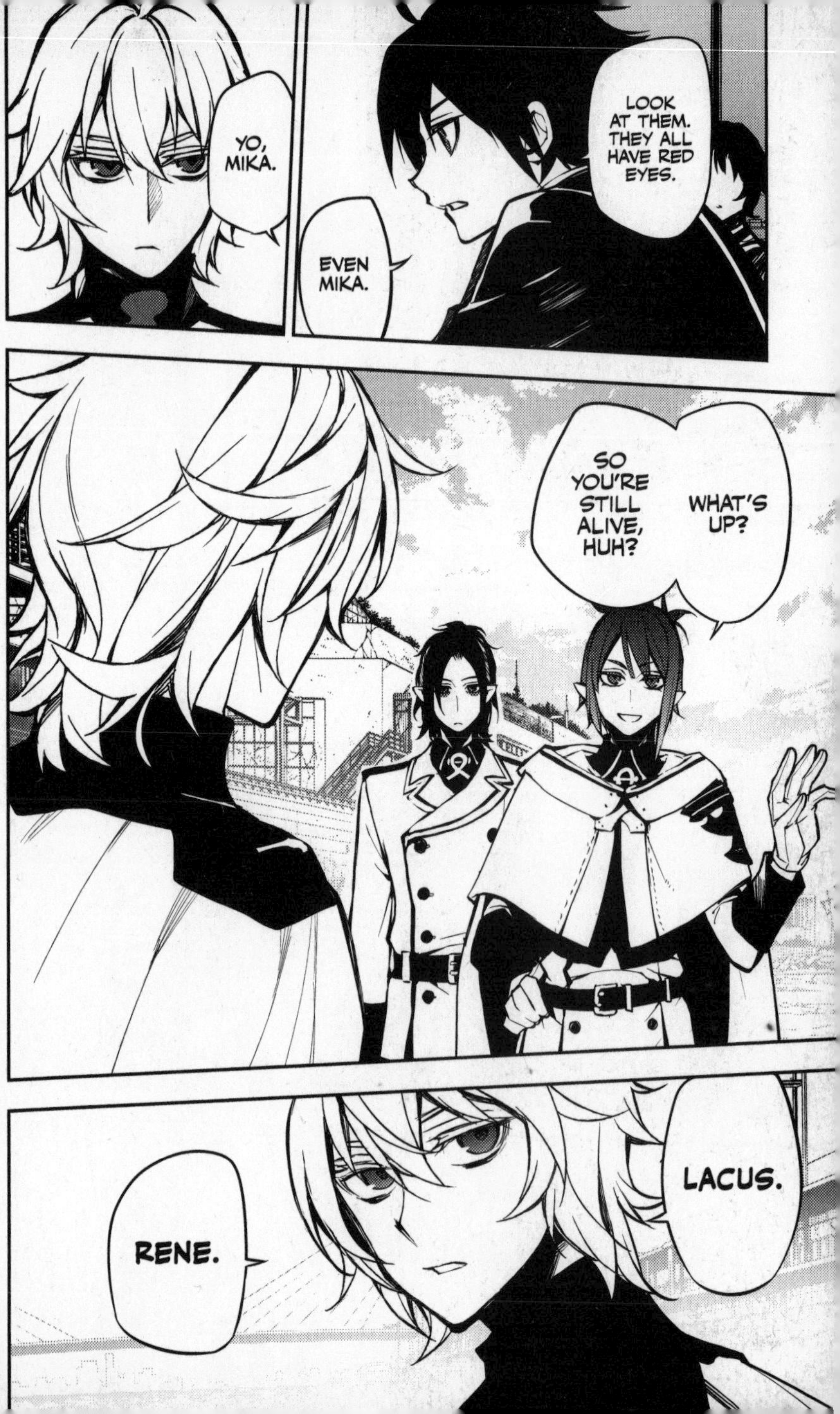
LOOK AT THEM. THEY ALL HAVE RED EYES.
EVEN MIKA.
YO, MIKA.
WHAT'S UP?
SO YOU'RE STILL ALIVE, HUH?
LACUS.
RENE.

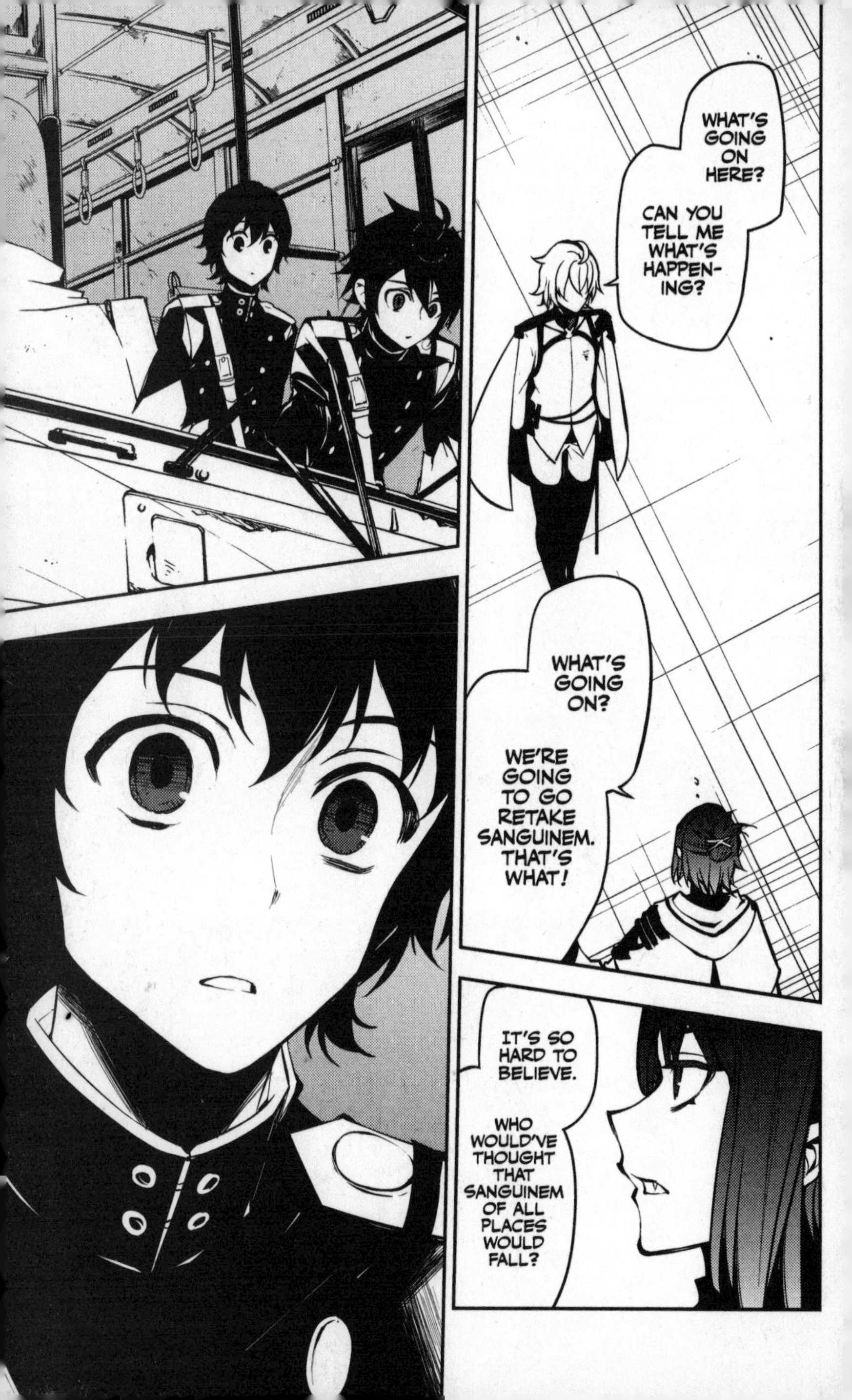
WHAT'S GOING ON HERE?
CAN YOU TELL ME WHAT'S HAPPEN-ING?
WHAT'S GOING ON?
WE'RE GOING TO GO RETAKE SANGUINEM. THAT'S WHAT!
IT'S SO HARD TO BELIEVE.
WHO WOULD'VE THOUGHT THAT SANGUINEM OF ALL PLACES WOULD FALL?

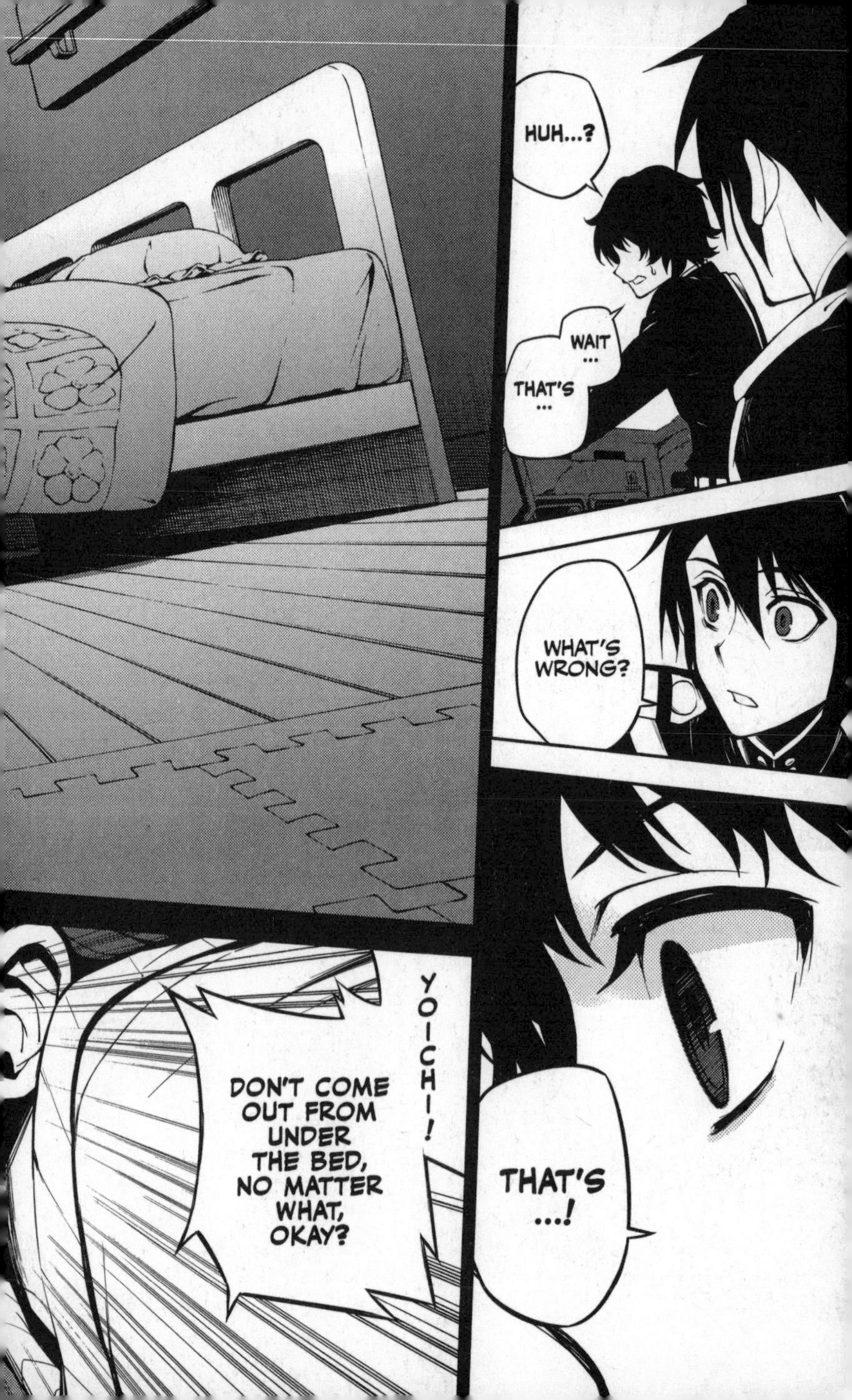
HUH...?
WAIT... THAT'S...
WHAT'S WRONG?
THAT'S...!
YOICHI!
DON'T COME OUT FROM UNDER THE BED, NO MATTER WHAT, OKAY?

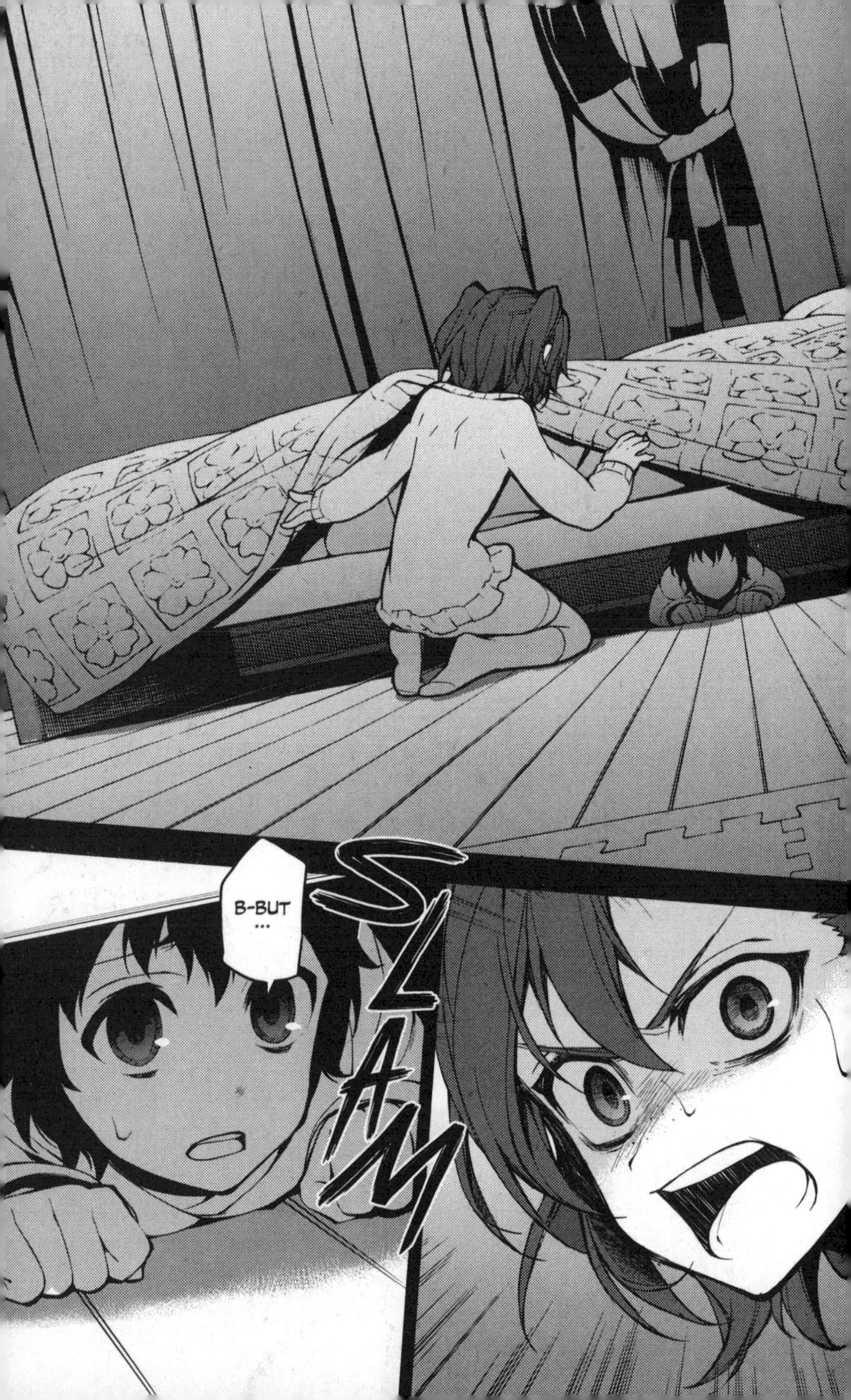
SLAM
B-BUT ...

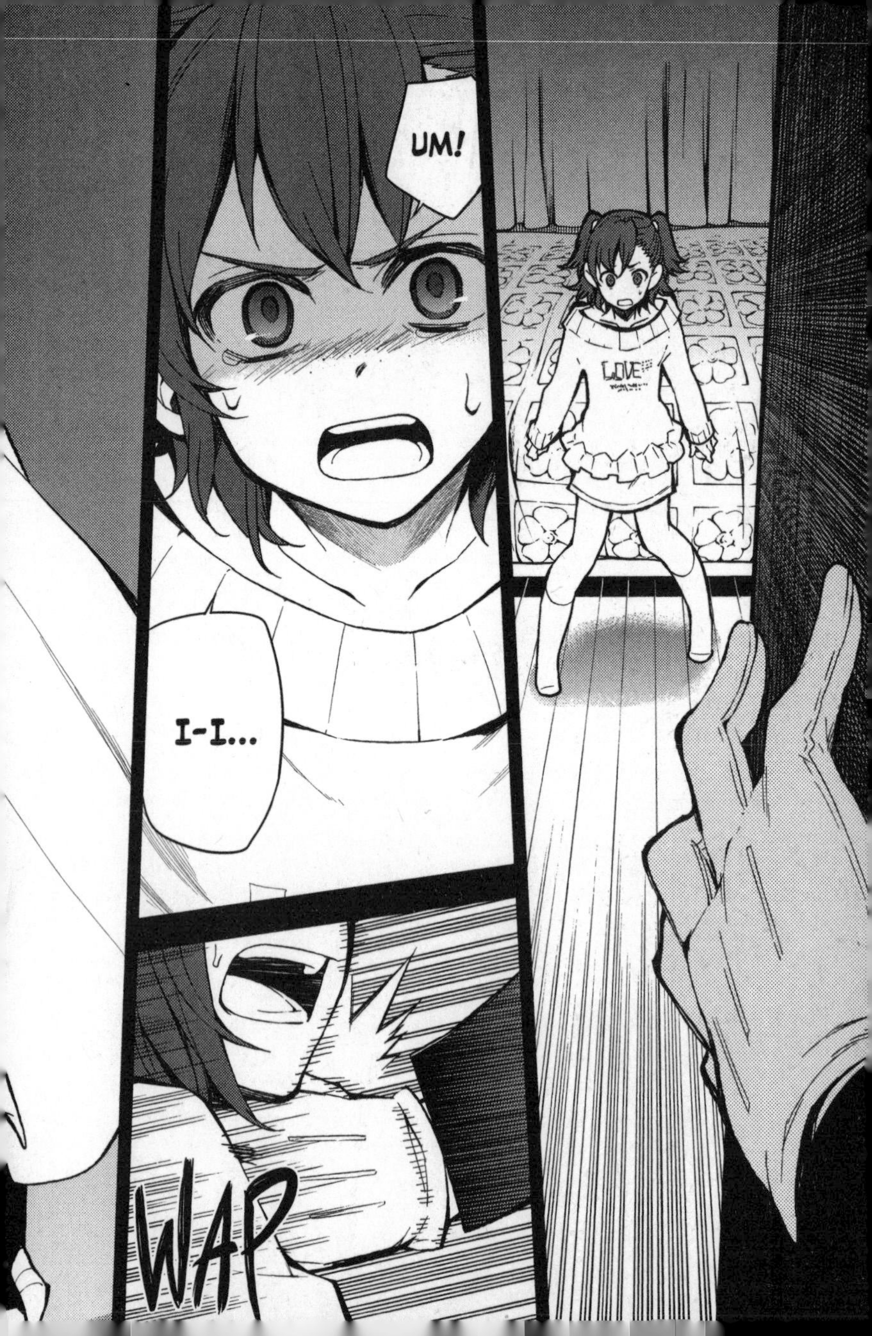
UM!
I-I...
WAP

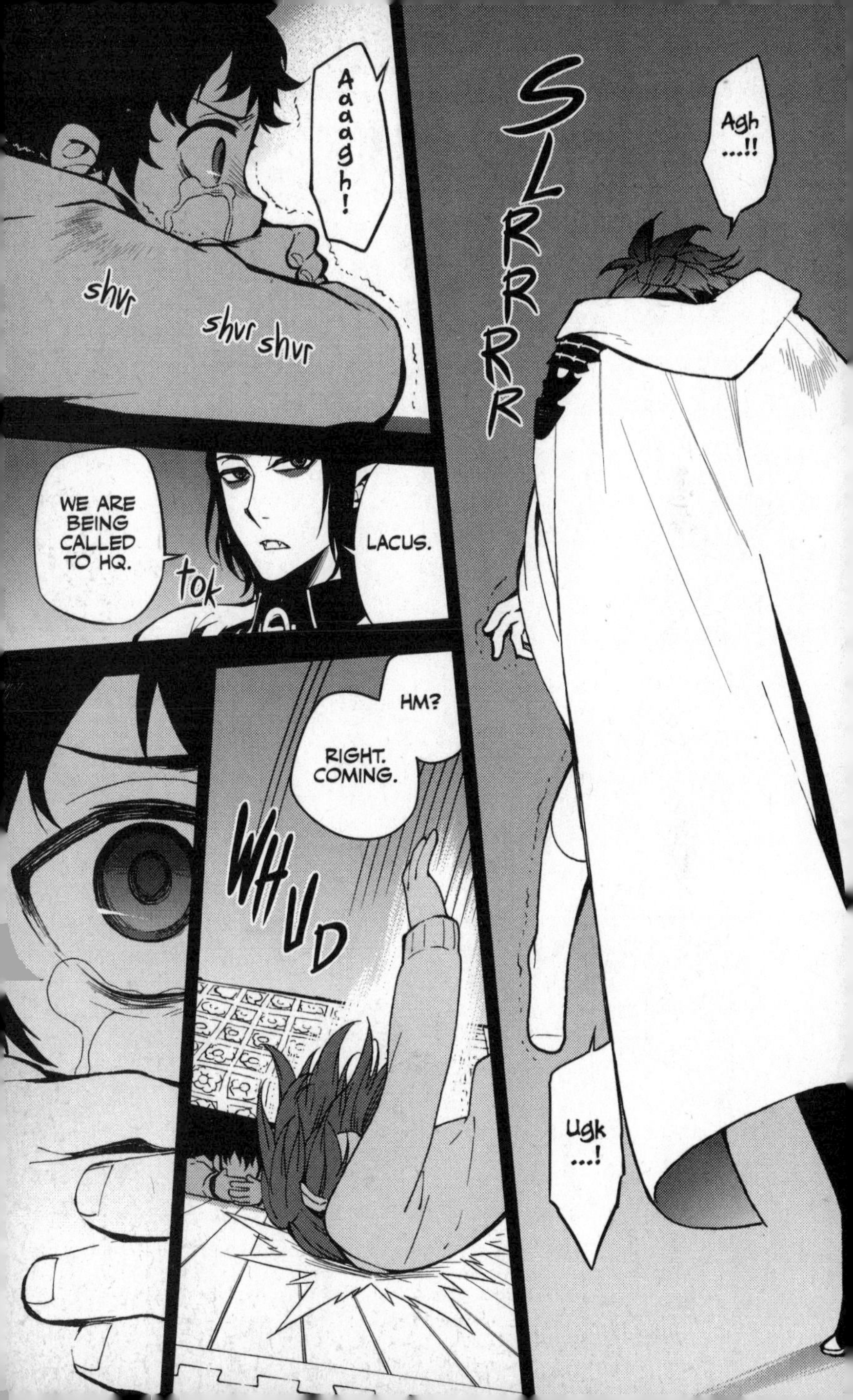
Agh ...!!
SLRRRR
Ugk ...!
Aaaagh!
shvr
shvr shvr
LACUS.
WE ARE BEING CALLED TO HQ.
tok
HM?
RIGHT. COMING.
WHUD

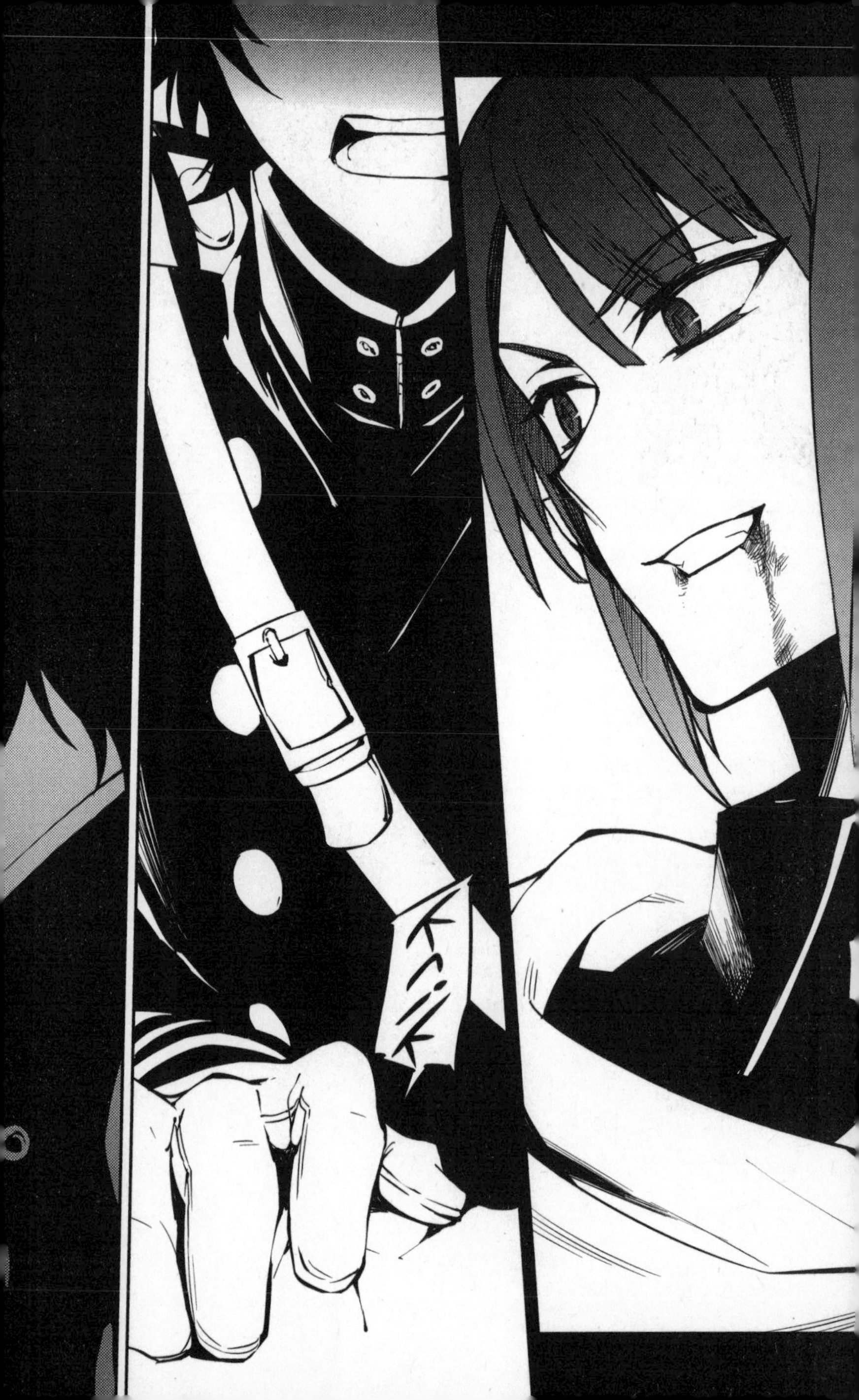
KRIK

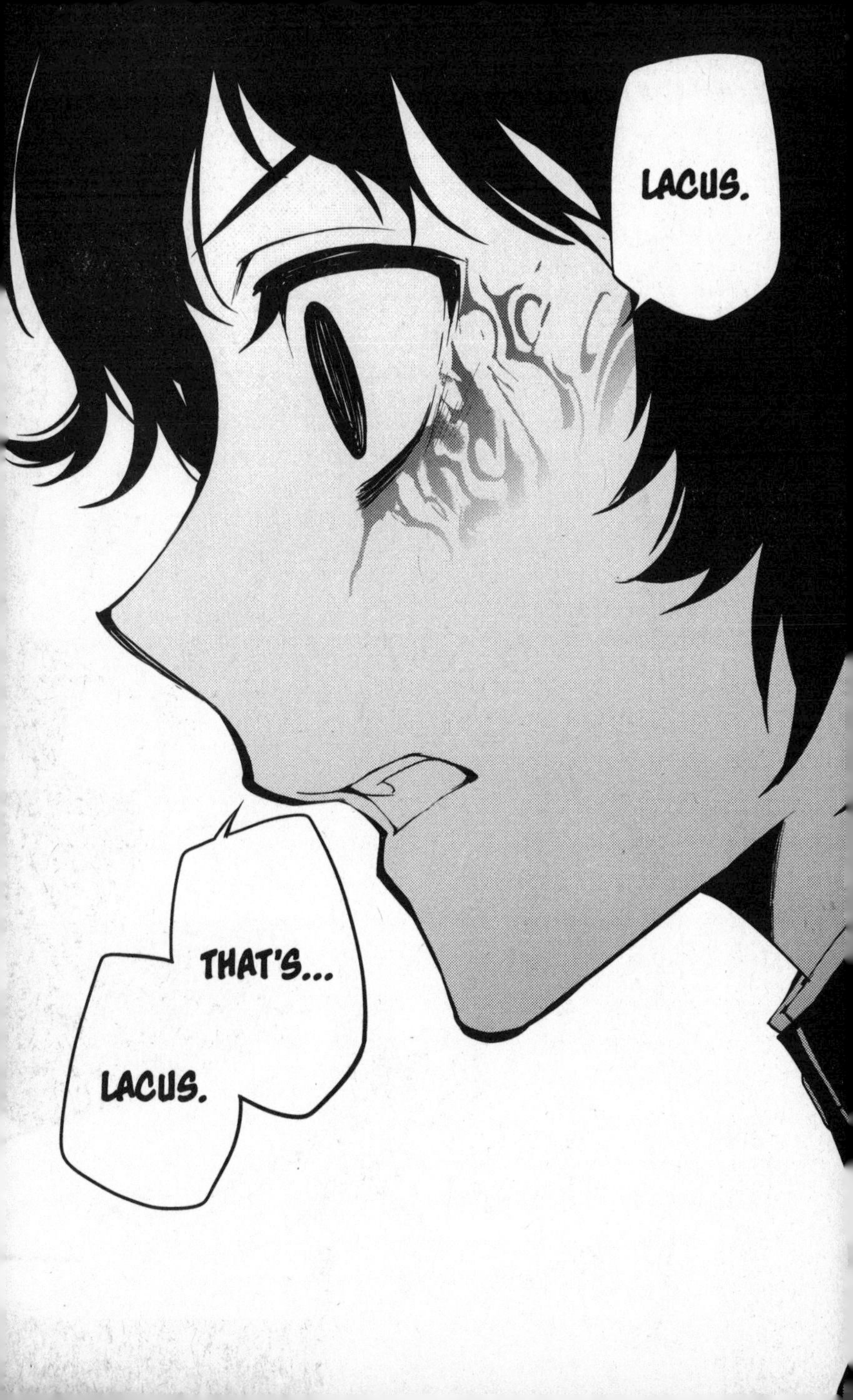
LACUS.
THAT'S...
LACUS.

Seraph of the End
VAMPIRE REIGN

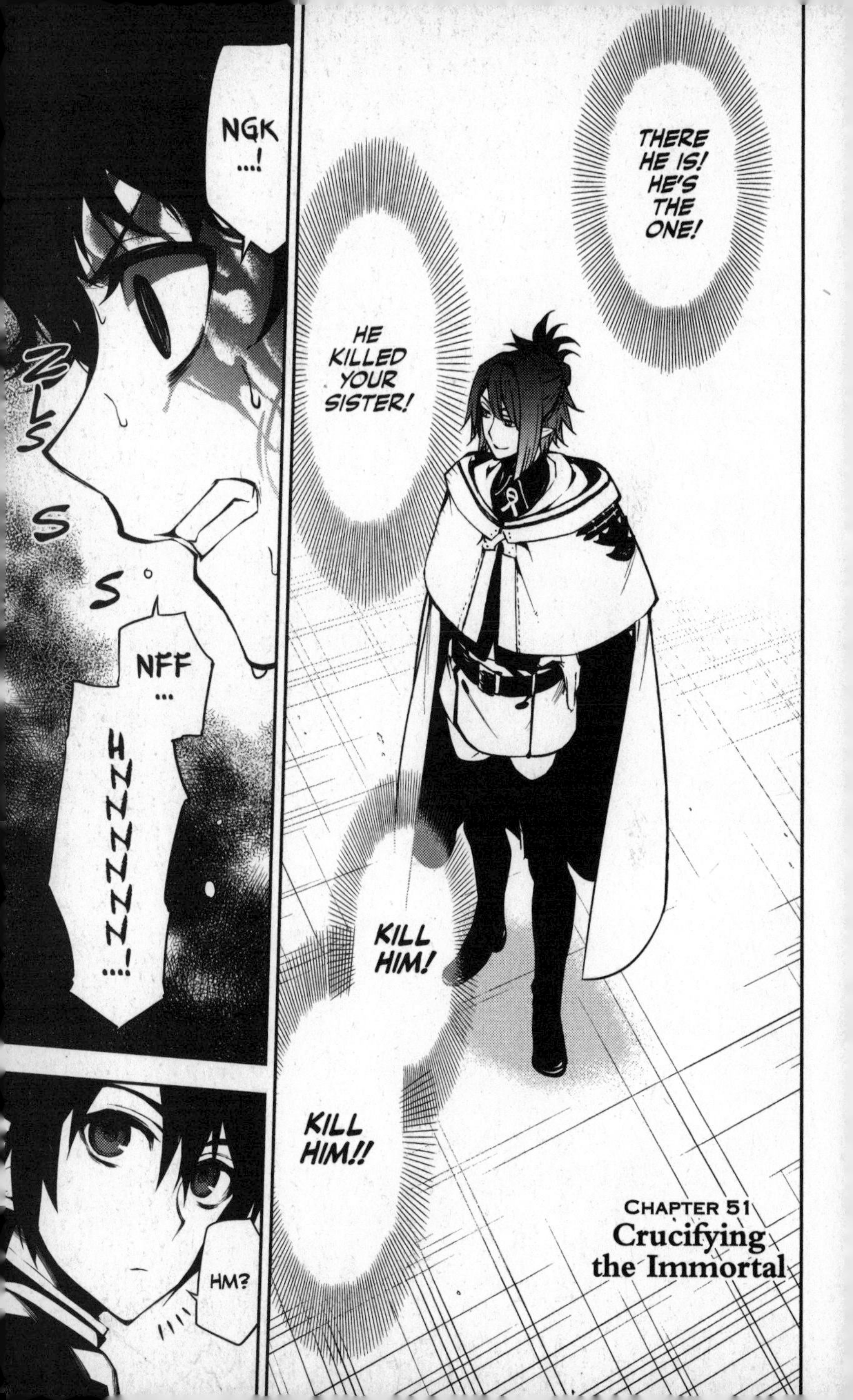
THERE HE IS! HE'S THE ONE!
HE KILLED YOUR SISTER!
KILL HIM!
KILL HIM!!
CHAPTER 51
Crucifying the Immortal
NGK ...!
ZLSSS
NFF ... HNNNNNN...!
HM?

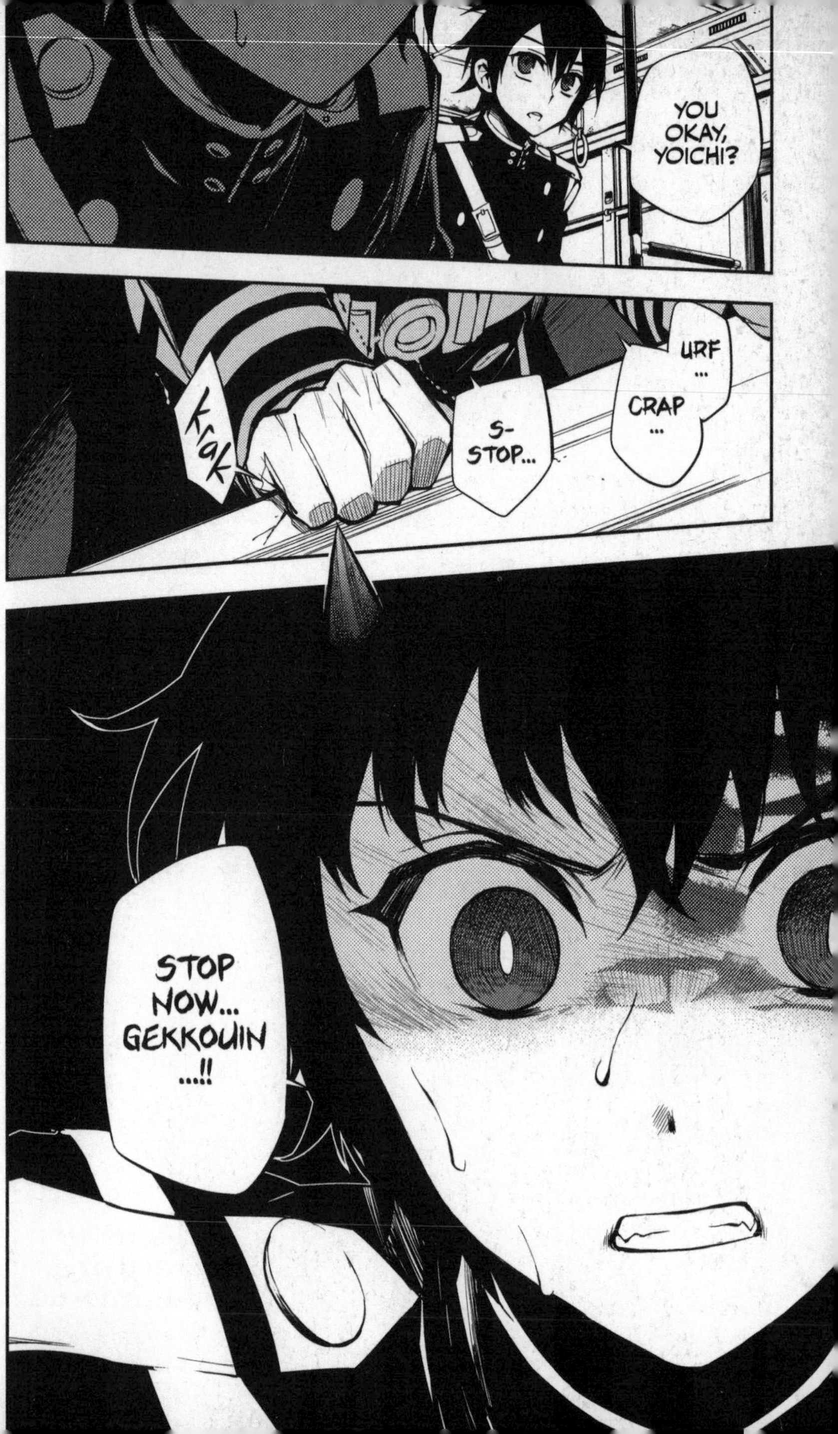
YOU OKAY, YOICHI?
URF ... CRAP ...
S-STOP...
krak
STOP NOW... GEKKOUIN ...!!

Chapter 51
Crucifying the Immortal

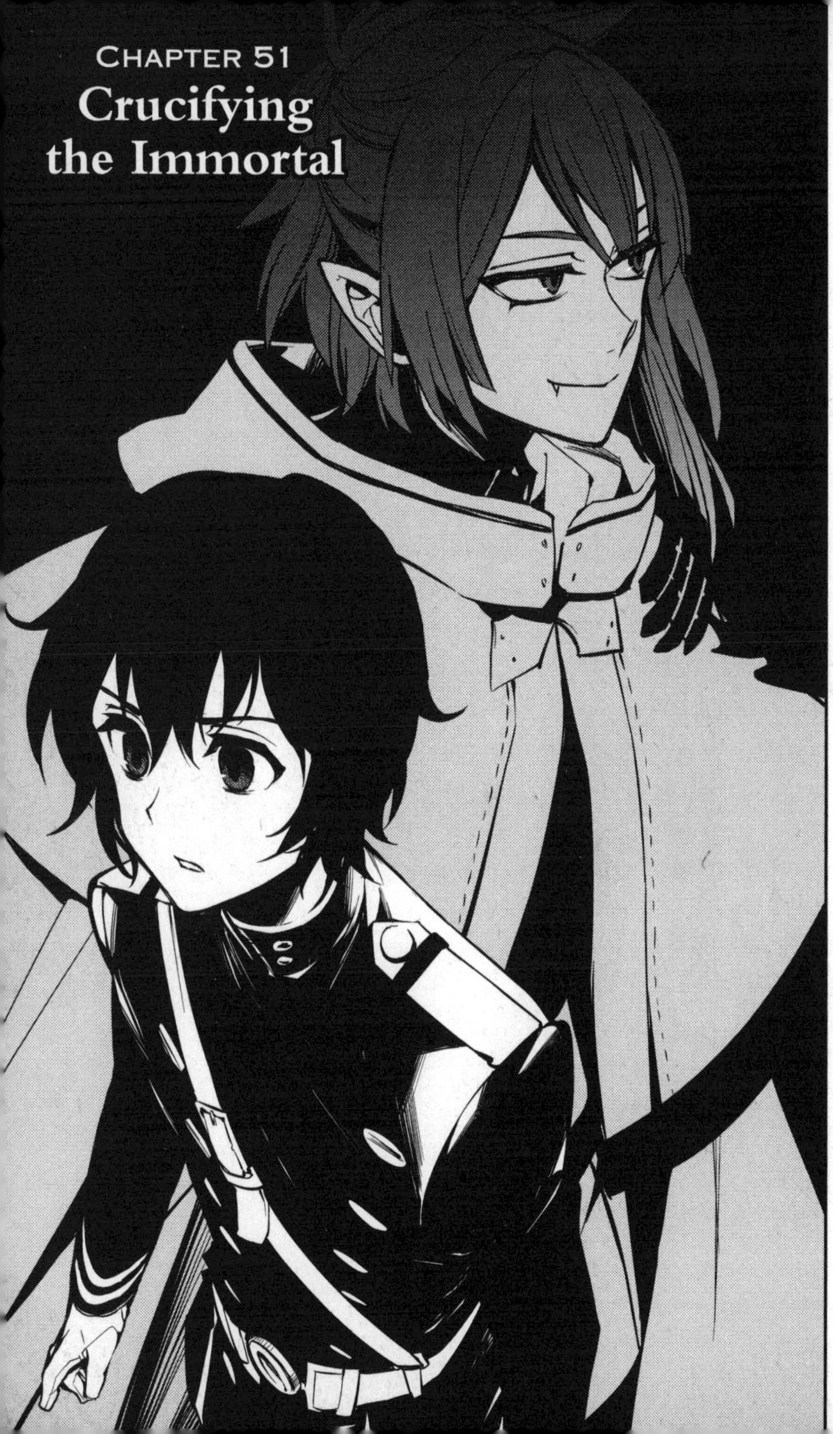

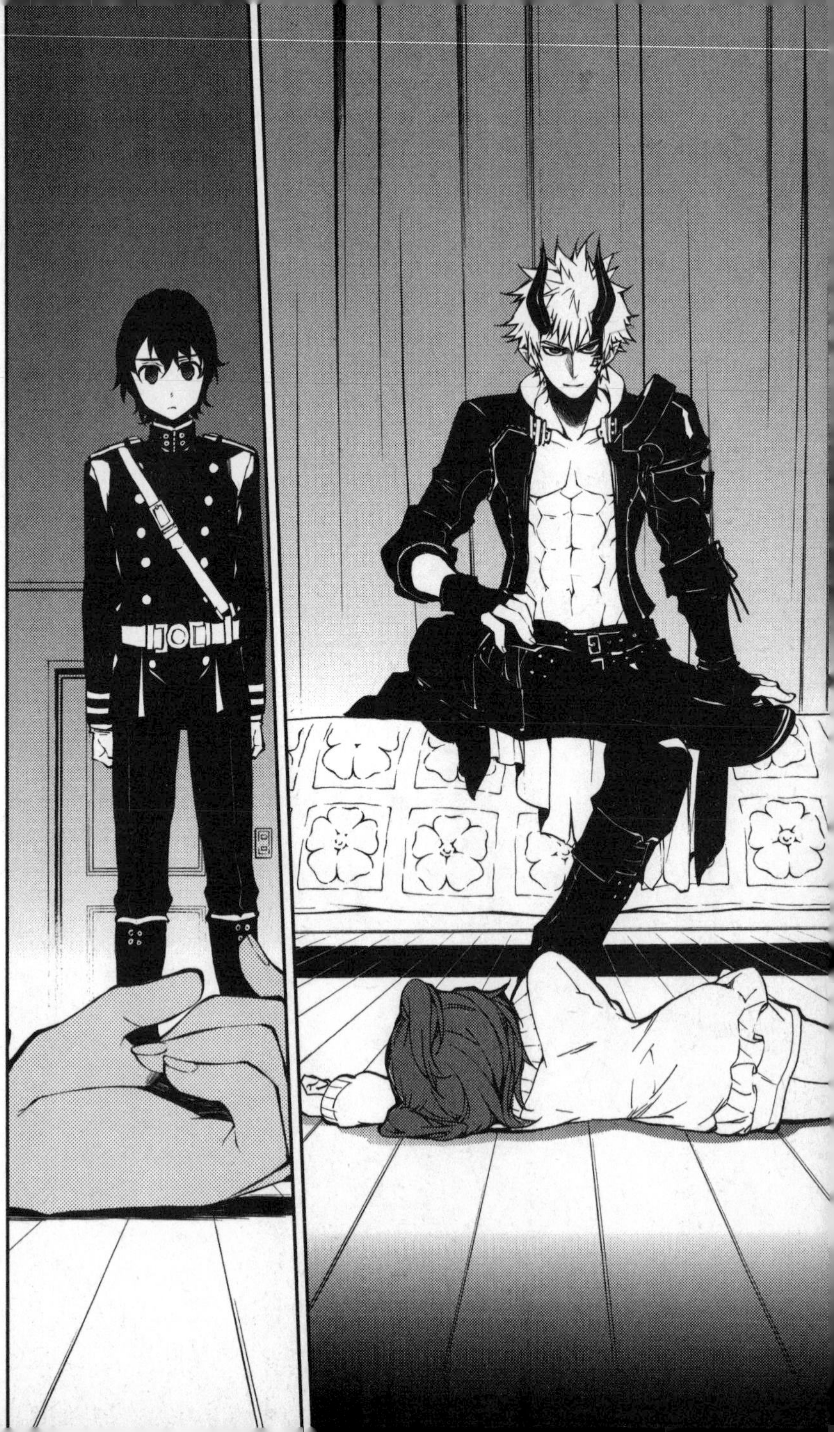

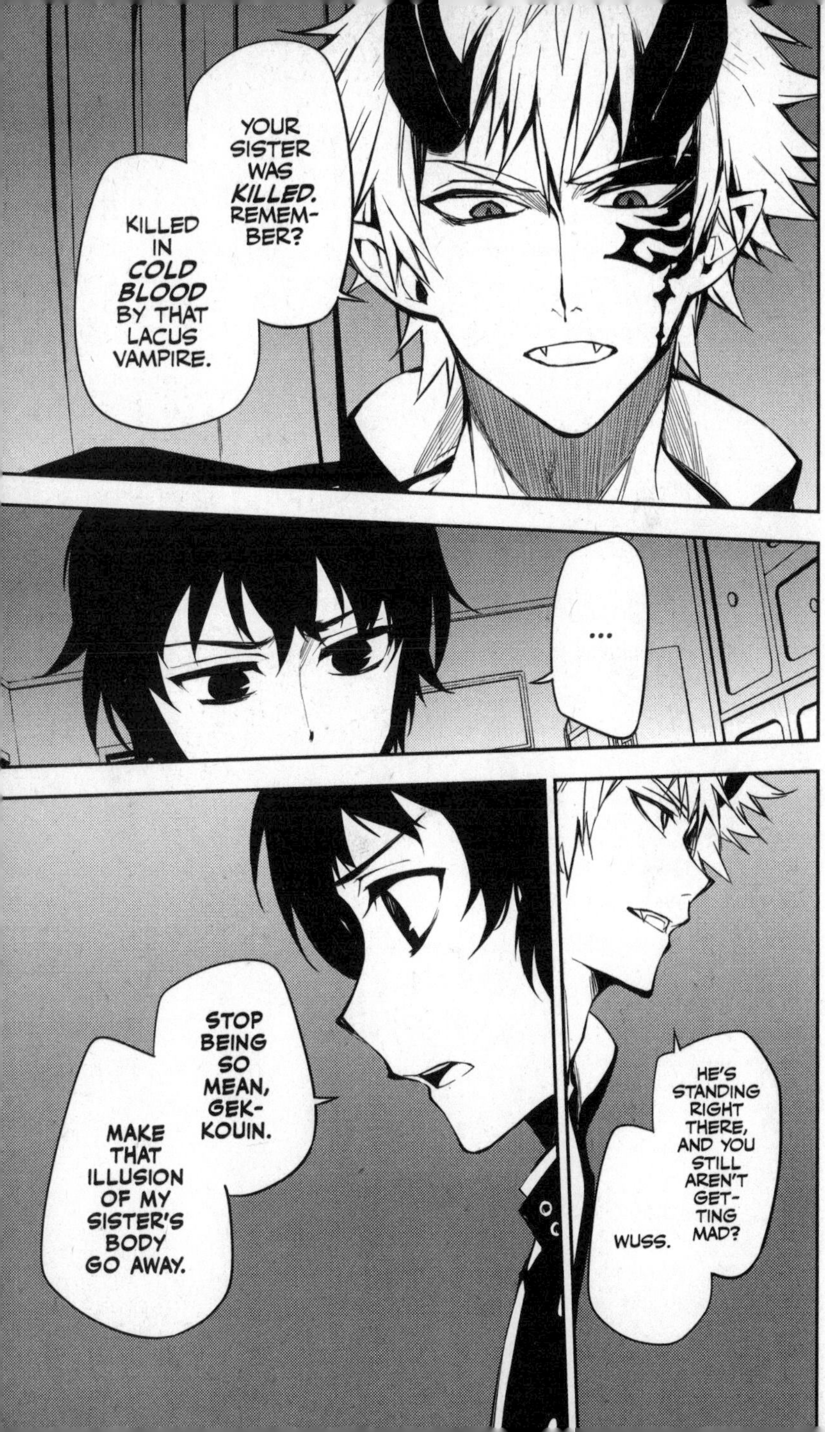
YOUR SISTER WAS *KILLED.* REMEMBER?
KILLED IN *COLD BLOOD* BY THAT LACUS VAMPIRE.
...
HE'S STANDING RIGHT THERE, AND YOU STILL AREN'T GETTING MAD?
WUSS.
STOP BEING SO MEAN, GEKKOUIN.
MAKE THAT ILLUSION OF MY SISTER'S BODY GO AWAY.

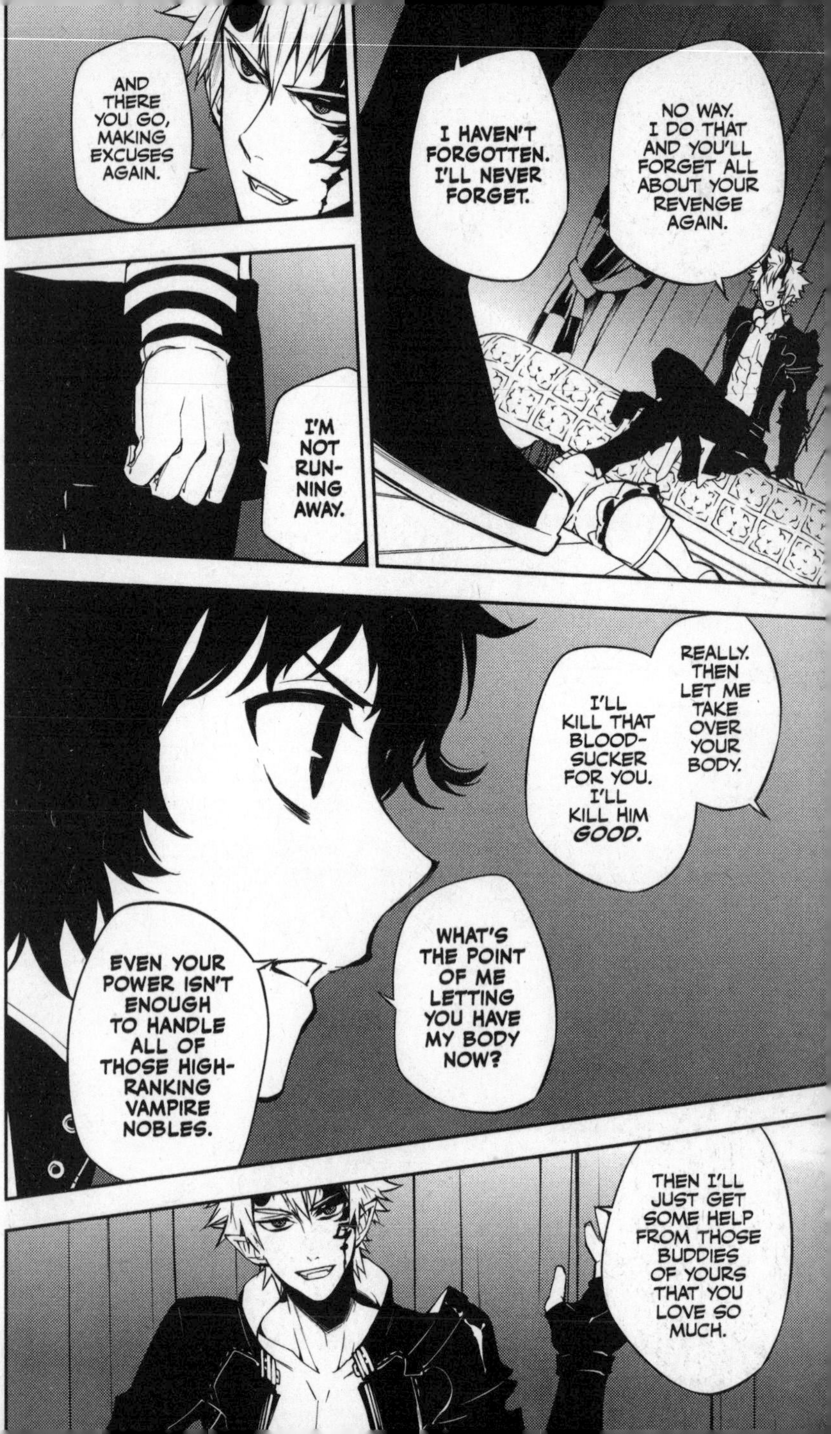
NO WAY. I DO THAT AND YOU'LL FORGET ALL ABOUT YOUR REVENGE AGAIN.
I HAVEN'T FORGOTTEN. I'LL NEVER FORGET.
AND THERE YOU GO, MAKING EXCUSES AGAIN.
I'M NOT RUN-NING AWAY.
REALLY. THEN LET ME TAKE OVER YOUR BODY.
I'LL KILL THAT BLOOD-SUCKER FOR YOU. I'LL KILL HIM *GOOD*.
WHAT'S THE POINT OF ME LETTING YOU HAVE MY BODY NOW?
EVEN YOUR POWER ISN'T ENOUGH TO HANDLE ALL OF THOSE HIGH-RANKING VAMPIRE NOBLES.
THEN I'LL JUST GET SOME HELP FROM THOSE BUDDIES OF YOURS THAT YOU LOVE SO MUCH.

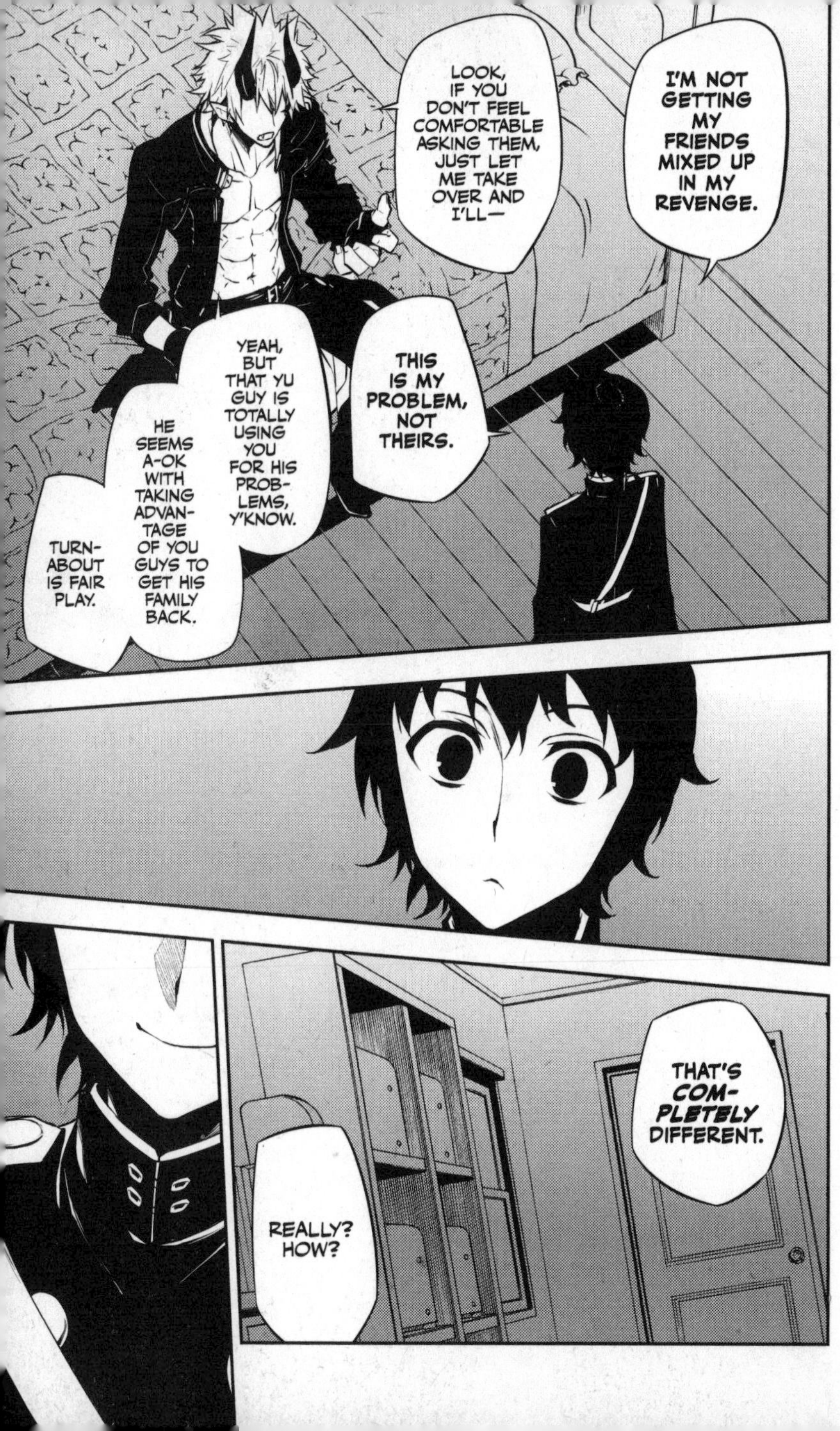
I'M NOT GETTING MY FRIENDS MIXED UP IN MY REVENGE.
LOOK, IF YOU DON'T FEEL COMFORTABLE ASKING THEM, JUST LET ME TAKE OVER AND I'LL—
THIS IS MY PROBLEM, NOT THEIRS.
YEAH, BUT THAT YU GUY IS TOTALLY USING YOU FOR HIS PROB-LEMS, Y'KNOW.
HE SEEMS A-OK WITH TAKING ADVAN-TAGE OF YOU GUYS TO GET HIS FAMILY BACK.
TURN-ABOUT IS FAIR PLAY.
THAT'S *COM-PLETELY* DIFFERENT.
REALLY? HOW?

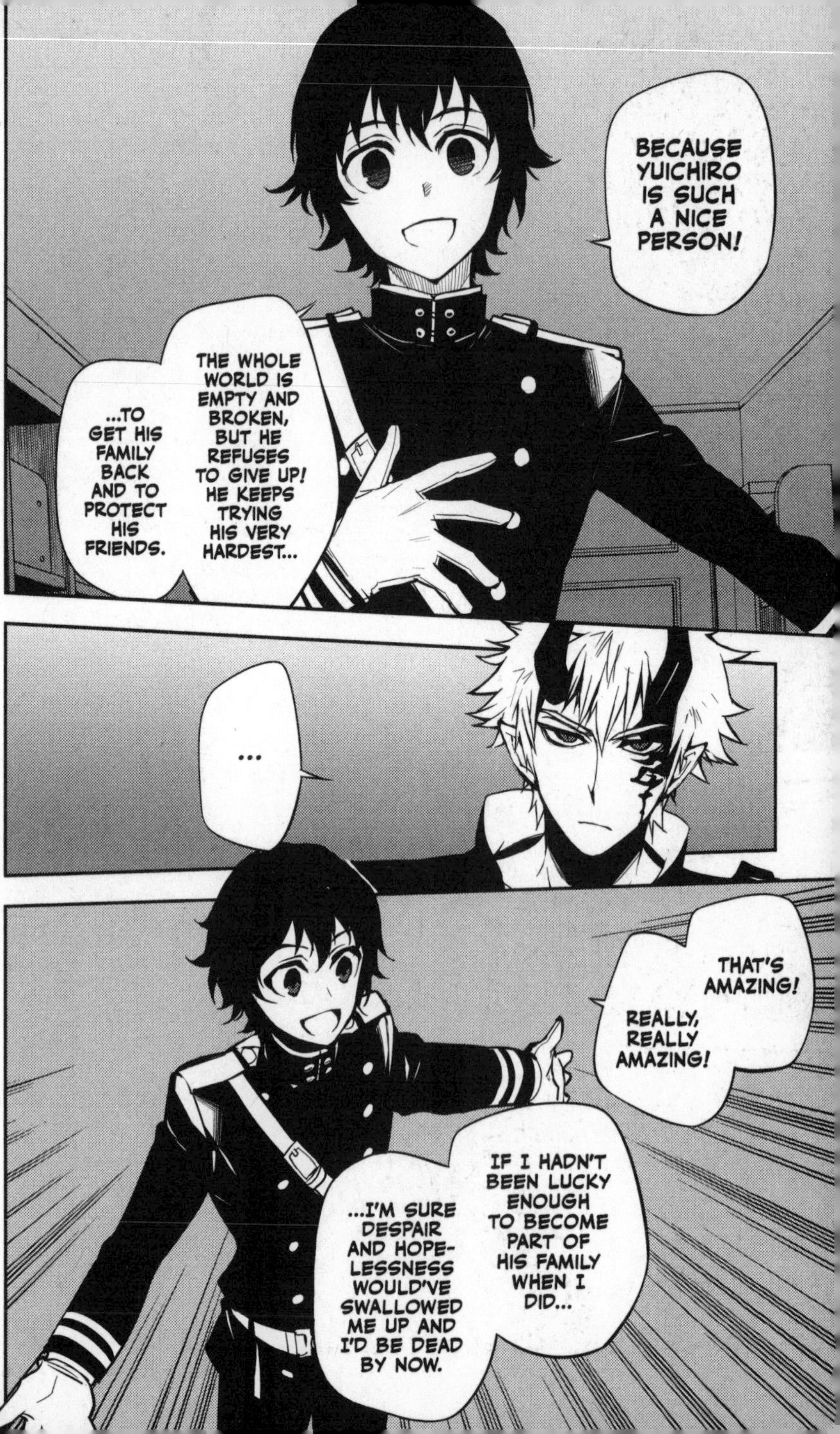
BECAUSE YUICHIRO IS SUCH A NICE PERSON!
THE WHOLE WORLD IS EMPTY AND BROKEN, BUT HE REFUSES TO GIVE UP! HE KEEPS TRYING HIS VERY HARDEST...
...TO GET HIS FAMILY BACK AND TO PROTECT HIS FRIENDS.
...
THAT'S AMAZING!
REALLY, REALLY AMAZING!
IF I HADN'T BEEN LUCKY ENOUGH TO BECOME PART OF HIS FAMILY WHEN I DID...
...I'M SURE DESPAIR AND HOPE-LESSNESS WOULD'VE SWALLOWED ME UP AND I'D BE DEAD BY NOW.

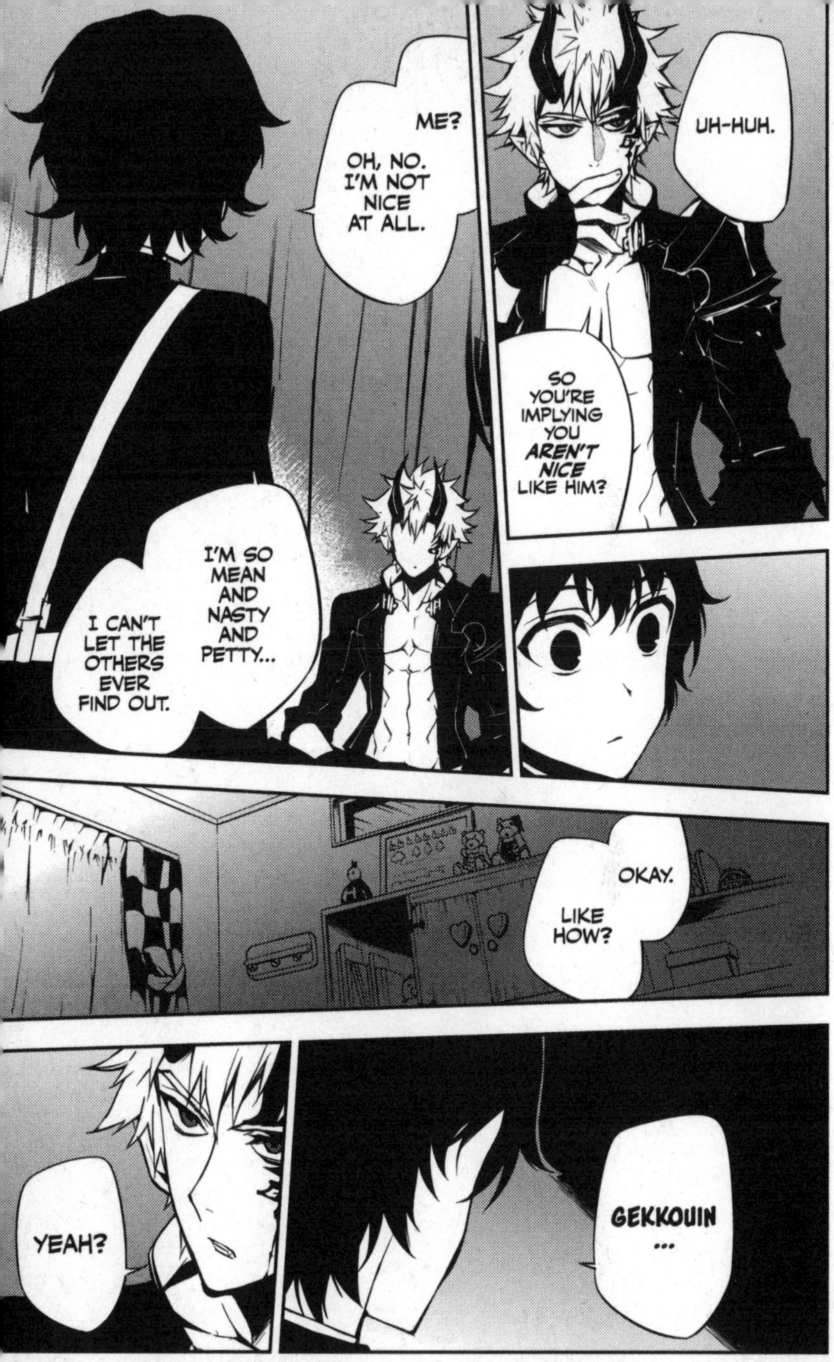
UH-HUH.
SO YOU'RE IMPLYING YOU ***AREN'T NICE*** LIKE HIM?
ME?
OH, NO. I'M NOT NICE AT ALL.
I'M SO MEAN AND NASTY AND PETTY...
I CAN'T LET THE OTHERS EVER FIND OUT.
OKAY.
LIKE HOW?
GEKKOUIN...
YEAH?

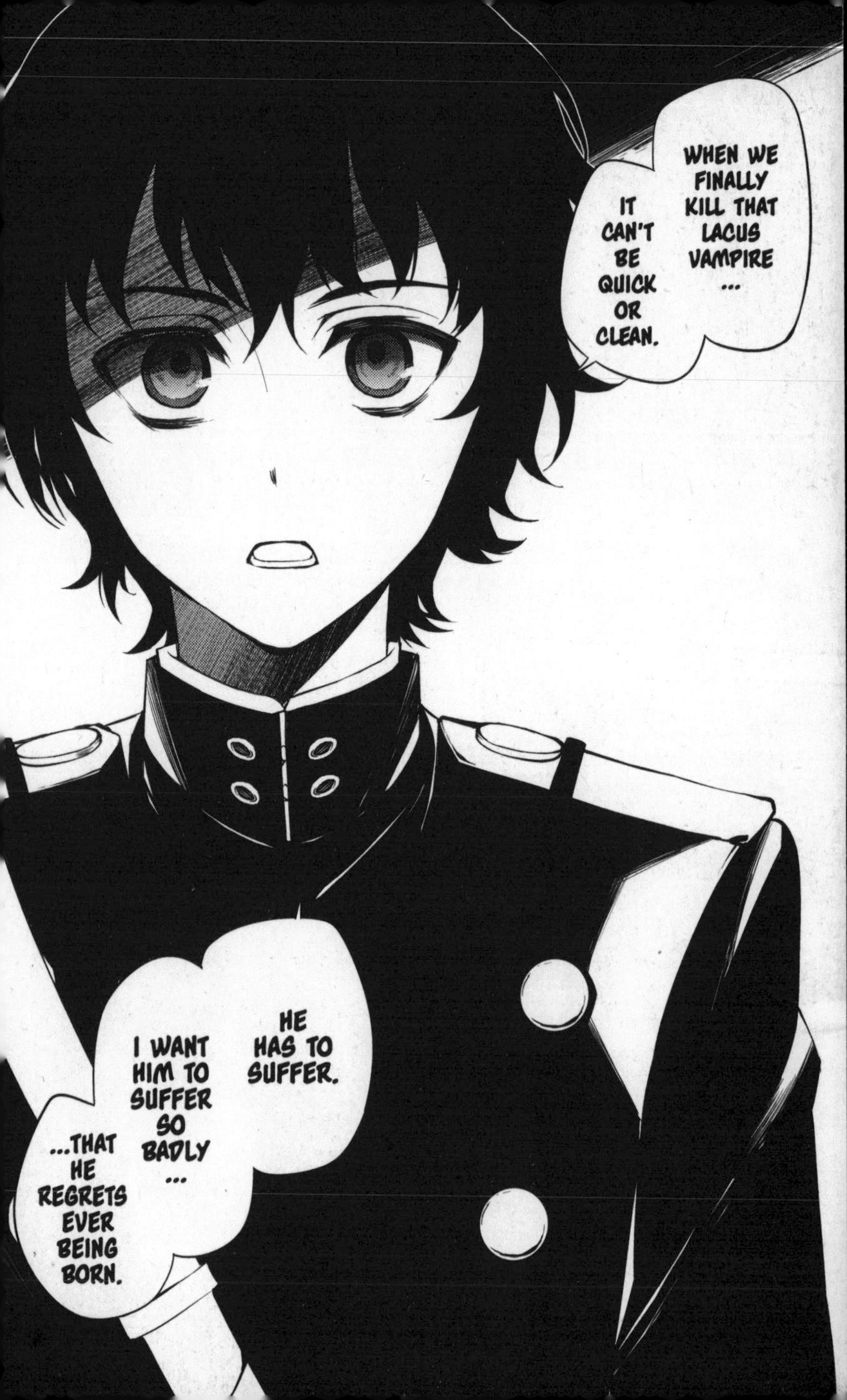
WHEN WE FINALLY KILL THAT LACUS VAMPIRE ...
IT CAN'T BE QUICK OR CLEAN.
HE HAS TO SUFFER.
I WANT HIM TO SUFFER SO BADLY ...
...THAT HE REGRETS EVER BEING BORN.

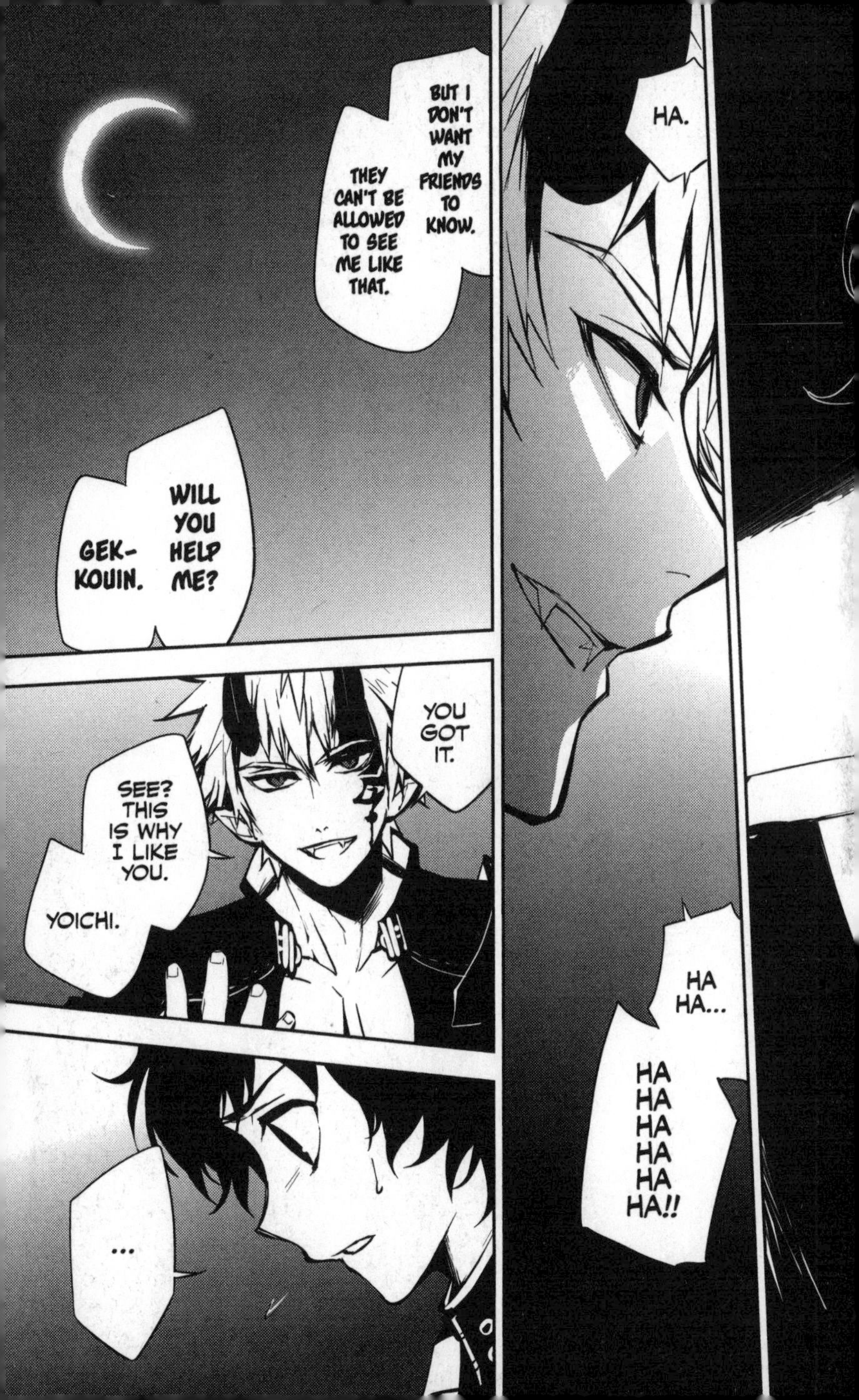
HA.
HA HA...
HA HA HA HA HA HA!!
BUT I DON'T WANT MY FRIENDS TO KNOW.
THEY CAN'T BE ALLOWED TO SEE ME LIKE THAT.
WILL YOU HELP ME?
GEK-KOUIN.
YOU GOT IT.
SEE? THIS IS WHY I LIKE YOU.
YOICHI.
...

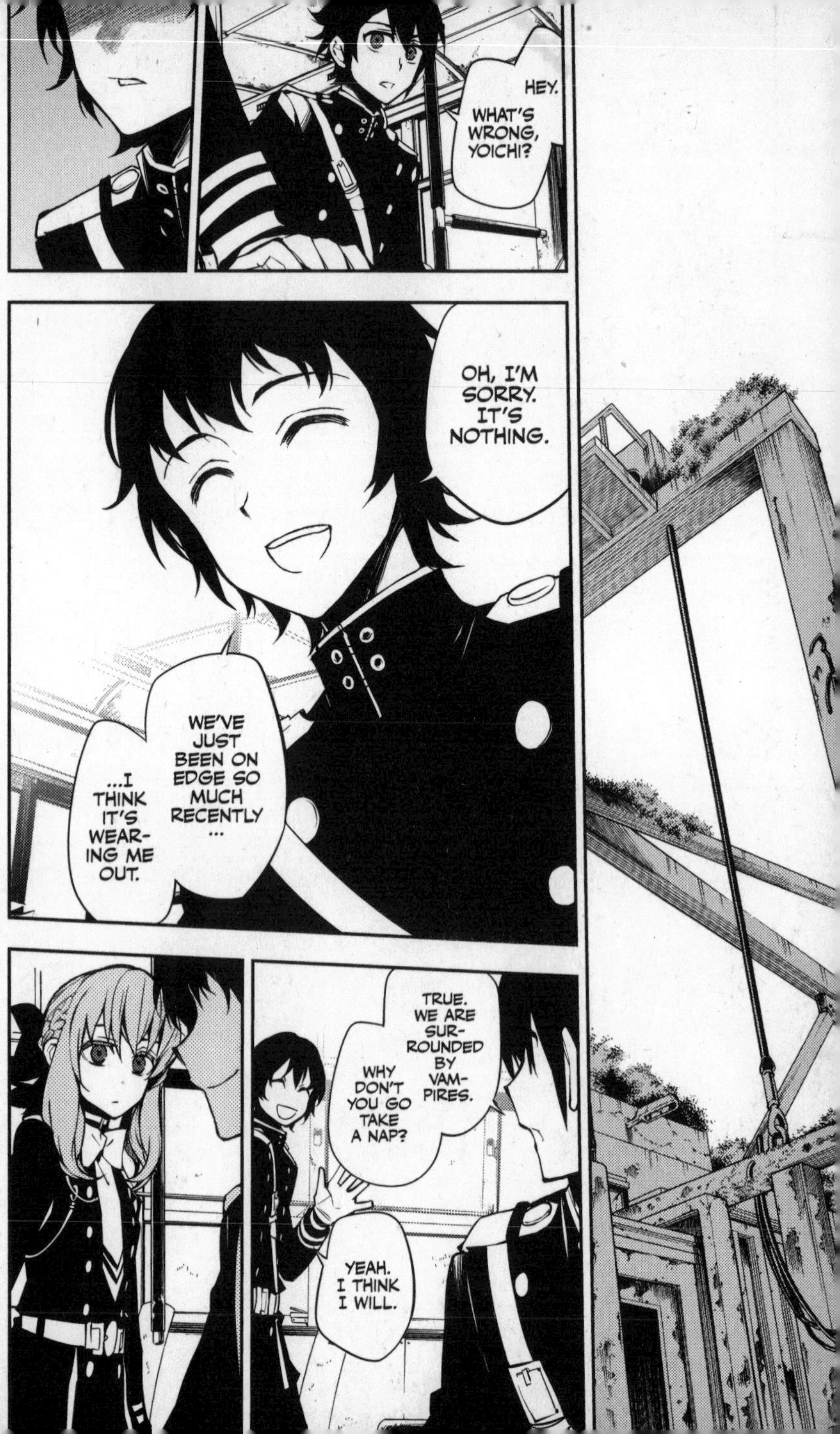
HEY.
WHAT'S WRONG, YOICHI?
OH, I'M SORRY. IT'S NOTHING.
WE'VE JUST BEEN ON EDGE SO MUCH RECENTLY...
...I THINK IT'S WEAR-ING ME OUT.
TRUE. WE ARE SUR-ROUNDED BY VAM-PIRES.
WHY DON'T YOU GO TAKE A NAP?
YEAH. I THINK I WILL.

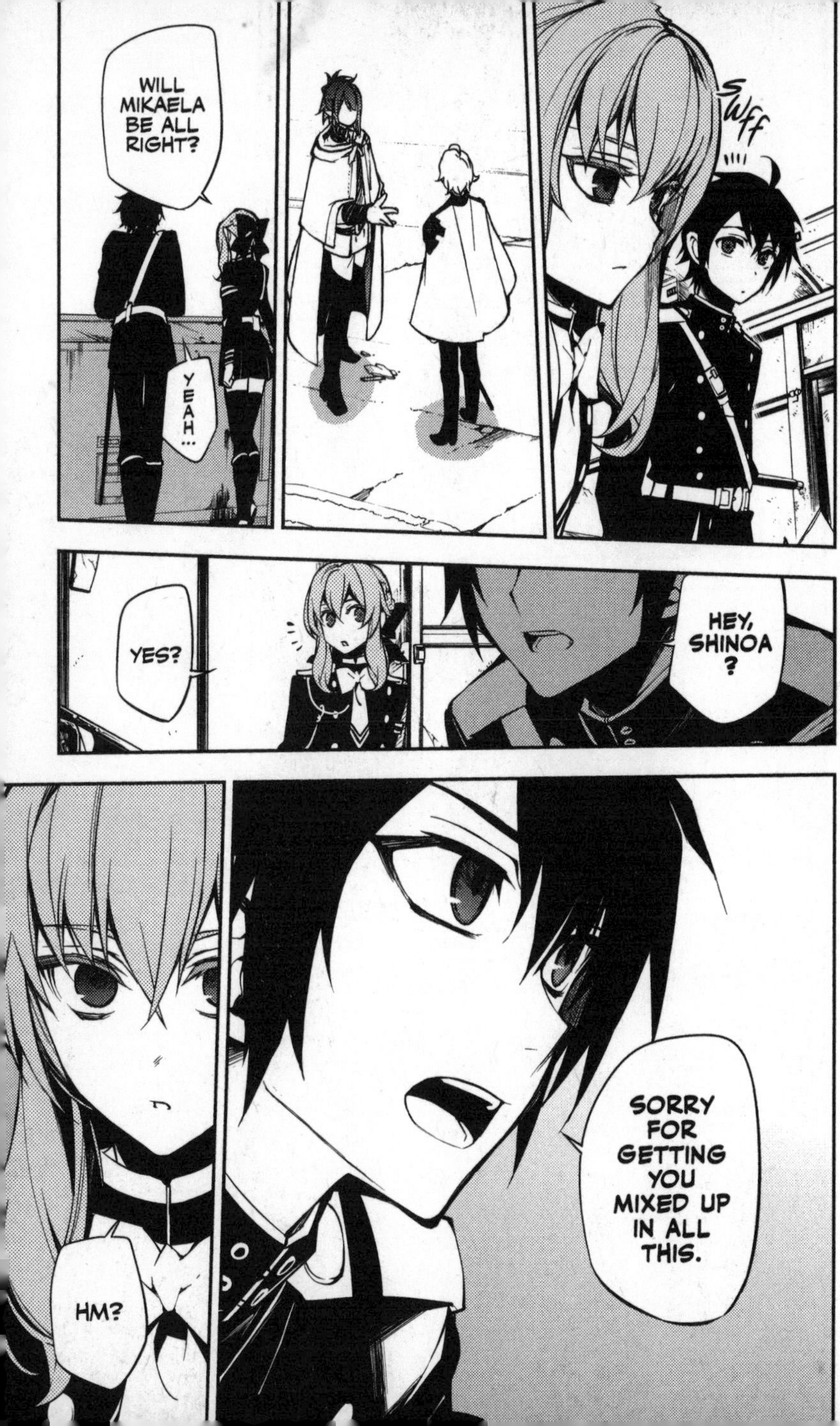
SWFF
WILL MIKAELA BE ALL RIGHT?
YEAH...
HEY, SHINOA?
YES?
SORRY FOR GETTING YOU MIXED UP IN ALL THIS.
HM?

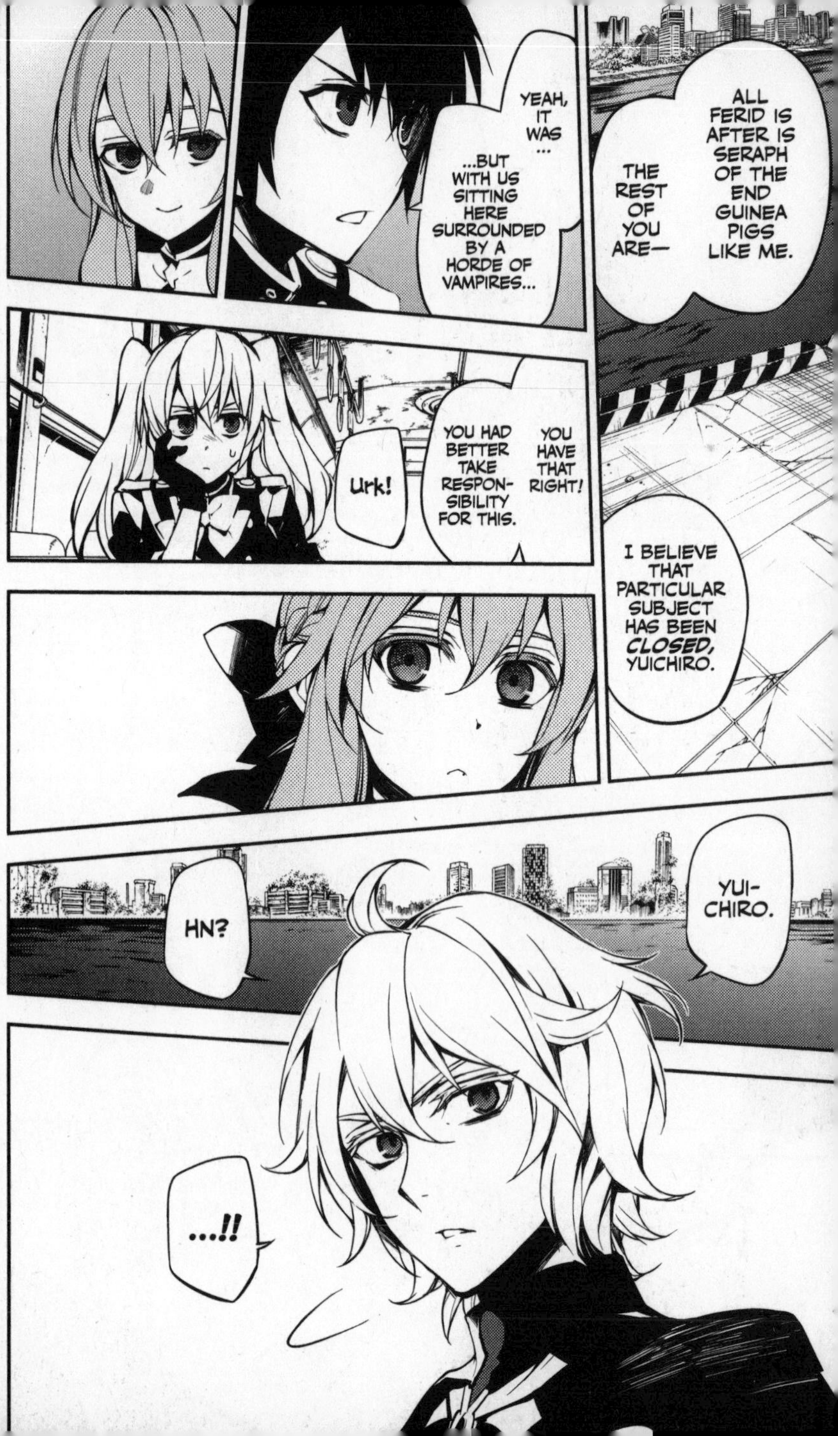

ALL FERID IS AFTER IS SERAPH OF THE END GUINEA PIGS LIKE ME.
THE REST OF YOU ARE—
I BELIEVE THAT PARTICULAR SUBJECT HAS BEEN *CLOSED,* YUICHIRO.
YEAH, IT WAS...
...BUT WITH US SITTING HERE SURROUNDED BY A HORDE OF VAMPIRES...
YOU HAVE THAT RIGHT!
YOU HAD BETTER TAKE RESPONSIBILITY FOR THIS.
Urk!
YUI-CHIRO.
HN?
...!!

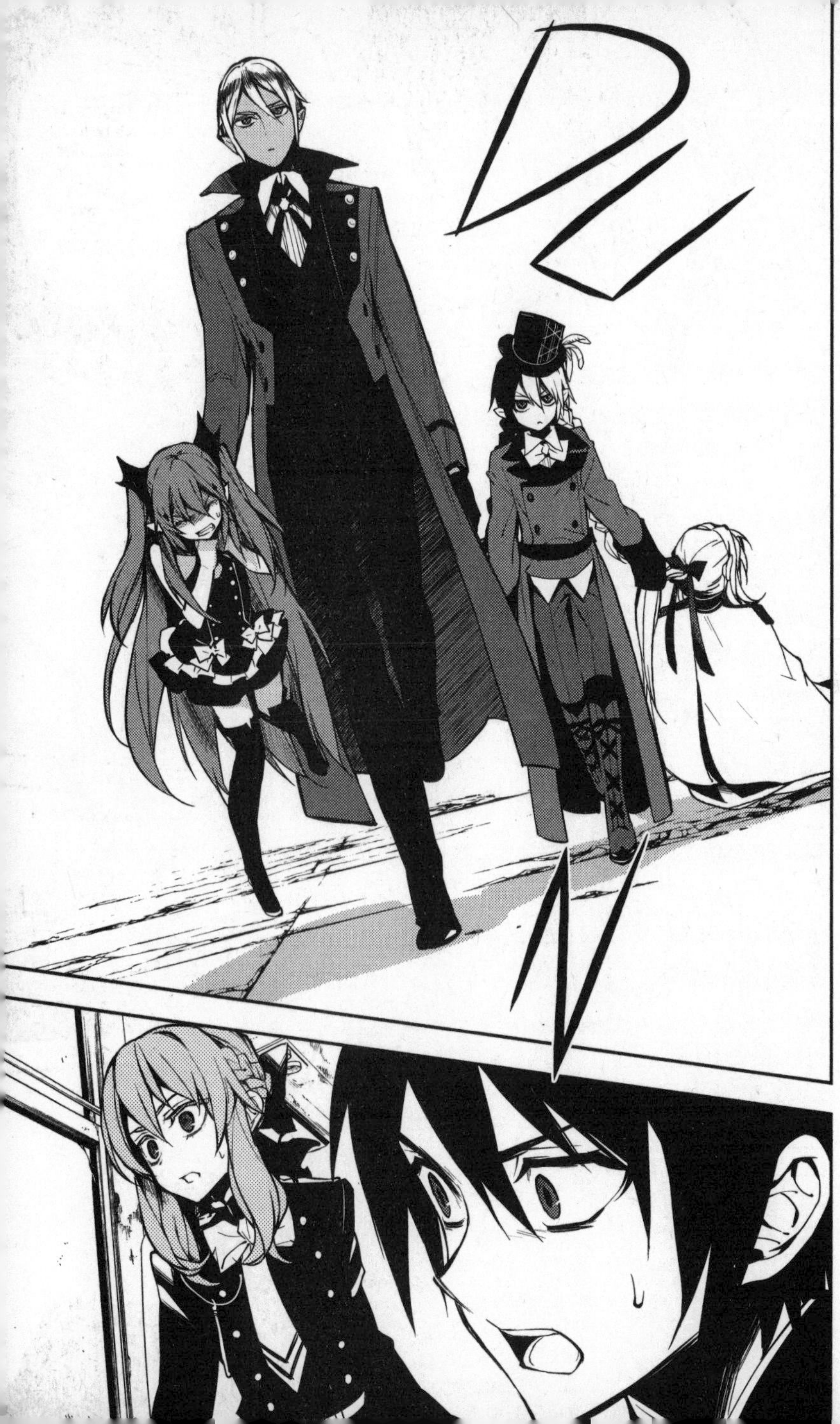

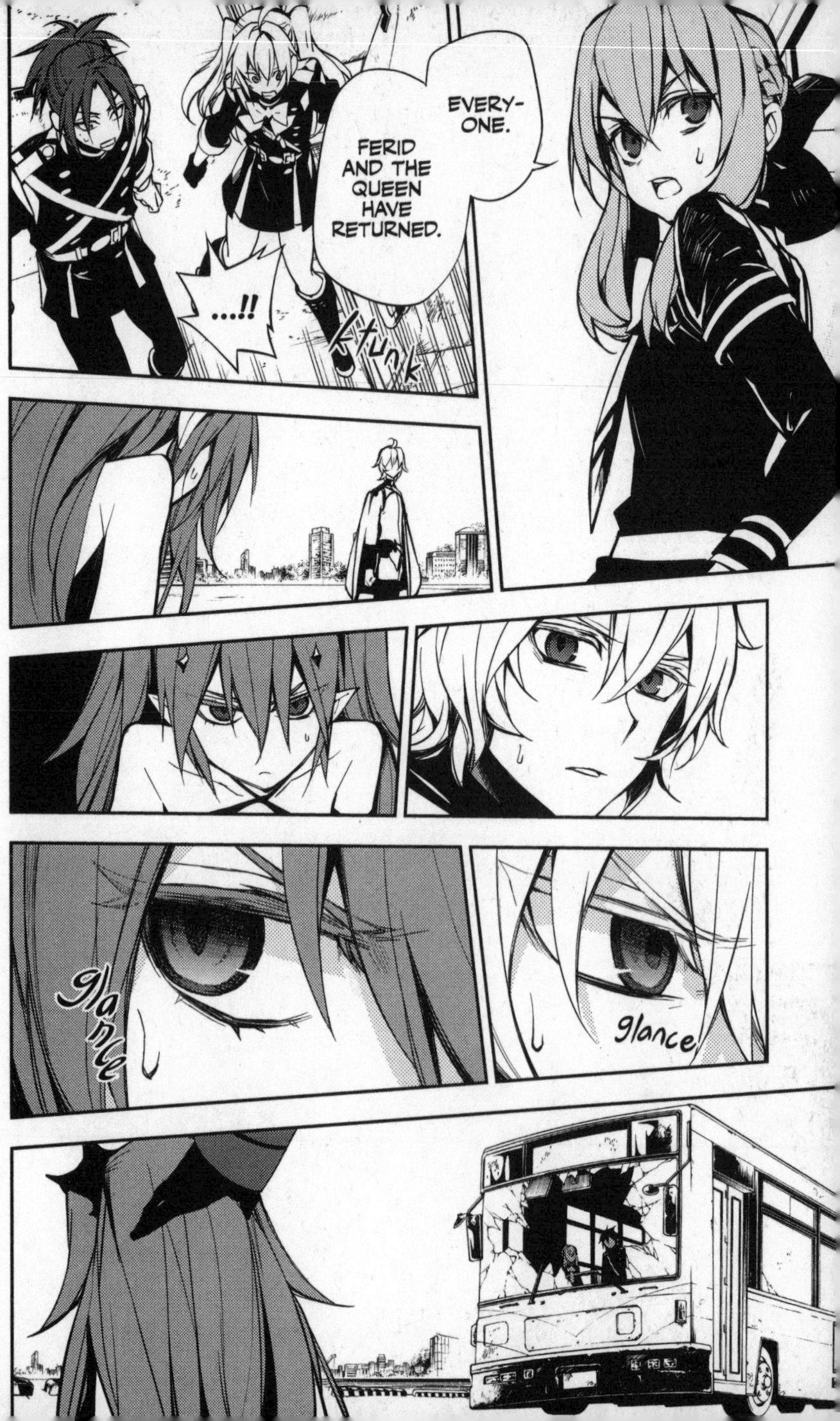
EVERY-ONE.
FERID AND THE QUEEN HAVE RETURNED.
...!!
ktunk
glance
glance

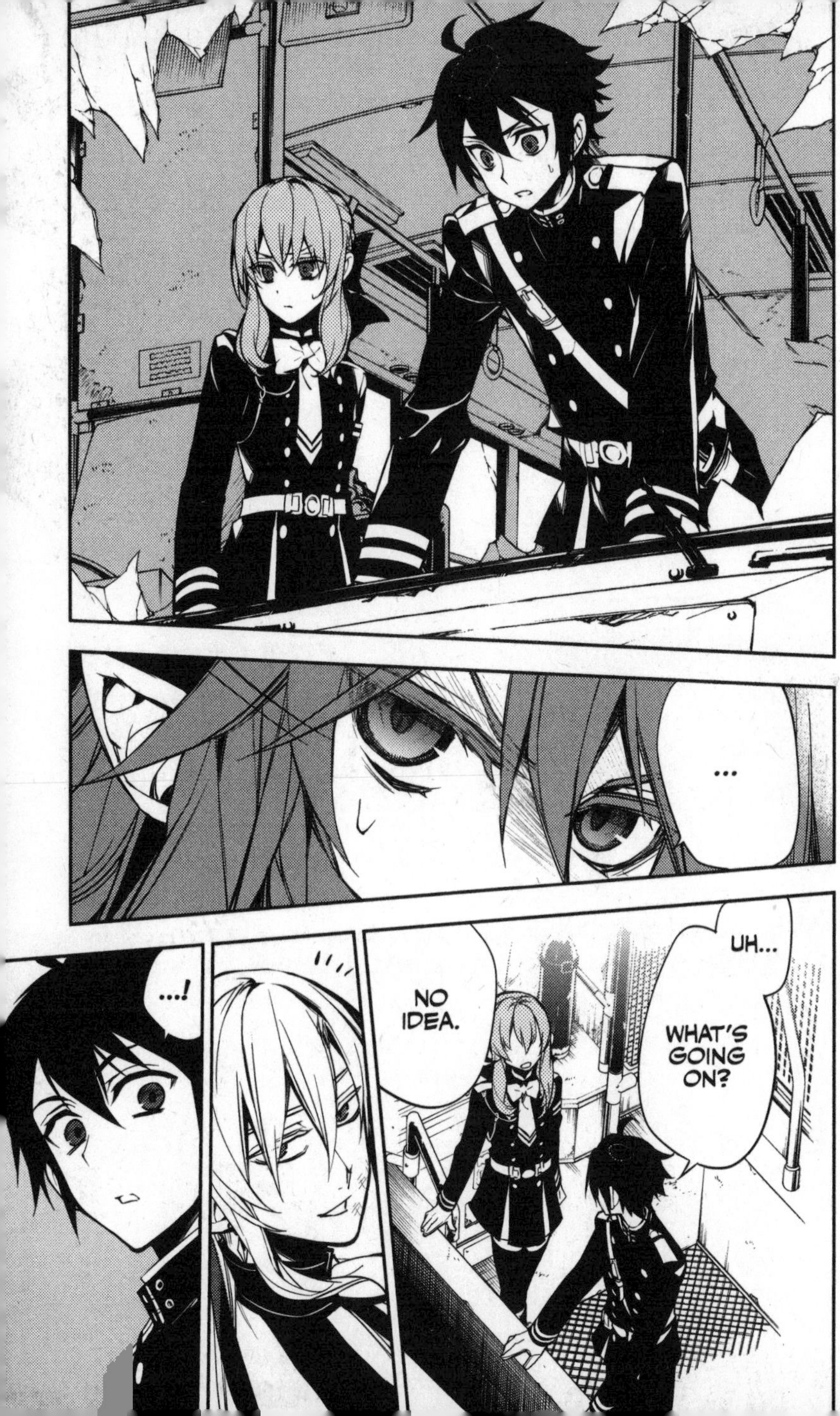
...
UH...
WHAT'S GOING ON?
NO IDEA.
...!

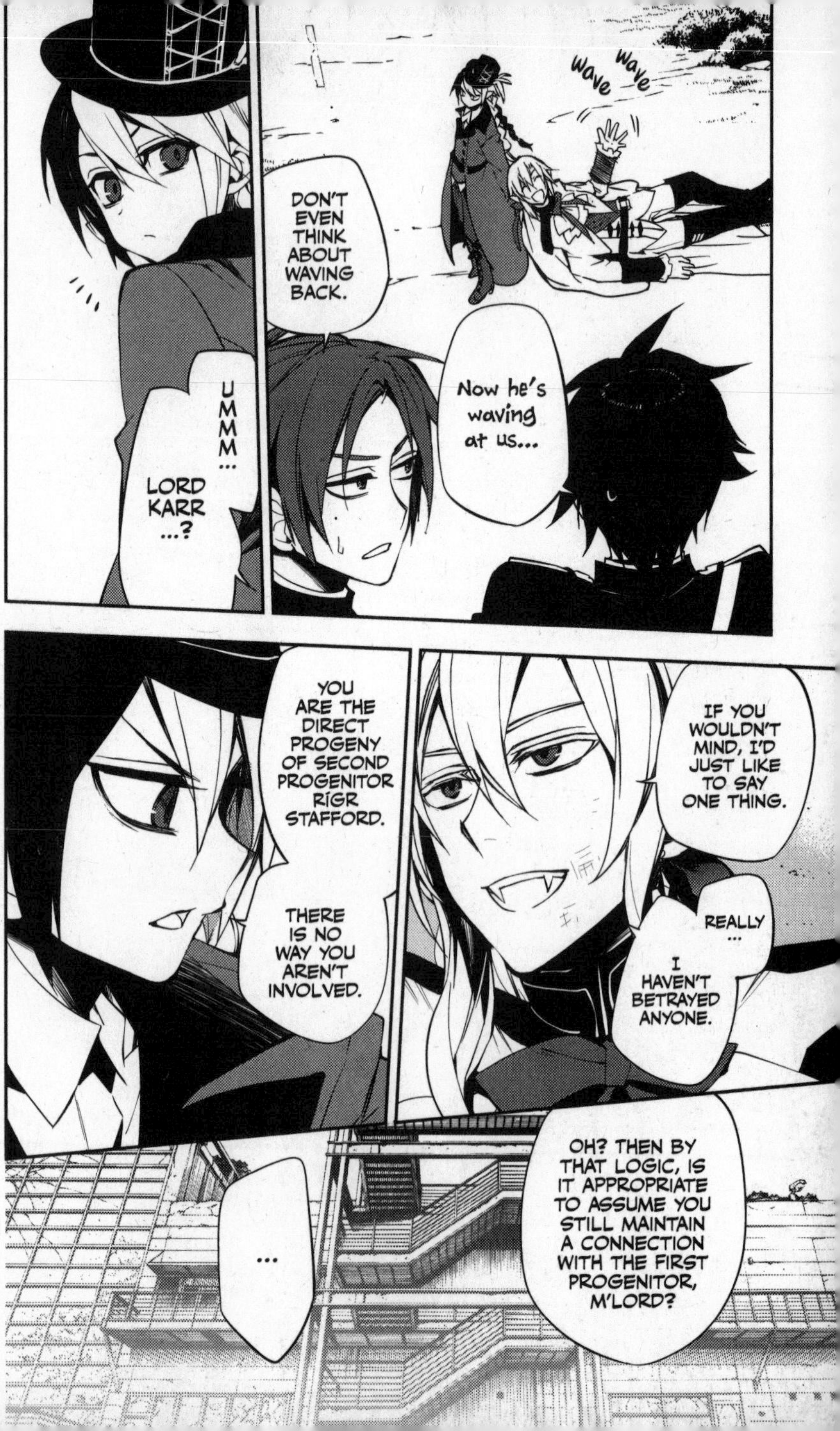
wave wave
Now he's waving at us...
DON'T EVEN THINK ABOUT WAVING BACK.
UMMM... LORD KARR...?
IF YOU WOULDN'T MIND, I'D JUST LIKE TO SAY ONE THING.
REALLY... I HAVEN'T BETRAYED ANYONE.
YOU ARE THE DIRECT PROGENY OF SECOND PROGENITOR RIGR STAFFORD.
THERE IS NO WAY YOU AREN'T INVOLVED.
OH? THEN BY THAT LOGIC, IS IT APPROPRIATE TO ASSUME YOU STILL MAINTAIN A CONNECTION WITH THE FIRST PROGENITOR, M'LORD?
...

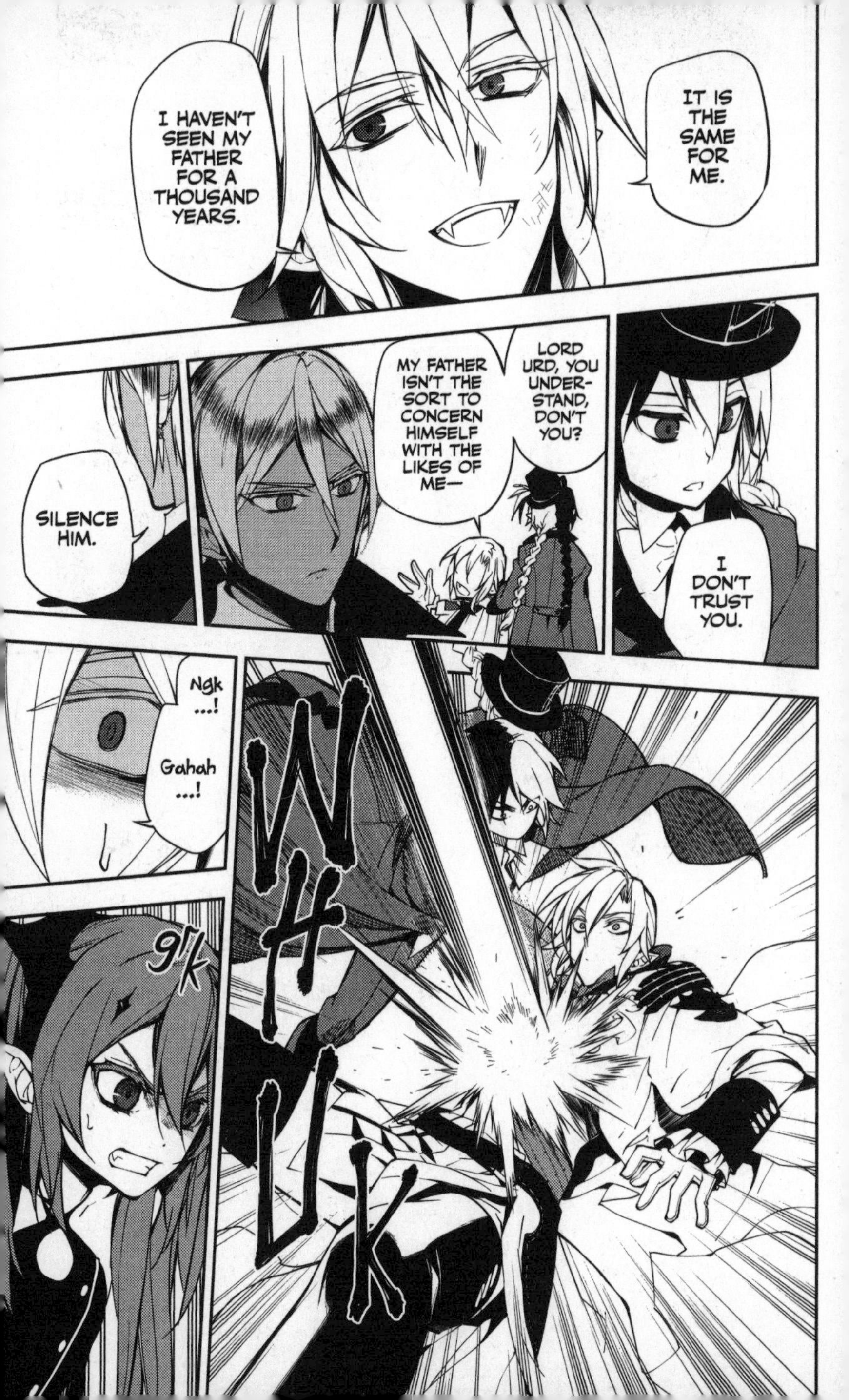
IT IS THE SAME FOR ME.
I HAVEN'T SEEN MY FATHER FOR A THOUSAND YEARS.
I DON'T TRUST YOU.
LORD URD, YOU UNDERSTAND, DON'T YOU?
MY FATHER ISN'T THE SORT TO CONCERN HIMSELF WITH THE LIKES OF ME—
SILENCE HIM.
WHACK
Ngk ...!
Gahah ...!
g'k

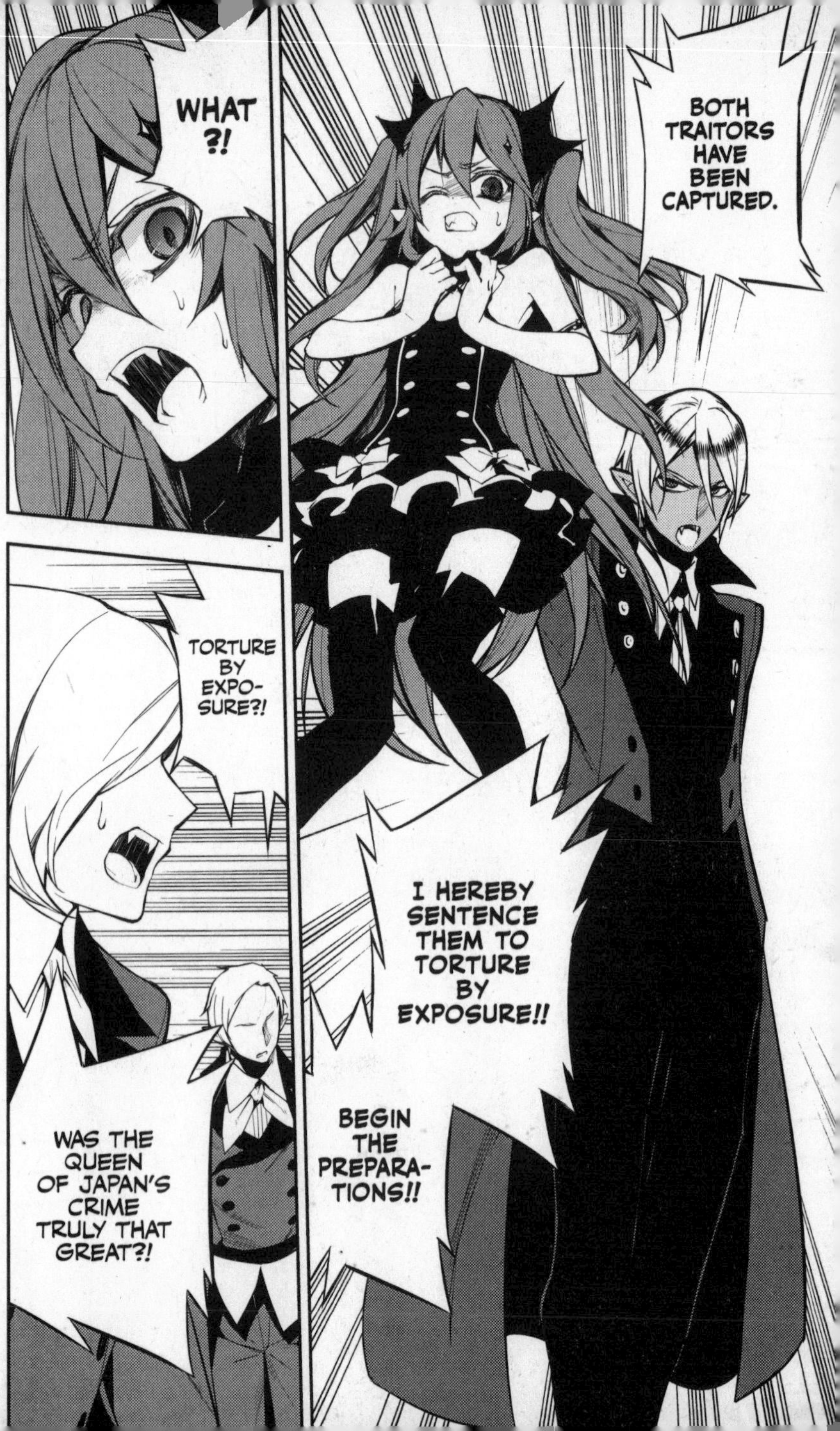
BOTH TRAITORS HAVE BEEN CAPTURED.
I HEREBY SENTENCE THEM TO TORTURE BY EXPOSURE!!
BEGIN THE PREPARATIONS!!
WHAT ?!
TORTURE BY EXPOSURE?!
WAS THE QUEEN OF JAPAN'S CRIME TRULY THAT GREAT?!

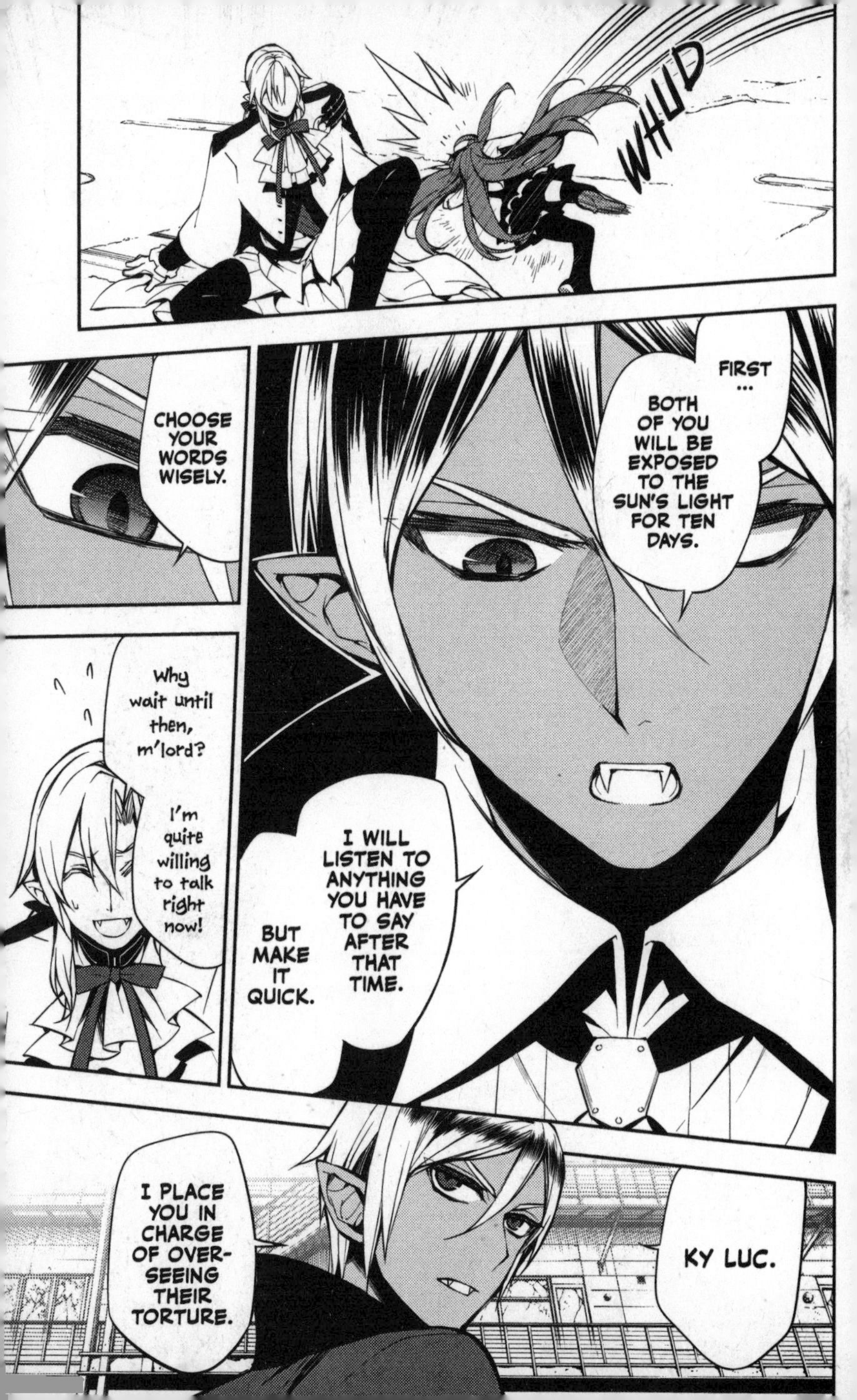
WHUD
FIRST... BOTH OF YOU WILL BE EXPOSED TO THE SUN'S LIGHT FOR TEN DAYS.
CHOOSE YOUR WORDS WISELY.
I WILL LISTEN TO ANYTHING YOU HAVE TO SAY AFTER THAT TIME.
BUT MAKE IT QUICK.
Why wait until then, m'lord?
I'm quite willing to talk right now!
KY LUC.
I PLACE YOU IN CHARGE OF OVER-SEEING THEIR TORTURE.

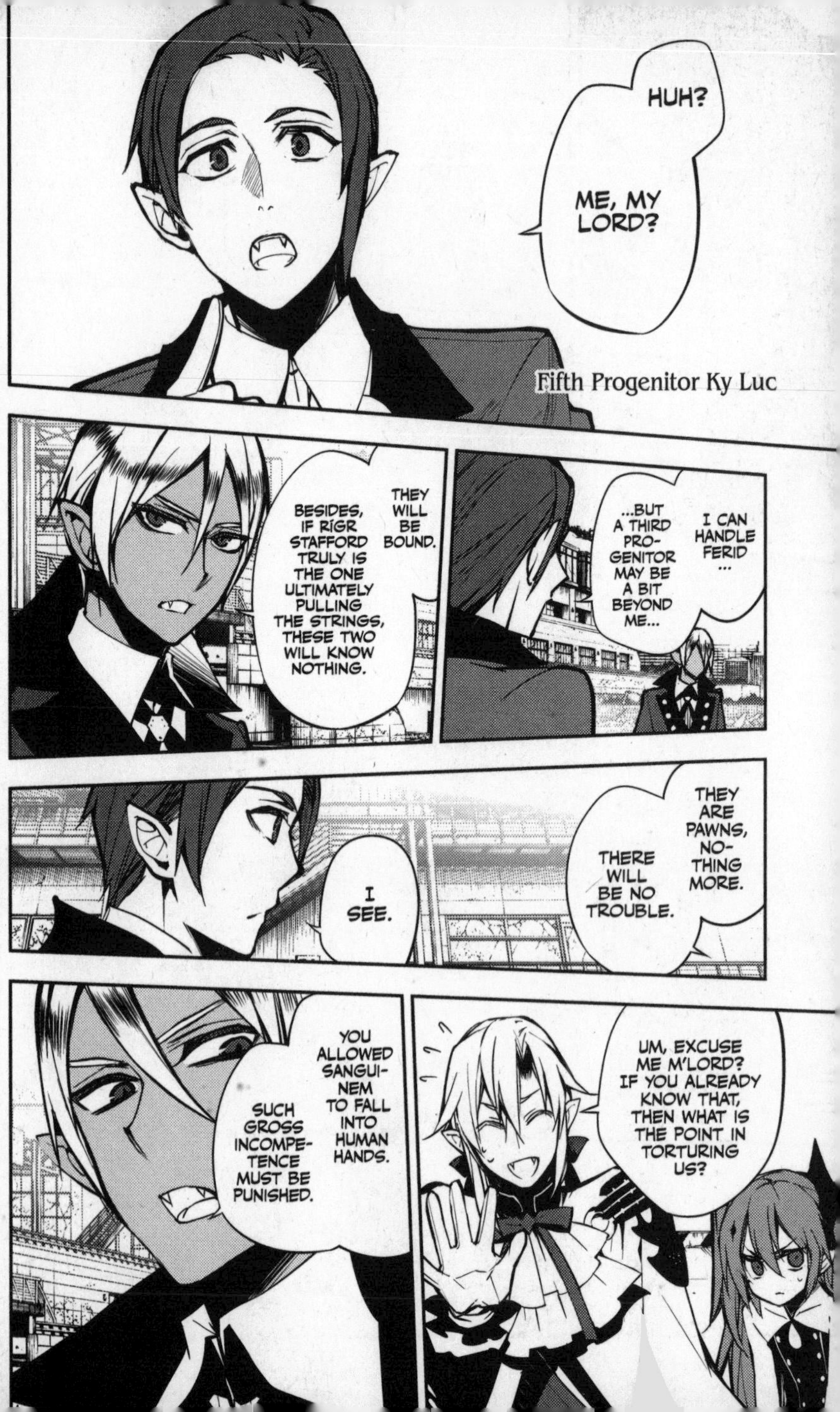
HUH?
ME, MY LORD?
Fifth Progenitor Ky Luc
I CAN HANDLE FERID ...
...BUT A THIRD PROGENITOR MAY BE A BIT BEYOND ME...
THEY WILL BE BOUND.
BESIDES, IF RIGR STAFFORD TRULY IS THE ONE ULTIMATELY PULLING THE STRINGS, THESE TWO WILL KNOW NOTHING.
THEY ARE PAWNS, NOTHING MORE.
THERE WILL BE NO TROUBLE.
I SEE.
UM, EXCUSE ME M'LORD? IF YOU ALREADY KNOW THAT, THEN WHAT IS THE POINT IN TORTURING US?
YOU ALLOWED SANGUINEM TO FALL INTO HUMAN HANDS.
SUCH GROSS INCOMPETENCE MUST BE PUNISHED.

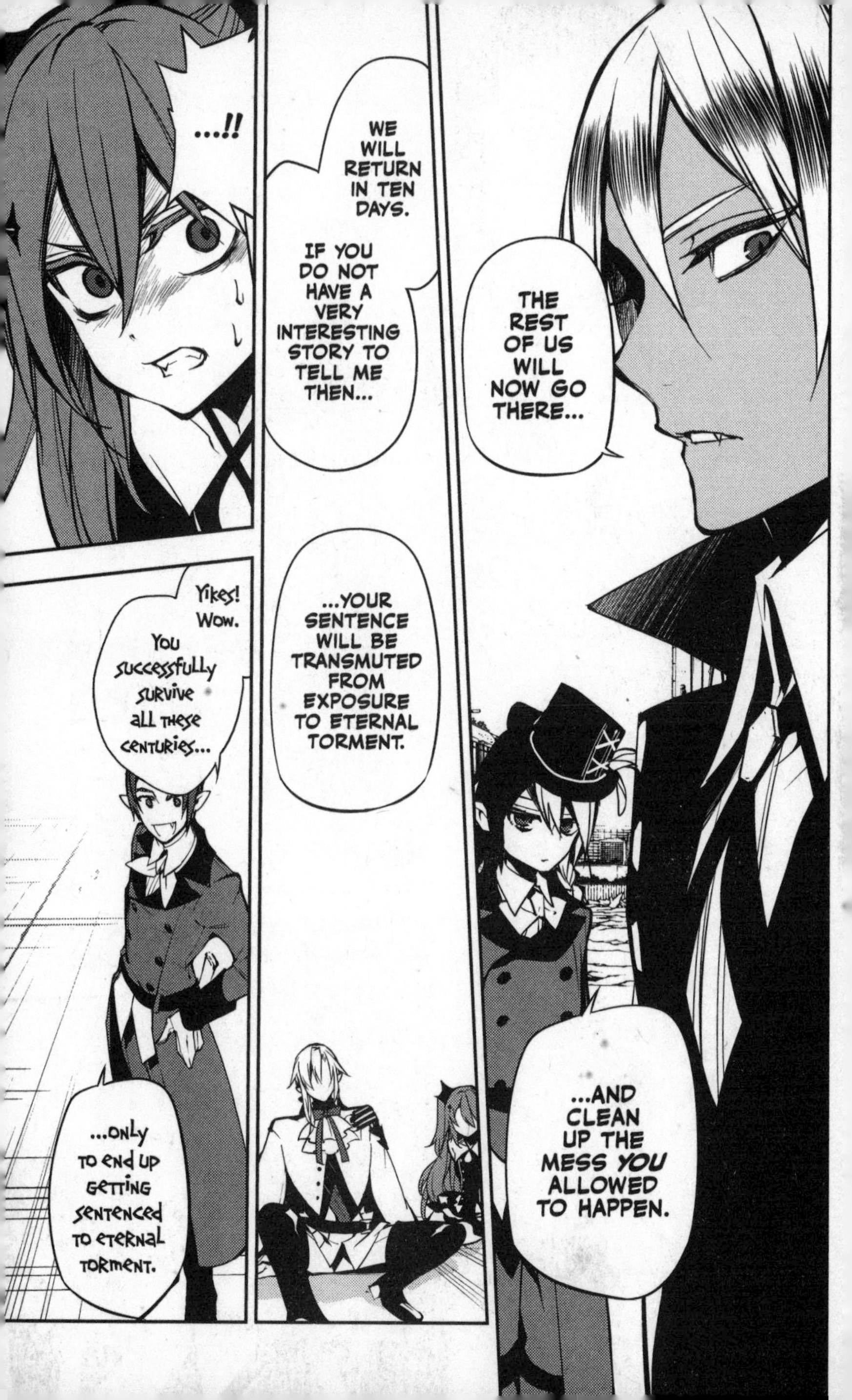
THE REST OF US WILL NOW GO THERE...
...AND CLEAN UP THE MESS *YOU* ALLOWED TO HAPPEN.
WE WILL RETURN IN TEN DAYS.
IF YOU DO NOT HAVE A VERY INTERESTING STORY TO TELL ME THEN...
...YOUR SENTENCE WILL BE TRANSMUTED FROM EXPOSURE TO ETERNAL TORMENT.
...!!
Yikes! Wow.
You successfully survive all these centuries...
...only to end up getting sentenced to eternal torment.

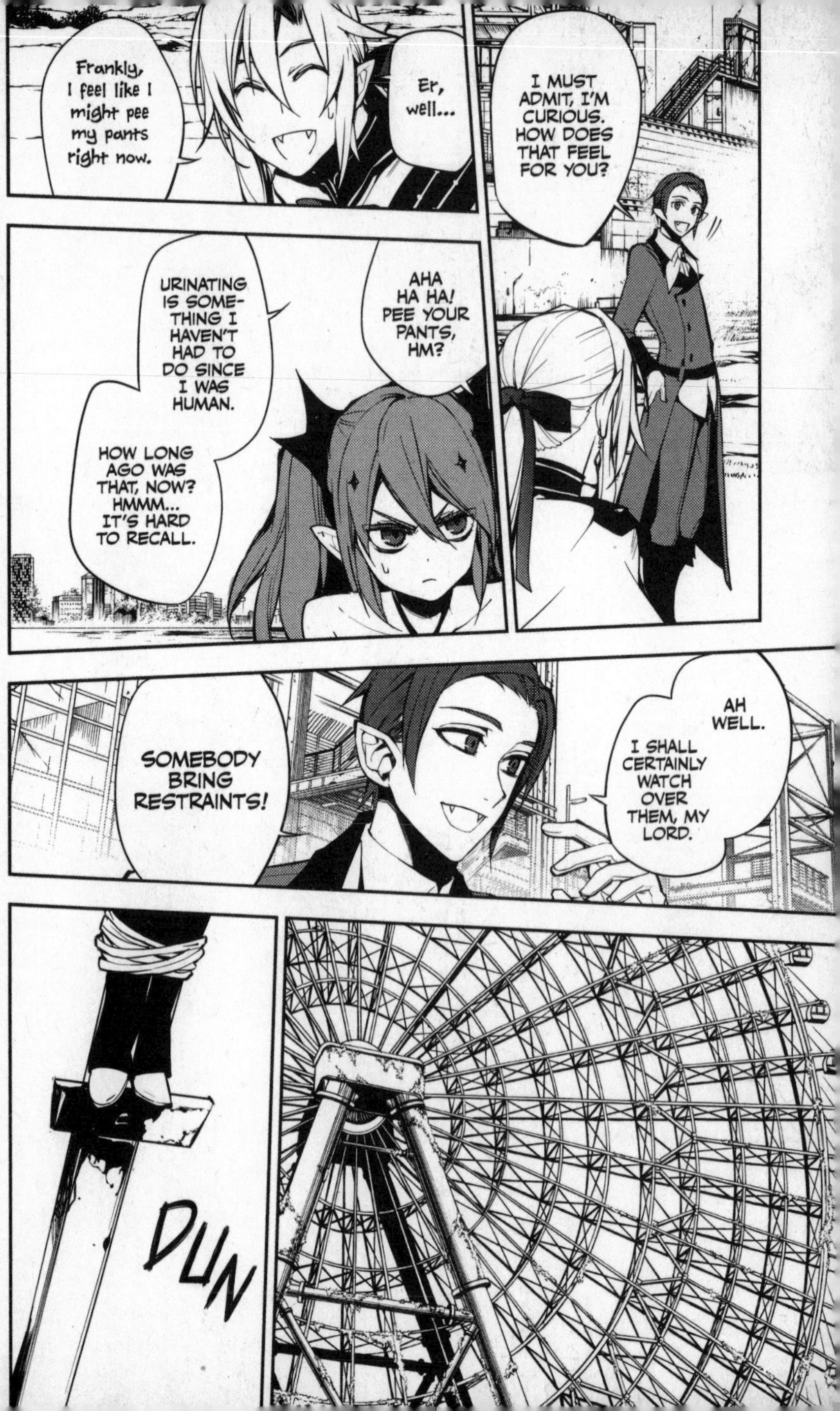
I MUST ADMIT, I'M CURIOUS. HOW DOES THAT FEEL FOR YOU?
Er, well...
Frankly, I feel like I might pee my pants right now.
AHA HA HA! PEE YOUR PANTS, HM?
URINATING IS SOME-THING I HAVEN'T HAD TO DO SINCE I WAS HUMAN.
HOW LONG AGO WAS THAT, NOW? HMMM... IT'S HARD TO RECALL.
AH WELL.
I SHALL CERTAINLY WATCH OVER THEM, MY LORD.
SOMEBODY BRING RESTRAINTS!
DUN

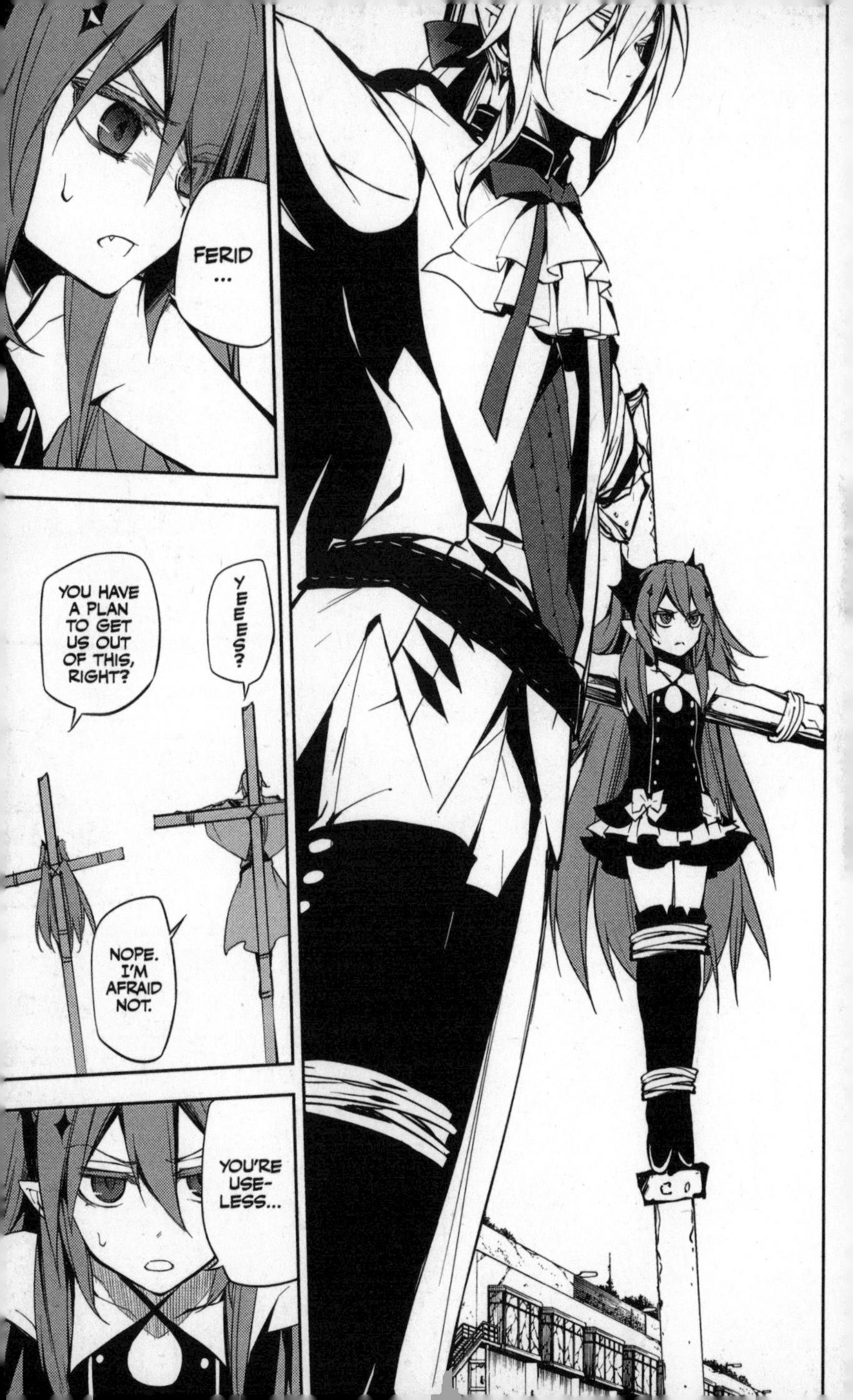
FERID ...
YEEES?
YOU HAVE A PLAN TO GET US OUT OF THIS, RIGHT?
NOPE. I'M AFRAID NOT.
YOU'RE USE-LESS...

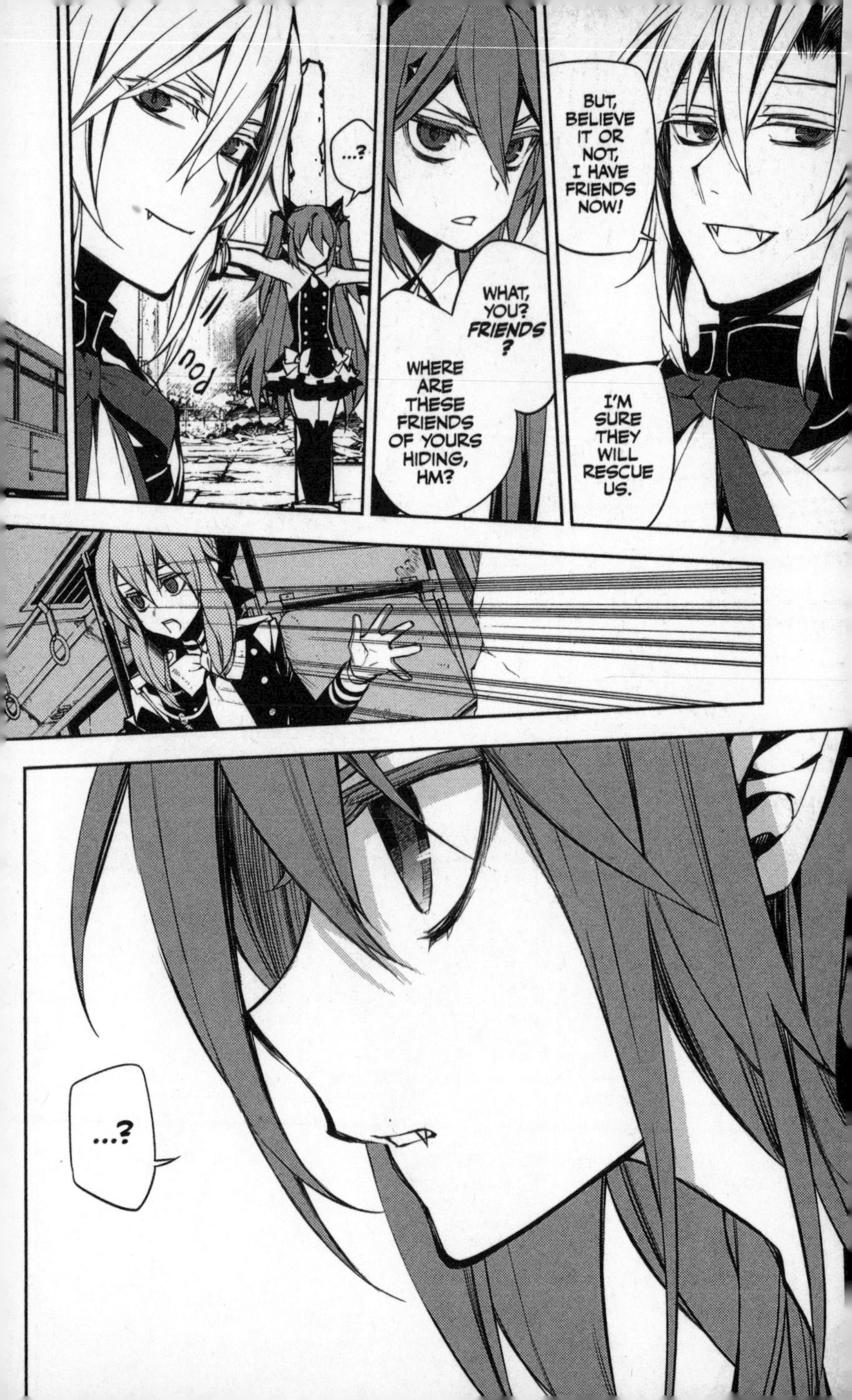

BUT, BELIEVE IT OR NOT, I HAVE FRIENDS NOW!
I'M SURE THEY WILL RESCUE US.
WHAT, YOU? *FRIENDS*?
WHERE ARE THESE FRIENDS OF YOURS HIDING, HM?
...?
...?

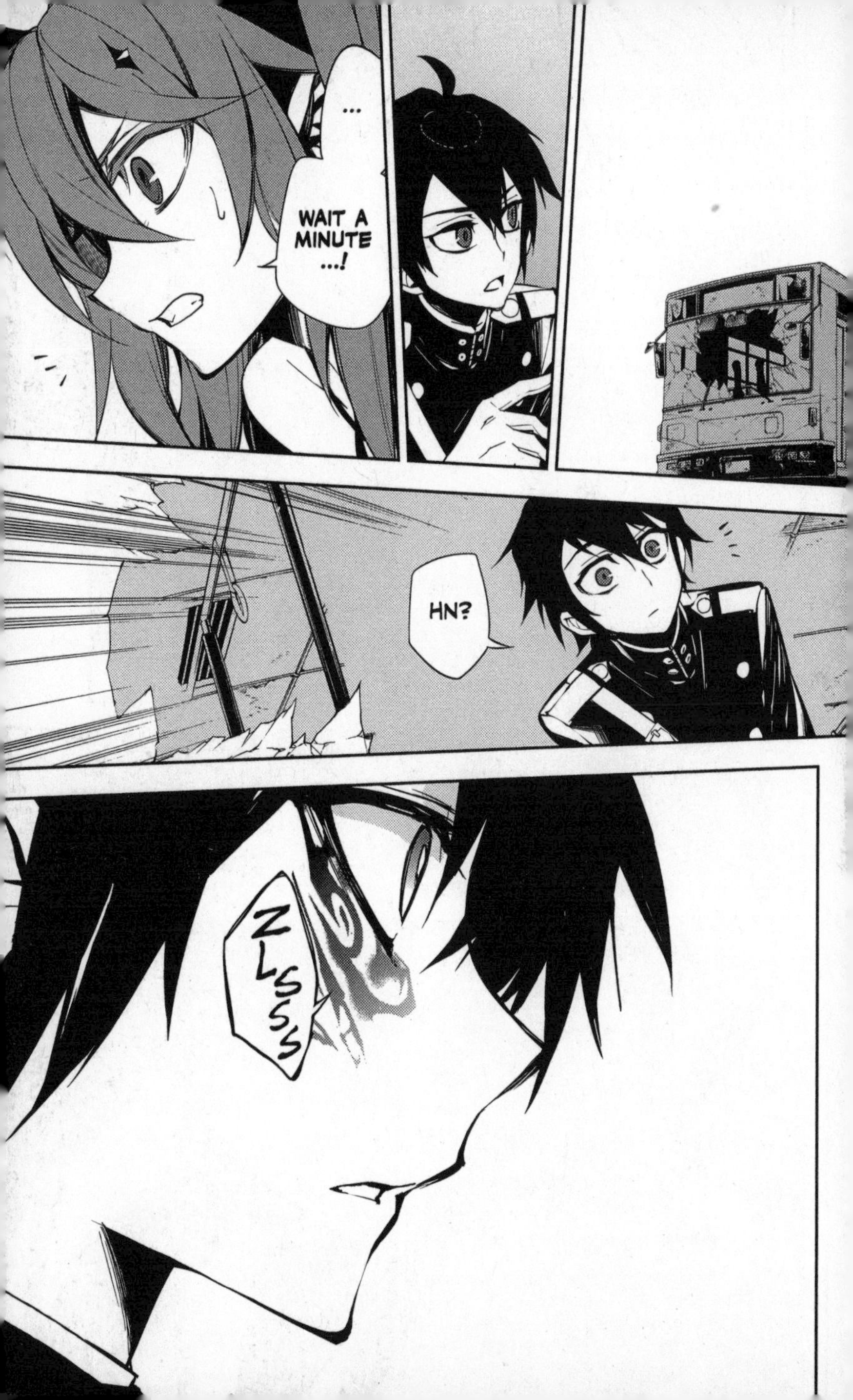
...
WAIT A MINUTE ...!
HN?
ZLSSS

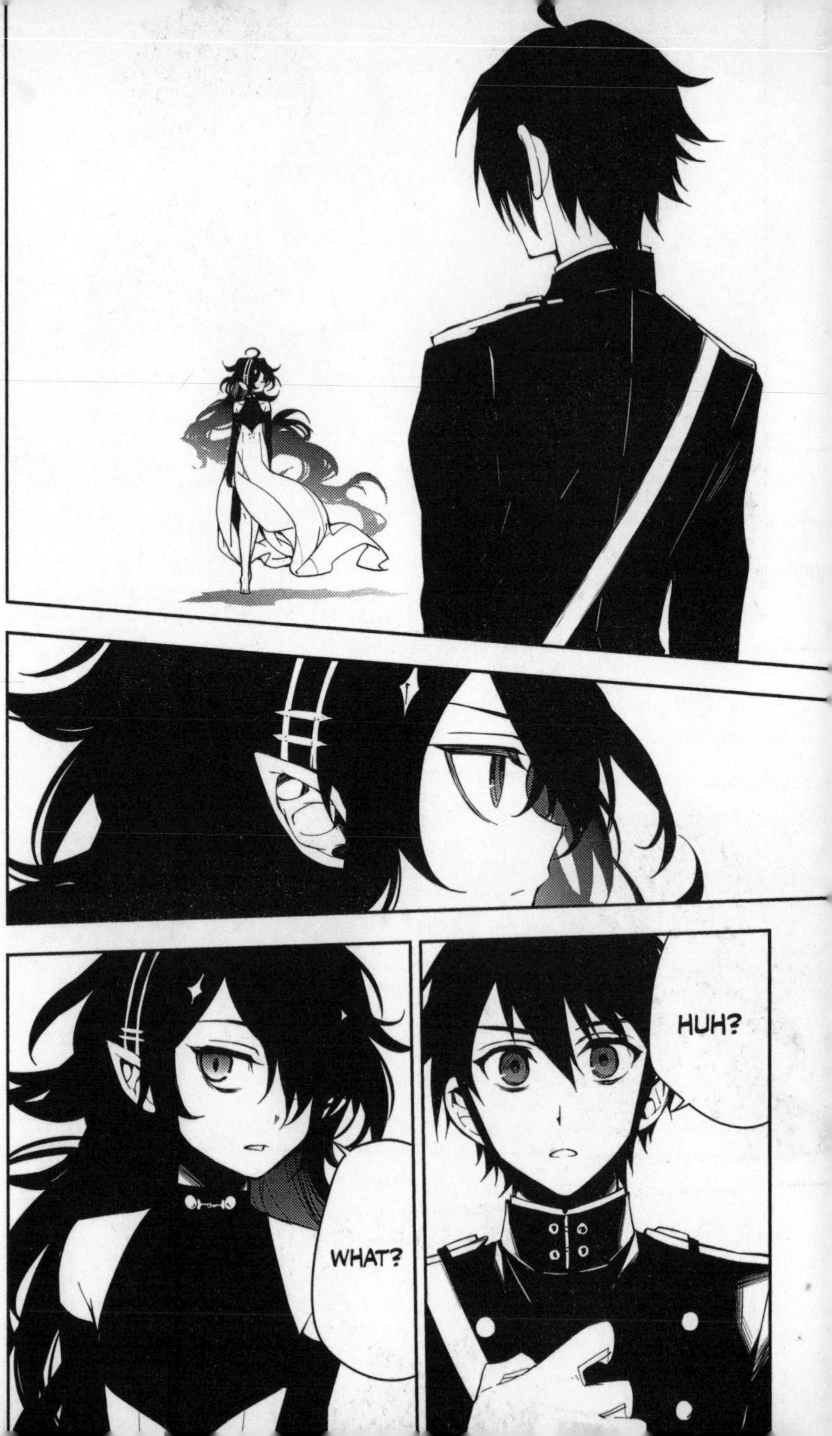
HUH?
WHAT?

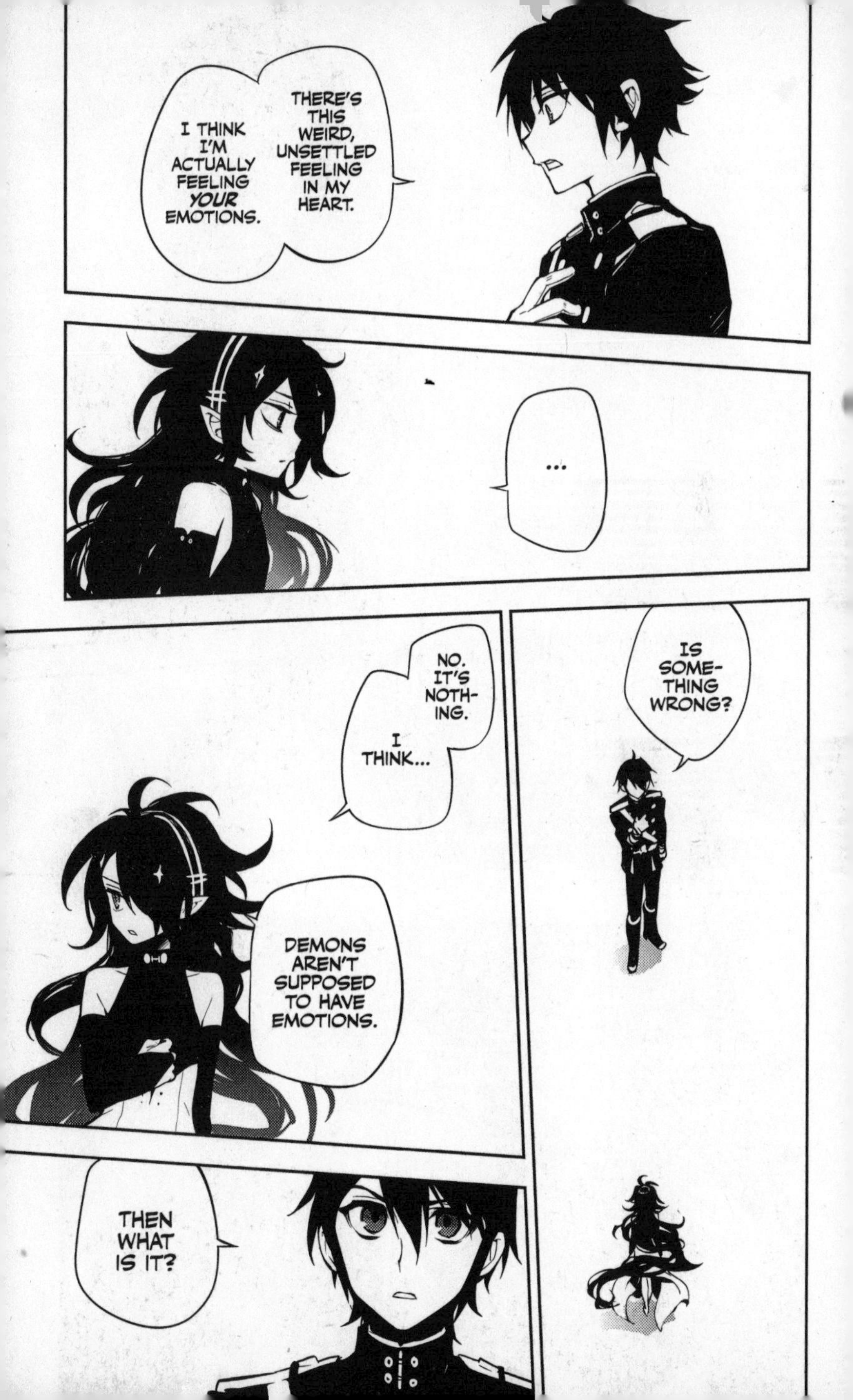
THERE'S THIS WEIRD, UNSETTLED FEELING IN MY HEART.
I THINK I'M ACTUALLY FEELING *YOUR* EMOTIONS.
...
IS SOME-THING WRONG?
NO. IT'S NOTH-ING.
I THINK...
DEMONS AREN'T SUPPOSED TO HAVE EMOTIONS.
THEN WHAT IS IT?

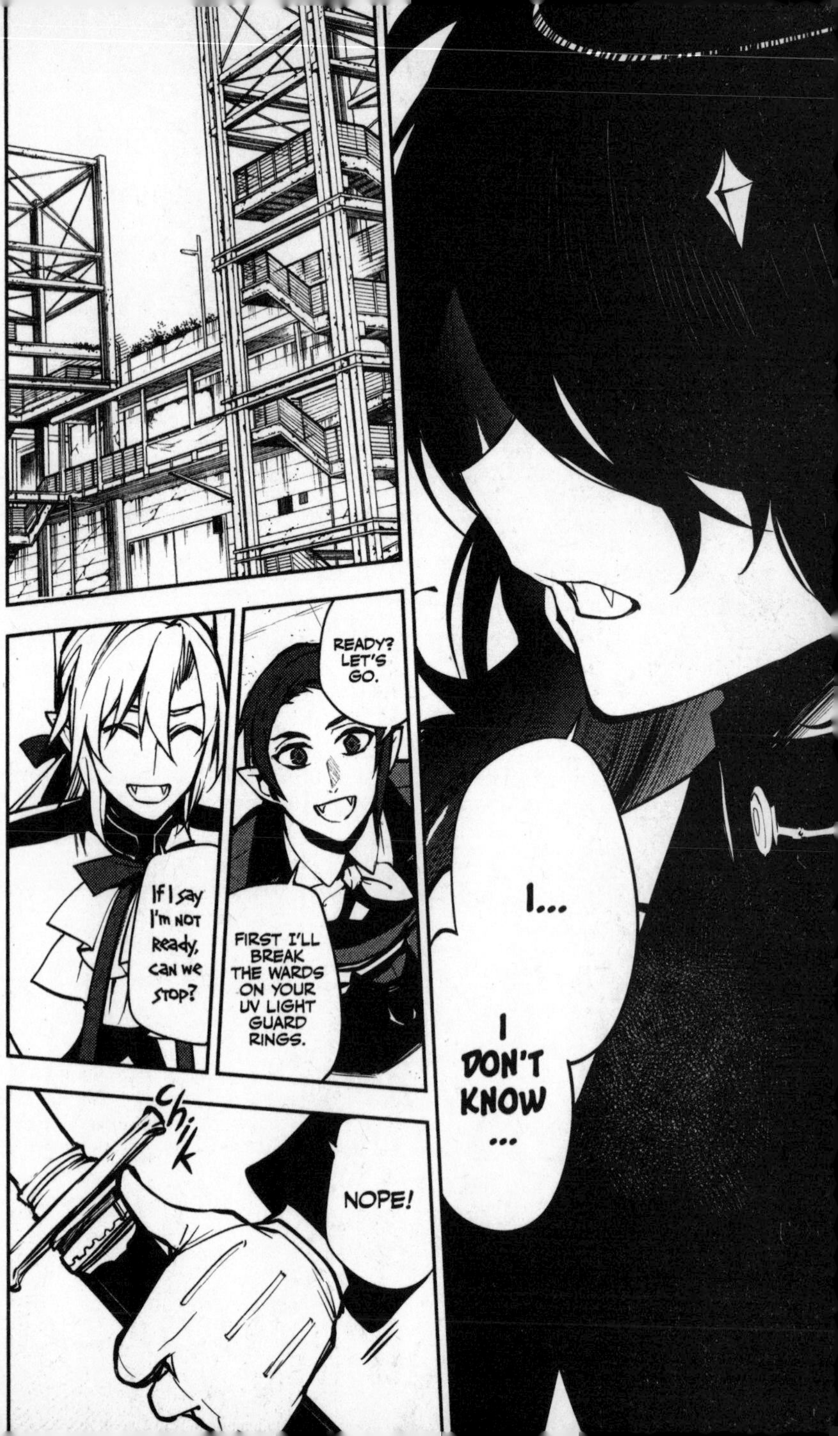
I...
I DON'T KNOW ...
READY? LET'S GO.
FIRST I'LL BREAK THE WARDS ON YOUR UV LIGHT GUARD RINGS.
If I say I'm NOT ready, can we stop?
NOPE!
Chik

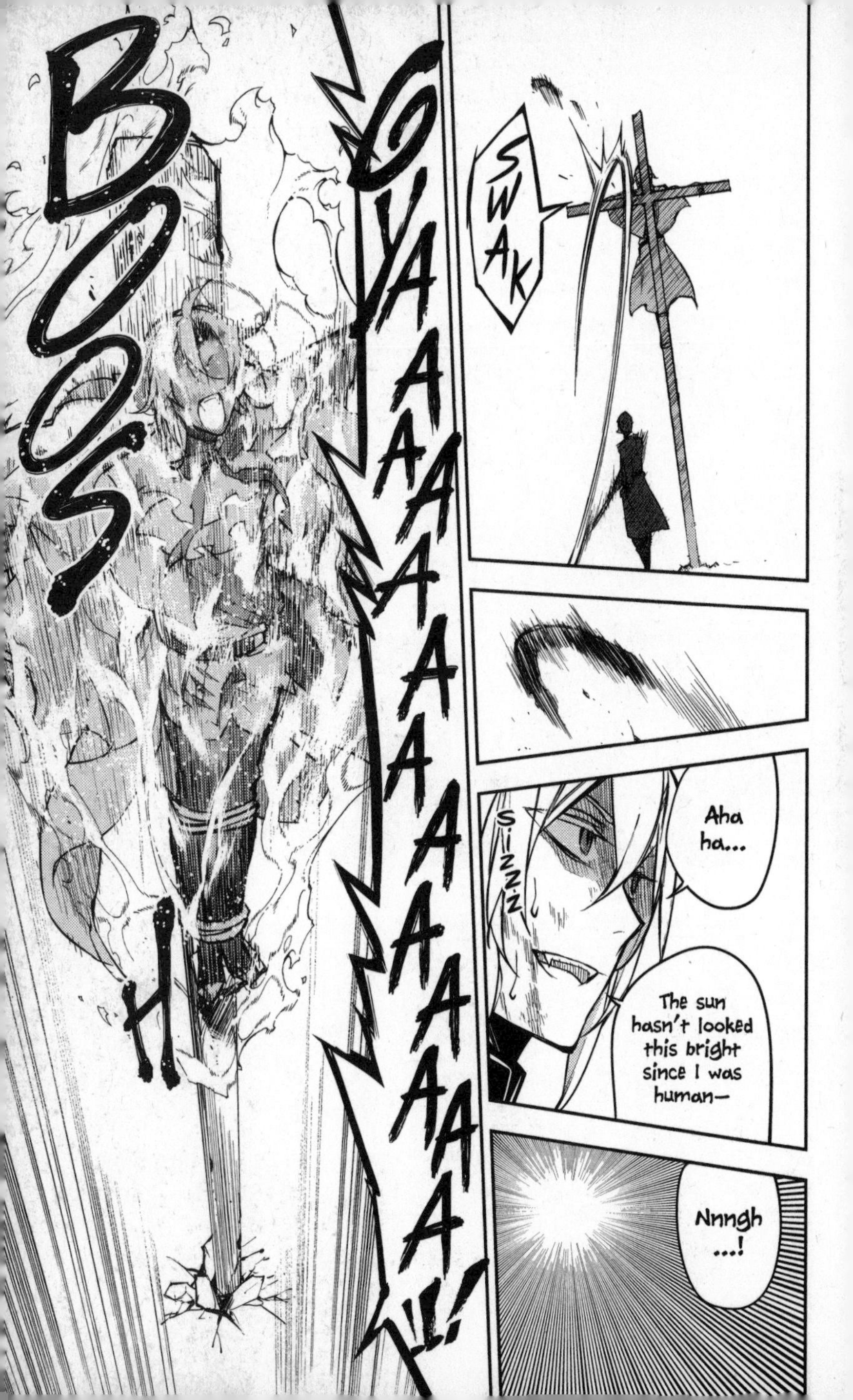
SWAK
SIZZZ
Aha ha...
The sun hasn't looked this bright since I was human—
Nnngh ...!
GYAAAAAAAAAAAAAA!!
BOOSH

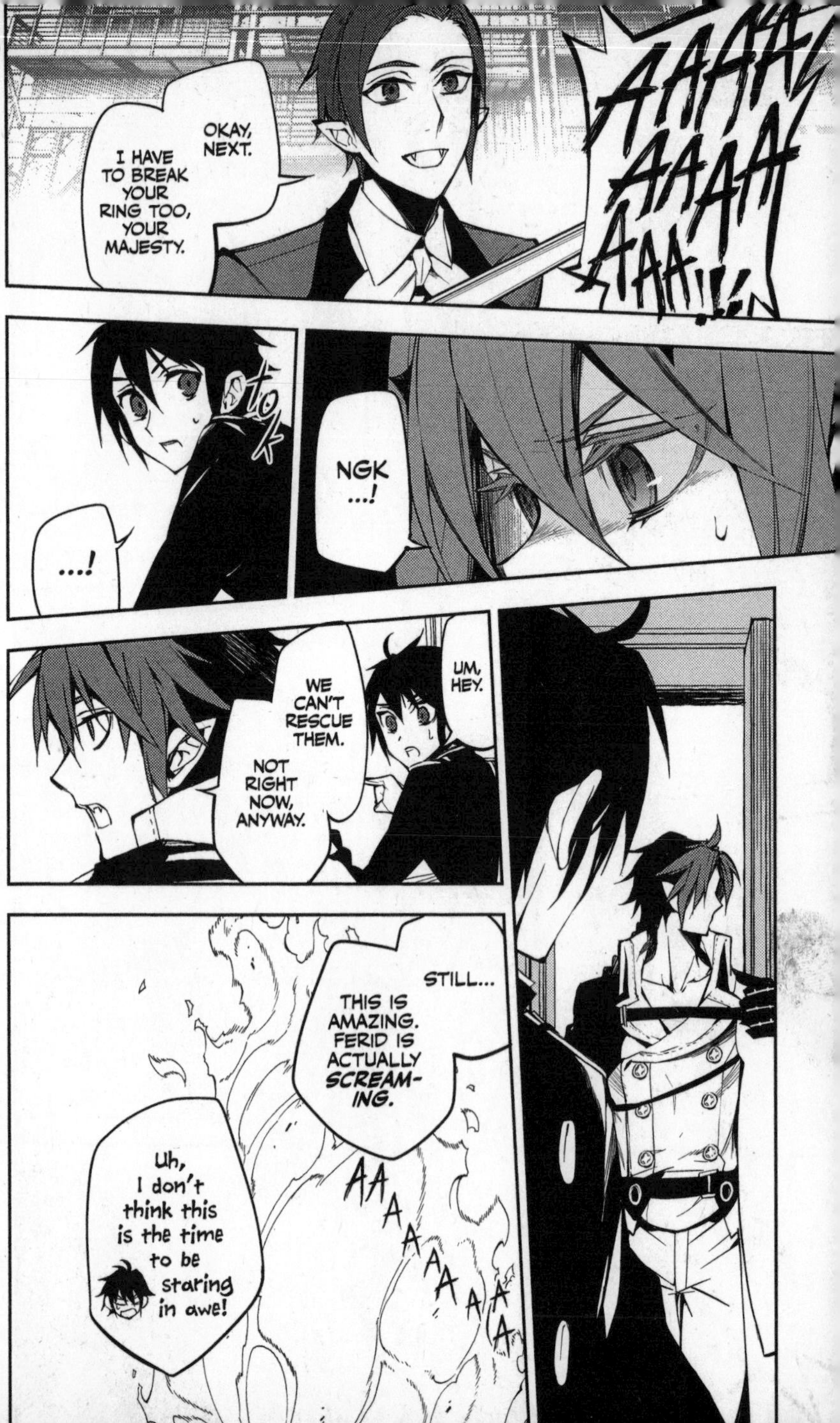
AAAA AAAA AA!!!!
OKAY, NEXT.
I HAVE TO BREAK YOUR RING TOO, YOUR MAJESTY.
NGK ...!
tok
...!
UM, HEY.
WE CAN'T RESCUE THEM.
NOT RIGHT NOW, ANYWAY.
STILL...
THIS IS AMAZING. FERID IS ACTUALLY SCREAMING.
Uh, I don't think this is the time to be staring in awe!
AAAAAAAAAA

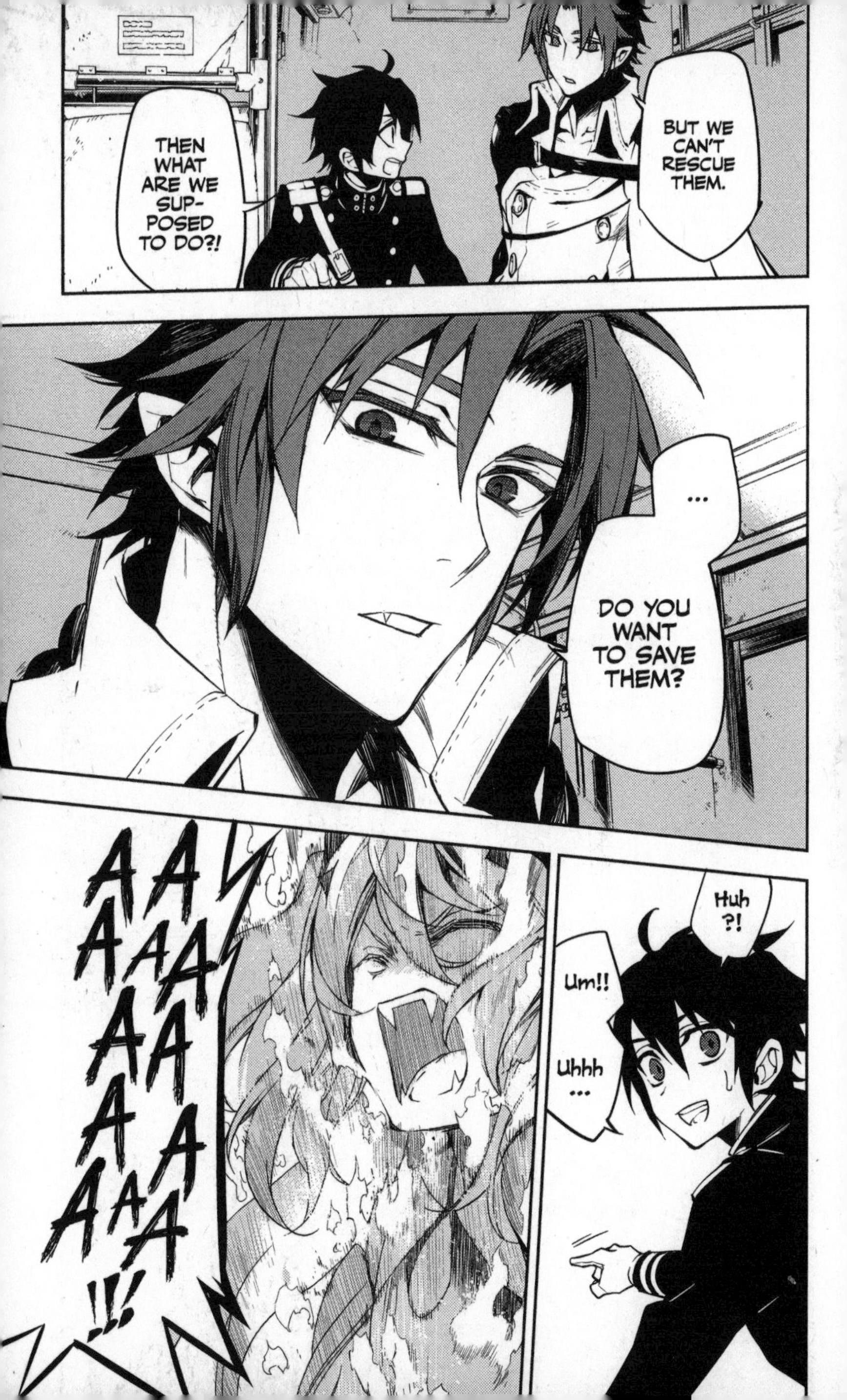
BUT WE CAN'T RESCUE THEM.
THEN WHAT ARE WE SUP-POSED TO DO?!
...
DO YOU WANT TO SAVE THEM?
Huh ?!
Um!!
Uhhh ...
AAAAAAAAAAAAAAAAA !!!

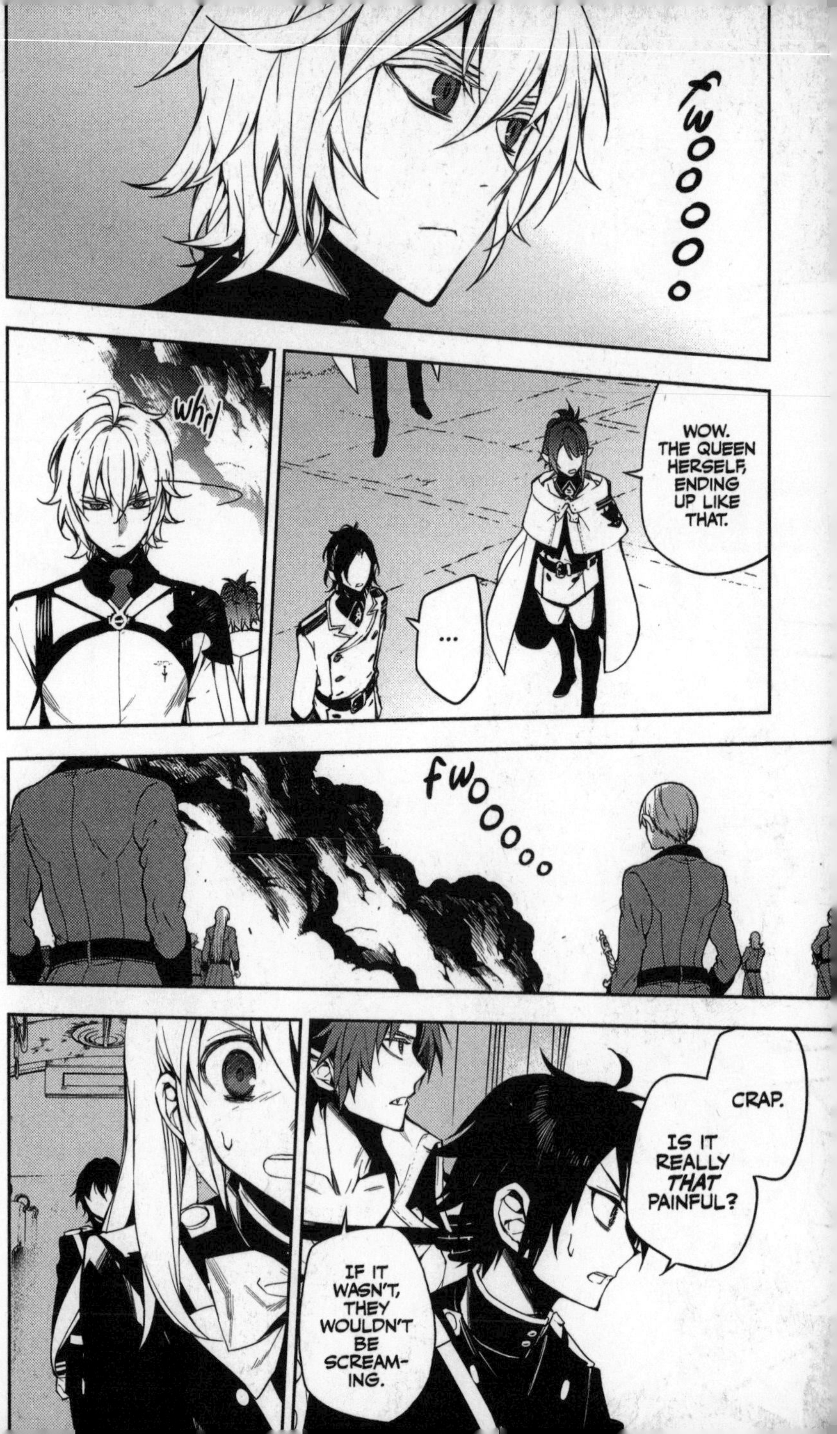
fwoooooo
WOW. THE QUEEN HERSELF, ENDING UP LIKE THAT.
...
whrl
fwoooooo
CRAP.
IS IT REALLY *THAT* PAINFUL?
IF IT WASN'T, THEY WOULDN'T BE SCREAM-ING.

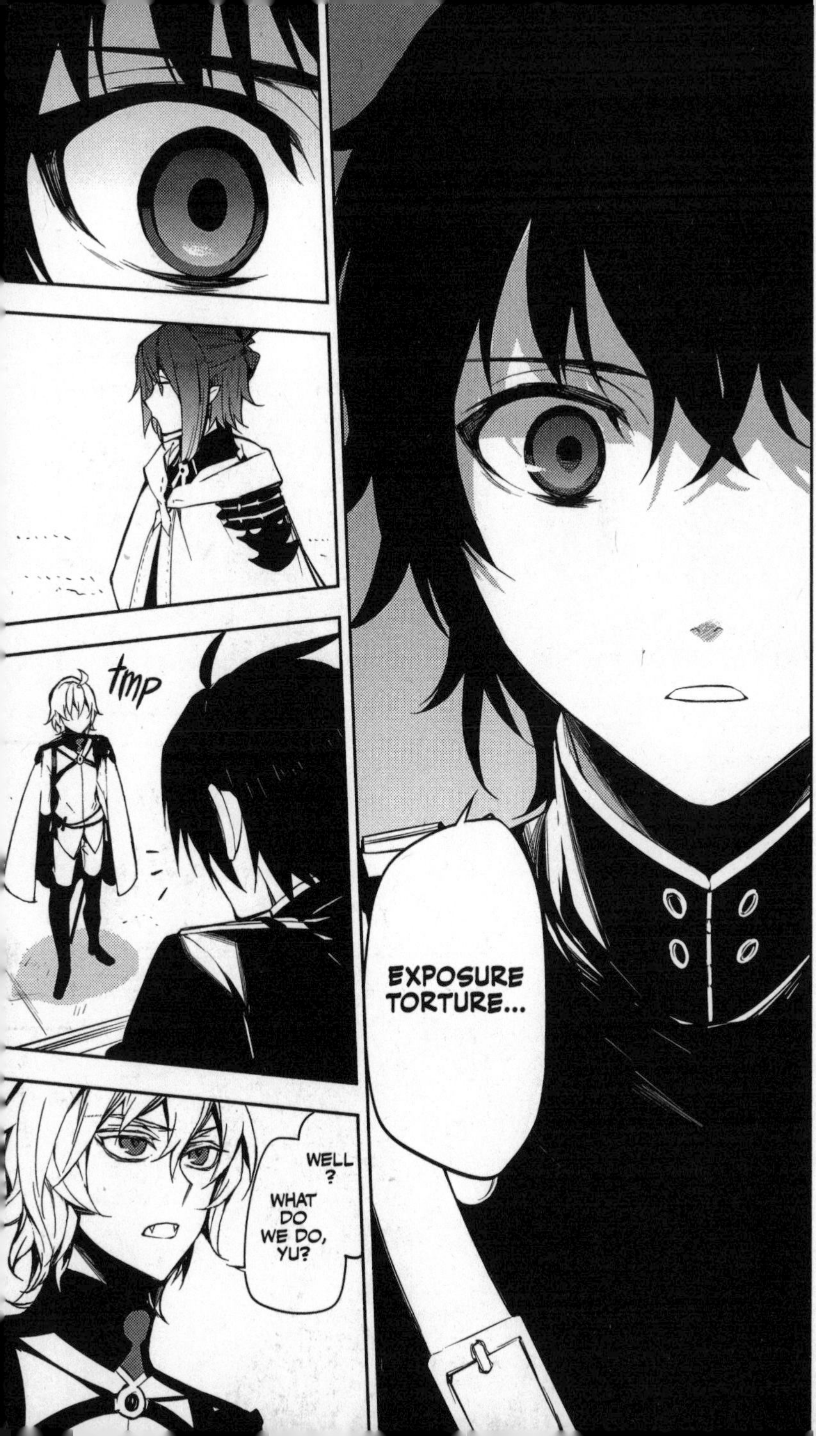
EXPOSURE TORTURE...
tmp
WELL?
WHAT DO WE DO, YU?

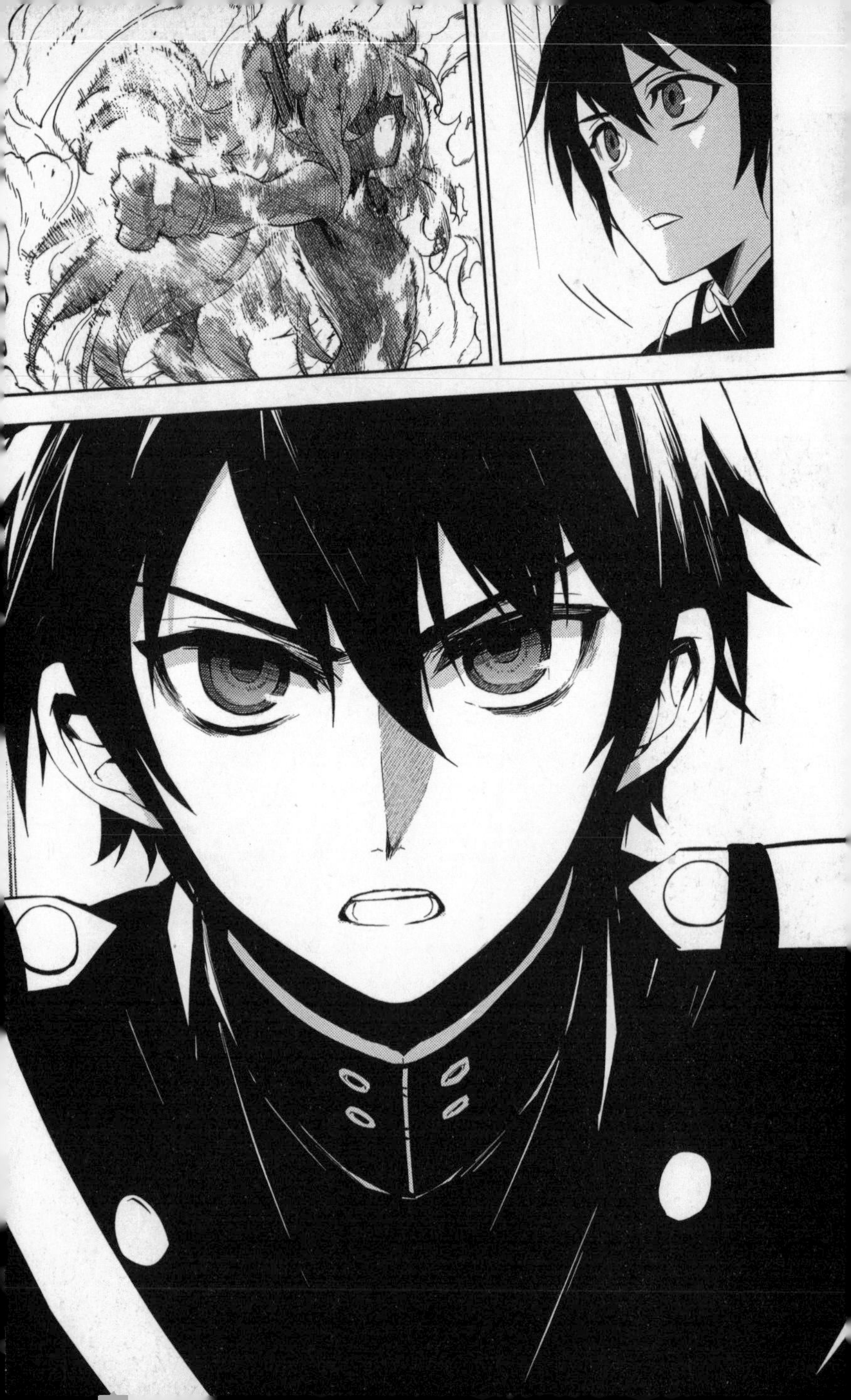

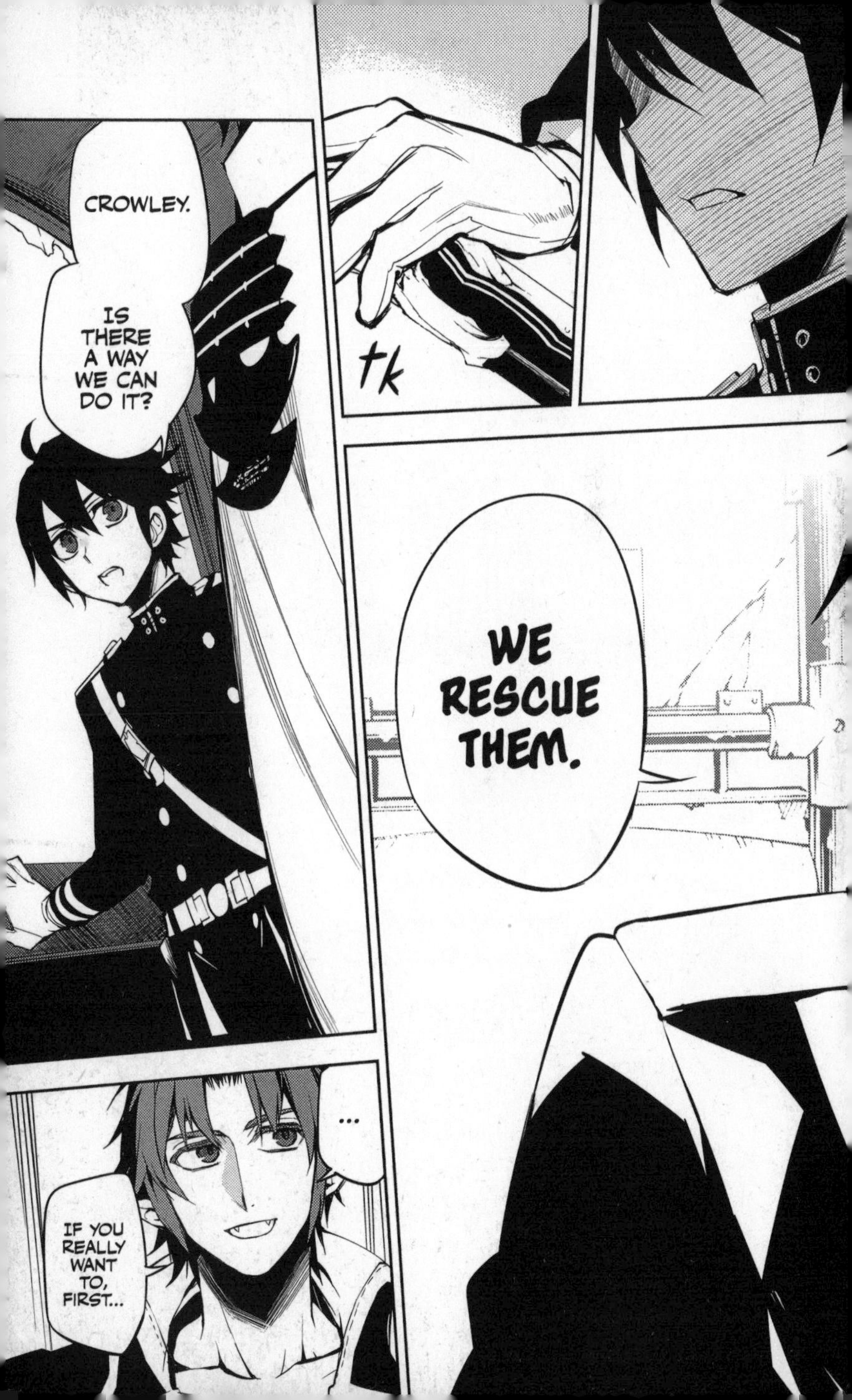
tk
CROWLEY.
IS THERE A WAY WE CAN DO IT?
WE RESCUE THEM.
...
IF YOU REALLY WANT TO, FIRST...

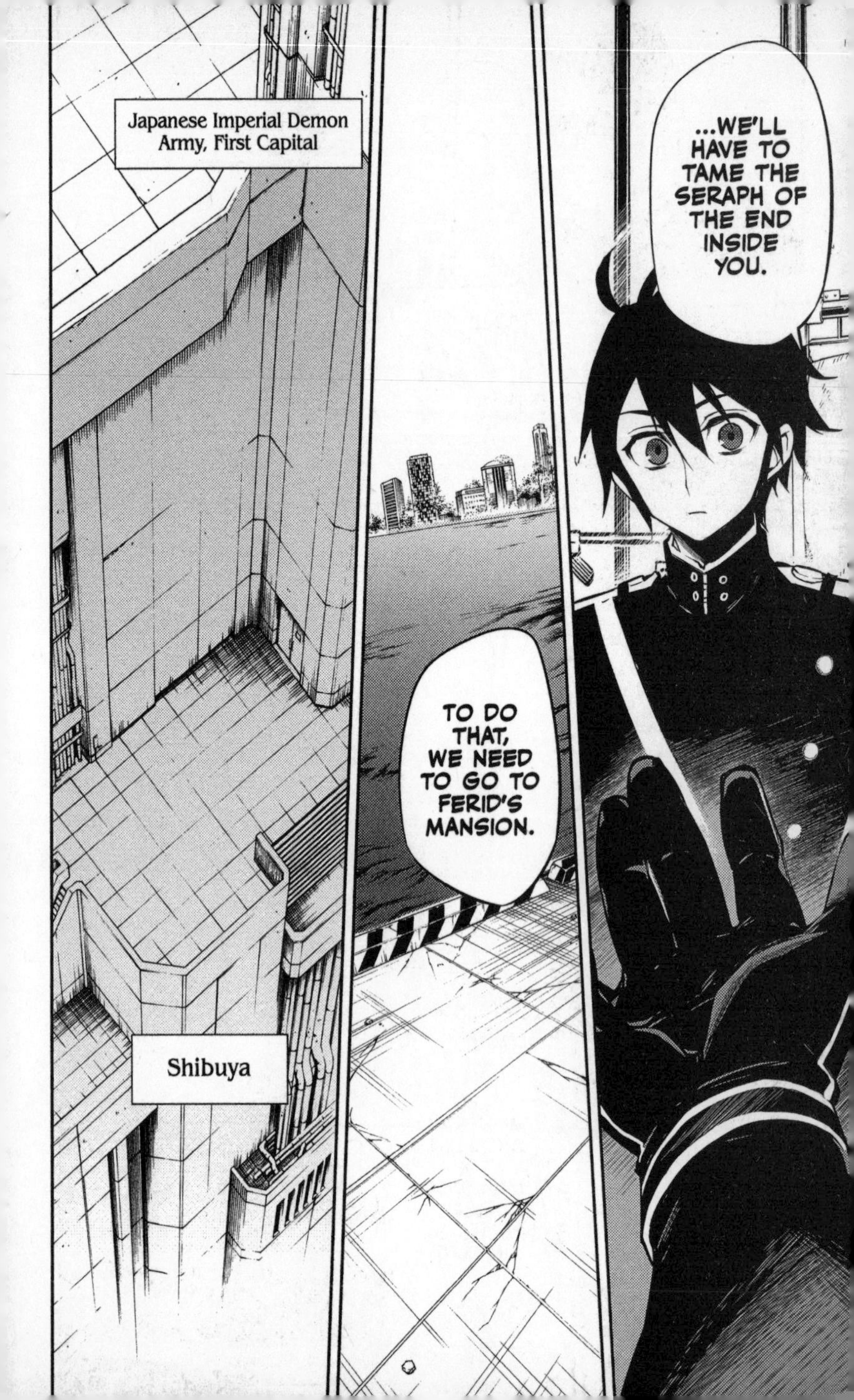
...WE'LL HAVE TO TAME THE SERAPH OF THE END INSIDE YOU.
TO DO THAT, WE NEED TO GO TO FERID'S MANSION.
Japanese Imperial Demon Army, First Capital
Shibuya

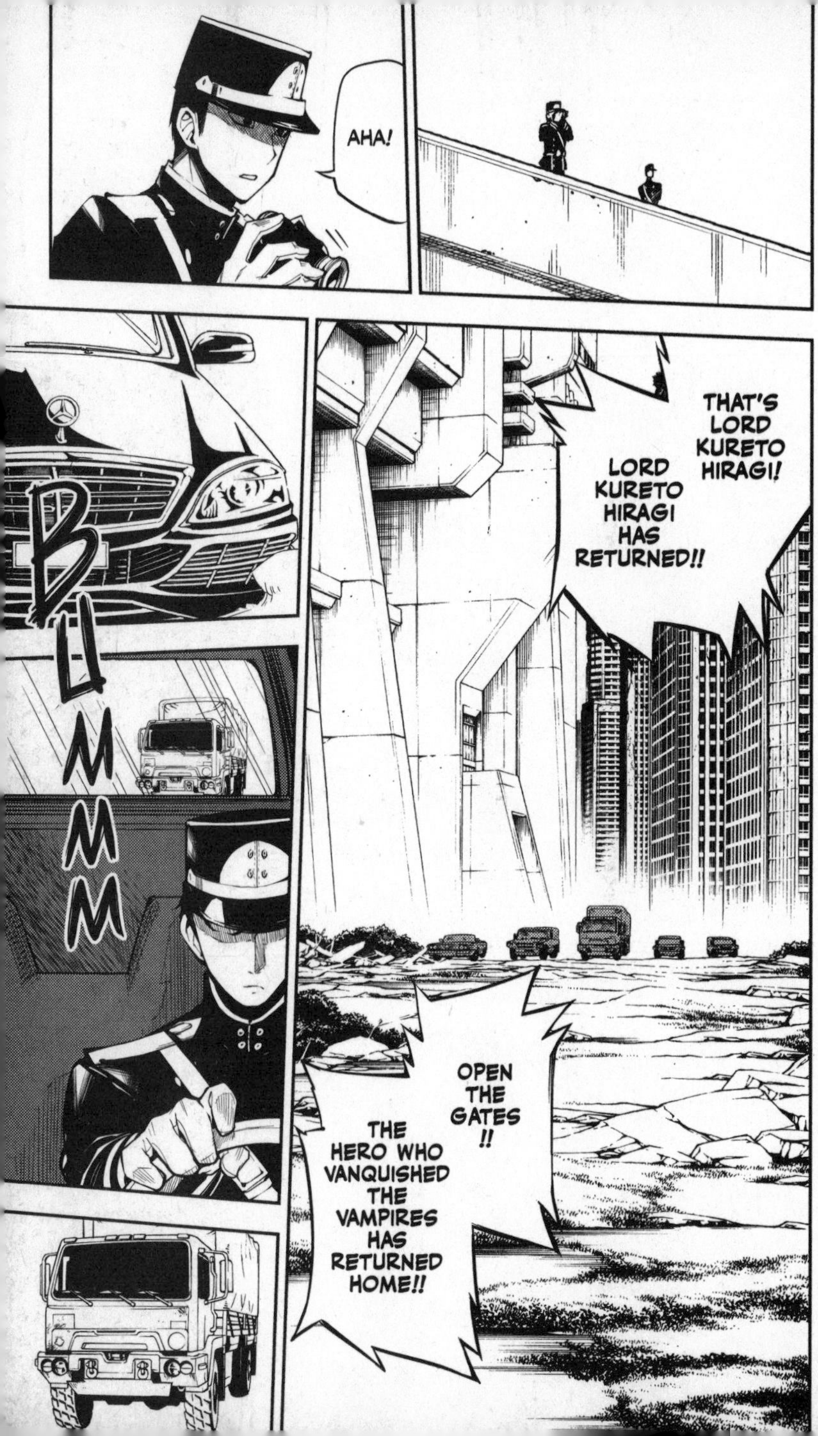
AHA!
THAT'S LORD KURETO HIRAGI!
LORD KURETO HIRAGI HAS RETURNED!!
OPEN THE GATES!!
THE HERO WHO VANQUISHED THE VAMPIRES HAS RETURNED HOME!!
BUMMMM

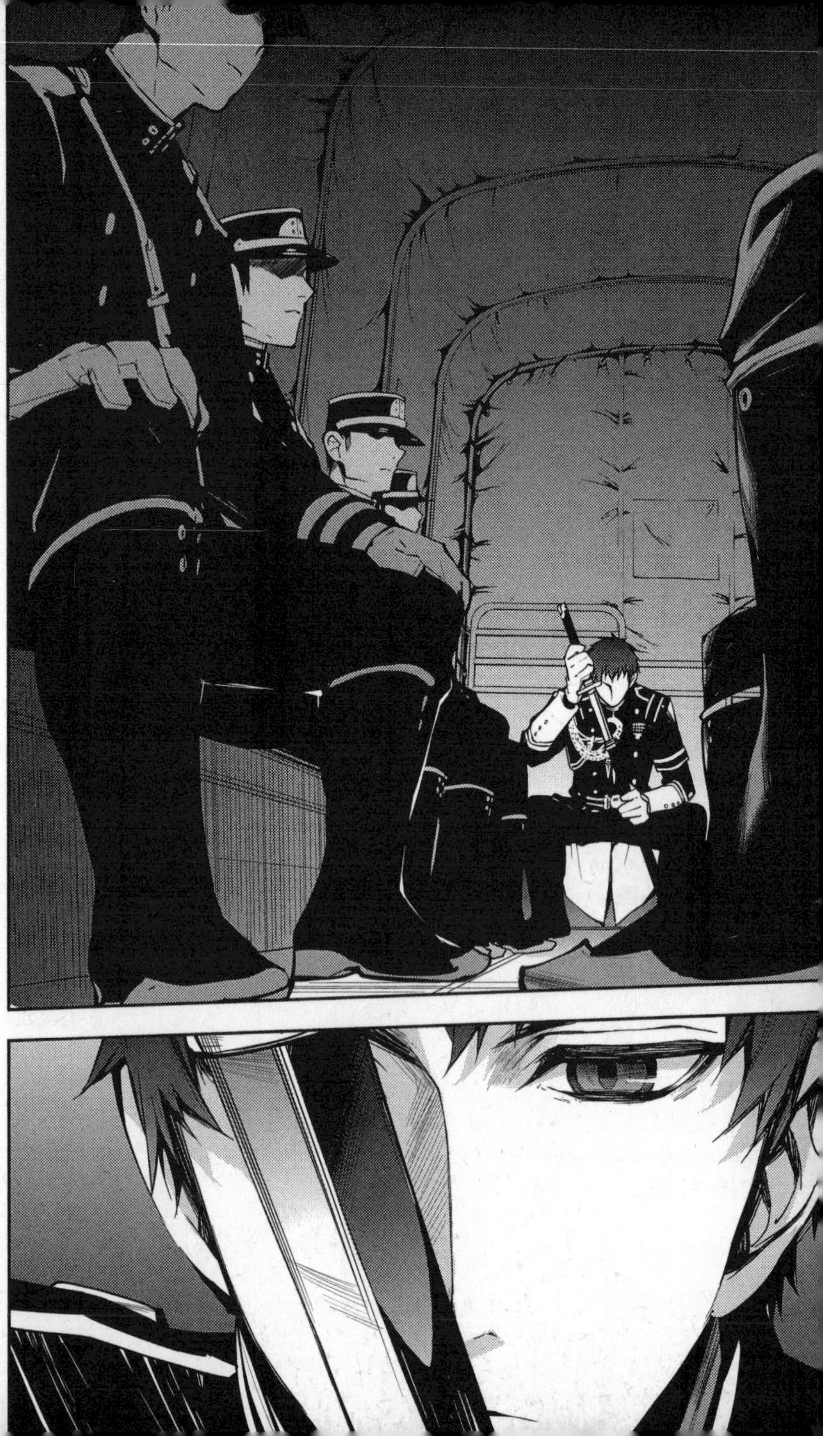

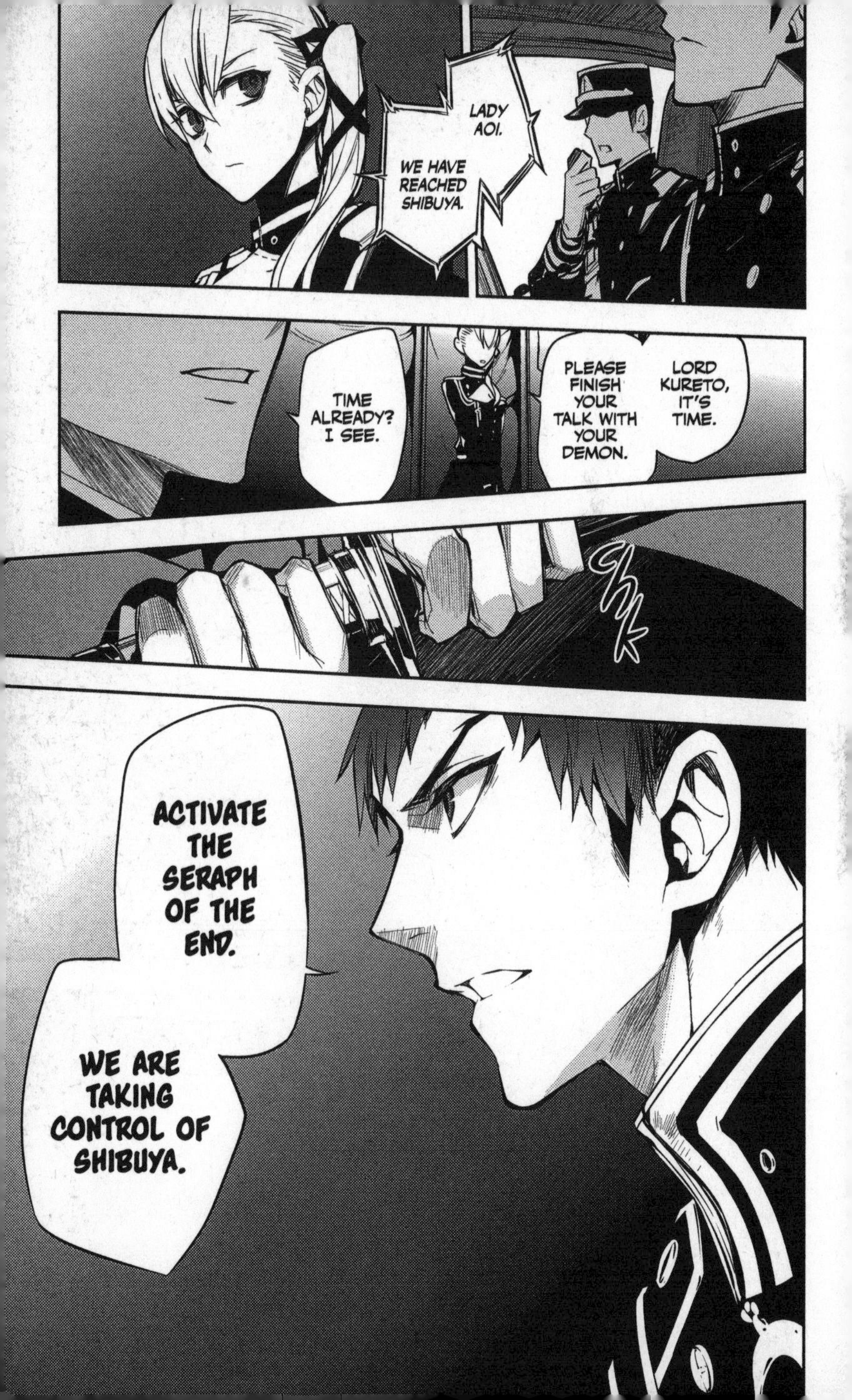
LADY AOI.
WE HAVE REACHED SHIBUYA.
LORD KURETO, IT'S TIME.
PLEASE FINISH YOUR TALK WITH YOUR DEMON.
TIME ALREADY? I SEE.
CHK
ACTIVATE THE SERAPH OF THE END.
WE ARE TAKING CONTROL OF SHIBUYA.

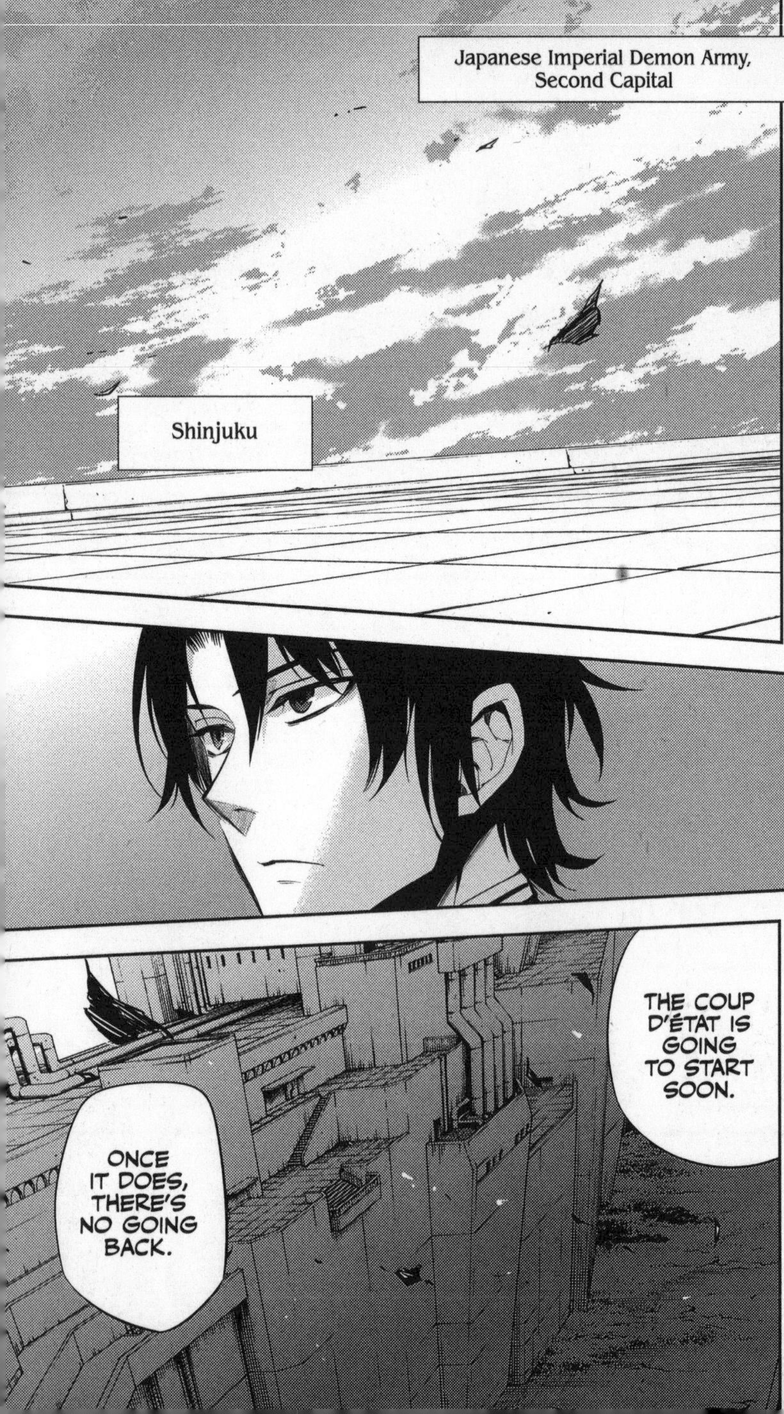
Japanese Imperial Demon Army, Second Capital
Shinjuku
THE COUP D'ÉTAT IS GOING TO START SOON.
ONCE IT DOES, THERE'S NO GOING BACK.

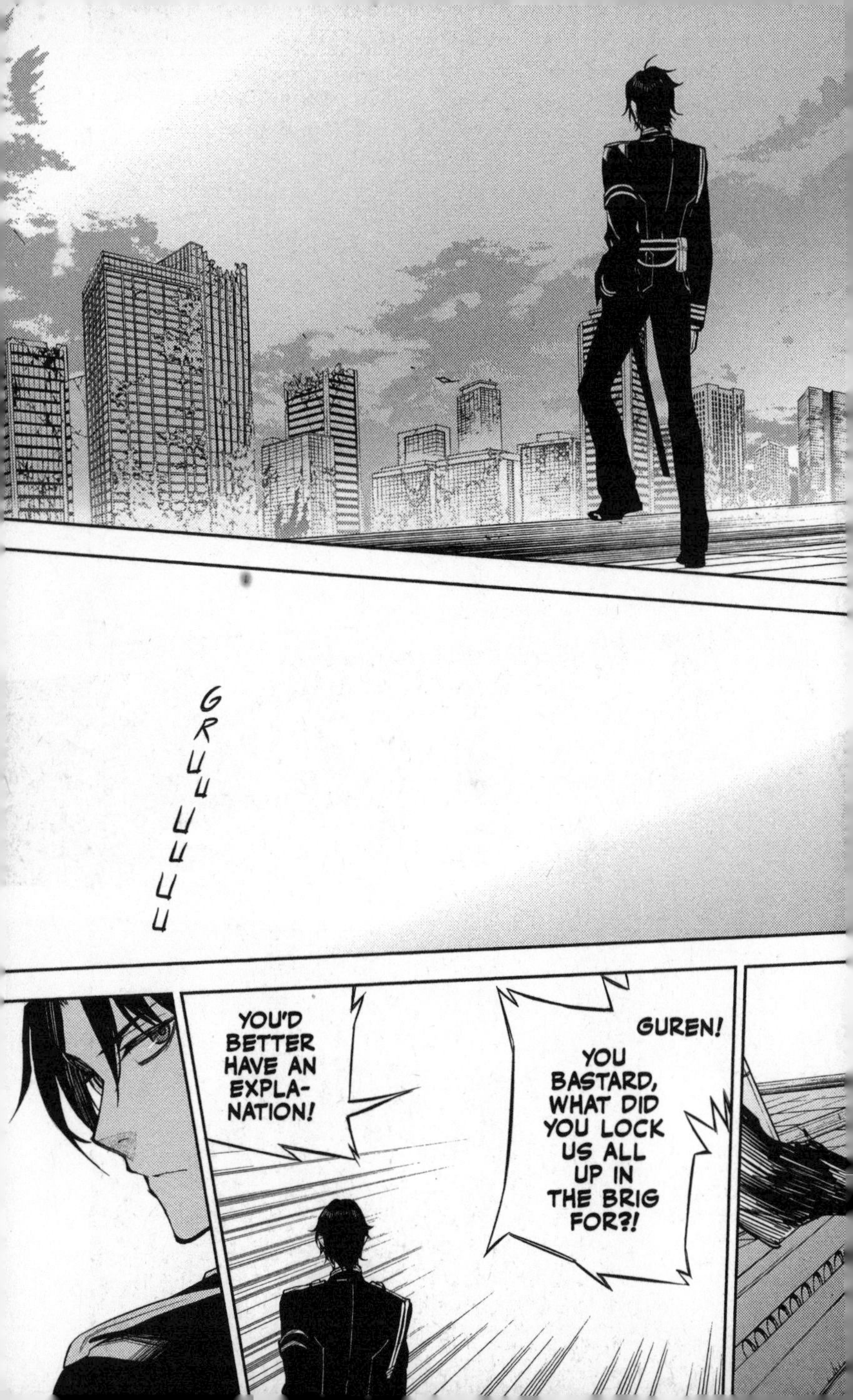
GRUUUUUUU
GUREN! YOU BASTARD, WHAT DID YOU LOCK US ALL UP IN THE BRIG FOR?!
YOU'D BETTER HAVE AN EXPLA-NATION!

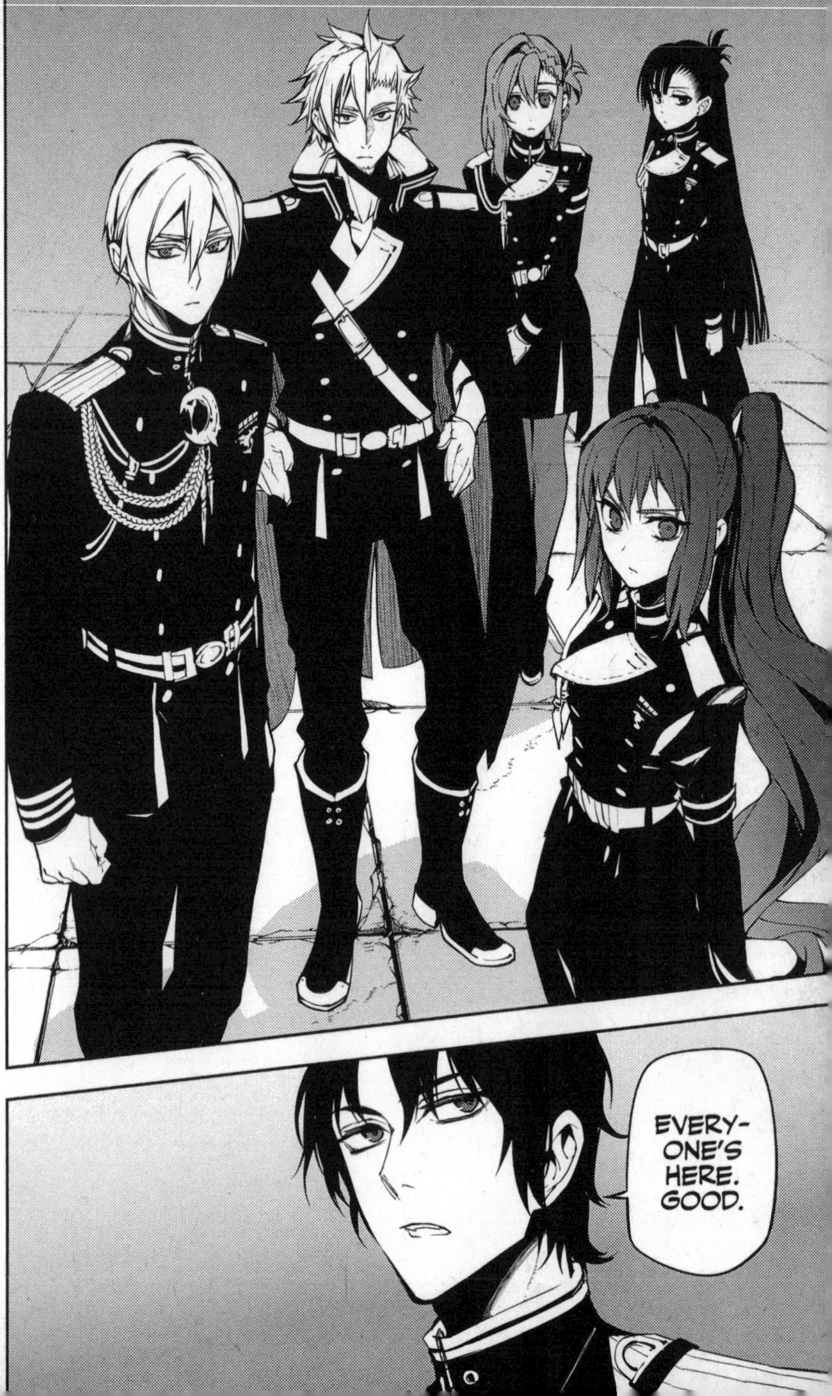
EVERY-ONE'S HERE. GOOD.

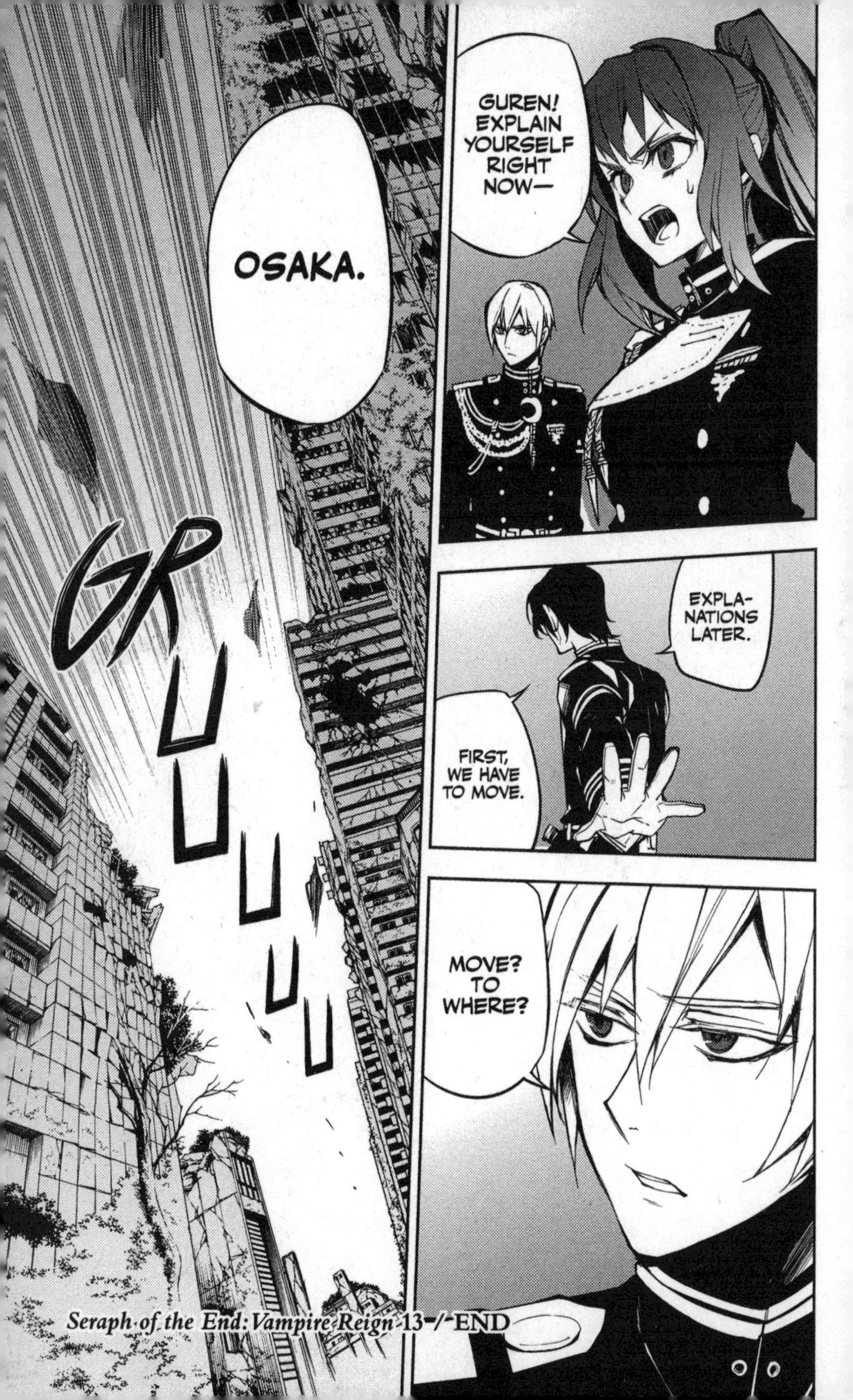
GUREN! EXPLAIN YOURSELF RIGHT NOW—
EXPLANATIONS LATER.
FIRST, WE HAVE TO MOVE.
MOVE? TO WHERE?
OSAKA.
GRUUUUU

Seraph of the End: Vampire Reign 13 / END

Seraph of the End
—VAMPIRE REIGN—

LEST KARR

LEST IS A THIRD PROGENITOR JUST LIKE KRUL. PRESENTLY, HE IS THE DESIGNATED RULER OF THE PART OF EUROPE THAT USED TO BE GERMANY. BOTH HE AND KRUL WERE TURNED INTO VAMPIRES AROUND THE SAME TIME. THEIR DIRECT MASTER IS THE FIRST PROGENITOR. IN FACT, ALL HIGHLY RANKED VAMPIRE PROGENITORS RECEIVED BLOOD DIRECTLY FROM THE FIRST PROGENITOR. DUE TO A CERTAIN EXPERIMENT THE FIRST PROGENITOR WAS DOING AT THE TIME, ALL THE THIRD PROGENITOR VAMPIRES LOOK TO BE ABOUT THE SAME AGE.

LEST: "WHAT, REALLY? OH, SO THAT'S WHY—"

KRUL: "YOU'RE SO SHORT."

LEST: "ME? Y-YOU'RE SHORTER!"

KRUL: "OH? WANT TO MEASURE AND FIND OUT? I BET I AM TALLER THAN YOU."

LEST: "YES, LET'S MEASURE AND PROVE WHO IS TALLER ONCE AND FOR ALL!"

KRUL: "TAKE YOUR HAT OFF."

LEST: "NO. WHY SHOULD I NEED TO TAKE IT OFF?"

URD GEALES

A SECOND PROGENITOR. WITH THE FIRST PROGENITOR LONG MISSING AND THE OTHER SECOND PROGENITOR, RÍGR STAFFORD (SAITO), GONE AWOL FOR CENTURIES, URD IS EFFECTIVELY THE SUPREME RULER OF VAMPIRE-KIND. IN OTHER WORDS, HE IS THE STRONGEST VAMPIRE IN THE WORLD. HE'S A SERIOUS PERSON. VERY SERIOUS. YOU CAN FIND OUT A LOT MORE ABOUT HIM, SAITO AND FERID IN THE *SERAPH OF THE END: MIKAELA'S STORY* NOVELS IN JAPAN. PLEASE CHECK THEM OUT.

URD: "THOUGH I ADMIT, I HAVE FORGOTTEN MUCH OF THE PAST."

SAITO: "TRUE. HOW MANY YEARS AGO WAS ALL THAT NOW?"

URD: "WHO KNOWS?"

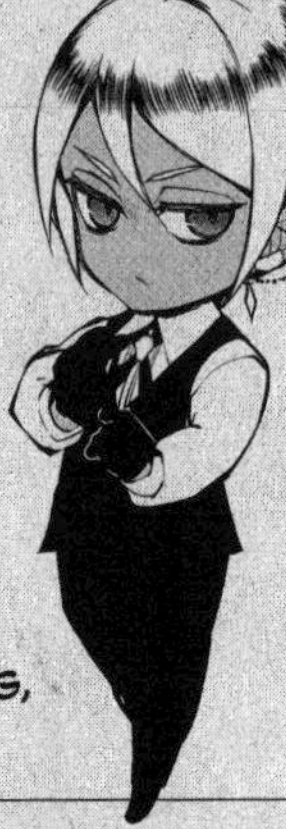

SAITO: "IF I'M REMEMBERING CORRECTLY, YOU WERE ON THE VERGE OF COMMITTING SUICIDE BECAUSE YOUR PRECIOUS LOVE JENNIFER HAD LEFT YOU WHEN YOU WERE TURNED INTO A VAMPIRE. RIGHT?"

URD: "N-NO..."

SAITO: "THERE, SEE? YOU DO REMEMBER."

URD: "*YOU* WERE THE ONE WITH A BROKEN HEART OVER JENNIFER."

SAITO: "IS THAT SO? I GUESS IF THAT'S WHAT YOU REMEMBER..."

URD: "DENY IT, YOU IDIOT. IT WAS A LIE."

SAITO: "AHA HA! WE'VE BOTH LIVED FAR TOO LONG, HAVEN'T WE?"

SAITO (a.k.a. Rígr Stafford, a.k.a. Makoto Kijima)

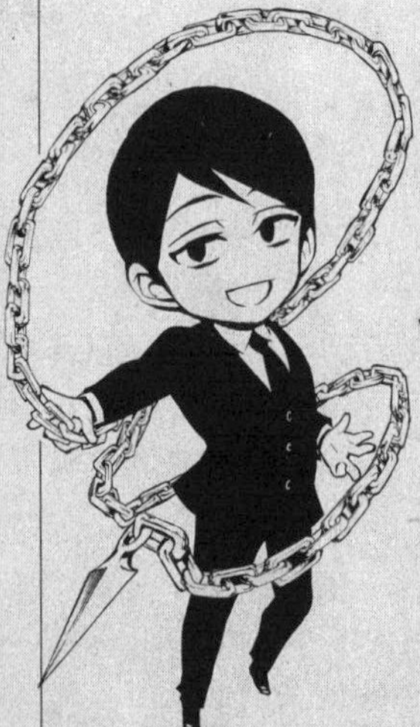

FORMERLY A SECOND PROGENITOR, HE, ALONG WITH URD, HAS BEEN AROUND SINCE THE DAWN OF VAMPIRE-KIND'S HISTORY. HE IS THE ONE WHO FIRST TURNED FERID INTO A VAMPIRE. IN THE MANGA, HE MADE HIS FIRST APPEARANCE WHEN HE DRAGGED A YOUNG YUICHIRO TO THE HYAKUYA ORPHANAGE FOR THE FIRST TIME. IN THE *SERAPH OF THE END* NOVEL SPINOFF *GUREN ICHINOSE: CATASTROPHE AT 16*, HE HAS BEEN A BIG THORN IN GUREN'S SIDE AS HYAKUYA SECT MEMBER MAKOTO KIJIMA. HE IS ONE OF THE KEY FIGURES AROUND WHOM MUCH OF THE SERAPH OF THE END STORY REVOLVES.

SAITO: "BUT I DID HAVE MY HEART BROKEN BY THE LOVELY JENNIFER."

URD: "YOU ARE REALLY GOING TO DRAG THAT OUT? WHO IS JENNIFER ANYWAY?"

FERID: "HELLO, EVERYONE. MY NAME IS JENNIFER."

SAITO: "HI, JENNIFER!"

URD: "WHATEVER..."

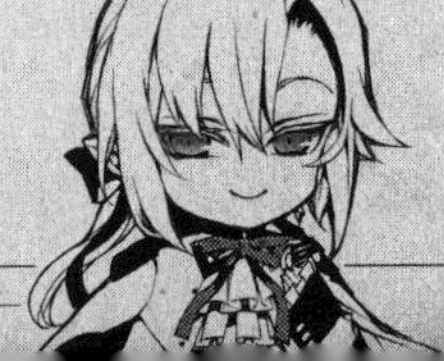

AFTERWORD

HELLO. I'M TAKAYA KAGAMI, ORIGINAL AUTHOR AND STORY WRITER FOR THE *SERAPH OF THE END* MANGA AND NOVELS. IT'S BEEN A WHILE. HOW HAVE YOU LIKED THE STORY SO FAR? THIS VOLUME SAW THE INTRODUCTION OF CHARACTERS AND DEVELOPMENTS THAT PULLED BACK THE CURTAIN ON SOME OF THE CORE EVENTS OF THIS STORY! AND NOT ONLY THAT, THE *SERAPH OF THE END* NOVEL *GUREN ICHINOSE: CATASTROPHE AT 16* VOLUME 7 IS FINALLY ON SALE IN JAPAN! WHAT'S GOING TO HAPPEN TO GUREN? TO SHINYA AND THE OTHERS? IT'S THIS VOLUME THAT SHEDS LIGHT ON HOW THE WORLD PLUNGED INTO THE CATASTROPHE. HECK, THIS NOVEL AND THE MANGA ARE JUST A COMPLETE COLLABORATION WORK NOW. YOU CAN ENJOY THEM BOTH TO GET THE FULL STORY!

ANYWAY, THERE ISN'T MUCH EXTRA SPACE IN THIS VOLUME, SO I'LL WRAP THINGS UP HERE. I HOPE TO SEE YOU AGAIN NEXT VOLUME OR IN THE NOVELS!

—TAKAYA KAGAMI

A brilliant sketch of Yuichiro by the author!

TAKAYA KAGAMI is a prolific light novelist whose works include the action and fantasy series *The Legend of the Legendary Heroes*, which has been adapted into manga, anime and a video game. His previous series, *A Dark Rabbit Has Seven Lives*, also spawned a manga and anime series.

❝ I'm on my way home from Shanghai. Just like when I visited Germany, when I go to new cities and countries, I can't help but think about what kinds of vampires would live there and what kind of story could be told about them. ❞

YAMATO YAMAMOTO, born 1983, is an artist and illustrator whose works include the *Kure-nai* manga and the light novels *Kure-nai*, *9S -Nine S-* and *Denpa Teki na Kanojo*. Both *Denpa Teki na Kanojo* and *Kure-nai* have been adapted into anime.

❝ Starting with this volume, more of the mystery surrounding the vampires' side of the story comes to light. How do you like it so far? I'm having a lot of fun drawing it. ❞

DAISUKE FURUYA previously assisted Yamato Yamamoto with storyboards for *Kure-nai*.

Seraph of the End
—VAMPIRE REIGN—

VOLUME 13
SHONEN JUMP ADVANCED MANGA EDITION

STORY BY **TAKAYA KAGAMI**
ART BY **YAMATO YAMAMOTO**
STORYBOARDS BY **DAISUKE FURUYA**

TRANSLATION **Adrienne Beck**
TOUCH-UP ART & LETTERING **Sabrina Heep**
DESIGN **Shawn Carrico**
EDITOR **Marlene First**

OWARI NO SERAPH © 2012 by Takaya Kagami,
Yamato Yamamoto, Daisuke Furuya
All rights reserved. First published in Japan in 2012 by SHUEISHA Inc., Tokyo.
English translation rights arranged by SHUEISHA Inc.

The stories, characters and incidents mentioned in this
publication are entirely fictional.

No portion of this book may be reproduced or transmitted
in any form or by any means without written permission from
the copyright holders.

Printed in the U.S.A.

Published by VIZ Media, LLC
P.O. Box 77010
San Francisco, CA 94107

10 9 8 7 6 5 4 3 2 1
First printing, November 2017

www.viz.com

www.shonenjump.com

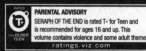
PARENTAL ADVISORY
SERAPH OF THE END is rated T+ for Teen and
is recommended for ages 16 and up. This
volume contains violence and some adult themes.
ratings.viz.com

A MULTIGENERATIONAL TALE OF THE HEROIC JOESTAR FAMILY
AND THEIR NEVER-ENDING BATTLE AGAINST EVIL!

JoJo's
BIZARRE ADVENTURE

HIROHIKO ★ ARAKI

PART I
PHANTOM BLOOD

Young Jonathan Joestar's life is forever changed when he meets his new adopted brother, Dio. For some reason, Dio has a smoldering grudge against him and derives pleasure from seeing him suffer. But every man has his limits, as Dio finds out. This is the beginning of a long and hateful relationship!

THE FIRST ARC OF THE SHONEN JUMP CLASSIC IN A DELUXE HARDCOVER EDITION!

Collect all 3 volumes!

www.viz.com

JOJO'S BIZARRE ADVENTURE © 1986 by Hirohiko Araki/SHUEISHA Inc.

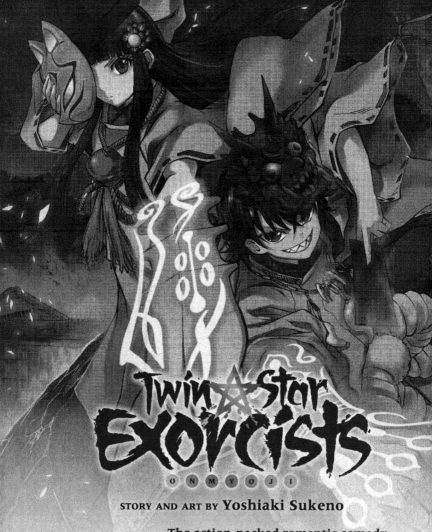

Twin★Star Exorcists

O N M Y O J I

STORY AND ART BY **Yoshiaki Sukeno**

The action-packed romantic comedy from the creator of *Good Luck Girl!*

Rokuro dreams of becoming *anything* but an exorcist! Then mysterious Benio turns up. The pair are dubbed the "Twin Star Exorcists" and learn they are fated to marry...

Can Rokuro escape both fates?

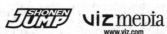

www.viz.com

SOUSEI NO ONMYOJI © 2013 by Yoshiaki Sukeno /SHUEISHA Inc.

A MULTIGENERATIONAL TALE OF THE HEROIC JOESTAR FAMILY AND THEIR NEVER-ENDING BATTLE AGAINST EVIL!

JoJo's
BIZARRE ADVENTURE

HIROHIKO ARAKI

PART 2
BATTLE TENDENCY

The Joestar family is called upon to do battle against evil again! This time, it's Joseph Joestar, the grandson of Jonathan Joestar! And his enemies are more powerful and diabolical than ever! Behold! The terror of the Pillar Men!

★ THE SECOND ARC OF THE SHONEN JUMP ★ CLASSIC IN A DELUXE HARDCOVER EDITION!

Collect all 4 volumes!

 SHONEN JUMP ADVANCED · VIZ media

www.viz.com

JOJO'S BIZARRE ADVENTURE © 1986 by Hirohiko Araki/SHUEISHA Inc.

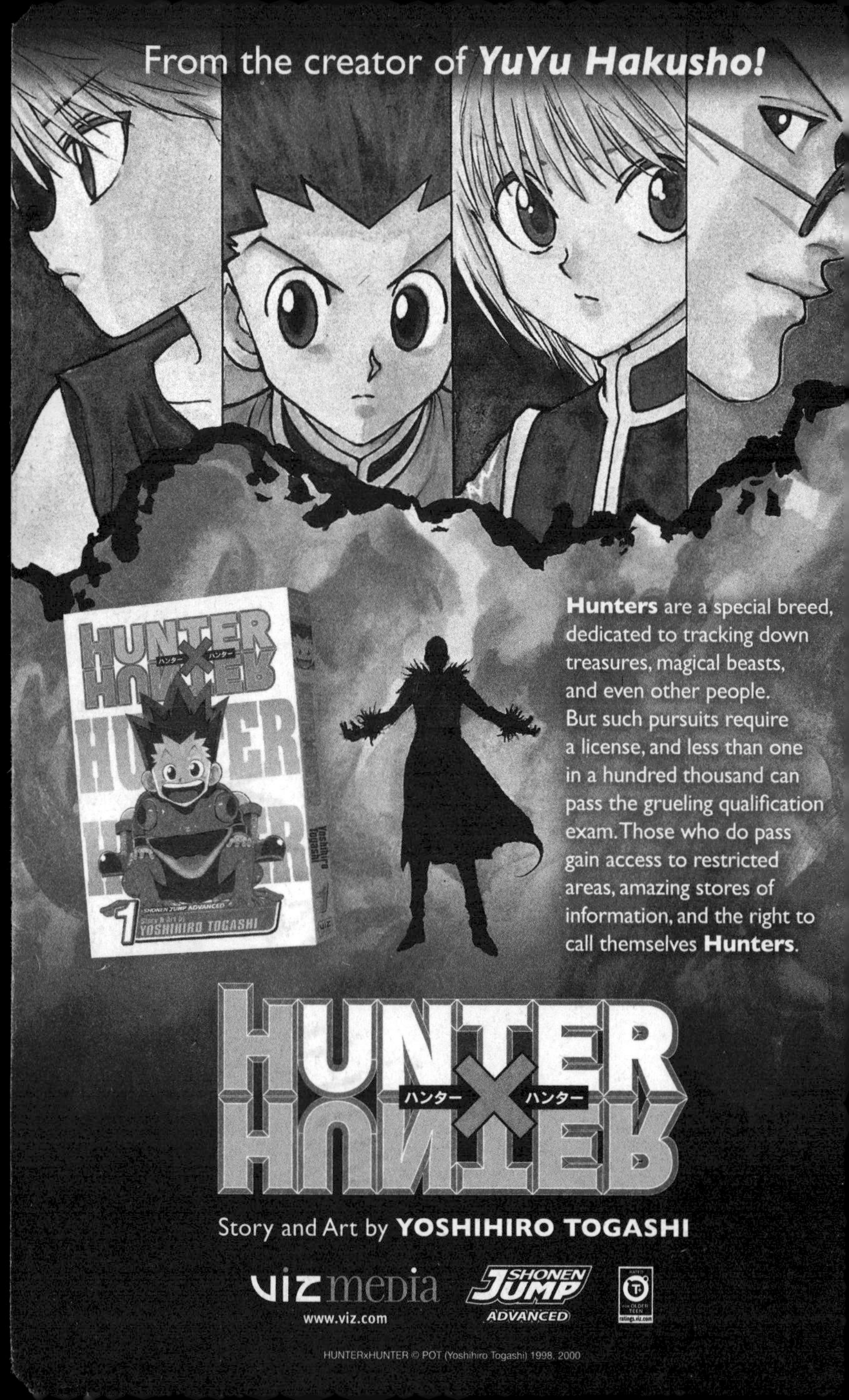
From the creator of YuYu Hakusho!
Hunters are a special breed, dedicated to tracking down treasures, magical beasts, and even other people. But such pursuits require a license, and less than one in a hundred thousand can pass the grueling qualification exam. Those who do pass gain access to restricted areas, amazing stores of information, and the right to call themselves Hunters.
HUNTER × HUNTER
ハンター ハンター
Story and Art by YOSHIHIRO TOGASHI
viz media
www.viz.com
SHONEN JUMP ADVANCED
HUNTERxHUNTER © POT (Yoshihiro Togashi) 1998, 2000

YOU'RE READING THE
WRONG WAY!

SERAPH OF THE END reads from right to left, starting in the upper-right corner. Japanese is read from right to left, meaning that action, sound effects, and word-balloon order are completely reversed from English order.

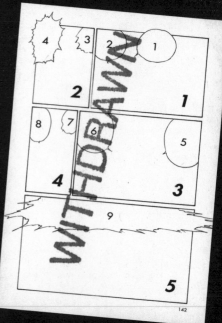